Hands-On Design Patterns with Delphi

Build applications using idiomatic, extensible, and concurrent design patterns in Delphi

Primož Gabrijelčič

BIRMINGHAM - MUMBAI

Hands-On Design Patterns with Delphi

Commissioning Editor: Richa Tripathi
Acquisition Editor: Karan Sadawana
Content Development Editor: Anugraha Arunagiri
Technical Editor: Aniket Iswalkar
Copy Editor: Safis Editing
Project Coordinator: Ulhas Kambali
Proofreader: Safis Editing
Indexer: Rekha Nair
Graphics: Tom Scaria
 Production Coordinator: Shraddha Falebhai

First published: February 2019

Production reference: 1220219

Published by Packt Publishing Ltd.
Livery Place
35 Livery Street
Birmingham
B3 2PB, UK.

ISBN 978-1-78934-324-3

www.packtpub.com

`mapt.io`

Mapt is an online digital library that gives you full access to over 5,000 books and videos, as well as industry leading tools to help you plan your personal development and advance your career. For more information, please visit our website.

Why subscribe?

- Spend less time learning and more time coding with practical eBooks and Videos from over 4,000 industry professionals

- Improve your learning with Skill Plans built especially for you

- Get a free eBook or video every month

- Mapt is fully searchable

- Copy and paste, print, and bookmark content

Packt.com

Did you know that Packt offers eBook versions of every book published, with PDF and ePub files available? You can upgrade to the eBook version at `www.packt.com` and as a print book customer, you are entitled to a discount on the eBook copy. Get in touch with us at `customercare@packtpub.com` for more details.

At `www.packt.com`, you can also read a collection of free technical articles, sign up for a range of free newsletters, and receive exclusive discounts and offers on Packt books and eBooks.

Contributors

About the author

Primož Gabrijelčič started coding in Pascal on 8-bit micros in the 1980s, and has never looked back. In the last 20 years, he was mostly programming high-availability server applications used in the broadcasting industry. A result of this focus was the open source parallel programming library for Delphi – the OmniThreadLibrary. He's also an avid writer and has written several hundred articles, and is a frequent speaker at Delphi conferences, where he likes to talk about complicated topics, ranging from memory management to creating custom compilers.

About the reviewer

Gaurav Aroraa has an M.Phil in computer science. He is a Microsoft MVP; a lifetime member of Computer Society of India; an advisory member of IndiaMentor; and certified as a Scrum trainer/coach, XEN for ITIL-F, and APMG for PRINCE-F and PRINCE-P. He is an open source developer, a contributor to TechNet Wiki, and the founder of Ovatic Systems Private Limited. In over the 20 years of his career, he has mentored thousands of students and industry professionals. You can tweet Gaurav on his Twitter handle at `@g_arora`.

To my wife, Shuby Arora, and my daughter, Aarchi Arora, an angel, who permitted me to steal time for this book from time I was supposed to spend with them. Thanks to the entire Packt team, especially Ulhas and Anugraha Arunagiri, whose coordination and communication during the writing period was tremendous, and who introduced me to this book.

Packt is searching for authors like you

If you're interested in becoming an author for Packt, please visit `authors.packtpub.com` and apply today. We have worked with thousands of developers and tech professionals, just like you, to help them share their insight with the global tech community. You can make a general application, apply for a specific hot topic that we are recruiting an author for, or submit your own idea.

Table of Contents

Section 4: Behavioral Patterns

Section 5: Concurrency Patterns

Preface

Design patterns - my friend and enemy!

I learned about design patterns in the formative phase of my life as a programmer. (Yes, that was long ago. I don't even remember, how long ago.) Since then, I've always been a great admirer of the concept. I like structured programming and I like algorithms and methodological approaches to coding, so this design patterns idea has always looked like a potentially very interesting topic to me.

Potentially; that's the word. Almost all of the books explaining design patterns were written with C++ (and later Java) programmers in mind. Well, I could swallow that. I know how to program in C, and I can read C++ and Java, so that was an obstacle that I could surmount with some work. A bigger problem were the UML diagrams explaining the patterns and code examples that had no connection to reality.

Problem one – UML diagrams. I don't do UML. I tried to learn it few times, but it doesn't speak to me, and for the sake of my sanity, I'm unable to remember what all those empty circles, full circles, and other line endings are supposed to mean. Each time I saw a UML diagram in a design patterns book, I lost my patience and walked away.

Finally, the time has come for some payback! This book contains no UML diagrams at all. What's more, this book contains only one diagram describing a state machine, but even this diagram uses no formal notation - it is just my ad hoc sketch. Take that, UML design pattern-lovers! (Not really. I have deep respect for people who fluently use UML.)

Rather than drawing all kinds of diagrams, here, I've tried to explain how each pattern works in simple words. I've also tried to find more-or-less appropriate and analogous examples from the real world. I can only hope you'll like my approach. If not, you can still read this book and use any website describing design patterns to look at pretty diagrams at the same time.

My second problem was with code examples. With some rare exceptions, design pattern books and websites all repeat examples that were cited in the original Gang of Four publication (more on that in `Chapter 1`, *Introduction to patterns*). Those examples are all terribly outdated and irrelevant to a Delphi programmer. Which one of you needs to know how to use the Decorator pattern to apply scroll bars to a text view? There are many other uses for this pattern in the modern world – see the `Chapter 5`, *Adapter, Proxy, Decorator, and Facade* and consider the Adapter, Proxy, Decorator, and Facade patterns as examples.

Because of my deeply rooted dislike of such examples, I tried to stay away from them as much as possible. There are still examples that draw shapes onscreen in this book – simply because some patterns were designed specifically with such problems in mind – but the big majority of examples try to be closer to the experience of an average Delphi programmer. I also added few standalone sections on Delphi-specific language enhancements that may not be known to a fresh Delphi programmer, or to a Pascal programmer that doesn't speak Delphi. Look for them in headings starting with Delphi idioms.

Did I succeed in writing a easier to understand and more practical design pattern book? Only you can tell. (And please, do tell! I'll be glad to receive any feedback – positive or negative.) I can only say that this book has helped me – now I finally understand what this "design pattern" stuff is all about.

Who this book is for

This book was written for all Delphi programmers. It doesn't matter whether you are a beginner or an expert this book is for you!

While a basic knowledge of Delphi programming language and IDE is definitely a boon, you can read this book even if you know nothing about Delphi. The Pascal language is simple to read and understand, and when we come to advanced topics, the book explains the Delphi syntax with clear and simple examples.

The only requirement this book has from the reader is that they like to explore and learn. This is not a when this happens, do that kind of book. It explores interesting topics and gives insights and sketches of solutions, but doesn't contain any recipes claiming that this is the only proper way to do X.

This book will teach you to think, not how to reuse code.

What this book covers

Chapter 1, Introduction to patterns, introduces the concept of patterns. We'll see why patterns are useful and how they should be used in programming. The book will explore the difference between design principles, patterns, and idioms. It will present a hierarchical overview of design patterns, talk a bit about anti-patterns, and finish with a description of some important design principles.

Chapter 2, *Singleton, Dependency Injection, Lazy Initialization, and Object Pool,* covers four patterns from the creational group. The chapter will firstly look into the singleton pattern, which makes sure that a class has only one instance. Next in line, the dependency injection pattern makes program architecture more flexible and appropriate for unit testing. In the second half, the chapter explores two optimization patterns. The lazy initialization pattern saves time and resources, while the object pool pattern speeds up creation of objects.

Chapter 3, *Factory Method, Abstract Factory, Prototype, and Builder,* examines four more creational patterns. The factory method pattern simplifies creation of dependent objects. The concept can be extended into the abstract factory pattern, which functions as a factory of factories. The prototype pattern is used to create copies of objects. Last in this group, the builder pattern separates instructions for creating an object from its representation.

Chapter 4, *Composite, Flyweight, Marker Interface, and Bridge,* covers four patterns from the structural group. The composite pattern allows client code to treat simple and complex objects the same. The flyweight pattern can be used to minimize memory usage by introducing data sharing between objects. The marker interface allows us to unleash a new level of programming power by introducing metaprogramming. The bridge pattern helps us separate an abstract interface from its implementation.

Chapter 5, *Adapter, Proxy, Decorator, and Facade,* explores four more structural patterns. The adapter pattern helps in adapting old code to new use cases. The proxy pattern wraps an objects and exposes an identical interface to facilitate caching, remoting, and access control, among other things. The decorator pattern specifies how the functionality of existing objects can be expanded, while the facade pattern shows us how to create a simplified view of a complex system.

Chapter 6, *Nullable Object, Template Method, Command, and State,* covers four patterns from the behavioral group. The null object pattern can reduce the need for frequent if statements in the code. The template method pattern helps with creating adaptable algorithms. The command pattern shows how we can treat actions as objects. It is a basis for Delphi *actions.* The state pattern allows an object to change its behavior on demand and is useful when we are writing state machines.

Chapter 7, *Iterator, Visitor, Observer, and Memento,* examines four more behavioral patterns. The iterator pattern allows us to effectively access data structures in a structure-independent way. This pattern is the basis of Delphi's for..in construct. The visitor pattern allows us to extend classes in accordance with the Open/Closed design principle. To write loosely coupled programs that react to changes in the business model, we can use the observer pattern. When we need to store the state of a complex object, the memento pattern comes to help.

Chapter 8, *Lock Patterns,* is entirely dedicated to data protection in a multithreaded world, and covers five concurrency patterns. The lock pattern enables the code to share data between threads and is basis for other patterns from this chapter. The lock striping pattern specifies how we can optimize locking when accessing a granular structure, such as an array. The double-checked locking pattern optimizes creation of shared resources, while the optimistic locking pattern speeds up this process even more. The readers-writer lock is a special version of the locking mechanism designed for situations where a shared resource is mostly read from, and only rarely written to.

Chapter 9, *Thread Pool, Messaging, Future, and Pipeline,* finishes the overview of design patterns by exploring four more concurrency patterns. As a specialized version of the object pool pattern, the thread pool pattern speeds up thread creation. The messaging pattern can be used to remove shared data access completely, and by doing so, can simplify and speed up the program. The future pattern specifies how we can integrate parallel execution of calculations into existing code. This chapter ends with a discussion of the pipeline pattern, which is a practical application of messaging designed to speed up tasks that are hard to parallelize with other approaches.

Chapter 10, *Designing Delphi Programs,* steps away from the design patterns and talks about concepts that are important for Delphi programmers. In this chapter, you will learn about event-driven programming and how the Delphi's event system can be extended with multicast events. We will explore the actions mechanism, which serves as a nice example of the command pattern. After that, the chapter will spend some time looking into the LiveBindings mechanism, an implementation of the observer pattern. In the second half of this chapter, we'll see how we can use form inheritance to create forms in an object-oriented way, and how we can use frames to create forms by compositions. At the end, we'll look into data modules; that is, tools that can be used to implement the table module enterprise pattern.

Chapter 11, *Other Kinds of Patterns,* wraps up the book by exploring patterns in three areas. The first part of the chapter deals with the exceptions and introduces exception patterns; that is, a set of recommendations that will help you write better code. After that, a short treatise of debugging patterns tries to bring some order to the messy world of code debugging. To end the book, a short exploration of functional programming is used to explain how this kind of programming paradigm can be used in Delphi.

To get the most out of this book

Although you can read this book in bed or on the beach, you will need a computer and Delphi to play with the code examples. The code was written in Delphi 10.2 Tokyo, but it should also work without a problem in the older versions. All the code was also tested with the newest version of Delphi (at the time of publishing) – Delphi 10.3 Rio.

This book does not refer to any functionality specific to the Enterprise edition of Delphi. You'll be able to test all the code with the Professional edition, or even with the Community edition.

Download the example code files

You can download the example code files for this book from your account at `www.packt.com`. If you purchased this book elsewhere, you can visit `www.packt.com/support` and register to have the files emailed directly to you.

You can download the code files by following these steps:

1. Log in or register at `www.packt.com`.
2. Select the **SUPPORT** tab.
3. Click on **Code Downloads & Errata**.
4. Enter the name of the book in the **Search** box and follow the onscreen instructions.

Once the file is downloaded, please make sure that you unzip or extract the folder using the latest version of:

- WinRAR/7-Zip for Windows
- Zipeg/iZip/UnRarX for Mac
- 7-Zip/PeaZip for Linux

The code bundle for the book is also hosted on GitHub at `https://github.com/PacktPublishing/Hands-On-Design-Patterns-with-Delphi`. In case there's an update to the code, it will be updated on the existing GitHub repository.

We also have other code bundles from our rich catalog of books and videos available at `https://github.com/PacktPublishing/`. Check them out!

Conventions used

There are a number of text conventions used throughout this book.

`CodeInText`: Indicates code words in text, database table names, folder names, filenames, file extensions, pathnames, dummy URLs, user input, and Twitter handles. Here is an example: "The project resides in a folder named adapter in the `Chapter05/` directory."

A block of code is set as follows:

```
type
  IProducer = interface ['{8E4001F9-11EC-4C9C-BAD9-97C9601699FF}']
    function NextData: TValue;
  end;
```

Bold: Indicates a new term, an important word, or words that you see onscreen. For example, words in menus or dialog boxes appear in the text like this. Here is an example: "Select **System info** from the **Administration** panel."

 Warnings or important notes appear like this.

 Tips and tricks appear like this.

Get in touch

Feedback from our readers is always welcome.

General feedback: If you have questions about any aspect of this book, mention the book title in the subject of your message and email us at `customercare@packtpub.com`.

Errata: Although we have taken every care to ensure the accuracy of our content, mistakes do happen. If you have found a mistake in this book, we would be grateful if you would report this to us. Please visit `www.packt.com/submit-errata`, selecting your book, clicking on the Errata Submission Form link, and entering the details.

Piracy: If you come across any illegal copies of our works in any form on the Internet, we would be grateful if you would provide us with the location address or website name. Please contact us at copyright@packt.com with a link to the material.

If you are interested in becoming an author: If there is a topic that you have expertise in and you are interested in either writing or contributing to a book, please visit authors.packtpub.com.

Reviews

Please leave a review. Once you have read and used this book, why not leave a review on the site that you purchased it from? Potential readers can then see and use your unbiased opinion to make purchase decisions, we at Packt can understand what you think about our products, and our authors can see your feedback on their book. Thank you!

For more information about Packt, please visit packt.com.

Section 1: Design Pattern Essentials

The objective of this part is to introduce the reader to the patterns, provide some historical background, and establish the context.

This section will comprise the following chapters:

Chapter 1, *Introduction to Patterns*

Introduction to patterns 1

Patterns are everywhere! In architecture, patterns help architects plan buildings and discuss their projects. In programming, they help programmers organize programs and think about the code. They also help to create beautiful knitwear, and help people navigate safely through traffic—in short, they affect your everyday life.

The human brain is a pattern—finding analog computer, so it is not surprising that we humans like to base our life around patterns. We programmers are especially fond of organized, pattern—based thinking.

There are different areas of programming where patterns can be applied, from organizational aspects to coding. This book deals mostly with a subset of programming patterns, namely design patterns. Before we start describing and implementing different design patterns, however, I'd like to talk to you a bit about the history of patterns, their best points, and how they are often misused in practice.

This chapter will cover the following topics:

- What design patterns are
- Why patterns are useful
- The difference between patterns and idioms
- The origins of design patterns
- The classification of common patterns
- Pattern misuse and anti-patterns

Patterns in programming

The concept of a pattern is simple to define. A pattern is something that you did in the past, was successful, and can be applied to multiple situations. Patterns capture experiences in software development that have been proven to work again and again, and thus provide a solution to specific problems. They are not invented: they arise from practical experience.

When many programmers are trying to solve similar problems, they arrive again and again at a solution that works best. Such a solution is later distilled into a solution template, something that we programmers then use to approach similar problems in the future. Such solution templates are often called **patterns**.

Good patterns are problem and language agnostic. In other words, they apply to C++ and Delphi, and to Haskell and Smalltalk. In practice, as it turns out, lots of patterns are at least partially specific to a particular environment. Lots of them, for example, work best with **object-oriented programming** (OOP) languages and do not work with functional languages.

In programming, patterns serve a dual role. Besides being a template for problem solving, they also provide a common vocabulary that programmers around the world can use to discuss problems. It is much simpler to say, for example, that we will use an observer pattern to notify subsystems of state changes than it is to talk at length about how that part will be implemented. Using patterns as a base for discussion therefore forces us to talk about implementation concepts, and not about the detailed implementation specifics.

It is important to note that patterns provide only a template for a solution and not a detailed recipe. You will still have to take care of the code and make sure that the pattern implementation makes sense and works well with the rest of the program.

Programming patterns can be split into three groups that cover different abstraction levels. At the very top, we talk about architectural patterns. They deal with program organization as a whole, with a wide, top-down view, but they do not deal with implementation. For example, the famous Model-View-ViewModel approach is an architectural pattern that deals with a user interface-business logic split.

Architectural patterns are not a topic of this book, but still I'll dedicate some space to them in `Chapter 11`, *Other Kinds of Patterns*.

A bit lower down the abstraction scale are design patterns. They describe the run—time behavior of a program. When we use design patterns, we are trying to solve a specific problem in code, but we don't want to go fully to the code level. Design patterns will be the topic of the first ten chapters.

Patterns that work fully on the code level are called **idioms**. Idioms are usually language specific and provide templates for commonly encountered coding problems. For example, a standard way of creating/destroying objects in Delphi is an idiom, as is iterating over an enumerable container with the `for..in` construct.

Idioms are not the topic of this book. I will, however, mention the most important Delphi idioms, while talking about their specific implementation for some of the patterns.

Patterns are useful

This is not a book about the theory behind patterns; rather, this book focuses on the aspects of their implementation. Before I scare you all off with all this talk about design patterns, their history, modern advances, anti-patterns, and so on, I have decided to present a very simple pattern using an example. A few lines of code should explain why a pattern—based approach to problem solving can be a good thing.

In the code archive for this chapter, you'll find a simple console application called `DesignPatternExample`. Inside, you'll find an implementation of a sparse array, as shown in the following code fragment:

```
type
  TSparseRec = record
  IsEmpty: boolean;
  Value : integer;
end;

TSparseArray = TArray<TSparseRec>;
```

Each array index can either be empty (in which case `IsEmpty` will be set to `True`), or it can contain a value (in which case `IsEmpty` will be set to `False` and `Value` contains the value).

If we have a variable of the data: `TSparseArray` type, we can iterate over it with the following code:

```
for i := Low(data) to High(data) do
  if not data[i].IsEmpty then
    Process(data[i].Value);
```

When you need a similar iteration in some other part of the program, you have to type this short fragment again. Of course, you could also be smart and just copy and paste the first two lines (`for` and `if`). This is simple but problematic, because it leads to the copy and paste anti-pattern, which I'll discuss later in this chapter.

For now, let's imagine the following hypothetical scenario. Let's say that at some point, you start introducing nullable types into this code. We already have ready to use nullable types available in the Spring4D library (`https://bitbucket.org/sglienke/spring4d`), and it was suggested that they will appear in the next major Delphi release after 10.2 Tokyo, so this is definitely something that could happen.

In Spring4D, nullable types are implemented as a `Nullable<T>` record, which is partially shown in the following code:

```
type
  Nullable<T> = record
    ...
    property HasValue: Boolean read GetHasValue;
    property Value: T read GetValue;
  end;
```

As far as we know, Delphi's implementation will expose the same properties: `HasValue` and `Value`.

You can then redefine `TSparseArray` as an array of `Nullable<integer>`, as the following code:

```
type
  TSparseArray = TArray<Nullable<integer>>;
```

This is all well and good, but we now have to fix all the places in the code where `IsEmpty` is called and replace it with `HasValue`. We also have to change the program logic in all of these places. If the code was testing the result of `IsEmpty`, we would have to use `not` `HasValue` and vice versa. This is all very tedious and error prone. When making such a change in a big program, you can easily forget to insert or remove the not, and that breaks the program.

Wouldn't it be much better if there were only one place in the program when that `for`/`if` iteration construct was implemented? We would only have to correct code at that one location and— voila!—the program would be working again. Welcome to the Iterator pattern!

We'll discuss this pattern at length in Chapter 7, *Iterator, Visitor, Observer, and Memento*. For now, I will just give you a practical example.

The simplest way to add an iterator pattern to `TScatteredArray` is to use a method that accepts such an array and an iteration method, that is, a piece of code that is executed for each non empty element of the array. As the next code example shows, this is simple to achieve with Delphi's anonymous methods:

```
procedure Iterate(const data: TSparseArray; const iterator:
TProc<integer>);
var
  i: Integer;
begin
  for i := Low(data) to High(data) do
```

```
    if not data[i].IsEmpty then
      iterator(data[i].Value);
  end;
```

In this example, data is the sparse array that we want to array over, and iterator represents the anonymous method that will be executed for each non null element. The TProc<integer> notation specifies a procedure accepting one integer argument (TProc<T> is a type declared in System.SysUtils).

As we don't want to make a full copy of the array data each time Iterate is called, the data parameter is marked with a const qualifier. This can make a big difference in the execution speed. The const on the iterator parameter is just a minor optimization that stops the iterator's reference count being incremented while the Iterate is executing. Anonymous methods are internally implemented as interfaces in Delphi, and they are managed in the same way.

In the following code, we call Iterate and pass it the array to be iterated upon (data), and an anonymous method will be executed for each non empty element:

```
Iterate(data,
  procedure (value: integer)
  begin
    Process(value);
  end);
```

If we had to adapt this code to a nullable-based implementation, we would just edit the Iterate method and change not data[i].IsEmpty into data[i].HasValue—simple, effective, and, most importantly, foolproof!

Delphi also offers us a nice idiom that we can implement in an iterator pattern: enumerators and the for..in language construct. Using this idiom we can iterate over our sparse array with the following elegant code:

```
for value in data.Iterator do
  Process(value);
```

I will leave the implementation details for Chapter 7, *Iterator, Visitor, Observer, and Memento*. You are, of course, welcome to examine the demonstration project DesignPatternExample to see how data.Iterator is implemented (hint: start at TSparseArrayHelper).

Delphi idioms – Creating and destroying an object

Patterns are mostly language independent. We could have written an equivalent of the `Iterate` method from the previous sections in most languages, even in old Turbo Pascal for DOS or in an assembler. The `for..in` construct, however, is specific to Delphi. We call such a low-level pattern an idiom.

Idioms are not that useful when we are thinking about or discussing the program design. The knowledge of a language's is, however, necessary for you to become fluent in a language. Idioms teach us about the best ways of performing common operations in a particular environment.

The most important Delphi idiom concerns how object creation and destruction should be handled in code. It is used whenever we require a common three-step operation: create an object, do something with it, destroy the object.

 It must be said that this idiom applies only to Windows and OS X development. Compilers for Android, iOS, and Linux support **Automatic Reference Counting** (**ARC**), which means that objects are handled the same way as interfaces.

This idiom also shows how we can run into problems if we stray from the path and try to manage objects in a different manner. But first, I'd like to show you the recommended ways of handling objects in code. All examples can be found in the demonstration project `ObjectLifecycle`.

For simplicity's sake, we'll be using two objects: `obj1` and `obj2` of type `TObject`, as shown in the following code:

```
var
   obj1, obj2: TObject;
```

In practice, you'll be using a different class, as there's not much that a `TObject` could be used for. But all other details (that is, the idiom) will remain the same.

The first idiomatic way of handling objects is shown in the following code. Let's call it Variant A:

```
obj1 := TObject.Create;
try
  // some code
finally
  FreeAndNil(obj1);
end;
```

Firstly, we create the object. Then we enter a `try..finally` construct and execute some code on object `obj1`. In the end, the object is destroyed in the `finally` part. If the `// some code` part raises an exception, it is caught, and the object is safely destroyed in the `finally` section.

> Is it better to use `obj1.Free` or `FreeAndNil(obj1)`? There is a big debate regarding this in the Delphi community, and verdict is inconclusive. I prefer `FreeAndNil` because it doesn't leave dangling references to uninitialized memory.

Variant A is short and concise, but it becomes unwieldy when you need more than one object. To create two objects, do something with them, and then destroy them, we have to nest the `try..finally` constructs, as shown in the following code fragment:

```
obj1 := TObject.Create;
try
  obj2 := TObject.Create;
  try
    // some code
  finally
    FreeAndNil(obj2);
  end;
finally
  FreeAndNil(obj1);
end;
```

This approach correctly handles the `obj1` destruction when an exception is raised inside any code dealing with `obj2`, including its creation.

The long-windedness of Variant A makes many programmers adopt the following designed approach:

```
try
  obj1 := TObject.Create;
  obj2 := TObject.Create;
  // some code
finally
  FreeAndNil(obj1);
  FreeAndNil(obj2);
end;
```

Let me say it loud and clear: this technique does not work correctly! If you are using such an approach in your code, you should fix the code!

The problem here is that creating `obj2` may fail. The `TObject.Create` phrase will succeed for sure (unless you run out of memory), but in a real-life example, a different object may raise an exception inside the constructor. If that happens, the code will firstly destroy `obj1` and then it will proceed with destroying `obj2`.

This variable, however, is not initialized, and so the code will try to destroy some random part of memory, which will in most cases lead to access violation—that is, if you're lucky. If you're not, it will just corrupt a part of another object and cause a random and potentially very wrong behavior of the program.

For the same reason, the following simplified version also doesn't work:

```
try
  obj1 := TObject.Create;
  // some code
finally
  FreeAndNil(obj1);
end;
```

If an `obj1` constructor fails, the code will try to free the object by referencing the uninitialized `obj1`, and that will again cause problems.

In such situations, we can use Variant B of the idiom as follows:

```
obj1 := nil;
try
  obj1 := TObject.Create;
  // some code
finally
  FreeAndNil(obj1);
end;
```

Now, we can be sure that `obj1` will either contain `nil` or a reference to a valid object. The code will work because `TObject.Free`, which is called from `FreeAndNil`, disposes of an object in the following manner:

```
procedure TObject.Free;
begin
  if Self <> nil then
    Destroy;
end;
```

If the object (`Self` in this code) is already `nil`, then calling `Free` does nothing.

Variant B also nicely expands to multiple objects, as shown in the following code:

```
obj1 := nil;
obj2 := nil;
try
  obj1 := TObject.Create;
  obj2 := TObject.Create;
  // some code
finally
  FreeAndNil(obj1);
  FreeAndNil(obj2);
end;
```

Again, all object variables are always correctly initialized and the destruction works properly.

The only problem with Variant B is that `obj2` doesn't get destroyed if the destructor for `obj1` raises an exception. Raising an exception in a destructor is, however, something that you should definitely not do, as that may also cause the object to be only partially destroyed.

Gang of Four started it all

The design pattern movement (as it applies to programming) was started by the **Gang of Four**. By Gang of Four, we don't mean the Chinese Cultural Revolution leaders from the seventies or a post-punk group from Leeds, but four authors of a prominent book: *Design Patterns: Elements of Reusable Object-Oriented Software*. This book, written by *Erich Gamma*, *Richard Helm*, *Ralph Johson*, and *John Vlissides*, was published in 1994, and thoroughly shook the programming community.

Back in 1994, when C++ was becoming more and more prominent, object orientation was all the rage, and people were programming in Smalltalk. Programmers were simply not thinking in terms of patterns. Every good programmer, of course, had their own book of recipes that work, but they were not sharing them or trying to describe them in a formal way. The *GoF* book, as it is mostly called in informal speech, changed all that.

The majority of the book is dedicated to 23 (now classic) software design patterns. The authors started with a rationale for each one, providing a formal description of the pattern and examples in Smalltalk and C++. These patterns now provide the very core of a programmer's toolset, although later, more patterns were discovered and formalized. Notably missing from the book are design patterns that relate to parallel programming (multi-threading).

In the first two chapters of their book, the authors explored the power and the pitfalls of OOP. They drew two important conclusions: you should program to an interface, not an implementation, and favor object composition over class inheritance.

The former rule corresponds to the **dependency inversion principle** (the **D** part of the **SOLID** principle, which I'll cover in more detail later in this chapter).

The latter contradicts the whole object-oriented movement, which preached class hierarchy and inheritance. As the distinction between the two approaches is not well known in the Delphi world, I have prepared a short example in the next section.

Don't inherit – compose!

If you are a programmer of a certain age, it will be hard for you, as it was for me, to accept the don't inherit—compose philosophy. After all, we were taught that OOP is the key to everything and that it will fix all our problems.

That was indeed the dream behind the OOP movement. The practice, however, dared to disagree. In most real-life scenarios, the OOP approach leads only to mess and ugly code. The following short example will succinctly demonstrate why this happens.

Let's say we would like to write a class that implements a list of only three operations. We'd like to add integer numbers (Add), get the size of the list (Count), and read each element (Items). Our application will use this list to simulate a data structure from which elements can never be removed and where data, once added, can never be modified. We would therefore like to prevent every user of this class, from calling methods that will break those assumptions.

We can approach this problem in three different ways. Firstly, we can write the code from scratch. We are, however, lazy, and we want Delphi's TList to do the actual work. Secondly, we can inherit from TList and write a derived class TInheritedLimitedList that supports only the three operations we need. Thirdly, we can create a new base class TCompositedLimitedList that uses TList for data storage. The second and third approach are both shown in the project called CompositionVsInheritance, which you can find in the code archive for this chapter.

When we start to implement the inherited version of TList, we immediately run into problems. The first one is that TList simply implements lots of functionality that we don't want in our class. An example of such methods would be Insert, Move, Clear, and so on.

The second problem is that inheriting from TList was simply not a factor when that class was designed. Almost all of its methods are static, not virtual, and as such cannot really be overridden. We can only reintroduce them, and that, as we'll see very soon, can cause unforeseen problems.

Another problematic part is the Clear method. We don't want to allow the users of our class to call it, but, still, it is implicitly called from TList.Destroy, and so we cannot fully disable it.

We would also like to access the elements as integer and not as Pointer data. To do this, we also have to reintroduce the Items property.

A full declaration of the TInheritedLimitedList class is shown next. You will notice that we have to reintroduce a whole bunch of methods:

```
type
  TInheritedLimitedList = class(TList)
  strict private
    FAllowClear: boolean;
  protected
    function Get(Index: Integer): Integer;
    procedure Put(Index: Integer; const Value: Integer);
  public
    destructor Destroy; override;
    function Add(Item: Integer): Integer; inline;
```

```
      procedure Clear; override;
      procedure Delete(Index: Integer); reintroduce;
      procedure Exchange(Index1, Index2: Integer); reintroduce;
      function Expand: TList; reintroduce;
      function Extract(Item: Pointer): Pointer; reintroduce;
      function First: Pointer; reintroduce;
      function GetEnumerator: TListEnumerator; reintroduce;
      procedure Insert(Index: Integer; Item: Pointer); reintroduce;
      function Last: Pointer; reintroduce;
      procedure Move(CurIndex, NewIndex: Integer); reintroduce;
      function Remove(Item: Pointer): Integer; reintroduce;
      function RemoveItem(Item: Pointer;
        Direction: TList.TDirection): Integer; reintroduce;
      property Items[Index: Integer]: Integer read Get write Put; default;
    end;
```

Some parts of the implementation are trivial. The next code fragment shows how `Delete` and `Exchange` are disabled:

```
procedure TInheritedLimitedList.Delete(Index: Integer);
begin
  raise Exception.Create('Not supported');
end;

procedure TInheritedLimitedList.Exchange(Index1, Index2: Integer);
begin
  raise Exception.Create('Not supported');
end;
```

Most of the implementation is equally dull, so I won't show it here. The demo project contains a fully implemented class that you can peruse in peace. Still, I'd like to point out two implementation details.

The first is the `Items` property. We had to reintroduce it, as we'd like to work with integers, not pointers. It is also implemented in a way that allows read-only access:

```
function TInheritedLimitedList.Get(Index: Integer): Integer;
begin
  Result := Integer(inherited Get(Index));
end;

procedure TInheritedLimitedList.Put(Index: Integer; const Value: Integer);
begin
  raise Exception.Create('Not supported');
end;
```

The second interesting detail is the implementation of the `Clear` method. It is normally disabled (because calling `Clear` would result in an exception). The `Destroy` destructor, however, sets an internal flag that allows `Clear` to be called from the inherited destructor, as shown in the following code:

```
destructor TInheritedLimitedList.Destroy;
begin
  FAllowClear := true;
  inherited;
end;

procedure TInheritedLimitedList.Clear;
begin
  if FAllowClear then
    inherited
  else
    raise Exception.Create('Not supported');
end;
```

There are numerous problems with this approach. We had to introduce some weird hacks, and write a bunch of code to disable functions that should not be used. This is partially caused by the bad `TList` design (bad from an object-oriented viewpoint), which does not allow us to override virtual methods. But worst of all is the fact that our inheritance based list still doesn't work correctly!

Looking at the following code fragment, everything seems OK. If we run it, we get an exception in the `list[1] := 42` statement:

```
var
  list: TInheritedLimitedList;

list.Add(1);
list.Add(2);
list.Add(3);
list[1] := 42;
```

If, however, we pass this list to another method that expects to get a `TList`, that method would be able to modify our list! The following code fragment changes the list to contain elements 1, 42, and 3:

```
procedure ChangeList(list: TList);
begin
  list[1] := pointer(42);
end;

var
```

```
   list: TInheritedLimitedList;

list.Add(1);
list.Add(2);
list.Add(3);
ChangeList(list);
```

This happens because `Get` and `Put` in the original `TList` are not `virtual`. Because of this, the compiler has no idea that a derived class can override them and just blindly calls the `TList` version. Assigning to `list[1]` in `ChangeList` therefore uses `TList.Put`, which doesn't raise an exception.

Raising exceptions to report coding errors is another problem with this approach. When working with strongly typed languages, such as Delphi, we would like such coding problems to be caught by the compiler, not during testing.

Compared to inheritance, implementing a list by using composition is totally trivial. We just have to declare a class that exposes the required functionality and write a few methods that use an internal `FList: TList` object to implement this functionality. All our public methods are very simple and only map to methods of the internal object. By declaring them `inline`, the compiler will actually create almost identical code to the one we would get if we are use `TList` instead of `TCompositedLimitedList` in our code. As the implementation is so simple, as you can see from the following code it can be fully included in the book:

```
type
  TCompositedLimitedList = class
  strict private
    FList: TList;
  strict protected
    function Get(Index: Integer): Pointer; inline;
    function GetCount: Integer; inline;
  public
    constructor Create;
    destructor Destroy; override;
    function Add(Item: Pointer): Integer; inline;
    property Count: Integer read GetCount;
    property Items[Index: Integer]: Pointer read Get; default;
  end;

constructor TCompositedLimitedList.Create;
begin
  inherited Create;
  FList := TList.Create;
end;
```

```
destructor TCompositedLimitedList.Destroy;
begin
  FList.Free;
  inherited;
end;

function TCompositedLimitedList.Add(Item: Pointer): Integer;
begin
  Result := FList.Add(Item);
end;

function TCompositedLimitedList.Get(Index: Integer): Pointer;
begin
  Result := FList[Index];
end;

function TCompositedLimitedList.GetCount: Integer;
begin
  Result := FList.Count;
end;
```

By using composition instead of inheritance, we get all the benefits fast code, small and testable implementation, and error checking in the compiler.

Pattern taxonomy

The original *Gang of Four* book separated patterns into three categories: creational, structural, and behavioral. To these three, another large category was added in recent years, concurrency patterns. Some concurrency patterns were covered in another classic book: *Pattern-Oriented Software Architecture: Patterns for Concurrent and Networked Objects, Volume 2*, by *Douglas C Schmidt, Michael Stal, Hans Rohnert*, and *Frank Buschmann*.

Creational patterns deal with delegation. They are focused on creating new objects and groups of related objects. These patterns will create objects for you, meaning that you don't have to create them directly.

The focus of structural patterns is aggregation. They define ways to compose objects in a way that creates new functionality from the constituent parts. They help us create software components.

Behavioral patterns are big on consultation they talk about responsibilities between objects. Unlike structural patterns, which only specify a structure, behavioral patterns define communication paths and messages.

Concurrency patterns deal with cooperation. They make a system composed of multiple components, running in parallel, work together. The main concerns of concurrency patterns are resource protection and messaging.

The next few pages will give an overview of the most important design patterns, organized by category and sorted by name.

Creational patterns

The patterns in the first group of patterns, creational patterns, are used when simple and composite objects are created. The following patterns belong to this group:

- **Abstract factory pattern**: You can use this pattern to create entire families of related objects but without the need to specify their classes. This pattern is described in Chapter 3, *Factory Method, Abstract Factory, Prototype, and Builder*.
- **Builder pattern**: This pattern abstracts the construction of a complex object, and allows the same process to create different representations. It is described in Chapter 2, *Singleton, Dependency Injection, Lazy Initialization, and Object Pool*.
- **Dependency injection pattern**: This is used to send specific instances of depended objects into a class (injecting them), instead of the class creating them directly. This pattern is described in Chapter 3, *Factory Method, Abstract Factory, Prototype, and Builder*.
- **Factory method pattern**: This pattern defines an interface for creating a single object. Subclasses can then decide which class to instantiate. This is described in Chapter 3, *Factory Method, Abstract Factory, Prototype, and Builder*.
- **Lazy initialization pattern**: This delays the creation of an object or the calculation of a value until it is actually needed. In the *GoF* book, it appeared as a *virtual proxy*. This pattern is described in Chapter 3, *Factory Method, Abstract Factory, Prototype, and Builder*.
- **Multiton pattern**: This pattern similar to singleton. It allows multiple named instances, while serving as the only way of accessing them. It is not covered in this book.
- **Object pool pattern**: This pattern recycles objects to avoid the expensive acquisition and creation of resources. A special case, connection pool, is well-known to all database programmers. This pattern is described in Chapter 2, *Singleton, Dependency Injection, Lazy Initialization, and Object Pool*.
- **Prototype pattern**: This specifies how to create objects based on a template object that is cloned to produce new objects. This pattern is described in Chapter 2, *Singleton, Dependency Injection, Lazy Initialization, and Object Pool*.

- **Resource acquisition is initialization pattern (RAII)**: This pattern ensures that resources are properly released by tying them to the lifespan of an object. In Delphi, we implement this pattern by using an interface as a resource owner. It is not covered in this book.
- **Singleton pattern**: This pattern ensures that a class has only one instance. It also provides a common point of access to that instance. This pattern is described in Chapter 2, *Singleton, Dependency Injection, Lazy Initialization, and Object Pool*.

Structural patterns

The second group of patterns, structural patterns, handles the way objects are composed into new objects. The following patterns belong to this group:

- **Adapter pattern**: This pattern, which is also known as a wrapper or a translator pattern, converts the interface of a class into another interface expected by a client. It is described in Chapter 5, *Adapter, Decorator, Facade, and Proxy*.
- **Bridge pattern**: This decouples an abstraction from its implementation, which allows the two to vary independently. This pattern is described in Chapter 4, *Composite, Flyweight, Marker Interface, and Bridge*.
- **Composite pattern**: This composes from the hierarchies of more basic objects. This pattern is described in Chapter 4, *Composite, Flyweight, Marker Interface, and Bridge*.
- **Decorator pattern**: This pattern allows an object to take additional responsibilities, in addition to its original interface. Decorators are an alternative to subclassing for an extending functionality. This pattern is described in Chapter 5, *Adapter, Proxy, Decorator, and Facade*.
- **Extension object pattern**: This pattern allows you to adding of a functionality to a hierarchy without changing that hierarchy. This is not covered in this book.
- **Facade pattern**: This pattern combines a set of interfaces exposed by subsystems into a simpler interface that is easier to use. This pattern is described in Chapter 5, *Adapter, Proxy, Decorator, and Facade*.
- **Flyweight pattern**: This pattern uses data-sharing to efficiently support large numbers of similar objects. It is described in Chapter 5, *Adapter, Proxy, Decorator, and Facade*.
- **Front controller pattern**: This pattern is used when designing web applications and provides a centralized entry point for request handling. It is not covered in this book.

- **Marker pattern**: This allows us to associate metadata with a class. This pattern is described in `Chapter 4`, *Composite, Flyweight, Marker Interface, and Bridge*.
- **Module pattern**: This pattern groups several related elements into one conceptual entity. It is not covered in this book.
- **Proxy pattern**: It provides a replacement for another object so it can control access to it. This pattern is described in `Chapter 5`, *Adapter, Proxy, Decorator, and Facade*.
- **Twin pattern**: This pattern helps simulating multiple inheritance in programming languages that don't support this feature. It is not covered in this book.

Behavioral patterns

The third group of patterns, behavioral patterns, deals with communication between objects and with the distribution of responsibilities. The following patterns belong to this group:

- **Blackboard pattern**: This is an **artificial intelligence** (**AI**) pattern for combining different data sources. It is not covered in this book.
- **Chain of responsibility pattern**: This is an object-oriented version of an `if` ladder idiom (`if ... else if ... else if ... else`). It works by constructing a chain of processing objects. It is not covered in this book.
- **Command pattern**: This pattern encapsulates a request as an object. It is especially useful for building user interfaces where it allows for the support of undoable operations. This pattern is described in `Chapter 6`, *Nullable Value, Template Method, Command, and State*.
- **Interpreter pattern**: This pattern defines a representation of a language grammar and gives an interpreter for that grammar. It is not covered in this book.
- **Iterator pattern**: This provides a way to access elements of an aggregate object (list, array, symbol table, tree, and so on) sequentially, without exposing the underlying implementation of that object. This pattern is described in `Chapter 7`, *Iterator, Visitor, Observer, and Memento*.
- **Mediator pattern**: This defines an object that handles interaction between other objects. This pattern supports loose coupling by preventing objects from referring to one another explicitly. It is not covered in this book.
- **Memento pattern**: This specifies how to store and restore an object's internal state without violating encapsulation. This pattern is described in `Chapter 7`, *Iterator, Visitor, Observer, and Memento*.

- **Null object pattern**: This removes the reason for using a `nil` pointer, by providing a special, default value for a class. This pattern is described in `Chapter` `6`, *Nullable Value, Template Method, Command, and State*.

- **Observer pattern**: This pattern is also known as a publish/subscribe pattern. It provides another way to prevent tight coupling in a system, by setting up a system where a change of objects results in all of its dependents being notified about the change. This pattern is described in `Chapter` `7`, *Iterator, Visitor, Observer, and Memento*.

- **Servant pattern**: This pattern defines an object that implements a common functionality for a group of classes. It is not covered in this book.

- **Specification pattern**: This pattern provides support for business logic that can be recombined by chaining the rules together with boolean operations. It is not covered in this book.

- **State pattern**: This allows an object to change its behavior when there is a change to its internal state. It is described in `Chapter` `6`, *Nullable Value, Template Method, Command, and State*.

- **Strategy pattern**: This pattern defines a family of algorithms that can be used interchangeably. It is not covered in this book.

- **Template method pattern**: This defines a skeleton of on operation and defers some steps to subclasses. This pattern is described in `Chapter` `6`, *Nullable Value, Template Method, Command, and State*.

- **Visitor pattern**: This pattern specifies an operation that is performed on all elements of an object's internal structure. It is described in `Chapter` `7`, *Iterator, Visitor, Observer, and Memento*.

Concurrency patterns

The last group, concurrency patterns, contains patterns that are needed in the world of parallel programming. The following patterns belong to this group:

- **Active object pattern**: This pattern hides the concurrency by implementing asynchronous method inside an object, which serves as a scheduler for handling requests. It is not covered in this book.

- **Binding properties pattern**: This pattern combines multiple observers to force synchronization on properties in different objects. It is not covered in this book.

- **Blockchain pattern**: This provides a decentralized way for storing data in a linked list protected with cryptographic means. It is not covered in this book.

- **Compute kernel pattern**: This pattern executes the same calculation many times in parallel, differing only on integer input parameters. It is frequently related to GPU calculation. It is not covered in this book.
- **Double-checked locking pattern**: This reduces the overhead of acquiring a lock in a safe manner. This pattern is described in `Chapter 8`, *Locking patterns*.
- **Event-based asynchronous pattern**: This pattern defines a way of executing parallel operations where a caller is notified when a worker finishes the execution. It is not explicitly described in this book, although it is used as a basis for concrete implementations in `Chapter 9`, *Thread pool, Messaging, Future and Pipeline*.
- **Future pattern**: This pattern pushes a calculation into a background and replaces it with a promise that a result will be available in the future. It is described in `Chapter 9`, *Thread pool, Messaging, Future and Pipeline*.
- **Guarded suspension pattern**: This pattern manages operations that depend on a two-part condition: a precondition that must be satisfied and a lock that must be acquired. It is not covered in this book.
- **Join pattern**: This pattern provides a way to write distributed and parallel systems, by message passing. It is not covered in this book.
- **Lock pattern**: This protects shared resources by implementing a locking mechanism. This pattern is described in `Chapter 8`, *Locking patterns*.
- **Lock striping pattern**: This pattern optimizes locking, by replacing a single global lock with a set of specialized locks. It is described in `Chapter 8`, *Locking patterns*.
- **Messaging design pattern (MDP):** This is based on the interchange of information between components in the system. This pattern is described in `Chapter 9`, *Thread Pool, Messaging, Future, and Pipeline*.
- **Monitor object pattern**: This pattern combines locking with a mechanism for signalling other threads that their condition was met. It is not covered in this book.
- **Optimistic initialization pattern**: This reduces the cost of locking by replacing it with the small probability of extraneous objects being created and thrown away. This pattern is described in `Chapter 8`, *Locking patterns*.
- **Pipeline pattern**: This pattern specifies a way of decoupling thread dependencies by passing small subsets of data from one worker thread to another through a message-passing pipeline. It is described in `Chapter 9`, *Thread Pool, Messaging, Future, and Pipeline*.
- **Reactor pattern**: This is a reactor object that provides an asynchronous interface to resources that must be handled synchronously. It is not covered in this book.

- **Read-write lock pattern**: This allows multiple objects to simultaneously read a shared resource, but forces exclusive access for write operations. This pattern is described in `Chapter 8`, *Locking patterns*.
- **Scheduler pattern**: This pattern controls when threads may execute single-threaded code. It is not covered in this book.
- **Thread pool pattern**: This is a parallel version of an object pool creational pattern that provides a pool of worker threads that execute numerous tasks. It is described in `Chapter 9`, *Thread Pool, Messaging, Future, and Pipeline*.
- **Thread-specific storage pattern**: This allows us to use global memory that is local to a thread. In Delphi, we implement this by declaring a variable with the `threadvar` directive. It is not covered in this book.

Criticism

While design patterns are undoubtedly a useful tool, many prominent computer scientists have expressed criticism directed both at the *Design Patterns: Elements of Reusable Object-Oriented Software* book and at the general way patterns are used in practice.

Over the years, programmers have learned that the patterns in the *GoF* book really aren't as widely applicable as the authors thought. Lots of them only apply to the object-oriented world. If we try to use them with a functional language, they are largely useless. They can also be greatly simplified when used in aspect-oriented languages.

Delphi, however, is an object-oriented language, so we can reuse most of the Gang of Four observations. Still, it is important to keep in mind how patterns should be used in practice.

As a main rule, you should never use design patterns to architect the software. Design patterns tell you how to write code to solve a specific problem while software design should be done on a higher abstraction level, without referring to implementation details. Rather, you should use them to approach specific problems that you run into while programming.

The second idea that should be present in your mind at all times is that patterns are not the goal: they are just a tool. Design patterns formalize only some aspects of programming, not all of it. You should also never follow a design pattern blindly. Think about what it says, think about how it applies to your problem, and then use it wisely. Programming is a craft, not a paint by numbers book, and patterns are not a silver bullet.

If you look at the code and the pattern stands out to you, it was not implemented correctly. A good pattern will hide in the code, and only a careful observer will be able to say: Oh! I see you used a visitor pattern here. Nice. It is important to understand the concepts behind the design patterns, and not the exact names of the methods and properties that were used in an implementation you found somewhere (even if that was in the *Design Patterns* book).

Design patterns *are* a great tool for refactoring and communication. Hey, gals and guys, this part of our system is completely messed up, and we should use a publish/subscribe pattern instead, is a type of a statement that should appear more frequently in our discussions!

Anti-patterns

Every yin has its yang, and every hero has their dark side, and so the very existence of patterns suggest that there exists the opposite. We could simply call it a mess, but programmers try to find an order to everything, even in chaos, and so they cataloged the mess and described the many kinds of anti-patterns. I will only briefly touch on this topic, as the goal of this book is to teach you about order, not disorder, but there is always something to learn from bad examples.

Design patterns are nicely classified, and most programmers agree on how they should be named and defined. Anti-patterns, on the other hand, are messier. They hide behind different names and they provide mere sketches of behavior, not fully defined templates.

The nastiest of the anti-patterns is sometimes called a **big ball of mud**. A typical sign of this anti-pattern is that the code is a mess, no matter how you look at it. It is unreadable: the data is global; every class uses every other class, except for the code that no one uses at all; and so on and so on. If you are ever hired to work on such a project, find a better job (just some friendly advice).

Another anti-pattern is the **blob**. It occurs when the problem was not correctly decomposed. One class is doing most of the work, while others represent just small fragments that don't do anything significant. In Delphi, we can find this anti-pattern in badly organized projects where most of the functionality is implemented in the main form of class. Such a project can usually be saved by applying SOLID design principles, which I'll discuss in the next section.

The golden hammer anti-pattern happens when a programmer uses one technology to solve everything. I've seen projects where every data structure was a `TStringList` and others where all data structures were implemented with in-memory datasets. The best way of rescuing such projects is to put them in the hands of programmers with a wide knowledge of programming, data structures, and available tools.

Everyone who programmed in old-school BASIC has an intimate knowledge of a spaghetti code pattern: the code jumps here and there, doesn't follow any logic, and definitely does not use standard flow-control constructs, such as `while`. It is usually too difficult to decode and fix such an implementation. A better approach is to write a decent set of unit tests and then rewrite the problematic part from scratch.

The last anti-pattern I want to mention is called **copy and paste programming**. A typical sign of this anti-pattern is longer sequences of code that are frequently repeated in the source. There are almost no shared methods; everything is copied all over the place. This is a direct violation of the DRY design principle, which will be described in the next section and can be more-or-less simply solved by applying the same principle.

Design principles

Patterns are not the only way of formalizing metaprogramming concepts. Patterns address specific problems, but sometimes we would like to express ideas that are not problem specific. Such formalizations are called **principles**. If they are related to program design, we call them, quite obviously, design principles.

Principles provide a view of a problem that is complementary to patterns. They don't give specific instructions on how to solve problems but rather instruct us how to write good code. A good programmer should, therefore, know both design patterns and design principles by heart. An excellent programmer, of course, also knows when to use patterns and principles and when to ignore them, but that's another story. You can only get such a level of knowledge by practicing programming for a long time.

Still, everyone has to start somewhere, and at the beginning, it is advantageous to know well-known and commonly appreciated principles. I'll finish this chapter with a short review of the most important design principles.

SOLID

The most important principle of OOP is undoubtedly SOLID. It covers five ideas that are a subset of many principles promoted by software engineer and author *Robert C Martin* (you may know him as *Dr. Bob*). SOLID is an acronym in which each letter represents one of the following principles:

- **Single responsibility principle**: This principle states that a class should only have one responsibility. It goes hand-in-hand with software decomposition. If we cannot nicely decompose software implementation into components, it will also be hard to implement classes with only one responsibility. Taking care of the single responsibility principle helps prevent the blob anti-pattern.

- **Open/closed principle:** This principle states that software entities should be open for extensions but closed for modification. In other words, a module (class) should be extensible (open for extensions) without having to modify its source code (closed for modification). This extensibility is usually achieved either with the careful use of object-oriented principles (inheritance, virtual functions) or delegation (for example, providing a custom comparison function to a sorting method).

- **Liskov substitution principle:** Introduced in 1987 by *Barbara Liskov*, this tells us that the program should continue to work correctly if we substitute one object with its sub-type (a derived class, for example). This principle requires that a derived class cannot have more strict requirements than its base class (the preconditions cannot be stronger in a derived class) and that it cannot give weaker guarantees about output data (post-conditions cannot be weaker).

- **Interface segregation principle:** This principle merely states that multiple interfaces with a specific functionality are better than one general-purpose interface. An interface segregation principle makes the system more decoupled and easier to refactor.

- **Dependency inversion principle:** The last SOLID principle states that you should depend on abstraction and not on the concrete implementation. When you use a class, you should only depend on the interface that is exposed and not on the specific implementation. This principle is frequently used to refer to programming for an interface, not for an implementation.

We could jokingly say that the SOLID principle doesn't respect its own rules. By the interface segregation principle, we would expect to read about five different principles and not one larger set. Other design principles in this chapter are simpler and cover only one idea.

Don't repeat yourself

The **don't repeat yourself** principle (**DRY**), states that every piece of knowledge should have a single representation within a system. In other words, you should implement each small part of functionality as one method, and not use copy and paste.

In practice, such detailed decomposition will also cause problems. We will usually use a function from multiple places in the code. If that shared function changes behavior, we have to explicitly check all call sites (all places that use it) to see whether the new functionality is indeed required and desired at that place. Still, this is much better than the mess introduced by copy and paste programming.

KISS and YAGNI

The **KISS** principle came into programming from the US Navy. It states that systems are more reliable when they are kept simple. Although many sources say that KISS stands for keep it simple, stupid, the original author described it as keep it simple stupid. In other words, it is not that the engineer is stupid, but that the implementation should be simple stupid, or as trivial as possible.

This principle goes hand in hand with another idea taken from the extreme programming world—**YAGNI**. Meaning *you ain't gonna need it*, this acronym teaches us to only implement parts of code that are actually needed. If you try to foresee what will be needed in the future and write it in advance, you will, in many cases, just lose time, as either you'll be mistaken or the software specification will change.

Both KISS and YAGNI require frequent refactoring when software specification is updated, so it is helpful if you know the refactoring tools in Delphi or use a software add-on, such as MMX Code Explorer.

Summary

This chapter provided a brief overview of a topic that will be discussed in the rest of the book: design patterns. We took a look at the broader picture and found that patterns are everywhere and that design patterns are only part of a larger group of programming patterns. We also learned about architectural patterns, which function on a higher level, and idioms, which are very low-level patterns. (We will talk more about architectural patterns in `Chapter 11`, *Other Kinds of Patterns*. Delphi idioms are introduced throughout this book, starting with this chapter.)

We then learned about at the history of patterns, and were introduced to Gang of Four and their *Design Patterns* book. We learned that patterns are not fixed in time, but are evolving, and that many patterns, especially ones dealing with parallel programming, were documented after that book was published.

After this, I gave an overview of design pattern classification, where we saw how patterns can be split into four big groups, and we learned what the most important patterns in each group are. This will help you research patterns that are not covered in this book.

The chapter ended with a short section on design principles, which represent more generic ideas than patterns. Design principles represent a foundation of a programmer's knowledge, and it is recommended that you know them, even before you start studying design patterns.

In the next chapter, we'll start discovering design patterns. I'll start with the first group (creational patterns) and give detailed examples of four design patterns: singleton, dependency injection, lazy initialization, and object pool.

Section 2: Creational Patterns 2

In this chapter, the reader will learn the most important patterns from one of the three Gang of Four categories—creational patterns.

This section will comprise the following chapters:

2
Singleton, Dependency Injection, Lazy Initialization, and Object Pool

In **Object-Oriented Programming (OOP)**, everything starts with an object, and if we want to use one, we have to create it first. In most cases, that simply means calling `TSomeClass.Create`, but in a more complex scenario, a specialized design pattern that creates an object for us can be quite handy.

In this chapter, we'll look into four patterns from the creational group. At the end of the chapter, you'll know the following:

- A singleton pattern, which makes sure that a class has only one instance
- A dependency injection pattern, which makes program architecture more flexible and suitable for test-driven development
- A lazy initialization pattern, which makes sure that we don't spend time and resources creating objects that we don't really need
- An object pool pattern, which speeds up the creation of objects that take a long time to create

Singleton

The **singleton** pattern was part of the original Design Patterns collection. It makes sure that a class, which we call a `singleton` class, has only one instance. In other words, only one object of that class may ever be created during the program's life. Such a class must also provide global access to this instance.

 Let me give a real-life example to clarify this definition. You probably live in a country that allows one, and only one, president (or monarch, head of state, and so on.) to exist at the same time. So, that person is a singleton.

You will notice that the pattern tells us nothing about how that one singleton instance should be destroyed. It also doesn't specify when the singleton instance should be created.

Whenever you need to create a singleton, you should first answer the following questions:

- Does the singleton have to be initialized on demand, or will it be created on first use?
- Can the singleton be destroyed when the program ends, or should it disappear when nobody is using it?
- And, most importantly, do you really need to use a singleton?

I believe the use of singletons should be kept to an absolute minimum. After all, a singleton is just a glorified global variable, and inherits all of its problems. It will, for example, cause problems with test-driven development and unit testing. It will also, unless it is created when the program starts, be hard to configure.

In most cases, you simply need an instance of a class and you don't need to bother with preventing this class from creating other instances (other objects). For example, Delphi VCL has a global variable, `Application` of the `TApplication` type, which is effectively a singleton. In a normal program, one and only one `Application` will exist. As the programmers are not idiots, they will not create new instances of `TApplication`, and the program will work just fine.

The code archive for this chapter contains the `Singleton` folder with the project, `SingletonPattern`. Inside this project, you'll find the `Singleton_GlobalVar` unit, which shows how such a singleton-like implementation could look. As it is short and simple, it is fully reproduced here:

```
unit Singleton_GlobalVar;

interface

uses
  Vcl.StdCtrls;

type
  TSingletonGV = class
  public
    procedure Log(logTarget: TListBox; const msg: string);
  end;

var
  SingletonGV: TSingletonGV;

implementation

procedure TSingletonGV.Log(logTarget: TListBox; const msg: string);
begin
  logTarget.ItemIndex := logTarget.Items.Add(
    Format('[%p] %s %s',
           [pointer(Self), FormatDateTime('hh:mm:ss', Now), msg]));
end;

initialization
  SingletonGV := TSingletonGV.Create;
finalization
  FreeAndNil(SingletonGV);
end.
```

In this example, the singleton instance is stored in the global variable, `SingletonGV`, which is created when an application is starting up and is destroyed when an application is shutting down. It implements the `Log` function which is used in the demo.

As the singleton is created when the program starts, we are quite limited in customizing it. We cannot, for example, pass the logging target (the `TListBox` parameter) to the singleton's constructor, as this listbox doesn't yet exist when the singleton is created. We are forced to accept this inflexibility and pass the `logTarget` parameter each time `Log` is called.

 In Delphi, the code in all `initialization` blocks is executed before the first statement of the `.dpr` program. Similarly, all `finalization` blocks are executed after the last statement of the program. You could say that initialization blocks are executed in the program's `begin` statement and that finalization blocks are executed in the program's `end` statement.

Still, sometimes, we really need a true singleton. How can we implement it? Maybe we could start by copying an implementation from a different language. So, how do other languages do it?

In C++, C#, and Java, the recommended solution is to make a constructor private. Access to that constructor is then limited to the method from the singleton class and we can implement a single-point access function. A naive Delphi implementation could try a similar approach, but, as we'll soon see, that wouldn't work.

Still, the `SingletonPattern` project contains the `Singleton_HiddenCreate` unit that implements a singleton class in that manner. I will soon tear this implementation apart, but first let's take a look at the full source code for that unit:

```
unit Singleton_HiddenCreate;

interface

uses
  Vcl.StdCtrls;

type
  TSingletonHC = class
  strict protected
    constructor Create;
  public
    class function Instance: TSingletonHC;
    procedure Log(logTarget: TListBox; const msg: string);
  end;

implementation

uses
  SysUtils;
```

```
var
  GSingleton: TSingletonHC;

constructor TSingletonHC.Create;
begin
  inherited Create;
end;

class function TSingletonHC.Instance: TSingletonHC;
begin
  if not assigned(GSingleton) then
    GSingleton := TSingletonHC.Create;
  Result := GSingleton;
end;

procedure TSingletonHC.Log(logTarget: TListBox; const msg: string);
begin
  logTarget.ItemIndex := logTarget.Items.Add(
    Format('[%p] %s %s',
           [pointer(Self), FormatDateTime('hh:mm:ss', Now), msg]));
end;

initialization
finalization
  FreeAndNil(GSingleton);
end.
```

This code tries to implement a singleton by hiding the constructor. This works in C++, C#, and Java, but Delphi implements constructors in a different way. If a code calls `TSingletonHC.Create`, the first visible constructor in the object hierarchy will be called and will happily create the object. In this instance, `TObject.Create` will be called and will construct a new object for us. This attempt therefore immediately fails.

The `Instance` function tries to make sure that there is one (and only one) instance of the `TSingletonHC` class created. The constructor problem, however, completely thwarts its work.

I should mention here that the code idiom used to create a global instance in the instance method (test whether the singleton exists, create the singleton, and use the singleton) works correctly only in a single-threaded code. If you are using a thread, you need better ways of creating the global instance. For more information, see the *Double-checked locking* and *Optimistic initialization* patterns in `Chapter 8`, *Locking Patterns*.

The singleton is destroyed when the program shuts down. This is completely acceptable, and I can say nothing bad about this part of the implementation.

 Delphi requires the `initialization` section to be present if we want to use the `finalization` section. The `initialization` section may be empty, as is in this example, but it must be present.

Besides being able to create multiple instances of `TSingletonHC`, this implementation suffers from another nasty problem. Any part of the code is capable of destroying the singleton object, but the implementation will think that the object is still alive.

Let's examine the following simple code sequence:

```
TSingletonHC.Instance.Log(listBox, 'A message');
TSingletonHC.Instance.Free;
TSingletonHC.Instance.Log(listBox, 'Another message');
```

Let's assume that the singleton was not created before. The first instance call creates a new `TSingletonHC` object and stores it in the `GSingletonHC` variable. This instance is then returned and its `Log` method is executed.

The second instance call retrieves the existing object. The code then executes `Free` on that object and destroys the singleton instance. The `GSingletonHC` variable, however, still contains a pointer to the memory location! (In Delphi, an object variable is nothing more than a simple pointer to the memory location where the object lies.)

The third instance call then retrieves the existing value of `GSingletonHC`. This value points to the object that was just destroyed! In real life, the third line would most probably execute correctly, as the program was not yet able to reuse this memory for a different purpose, and that makes the problem even bigger. We cannot even be sure that it will be noticed immediately after the singleton object has been destroyed. The program will just start throwing out weird errors some undefined time after that!

The following code from the `SingletonPattern` project demonstrates both problems. You can execute it by clicking on the `TestHiddenCreate` button:

```
procedure TfrmSingleton.btnTestHiddenCreateClick(Sender: TObject);
var
  Singleton1: TSingletonHC;
  Singleton2: TSingletonHC;
  Singleton3: TSingletonHC;
begin
  Singleton1 := TSingletonHC.Instance;
  Singleton2 := TSingletonHC.Instance;
```

```
    // It is still possible to create a new instance of this "singleton"
    Singleton3 := TSingletonHC.Create;

    Singleton1.Log(ListBox1, 'TSingletonHC[1]');
    Singleton2.Log(ListBox1, 'TSingletonHC[2]');
    Singleton3.Log(ListBox1, 'TSingletonHC[3]');
    if Singleton1 <> Singleton2 then
      Singleton2.Log(ListBox1, 'TSingletonHC: Singleton1 <> Singleton2');
    if Singleton2 <> Singleton3 then
      Singleton3.Log(ListBox1, 'TSingletonHC: Singleton2 <> Singleton3');

    Singleton3.Free; // no problem, this is a separate instance
    // Uncommenting the next line will actually free Singleton1,
    // too, as they are the same object
    // Singleton1.Log call below may still work,
    // but program may raise access violations on exit
    // Singleton2.Free;

    Singleton1.Log(ListBox1, 'TSingletonHC alive');
  end;
```

At the beginning of this method, the singleton is accessed twice via the `Instance` method. This works correctly and stores the same object (the same pointer) into both the `Singleton1` and `Singleton2` variables. Immediately after that, however, `TSingletonHC.Create` creates a new object, which destroys the whole singleton idea.

Logging code in the middle of the method checks whether all singleton instances are the same. If you run the program and execute this code, you'll notice that the message **TSingletonHC: Singleton2 <> Singleton3** is displayed. The following screenshot shows the output from the program:

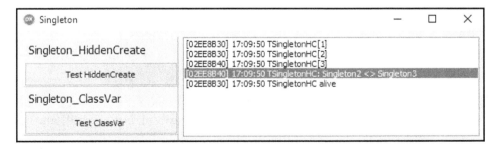

Proof that Singleton_HiddenCreate doesn't work correctly

At the end of the method, the code destroys the `Singleton3` object. This doesn't represent a problem, because this singleton is actually a separate instance of the `TSingletonHC` class. If you uncomment a call to `Singleton2.Free`, however, you'll run into problems. This statement will also destroy `Singleton1`. Also, all future calls to `TSingletonHC.Instance` will return a destroyed object!

As a workaround, we could make the constructor public and throw an exception from it if a global singleton variable is not nil. That would more-or-less work, but it is an ugly solution that just masks a bad approach. As we'll see in a moment, Delphi offers a better way to prevent the creation of multiple instances.

As a bonus, the sample project also includes the `Singleton_ClassVar` unit. This unit stores the singleton in a class variable and not in a global variable. It suffers from the same problems as the hidden constructor variation. I have included this implementation, because you can find some similar solutions on the web, and I don't want them to mislead you.

NewInstance

The proper way to create a singleton in Delphi is not to mess with constructors, but to override the `NewInstance` and `FreeInstance` methods.

When an object is created, the compiler firstly calls the `NewInstance` class method of that object and only then executes the constructor. The `NewInstance` method is `virtual`, and so we can easily override it in our singleton class.

The default implementation in `TObject.NewInstance` calls the `InstanceSize` method to get the number of bytes that are needed to store the new object, then calls `GetMem` to allocate that number of bytes, and in the end, it calls `InitInstance` to fill this memory with zeros.

Instead of all of that, we can change our overridden `NewInstance` method to always return the same memory—our singleton object.

Similarly, the `FreeInstance` method is called to release the memory when the object is destroyed. This method is a normal method, not a class method, but it is still marked as `virtual`, and we can easily change its implementation in the singleton class.

Both techniques are combined in the `Singleton_NewInstance` unit. The full content of that unit is shown here:

```
unit Singleton_NewInstance;

interface

uses
  Vcl.StdCtrls;

type
  TSingletonNI = class
  strict private
  class var
    FSingleton : TSingletonNI;
    FShuttingDown: boolean;
  strict protected
    class function GetInstance: TSingletonNI; static;
  public
    class destructor Destroy;
    class function NewInstance: TObject; override;
    class property Instance: TSingletonNI read GetInstance;
    procedure FreeInstance; override;
    procedure Log(logTarget: TListBox; const msg: string);
  end;

implementation

class destructor TSingletonNI.Destroy;
begin
  FShuttingDown := true;
  FreeAndNil(FSingleton);
  inherited;
end;

procedure TSingletonNI.FreeInstance;
begin
  if FShuttingDown then
    inherited;
end;

class function TSingletonNI.GetInstance: TSingletonNI;
begin
 Result := TSingletonNI.Create;
end;

class function TSingletonNI.NewInstance: TObject;
begin
```

```
    if not assigned(FSingleton) then
      FSingleton := TSingletonNI(inherited NewInstance);
    Result := FSingleton;
  end;

  procedure TSingletonNI.Log(logTarget: TListBox; const msg: string);
  begin
    logTarget.ItemIndex := logTarget.Items.Add(
      Format('[%p] %s %s',
             [pointer(Self), FormatDateTime('hh:mm:ss', Now), msg]));
  end;

  end.
```

In this implementation, `NewInstance` is overridden to create only the singleton instance, `FSingleton` the first time it is called. That takes care of the instances that are created by calling `TSingletonNI.Create`. To provide a nicer global access to this instance, the class implements an `Instance` property. Reading that property calls the `GetInstance` class function, which simply creates a new object and returns it. That way, the singleton is always accessed through the constructor.

On the other hand, `FreeInstance` simply refuses to do anything unless the `FShuttingDown` flag is set. This can only happen when a class destructor is called, and this can only happen when the program is shutting down.

 Class destructors are called after all `finalization` sections have been executed.

The `SingletonPattern` project demonstrates that this implementation really always returns the same object. Click on the `Test NewInstance` button and see for yourself!

This implementation still suffers from a design problem. It offers two ways of accessing the singleton instance. You can either call the `Create` constructor or access the `Instance` property. We could fix this by removing the `Instance` function, and that's exactly what the next example will do. This, however, is not as practical, as using `Instance` in code is simpler than using `Create`. A forthcoming demonstration will prove that.

But, first, let's examine a different problem. Can we change the singleton implementation so that the singleton instance will still be created on demand but also be destroyed when nobody is using it? Well, to do that, we must always know how many users of the singleton are out there, and to do that we must somehow count them. The implementation in Singleton_NewInstanceCounted does that by removing the access via the Instance property. You can only access the singleton by calling TSingletonNIC.Create, and you must release it by calling TSingletonNIC.Free. The following code shows this implementation:

```
unit Singleton_NewInstanceCounted;

interface

uses
  Vcl.StdCtrls;

type
  TSingletonNIC = class
  strict private
  class var
    FInstanceCount: integer;
    FSingleton    : TSingletonNIC;
  public
    class destructor Destroy;
    procedure FreeInstance; override;
    class function NewInstance: TObject; override;
    procedure Log(logTarget: TListBox; const msg: string);
  end;

implementation

class destructor TSingletonNIC.Destroy;
begin
  FreeAndNil(FSingleton);
  inherited;
end;

procedure TSingletonNIC.FreeInstance;
begin
  Dec(FInstanceCount);
  if FInstanceCount = 0 then begin
    inherited;
    FSingleton := nil;
  end;
end;

class function TSingletonNIC.NewInstance: TObject;
```

```
begin
  if not assigned(FSingleton) then
    FSingleton := TSingletonNIC(inherited NewInstance);
  Result := FSingleton;
  Inc(FInstanceCount);
end;

procedure TSingletonNIC.Log(logTarget: TListBox; const msg: string);
begin
  logTarget.ItemIndex := logTarget.Items.Add(
    Format('[%p] %s %s',
           [pointer(Self), FormatDateTime('hh:mm:ss', Now), msg]));
end;

end.
```

This implementation works, but using the `TSingletonNIC` singleton is very clumsy. As the secondary form, `TfrmSecondary`, of the `SingletonPattern` demo shows, most singleton implementation can be used through the `Instance` property. The following code fragment shows how some of the implementations can be used:

```
SingletonGV.Log(frmSingleton.ListBox1, 'SingletonGV');
TSingletonHC.Instance.Log(frmSingleton.ListBox1, 'TSingletonHC');
TSingletonNI.Instance.Log(frmSingleton.ListBox1, 'TSingletonNI');
```

The counted implementation, however, requires the following clumsy approach:

```
var
  logger: TSingletonNIC;

logger := TSingletonNIC.Create;
logger.Log(frmSingleton.ListBox1, 'TSingletonNIC');
logger.Free;
```

This approach is required because we have to manually count the instances in use. Wouldn't it be nice if there existed a mechanism that would do that for us? Oh, but there is one! Delphi interfaces do exactly what we need!

Lateral thinking

Delphi gives us a very nice way to implement something that is, for all practical purposes, a singleton—an interface. An interface-based singleton doesn't strictly confront to the singleton design pattern, but we'll see later that the same property that makes it an almost singleton also gives it additional powers.

As I said before, a singleton pattern is not really a practical solution for (almost) anything. It is better to use a practical solution that is not a full singleton but can be used as one.

The singleton implementation in the `Singleton_Factory` unit borrows from the design patterns book and implements a `Factory` method design pattern. As shown next, this allows us to replace the singleton class with an interface and a method that returns the one and only instance of that class:

```
unit Singleton_Factory;

interface

uses
  Vcl.StdCtrls;

type
  ISingletonF = interface ['{5182E010-121F-4CD9-85EB-4F31D34354F2}']
    procedure Log(logTarget: TListBox; const msg: string);
  end;

function SingletonF: ISingletonF;

implementation

uses
  System.SysUtils;

type
  TSingletonF = class(TInterfacedObject, ISingletonF)
  public
    destructor Destroy; override;
    procedure Log(logTarget: TListBox; const msg: string);
  end;

var
  GSingletonF: TSingletonF;

function SingletonF: ISingletonF;
begin
  if not assigned(GSingletonF) then
    GSingletonF := TSingletonF.Create;
  Result := GSingletonF;
end;

destructor TSingletonF.Destroy;
begin
  GSingletonF := nil;
```

```
    inherited;
end;

procedure TSingletonF.Log(logTarget: TListBox; const msg: string);
begin
  logTarget.ItemIndex := logTarget.Items.Add(
    Format('[%p] %s %s',
           [pointer(Self), FormatDateTime('hh:mm:ss', Now), msg]));
end;

end.
```

This almost-trivial implementation stores the singleton instance inside the global variable, GSingletonF. The factory function, SingletonF, uses the standard test, and use idiom to create the global instance. I would like to stress again that this idiom works only in a single-threaded code and that you should check Chapter 8, *Locking Patterns*, for approaches that work in the parallel world.

 This tests, creates, uses idiom is actually an example of a lazy initialization pattern. We will cover it later in this chapter.

The singleton instance is automatically destroyed when all references to it (all interfaces created by the SingletonF factory and all copies of these interfaces) are no longer in use. A standard destructor makes sure that the global reference, GSingletonF, is also cleared.

If you don't want the singleton to be automatically destroyed when nobody is using it, you just have to change GSingletonF: TSingletonF to GSingletonF: ISingletonF. This will store an additional reference to the interface in GSingletonF, and the singleton will be destroyed only when the program exits.

What about the almost-singleton part I mentioned before? Well, nobody can stop a programmer from creating another class that implements the same ISingletonF interface and then passes the instance of that interface around. In real life, this doesn't represent any problem. If anything, it makes the code more flexible and simplifies testing.

At the end of this long discussion, I'd like to present another singleton implementation where Delphi will do everything for us. Its only limitation is that the singleton instance is always created when the program starts and is destroyed when the program ends.

The trick lies in Delphi's concept of class constructors, class methods, and class variables. In essence, every definition inside a class that is prefixed by the class directive can be thought of as a method/variable of another meta class that always has only one instance. This hidden class is created when the code starts up and is destroyed when the program terminates. We therefore don't have to take any care managing the instance and so on.

The following code shows the full implementation of such a singleton, stored in the `Singleton_Class` unit:

```
unit Singleton_Class;

interface

uses
  Vcl.StdCtrls;

type
  SingletonCl = class
  public
    class procedure Log(logTarget: TListBox; const msg: string);
  end;

implementation

uses
  System.SysUtils;

class procedure SingletonCl.Log(logTarget: TListBox; const msg: string);
begin
  logTarget.ItemIndex := logTarget.Items.Add(
    Format('[%p] %s %s',
            [pointer(Self), FormatDateTime('hh:mm:ss', Now), msg]));
end;

end.
```

This brings us to the end of the singleton story. As I mentioned a few times, singletons cause problems with unit testing. Mostly, that happens because they are hard to be replaced with a different implementation (they are hard to mock).

Another problem with singletons is that it is hard to configure them. If the singleton instance is created automatically when the program starts, there's no way to provide any configuration. If, however, the singleton is created on first use, we must pass this configuration each time we access the singleton. That is a) not practical and b) fragile, as one part of the code can pass in a different configuration than the others.

There's a hacky way out of this conundrum. We can push the configuration into some global state that is then used by the singleton class when the singleton instance is created. Still, this is bad from the design view.

There's a much better way to solve this problem. We can simply move away from the singleton pattern and replace it with a dependency injection.

Dependency injection

The **Dependency injection** (**DI**) pattern is the first of many design patterns in this book that were not described in the Gang of Four book. There's a good reason for that. The DI pattern has sprung from the unit-testing movement, and in 1994, unit testing was not yet a thing. In that era, applications were treated as monolithic blocks of code, and not as collections of loosely connected units.

DI works by changing responsibility for object creation. In classical OOP, each object creates new objects that it needs for functioning. This makes the program very rigid and hard to test. DI turns this on its head. If an object needs other objects to functions, the owner (the code which creates the first objects) should also create these other objects and pass them to the first one. In short, a dependency injection says this: Don't create things yourself; your owner should provide them. This decouples objects (makes interconnections between them less tight) and simplifies testing.

> For a real-life example, imagine a remote-controlled model car with a fixed rechargeable battery. Do whatever you want, but you are not able to exchange this battery for a better model. This is how coding was approached in a classical object-oriented style.

> The same car, built according to dependency injection principles, uses an interchangeable battery pack. When you want to play with the car, you insert (inject) a fresh battery pack and start driving. You can also do long-term tests of the motor by replacing the battery pack with an adapter plugged into the A/C power.

> Dependency injection gives you flexibility in exchange for slightly increased complexity. (A car with an interchangeable battery pack has more parts and is harder to make.)

Some programmers argue that DI is actually a case of a strategy design pattern from the design patterns book. (A strategy pattern is not covered in this book.) Indeed, they look very similar, but the difference is, at least in my opinion, in the way they are used. Strategy helps us to write code where different implementations are part of solving a problem. DI, on the other hand, is used when different implementations are parts of testing. A strategy pattern introduces true implementations, while a dependency injection introduces fake implementations, used only for testing.

We could argue that DI is much more than a pattern, and, in a way, this is true. This pattern is so comprehensive that we can easily treat it as a design principle. (Design principles are covered in `Chapter 1`, *Introduction to patterns*).

To simplify the topic, I decided to cover only the basics of dependency injection. This book will therefore abstain from discussing the **Inversion Of Control** (**IOC**) approach, which really is more a design principle than a pattern. If you want to know more about DI, I would strongly recommend a great book by *Nick Hodges, Dependency Injection in Delphi* (`https://leanpub.com/dependencyinjectionindelphi`).

The simplest way to explain DI is through an example. I will start with an old-school object-oriented code and, in a few steps, introduce the dependency injection pattern. At the end, I'll add unit tests to prove that the code has become more testable and maintainable. The main project used in this section is stored in the `Dependency Injection` folder in the `DependencyInjectionPattern` project. You can also start by opening a `DependencyInjection` project group that contains both a demo project and a `DUnit` test project.

The demonstration project is a trivial VCL application with four buttons, each executing a different implementation of the code that we want to convert. The first button, `No Dependency Injection`, executes the following code, which runs the `TDataProcessor.ProcessData` method from the `DataProcessing.NoDI` unit:

```
procedure TfrmDI.btnNoDIClick(Sender: TObject);
var
  processor: DataProcessing.NoDI.TDataProcessor;
begin
  processor := DataProcessing.NoDI.TDataProcessor.Create;
  try
    processor.ProcessData;
  finally
    FreeAndNil(processor);
  end;
end;
```

The `ProcessData` method is shown next:

```
procedure TDataProcessor.ProcessData;
var
  count: integer;
  reader: TReader;
  sum: int64;
  value: integer;
  writer: TWriter;
begin
  reader := TReader.Create('..\..\data.txt');
  try
    sum := 0;
    count := 0;
    while reader.GetNext(value) do
    begin
      Inc(sum, value);
      Inc(count);
    end;
    writer := TWriter.Create('..\..\data.csv');
    try
      writer.WriteOut(count, sum, sum/count);
    finally
      FreeAndNil(writer);
    end;
  finally
    FreeAndNil(reader);
  end;
end;
```

The code firstly creates a data reader, `TReader`. It is implemented in the `DataProcessing.Reader` unit. This is a very simple text file reader class that, on each call of the `GetNext` method, reads the next line from the file, converts it into the integer value, and returns it in the `value` parameter. When there's no more data in the file, the function returns `False`.

The code then calls this `GetNext` method, adds all numbers together, and maintains a count of read numbers.

In the last step, the code creates a `TWriter` class and writes three values into a **Comma Separated Values** (**CSV**) text file. The first value contains a number of read values, the second a sum of all numbers, and the last one the average value of all data.

The statistical part of that code is really hard to test. We have to create an input text file in an expected format, run the code, and then open and parse the output file. That means lots of work, and, besides that, this defeats the whole idea of unit testing, because we are actually testing an integration of three units: reader, data processor, and writer.

The dependency injection pattern states that it is the owner who should pass the required dependency to the worker class. This approach is implemented in the `DataProcessing.InjectedParam` unit and is activated by the `Injected parameters` button. A click on this button executes the following code:

```
procedure TfrmDI.btnInjectedParamsClick(Sender: TObject);
var
  processor: DataProcessing.InjectedParam.TDataProcessor;
  reader: TReader;
  writer: TWriter;
begin
  reader := TReader.Create('..\..\data.txt');
  try
    writer := TWriter.Create('..\..\data.csv');
    try
      processor := DataProcessing.InjectedParam.TDataProcessor.Create;
      try
        processor.ProcessData(reader, writer);
      finally
        FreeAndNil(processor);
      end;
    finally
      FreeAndNil(writer);
    end;
  finally
    FreeAndNil(reader);
  end;
end;
```

An implementation of `TDataProcessor.ProcessData` is now much simpler:

```
procedure TDataProcessor.ProcessData(AReader: TReader; AWriter: TWriter);
var
  count: integer;
  sum: int64;
  value: integer;
begin
  sum := 0;
  count := 0;
  while AReader.GetNext(value) do begin
    Inc(sum, value);
    Inc(count);
```

```
    end;
    AWriter.WriteOut(count, sum, sum/count);
  end;
```

This version already looks much better. The reader and writer are created in the part of code that would also set the correct file names in a real application. The `ProcessData` method does not need to know where the data lies anymore.

From classes to interfaces

Such an approach, while more maintainable, still isn't good for unit testing. We cannot simply create a replacement for `TReader`, as `GetNext` is not a virtual method. (The same goes for `TWriter` and `WriteOut`.) Even if we fix that, the fact remains that creating mock classes (classes used only for testing other classes) by deriving from real implementation is a recipe for trouble. Doing it that way just brings in lots of dependencies and interconnectedness.

A better way is to extract the public interface of a class to an interface and change the code to depend on an interface, not on a class. In this example, both interfaces are intentionally simple, as the following code fragment shows:

```
type
  IReader = interface ['{9B32E26A-456F-45D1-A494-B331C7131020}']
    function GetNext(var value: integer): boolean;
  end;

  IWriter = interface ['{ED6D0678-5FCE-41BA-A161-BE691FCB6B7B}']
    procedure WriteOut(count: integer; sum: int64; average: real);
  end;
```

This approach is implemented in the `DataProcessing.InjectedProperties` unit and is activated with a click on the `Injected properties` button. The following method shows how to create appropriate interfaces and pass them to `ProcessData`:

```
procedure TfrmDI.btnInjectedPropsClick(Sender: TObject);
var
  processor: DataProcessing.InjectedProperties.TDataProcessor;
  reader: IReader;
  writer: IWriter;
begin
  reader := TReader.Create('..\..\data.txt');
  writer := TWriter.Create('..\..\data.csv');
  processor := DataProcessing.InjectedProperties.TDataProcessor.Create;
  try
```

```
      processor.Reader := reader;
      processor.Writer := writer;
      processor.ProcessData;
    finally
      FreeAndNil(processor);
    end;
  end;
```

In this example, I' have changed the way dependent implementations are injected into the worker method. Instead of passing them as parameters to `ProcessData`, they are injected into `TDataProcessor` properties. This was done for demonstration purposes and is not connected to the change from object-based to interface-based implementation. I just wanted to show that there are other options on how dependencies are injected. At the very end of this section, I will enumerate and evaluate them all.

The new `TDataProcessor` implementation is shown next:

```
type
  TDataProcessor = class
  strict private
    FReader: IReader;
    FWriter: IWriter;
  public
    procedure ProcessData;
    property Reader: IReader read FReader write FReader;
    property Writer: IWriter read FWriter write FWriter;
  end;

procedure TDataProcessor.ProcessData;
var
  count: integer;
  sum: int64;
  value: integer;
begin
  sum := 0;
  count := 0;
  while FReader.GetNext(value) do begin
    Inc(sum, value);
    Inc(count);
  end;
  FWriter.WriteOut(count, sum, sum/count);
end;
```

Now we have a fully testable implementation. A `UnitTestDependencyInjection` project shows how unit tests can be done in practice. This project is implemented with the `DUnit` framework because it is included in standard Delphi installation, but it could be implemented equally well with `DUnit2`, `DUnitX`, or any other testing framework. Let's take a look at one test taken from the `DataProcesing.DUnit` unit:

```
procedure TestTDataProcessor.TestSequence;
var
  writer: ITestWriter;
begin
  writer := TTestWriter.Create;
  FDataProcessor.Reader := TTestReader.Create([1, 1, 2, 2]);
  FDataProcessor.Writer := writer as IWriter;
  FDataProcessor.ProcessData;
  CheckEquals(4, writer.Count);
  CheckEquals(6, writer.Sum);
  CheckEquals(double(1.5), double(writer.Average));
end;
```

The `TTestReader` and `TTestWriter` classes are now true mock classes and have no connection to the actual `TReader` and `TWriter` implementations. `TTestReader` (implemented in the `DataProcessing.Reader.DUnit` unit) is a simple class that enumerates over an array and returns one value in each `GetNext` call. Although simple, the implementation is quite interesting, and I urge you to explore this code.

The `TTestWriter` class is a bit more complicated. It must implement the `WriteOut` method and allow us to check the values that we passed to that call. To do that, it implements two interfaces: the original `IWriter` and a test interface `ITestWriter`. This class is implemented in the `DataProcessing.Writer.DUnit` unit.

I' have implemented several tests, and one of them pointed to a deficiency in the `ProcessData` implementation. The next method tests what happens when `GetNext` returns no data (`False` is returned from the first call):

```
procedure TestTDataProcessor.TestZero;
var
  writer: ITestWriter;
begin
  writer := TTestWriter.Create;
  FDataProcessor.Reader := TTestReader.Create([]);
  FDataProcessor.Writer := writer as IWriter;
  FDataProcessor.ProcessData;
  CheckEquals(0, writer.Count);
  CheckEquals(0, writer.Sum);
```

```
    CheckEquals(double(0), double(writer.Average));
  end;
```

Instead of working as expected, `ProcessData` raises a floating point invalid operation exception.

The reason is not hard to find. `ProcessData` executes the following line:

```
  FWriter.WriteOut(count, sum, sum/count);
```

As the `count` is zero in this test, the code tries to divide by zero and raises an exception.

Using a factory method

One way to fix this problem would be to add a simple test to the `ProcessData` method and write out three zeros (or some other value). This solution is simple but provides no educational value, so I decided to do something different. My solution is to simply not create an output file if the input data is empty.

Once we do that, the code doesn't always need the `IWriter` interface. It is therefore wasteful to create this interface before we call the `ProcessData` method. We can instead use a lazy initialization pattern, which I already mentioned while discussing different singleton implementations.

The lazy initialization will be covered in the next section, but it is so simple and intuitive that I won't confuse you if I use it in the dependency injection example. After all, I already used it to implement singletons, and you didn't think twice about it, I'm sure.

The simplest possible way to introduce lazy initialization to a dependency injection is to use yet another design pattern, `factory method`. (This pattern will be covered in depth in Chapter 3, *Factory Method, Abstract Factory, Prototype, and Builder*.) Instead of injecting an interface, we will inject an anonymous method that creates this interface. The worker code will only call this anonymous method when an interface is actually required.

The fourth button in the demo application, `Injected factory`, executes the following code, which calls the new and improved implementation:

```
procedure TfrmDI.btnInjectedFactoryClick(Sender: TObject);
var
  processor: DataProcessing.Factory.TDataProcessor;
begin
  processor := DataProcessing.Factory.TDataProcessor.Create;
  try
    processor.Reader := TReader.Create('..\..\data.txt');
```

```
      processor.WriterFactory :=
        function: IWriter
        begin
          Result := TWriter.Create('..\..\data.csv');
        end;
      processor.ProcessData;
    finally
      FreeAndNil(processor);
    end;
  end;
```

The new `TDataProcessor` is stored in the `DataProcessing.Factory` unit. Its implementation is shown here:

```
type
  TDataProcessor = class
  strict private
    FReader: IReader;
    FWriterFactory: TFunc<IWriter>;
  public
    procedure ProcessData;
    property Reader: IReader read FReader write FReader;
    property WriterFactory: TFunc<IWriter> read FWriterFactory
      write FWriterFactory;
  end;

procedure TDataProcessor.ProcessData;
var
  count: integer;
  sum: int64;
  value: integer;
begin
  sum := 0;
  count := 0;
  while FReader.GetNext(value) do begin
    Inc(sum, value);
    Inc(count);
  end;

  if count > 0 then
    FWriterFactory.WriteOut(count, sum, sum/count);
end;
```

This version of `ProcessData` creates the `IWriter` interface (by calling the `FWriterFactory` anonymous method) only if a number of values read from the source is greater than zero.

TIP

Delphi allows us to use the `FWriterFactory.WriteOut` or the `FWriterFactory().WriteOut` syntax to call the anonymous method. In such cases, a method stored in the `FWriterFactory` parameter is implicitly executed. Some still like to write parentheses after it so that the intent of the code is more explicit.

This revised implementation is tested with the `TestZeroFixed` and `TestSequenceFixed` in the `DataProcessing.DUnit` unit.

Wrapping up

The examples in this section have demonstrated two of three common ways to inject dependencies:

- **Constructor injection**: When concrete implementations are used for proper functioning of the entire class, we can inject them as parameters to the constructor. This approach was not used in examples from this section, but I did implement a version of `TDataProcessor` that uses a constructor injection. You can explore the `DataProcessing.ClassParams` unit yourself to see how the constructor injection could be used in practice.
- **Property injection**: Sometimes, concrete implementations are used only under specific circumstances. In such cases, we can inject them as properties. Implementations in `DataProcessing.InjectedProperties` and `DataProcessing.Factory` are using this approach.
- **Method injection**: If concrete implementations are only used inside one method, we can inject them as parameters to that method. An implementation in the `DataProcessing.InjectedParam` unit uses this approach.

At the end of this lengthy introduction to dependency injection, I would like to return to the `SingletonPattern` project from the previous section. The secondary form, `SingletonPatternSecondary` implements (in addition to all singleton examples), logging via the injected `InjectedLogger` property.

A proper way to introduce this logger would be the constructor injection (because the logger may be used each time the form is displayed), but that's hard to do with forms that are automatically created, and so the example uses the next best approach: property injection.

Lazy initialization

After two lengthy discussions, a section about a lazy initialization pattern should present a comfortable change. This pattern appeared in the *Gang of Four* book under the name of virtual proxy, which virtually nobody is using today. Lazy initialization, on the other hand, has become a common household name.

Lazy initialization is a very simple pattern that merely states whether an object is not always required, creating it only when it is needed. We would use this pattern on two occasions: when the creation of an object or its initialization is a slow process, or when the very existence of the object signifies something.

Whenever I go somewhere with a car, I have to take into account the small possibility that the car will not start. If that happens, I call my mechanic. That's lazy initialization.

Doing it in a classical object-oriented way would be entirely stupid. Just imagine, I want to go out, and so I call my mechanic and say: Please come here; I intend to start the car, and maybe I'll need you... probably not, but still...

Implementing lazy initialization is trivial, so we usually don't even think about it. Instead of initializing an object when the program starts or when the owner object is created, we use the `test`, `create`, `use` idiom, as shown here:

```
if not assigned(lazyObject) then
  lazyObject := TLazyObject.Create;
Use(lazyObject);
```

The problem with lazy initialization is that the programmer may forget to code the initialization part. For example, we could by mistake call `Use(lazyObject)` directly before firstly checking whether `lazyObject` had been created. A good implementation of a lazy object therefore makes sure that the object can never be accessed directly.

Let's say that this lazily created object (let's call it a `lazy` object) is part of another object (`parent` object). If the parent object never uses the lazy object directly, we can simply hide the lazy object behind a property getter. This getter will take care of a lazy initialization when the lazy object is accessed for the first time.

The example project `LazyInitializationPattern` contains the class `TLazyOwner` in the `Lazy` unit. Inside this class, you'll find a `FLazyObject: TLazyObject` field. This field is not used inside the `TLazyOwner` class. From the viewpoint of the external code, it can only be accessed through the `LazyObject` property. The following code fragment shows the relevant parts of the `TLazyOwner` class:

```
type
  TLazyOwner = class
  strict private
    FLazyObject: TLazyObject;
  strict protected
    function GetLazyObject: TLazyObject;
    property LazyInternal: TLazyInternal read GetLazyInternal;
  public
    destructor Destroy; override;
    property LazyObject: TLazyObject read GetLazyObject;
  end;

destructor TLazyOwner.Destroy;
begin
  FreeAndNil(FLazyObject);
  inherited;
end;

function TLazyOwner.GetLazyObject: TLazyObject;
begin
  if not assigned(FLazyObject) then
    FLazyObject := TLazyObject.Create;
  Result := FLazyObject;
end;
```

This code shows how an object can be lazily initialized in a single-threaded program. On the other hand, it is completely broken in a multi-threaded code! To see how a project should be properly initialized in a multithreaded program, check the patterns *Double-Checked Locking* and *Optimistic initialization* in `Chapter 8`, *Locking Patterns*.

The example program contains some logging code that I removed from the previous code sample. If you run the program and click on the **Create/destroy owner** button, followed by a click on the **Access lazy object** button, you should get the same result, as shown in the next screenshot:

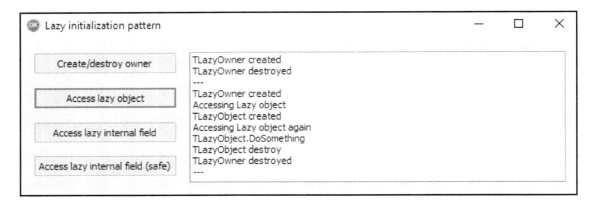

The lazy object is only created when the LazyObject property is accessed.

We can see from this screenshot that the lazy object is not created if the parent object is created and then immediately destroyed. Only if the code accesses the `LazyObject` property is the underlying object created.

Safe programming is not so easily enforced if the parent object itself is using the lazy object. The `TLazyOwner` class also implements a `FLazyInternal` object that's used inside the `TLazyOwner.ProcessUsingLazy` method. In this case, we can easily make a mistake and use `FLazyInternal` directly, instead of accessing it through the `LazyInternal` property.

If we want to protect ourselves from such mistakes, we have to make it impossible to access the lazy object directly. One of the possible solutions is to hide it inside a nested class. If we put it inside a `strict private` section, even the parent object won't have access to it! The declaration is shown in the next code fragment:

```
type
  TLazyOwner = class
  strict private
  type
    THiddenLazyInternal = class
    strict private
      FLazyInternalSafe: TLazyInternal;
    public
      constructor Create;
```

```
    destructor Destroy; override;
    property LazyInternal: TLazyInternal read FLazyInternalSafe;
  end;
var
  FLazyInternalSafe: THiddenLazyInternal;
strict protected
  function LazyInternalSafe: TLazyInternal;
public
  constructor Create;
  destructor Destroy; override;
end;
```

The real lazy object is stored inside the FLazyInternalSafe field of
the THiddenLazyInternal class. Because it is marked as strict private, the code in
the TLazyOwner class cannot access it directly. It can, however, be accessed through
the LazyInternalSafe function, which creates the internal THiddenLazyInternal object
and returns its LazyInternal property, as shown:

```
constructor TLazyOwner.THiddenLazyInternal.Create;
begin
  inherited Create;
  FLazyInternalSafe := TLazyInternal.Create;
end;

destructor TLazyOwner.THiddenLazyInternal.Destroy;
begin
  FreeAndNil(FLazyInternalSafe);
  inherited;
end;

function TLazyOwner.LazyInternalSafe: TLazyInternal;
begin
  if not assigned(FLazyInternalSafe) then
    FLazyInternalSafe := THiddenLazyInternal.Create;
  Result := FLazyInternalSafe.LazyInternal;
end;
```

This code exposes lazy object through a function, not through a property as the previous
example did. Both approaches are equally valid.

Using Spring

If you intend to use a large number of lazily created objects, you will soon get fed up of writing all of the management code. A simpler solution is to use a pre-made lazy initialization wrapper, such as `Lazy<T>` from the Spring4D library (`https://bitbucket.org/sglienke/spring4d`).

I have prepared an example, `LazyInitializationSpring4D` that uses `Lazy<T>` to do the hard work. It requires the Spring4D library to function. To run the example program, you'll have to install this library and then add its `Source` and `Source\Base` folders to Delphi's Library path or to the project's `Search` path. If you unpack the library into the `Chapter2\Spring4D` folder, the project's search path will already be correctly configured.

If you have `git` installed, you can execute the following command in the folder `Chapter 2` folder to install Spring4D: `git clone https://bitbucket.org/sglienke/spring4d`.

The following code fragment shows how to lazily initialize an object using this method. This implementation can be found in the `LazySpring4D.Lazy` unit:

```
type
  TLazyOwner = class
  strict private
    FLazyObj: Lazy<TLazyObj>;
  strict protected
    function GetLazy: TLazyObj;
  public
    constructor Create;
    destructor Destroy; override;
    property Lazy: TLazyObj read GetLazy;
  end;

constructor TLazyOwner.Create;
begin
  inherited Create;
  FLazyObj := Lazy<TLazyObj>.Create;
end;

destructor TLazyOwner.Destroy;
begin
  FLazyObj.Value.Free;
  inherited;
end;
```

```
function TLazyOwner.GetLazy: TLazyObj;
begin
  Result := FLazyObj;
end;
```

In the constructor, we have to make sure that Lazy<TLazyObj> is correctly initialized. The call to Lazy<TLazyObj>.Create will not create the TLazyObj object; it will just set up everything so that the lazy wrapper can be properly used.

The code in the destructor destroys the lazy object if it was created before. As Free works correctly when executed on a nil object, we can call it freely without firstly checking whether the lazy object was indeed initialized.

The GetLazy function retrieves the lazy object. At the first use of this function, the object will be initialized. All ugly plumbing code is hidden inside the Spring4D library.

> This approach to lazy initialization is also thread-safe, so you can use it without any reservations in a multi-threaded program.

The same project also shows how we can lazily initialize an interface. In this case, we don't have to take care about destruction. We must, however, provide an additional piece of code, a factory method that will create the interface. The factory method pattern will be discussed in the next chapter. Relevant parts of the TLazyOwner class are shown in the next code fragment:

```
type
  TLazyOwner = class
  strict private
    FLazyInt: Lazy<ILazyInt>;
  strict protected
    function GetLazyInt: ILazyInt;
  public
    constructor Create;
    property LazyInt: ILazyInt read GetLazyInt;
  end;

constructor TLazyOwner.Create;
begin
  inherited Create;
  FLazyInt := Lazy<ILazyInt>.Create(
    function: ILazyInt
    begin
      Result := TLazyInt.Create;
    end);
```

```
end;

function TLazyOwner.GetLazyInt: ILazyInt;
begin
  Result := FLazyInt;
end;
```

The factory method that creates an object implementing the `ILazyInt` interface is passed as an anonymous method parameter to the `Lazy<ILazyInt>.Create` constructor. All other pieces of the solution are the same as in the previous example.

As you can see, the lazy initialization pattern really isn't complicated, as long as you know whether it will be used in a single-threaded or a multi-threaded environment and uses an appropriate implementation.

Object pool

The last pattern in this chapter, object pool, is again not part of the original design patterns book. Object pools as a concept appeared early in the history of OOP, but somehow the Gang of Four didn't see them as a design pattern.

Object pool functions as storage for objects. When we have an object that takes a long time to create and initialize, we sometimes don't want to spend time doing it all over again. Instead of destroying such an object, we can simply put it away in a special container: an object pool. Later, we can just ask the object pool to return the already-created object, an operation that's much faster than creating a new object.

If you have to write a letter (yes, a physical one, on paper!), you need a pen. If there is no pen in the house, you will go to the shop and buy one. Acquiring a new pen is therefore a costly operation. Because of that, you don't throw a pen away once you've finished the letter. Instead, you store it in a drawer.

The next time you have to write a letter, you just take a pen from a drawer, bypassing all of the costly creation of a new pen. You can also have multiple pens in the drawer, hence easily satisfying the writing urges of other family members.

A standard example of an object pool is a database-connection pool. Connecting to a database is a relatively slow operation, and if you want fast response times, you'll store already-open but unused connections in a pool.

Another typical example comes from a parallel world. Creating a new thread is a costly operation. It can easily take ten milliseconds and more. Sometimes, for example when you are debugging a program in Delphi IDE, it can take up to half a second to create a new thread. A well-designed framework for multithreaded computing therefore stores inactive threads in a thread pool.

An object pool is less important in Delphi than in garbage-collected environments (Java and .NET). In the latter, object pools are also used to fight memory fragmentation. That represented a problem in early Delphi versions, too, but since the 2006 release, the FastMM memory manager takes care of the fragmentation problem.

An object pool needs a storage mechanism to store our objects when they are not used. We can use any data container for this storage: an array, a list, or something else. In most cases, we will set the maximum size for an object pool at the time it is created. Sometimes, though, we will want the object pool to grow as required. Both approaches are perfectly valid. You will use the one that fits your problem better.

The life cycle of objects stored inside a pool (pooled objects) is managed by the pool itself. If a pool cannot retrieve a pooled object and there is still room to grow (or size is not limited), then it will create a new instance of a pooled object and will return it. When a pool is destroyed, it will destroy the pooled objects too.

When a pool is empty (all objects are in use) and the maximum size has been reached, a caller cannot retrieve a new object from the pool. A pool can in such a case either return a failure (by returning a `nil` object or failure status or raising an exception), or it can block and wait until an object is available. The last approach is especially useful in a multithreaded application. One thread can wait for a pooled object (can block) until another thread has finished with it.

To create a new pooled object, a pool can call the default constructor `Create`. Alternatively, we can provide a `factory` method that will create a new pooled object when required. The `factory` method design pattern is described in the next chapter.

Sometimes, an object pool can implement a timeout mechanism. If an object has not been used for a configured time period, the pool will destroy the object, and with that release some resources. You will see such behavior in most thread pool implementations.

You must be careful not to leave any secret information stored inside a pooled object when it is not in use. If you are implementing an object pool in a server application where multiple clients can use objects created from a pool, it would be especially bad if information put there by one client somehow leaked to the next one. Make sure that you always clear such parts of an object before it is put back into use.

It is quite hard to find a problem where an object pool is really necessary in Delphi, apart from the standard candidates, connection, and thread pool. As the thread pool pattern will be described in `Chapter 9`, *Thread pool, Messaging, Future and Pipeline*, this chapter focuses on a connection pool, not one that's connecting to databases, though, but a pool that stores https connections.

 Object pools can be very useful in multithreaded applications. When multiple threads are allocating and releasing objects at the same time, access to the memory manager can become very slow.

If you think that you need an object pool in your code, measure execution times first. Many times, you'll find that the slow part of the program lies somewhere else, not in object creation and initialization.

Stock quote connection pool

As a short example, I've created an application that reads data about stock symbols (**AAPL** (**Apple**), IBM, and **MSFT** (**Microsoft**)) and returns some basic information about the symbol, such as the latest stock value. This information is retrieved from a public server provided by the company IEX (`https://iextrading.com/developer/docs/#attribution`).

The demonstration program, `ObjectPoolPattern` allows you to enter the name of a stock symbol and then query the server for this symbol's data by clicking the `Get data` button. This will generate a request in the `https://api.iextrading.com/1.0/stock/SYMB/quote` form, where SYMB will be replaced with the actual symbol (for example, MSFT).

As connecting to a https server is a relatively lengthy operation, it makes sense to store currently unused connections in an object pool.

The actual https query is implemented by using Delphi's standard `TNetHTTPClient` component. This component supports asynchronous operation. We can start a query and provide a callback (similar to an event handler) that will be called when the operation completes. Our program is still responsive during that time, and the user can request data for another stock, even when the first query didn't return the result.

This connection mechanism is implemented in the class `TStockQuoteConnection` in the unit `ObjectPool.StockQuotePool`. Besides the constructor and destructor, which you can look up in the code, this class implements the method `Query`, which is called from the main program to fetch the data for a stock symbol. When the https query returns, the function `HandleHttpRequestCompleted` is called. Both functions are shown next:

```
type
  TStockQuoteResponse = reference to procedure (const symbol, content:
string);

procedure TStockQuoteConnection.HandleHttpRequestCompleted(
  const Sender: TObject; const AResponse: IHTTPResponse);
begin
  if assigned(AResponse) then
    FResponseProc(FSymbol, AResponse.ContentAsString)
  else
    FResponseProc(FSymbol, '');
end;

procedure TStockQuoteConnection.Query(const symbol: string;
  const responseProc: TStockQuoteResponse);
begin
  FSymbol := symbol;
  FResponseProc := responseProc;
  FHttpClient.Get('https://api.iextrading.com/1.0/stock/'
    + symbol + '/quote');
end;
```

A caller will call the `Query` method with two parameters: a name of the stock symbol and a callback method. This callback is implemented as an anonymous method because that, as we'll see later, simplifies the code in the main program.

The `Query` method simply stores both parameters in class fields and then composes and executes a GET request to a `https://` address. The `Get` method soon returns, and the program can continue with execution.

Some time later, depending on how quickly the web server responds, the `HandleHttpRequestCompleted` is called from the `TNetHTTPClient` code. This method simply uses previously stored callback (`FResponseProc`) and a stock symbol (`FSymbol`) and executes the callback.

Let's now see how this is used in the program. The main form uses an object pool, `FStockQuotePool: TStockQuotePool` to manage the connection. (We will see soon how this pool is implemented.) To retrieve a new connection, the code must call the `GetConnection` method. When a connection is not needed anymore, it must be returned to the pool with a call to the `ReleaseConnection` method. The following code fragment shows how the pool is used in the main program:

```
procedure TfrmObjectPool.QuerySymbol(const symbol: string);
var
  connection: TStockQuoteConnection;
begin
  connection := FStockQuotePool.GetConnection;
  if not assigned(connection) then
    Log(symbol + ': All connections are busy!'#13#10)
  else
    connection.Query(symbol,
      procedure (const symbol, response: string)
      begin
        Log(Format('%s [%p]', [symbol, pointer(connection)])
            + #13#10 + response + #13#10);
        FStockQuotePool.ReleaseConnection(connection);
      end);
end;
```

The code firstly requests a new connection. As the connection pool is limited in size (we will see soon how this is done), `GetConnection` may fail and return `nil`. In such a case, the code will log `All connections are busy!`

When a connection object is successfully acquired, the code calls its `Query` method and passes in a stock symbol name `symbol` and an anonymous method that is constructed in its place. This anonymous method will be called from the `HandleHttpRequestCompleted` method.

In the anonymous method, we simply log the response and release the connection back to the pool by calling `ReleaseConnection`. Through the magic of anonymous methods and variable capturing, we can simply reuse the `connection` variable in the anonymous method.

This is the afore-mentioned part, when using an anonymous method simplifies the code. If we were using a standard event handler (`procedure ... of object`), we would have to store `connection` into a form field so that the event handler would be able to access it later. We would also have to manage multiple connections, as the user can execute multiple simultaneous requests. By using the anonymous methods and variable capturing, the code gets simplified a lot.

For testing purposes, the object pool is limited to two objects. You can easily change this by editing the `FormCreate` method, shown next:

```
procedure TfrmObjectPool.FormCreate(Sender: TObject);
begin
  FStockQuotePool := TStockQuotePool.Create(2);
end;
```

If you click the **Get all 3** button, three simultaneous queries will be activated, one for each stock symbol. As the pool can only provide two connections, the third query will immediately fail. Moments later, results from other two queries will appear. The next screenshot shows a screenshot of the demo program in that state:

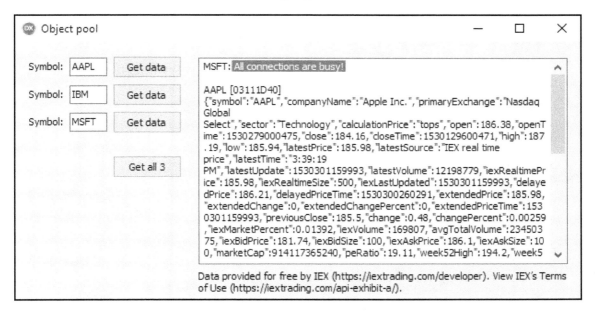

Stock quote connection pool in action.

The two succeeding requests will both have [somenumber] displayed next to the stock symbol. In the previous screenshot, for example, a line, **AAPL [03111D40],** contains that number. This number is the address of the connection object used to query the server. If you continue clicking on the *Get data* buttons, you'll notice that only two addresses are used. They correspond to two connection objects stored in the object pool.

Let's now look at the object pool implementation. `Object pool` is implemented in class `TStockQuotePool,` stored in unit `ObjectPool.StockQuotePool`. Its implementation is as follows:

```
type
  TStockQuotePool = class(TInterfacedObject)
  strict private
    FMaxConnections: integer;
    FNumConnections: integer;
    FConnections : TStack<TStockQuoteConnection>;
  public
    constructor Create(AMaxConnections: integer);
    destructor Destroy; override;
    function GetConnection: TStockQuoteConnection;
    procedure ReleaseConnection(connection: TStockQuoteConnection);
  end;

constructor TStockQuotePool.Create(AMaxConnections: integer);
begin
  inherited Create;
  FMaxConnections := AMaxConnections;
  FConnections := TStack<TStockQuoteConnection>.Create;
end;

destructor TStockQuotePool.Destroy;
begin
  while FConnections.Count > 0 do
    FConnections.Pop.Free;
  FreeAndNil(FConnections);
  inherited;
end;

function TStockQuotePool.GetConnection: TStockQuoteConnection;
begin
  if FConnections.Count > 0 then
    Exit(FConnections.Pop);
  if (FMaxConnections > 0) and (FNumConnections >= FMaxConnections) then
    Exit(nil);
  Result := TStockQuoteConnection.Create;
  Inc(FNumConnections);
end;

procedure TStockQuotePool.ReleaseConnection(connection:
TStockQuoteConnection);
begin
  FConnections.Push(connection);
end;
```

The stock connection pool stores pooled objects in a `TStack` structure. I selected this structure because it is simple and fast. We can only store data on a stack (`Push`) and retrieve data from the top of the stack (`Pop`), but that is enough for our purposes.

The constructor creates a background storage and sets the field `FMaxConnections`, which limits the maximum pool size. You can set it to 0, and that will allow the pool to grow without any limits.

The destructor takes all the connections from the stack and destroys each one. In the end, it destroys the stack storage.

Getting a connection from the pool is the most complicated part. Firstly, a connection is taken from the stack if it is not empty. If that fails and the pool can still grow, a new connection is created and the total number of managed connections is updated.

To release a connection back to the pool, the code simply pushes it on to the stack.

As we are only using the connection pool from the main thread, it was not designed to function correctly in a multithreaded environment!

If you need the object pool to function in a multi-threaded code, you should implement locking. See the `DPObjectPool` unit (discussed next) for an example of this.

The code in the archive for this chapter also contains the unit `DPObjectPool` that implements a generic object pool class `TObjectPool<T>`. You can use it freely in your applications whenever you need an object pool. This pool implements an interface that is very similar to `TStockQuotePool`. The next code fragment shows relevant parts of the class definition:

```
type
  TObjectPool<T:class, constructor> = class
  public
    constructor Create(maxSize: integer = 0;
      const factory: TFunc<T> = nil); overload;
    constructor Create(const factory: TFunc<T>); overload;
    destructor Destroy; override;
    function Allocate: T;
    procedure Release(const obj: T);
  end;
```

This pool will be limited in size if you set the `maxSize` to a positive number. If the `factory` parameter is provided, it will be used to create new pooled objects. You can, for example, create the pool as in the following code fragment to pass some additional information to the object's constructor:

```
pool := TObjectPool<TPoolObject>.Create(
  function: TPoolObject
  begin
    Result := TPoolObject.Create(42);
  end);
```

The `Allocate` method retrieves an object from the pool (possibly creating it in the process). The `Release` method releases a pooled object back to the pool.

The implementation closely matches stock connection pool implementation, so I will not show it in the book. I would only like to point out that the `TObjectPool<T>` implementation uses *locking* to protect the critical code, so this pool can be safely used in a multithreaded environment. For a longer discussion on locking, see `Chapter 8`, *Locking patterns*. A full implementation of the `Release` method is shown here:

```
procedure TObjectPool<T>.Release(const obj: T);
begin
  MonitorEnter(Self); // lock
  try
    FPool.Push(obj);
  finally
    MonitorExit(Self); // unlock
  end;
end;
```

Summary

In this chapter, I have explored four basic creational patterns.

The first one was singleton, a pattern used when we need exactly one instance of a class. The chapter looked at a few bad and a few good implementations and explored alternatives.

After that, I switched to the DI pattern, which can sometimes be used to replace a singleton. As DI is incredibly large area, the chapter has focused on basics and explored different injection mechanisms.

The third pattern in this chapter was lazy initialization. The mechanism behind the lazy initialization (the test, create, use idiom) is so simple that most of the time we don't think about this concept as a pattern. It can still be tricky to implement this pattern correctly, and I have pointed to few potential problems and offered a way to overcome them.

For the last pattern in this chapter, I have looked into the object pool. This pattern is used when creating and initializing new object is a costly operation. The object pool represents a storage for objects that are not currently in use. For this demonstration, I have built a connection pool that caches https connections to a stock quote service.

In the next chapter, we'll look into four more complex creational patterns: Factory method, Abstract Factory, Prototype, and Builder.

3
Factory Method, Abstract Factory, Prototype, and Builder

Creating an object can sometimes be a complicated operation, especially if we are dealing with a complicated hierarchy of interdependent objects. Patterns can introduce order into chaos in such situations.

In this chapter, we'll look into four more patterns from the creational group. You will learn about the following:

- A factory method pattern that simplifies the creation of dependent objects
- An abstract factory pattern that functions as a factory for factories and creates whole families of objects
- A prototype pattern that produces perfect copies of objects
- A builder pattern that separates instructions for creating an object from its representation

Factory method

The factory method pattern specifies how an object can defer creation of some internal data and leave the actual task of creation for the derived class. It is part of the original *Gang of Four* book.

Imagine a kid making cookies out of dough. They can do nothing until they invoke the `factory` method and say, Give me a cutter. So, you provide them with a cookie cutter (the result of the `factory` method), and they can finally start making cookies.

By implementing this approach, you can be flexible and select the appropriate cookie shape for the occasion. Output from the factory method therefore changes the final result.

The functionality of this pattern, as described in the original Design Patterns publication, looks very similar to the dependency injection approach, but implemented with pure object-oriented tools. This section will mostly focus on the original approach, but at the end, I will spend some time modernizing this technique.

The pure GoF example is stored in the folder of the `Factory` method in the project example. It implements the base class `TBaseClass`, which uses the factory method `MakeSomething` to create an instance of the `TSomething` class. As we'll soon see, this instance is used for further calculations.

Both classes are defined as follows:

```
type
  TSomething = class
  public
    function Value: integer; virtual; abstract;
  end;

  TBaseClass = class
  strict protected
    FSomething: TSomething;
  protected
    function MakeSomething: TSomething; virtual; abstract;
  public
    constructor Create;
    destructor Destroy; override;
    function Value: integer;
  end;
```

As you can see, TBaseClass is not directly usable, because the declaration of MakeSomething is marked as abstract. This tells the Delphi compiler that we are intentionally skipping the declaration part of this method and that we know that the resulting class will be incomplete. If you still try to create TBaseClass in the code by calling TBaseClass.Create, you will get the compiler warning W1020. If you insist on running such a program, TBaseClass.Create will raise an exception: EAbstractError. The following diagram shows this warning, exception, and code that caused both:

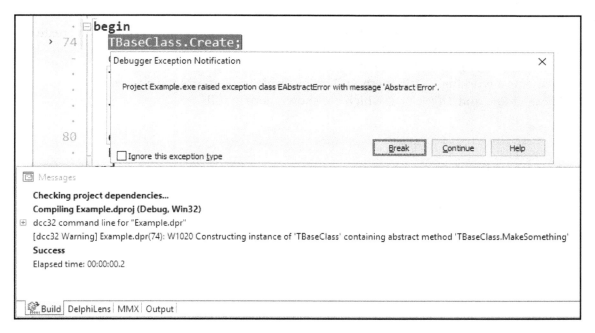

Delphi does not allow you to create an instance of a class containing abstract methods

For a similar reason, you cannot create an instance of the TSomething class. This class actually functions just like an interface in modern languages: it provides method declaration but no implementation.

The something object is created inside TBaseClass.Create and is used in TBaseClass.Value. The following code fragment shows both methods:

```
constructor TBaseClass.Create;
begin
  inherited;
  FSomething := MakeSomething;
end;
```

```
function TBaseClass.Value: integer;
begin
  Result := FSomething.Value * 2;
end;
```

At this moment, we have two classes. One calls a method that does not exist (MakeSomething) to create an object. The other exposes the Value method, which also doesn't exist. It looks as if we have produced a bunch of useless code. How can we make it do anything useful?

The answer, as is usual with pure object-oriented code, is subclassing. We have to create a new class, derived from TBaseClass, which implements a working MakeSomething method. We also need a new class, derived from TSomething, which implements a working Value method. This example implements the classes T21Something and T42Class, which are shown here in full:

```
type
  T21Something = class(TSomething)
  public
    function Value: integer; override;
  end;

  T42Class = class(TBaseClass)
  protected
    function MakeSomething: TSomething; override;
  end;

  function T21Something.Value: integer;
  begin
    Result := 21;
  end;

  function T42Class.MakeSomething: TSomething;
  begin
    Result := T21Something.Create;
  end;
```

As you can see, there is really not much to these two classes. All basic functionality already exists in the TBaseClass class, and we are merely plugging the holes.

To use this class, we have to create not the TBaseClass but an instance of a derived class: T42Class. The following code fragment, taken from the preceding example, shows how:

```
var
  data: TBaseClass;
```

```
begin
  data := T42Class.Create;
  try
    Writeln(data.Value);
  finally
    FreeAndNil(data);
  end;
end.
```

Let's go through the steps the code is taking to return a value from the `Value` method:

1. The code calls `T42Class.Create` to create an instance of this class.
2. As there is no constructor defined in the `T42Class`, the compiler calls the constructor from the parent class, `TBaseClass`.
3. During `TBaseClass.Create`, the `MakeSomething` method is called.
4. As this method is marked as `virtual`, the program tries to find the overridden version of this method in the `T42Class`.
5. This search succeeds and `T42Class.MakeSomething` is called.
6. `MakeSomething` creates and returns the `T21Something` object. As `T21Something` is derived from `TSomething`, we can return such an object, even though the function returns a `TSomething`.
7. The result of `MakeSomething` is stored in the field `FSomething`. Although the field is declared as `TSomething`, it actually contains a `T21Something` object.
8. The object is fully constructed, and `Value` is called.
9. There is no `T42Class.Value`, so `TBaseClass.Value` is executed.
10. `TBaseClass.Value` calls `FSomething.Value`.
11. As the `Value` method is declared `virtual` in the `TSomething` class, the code searches for this method in the actual `T21Something` object once more.
12. `T21Something.Value` is found and called. It returns the value 21.
13. `TBaseClass.Value` multiples that 21 by 2 and returns 42.

Wow! What a convoluted trip! Don't worry; this is something that is happening all the time when you are using derived objects (also known as subclassing) and virtual methods, and you don't need to spend much time thinking about it.

Painter

I have also prepared a more useful example of a simple painting application. As shown in the following image, the Painter project allows you to draw with two tools: one drawing squares and another drawing circles:

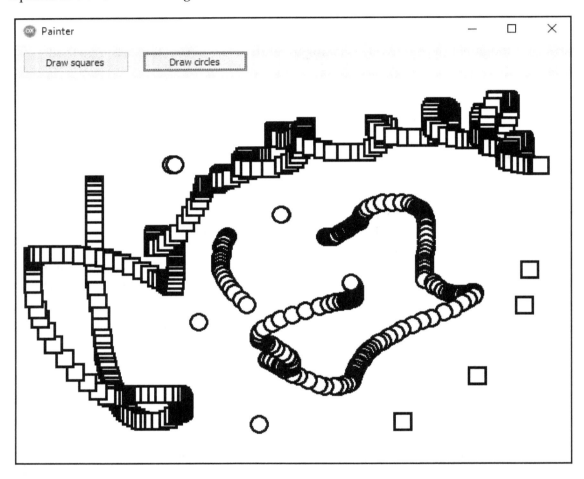

Painter project in action.

The painting tools are implemented in the `Painter.Tools` unit. As in the first example, they are implemented in a true GoF manner by deriving from the base abstract class. The following code fragment shows tool definitions:

```
type
  TPaintStamp = class
  public
    procedure Apply(canvas: TCanvas; x, y: integer); virtual; abstract;
  end;

  TSquareStamp = class(TPaintStamp)
  public
    procedure Apply(canvas: TCanvas; x, y: integer); override;
  end;

  TCircleStamp = class(TPaintStamp)
  public
    procedure Apply(canvas: TCanvas; x, y: integer); override;
  end;

  TPaintTool = class
  protected
    function MakeStamp: TPaintStamp; virtual; abstract;
  public
    constructor Create(canvas: TCanvas);
    procedure PaintStampAt(x, y: integer);
  end;

  TPaintSquare = class(TPaintTool)
  protected
    function MakeStamp: TPaintStamp; override;
  end;

  TPaintCircle = class(TPaintTool)
  protected
    function MakeStamp: TPaintStamp; override;
  end;
```

As in the original example, we have one base class, TPaintTool, that provides basic painting functionality but is missing the MakeStamp method. This method creates an object that can actually do some painting. The two derived classes, TPaintSquare and TPaintCircle override this method to create an appropriate instance, as shown in the following code:

```
function TPaintSquare.MakeStamp: TPaintStamp;
begin
  Result := TSquareStamp.Create;
```

```
  end;

  function TPaintCircle.MakeStamp: TPaintStamp;
  begin
    Result := TCircleStamp.Create;
  end;
```

In the main unit, `PatternMain`, the code merely creates an appropriate tool when a button is clicked:

```
  procedure TfrmPainter.btnSquareClick(Sender: TObject);
  begin
    FreeAndNil(FTool);
    FTool := TPaintSquare.Create(PaintImage.Canvas);
  end;

  procedure TfrmPainter.btnCirclesClick(Sender: TObject);
  begin
    FreeAndNil(FTool);
    FTool := TPaintCircle.Create(PaintImage.Canvas);
  end;
```

An actual drawing is performed in the `OnMouseDown` and `OnMouseMove` handlers. As the following code fragment shows, they merely call the `PaintStampAt` method, which then calls the `Apply` method of the `TPaintStamp` descendant to do the painting:

```
  procedure TfrmPainter.PaintImageMouseDown(Sender: TObject;
    Button: TMouseButton; Shift: TShiftState; X, Y: Integer);
  begin
    if assigned(FTool) then
      FTool.PaintStampAt(X, Y);
    FMouseDown := true;
  end;

  procedure TfrmPainter.PaintImageMouseMove(Sender: TObject;
    Shift: TShiftState; X, Y: Integer);
  begin
    if assigned(FTool) and FMouseDown then
      FTool.PaintStampAt(X, Y);
  end;
```

Modernizing the factory method pattern

The factory method, as specified originally, is almost useless in current times. It is not very flexible and requires a complicated hierarchy of classes. Nowadays, we still use the general idea, providing a method that creates something, but we wrap it into modern concepts. Usually, we use some form of dependency injection. An example of such a modification can be found in the project ExampleDI. For more information on dependency injection, see Chapter 2, *Singleton, Dependency Injection, Lazy Initialization, and Object Pool*.

As I have mentioned before, the whole reason for the TSomething class is to specify an interface. We can therefore replace it with a pure interface ISomething as shown in the following code:

```
type
  ISomething = interface
    function Value: integer;
  end;
```

There is also no need to create classes that are derived from the TBaseClass. We can simply pass in the correct implementation of ISomething to the constructor, as the following code fragment shows:

```
type
  TBaseClass = class
  strict protected
    FSomething: ISomething;
  public
    constructor Create(const something: ISomething);
    function Value: integer;
  end;

  constructor TBaseClass.Create(const something: ISomething);
  begin
    inherited Create;
    FSomething := something
  end;
```

An actual implementation of ISomething, T21Something is very similar to the implementation from the previous example. We just have to derive from TInterfacedObject, not TSomething (the latter doesn't exist in this approach) and implement ISomething. The following code fragment shows the full declaration and implementation of T21Something:

```
type
  T21Something = class(TInterfacedObject, ISomething)
  public
    function Value: integer;
  end;

  function T21Something.Value: integer;
  begin
    Result := 21;
  end;
```

To use a concrete implementation, we can just pass an instance of the T21Something class to the TBaseClass constructor, as shown here:

```
data := TBaseClass.Create(T21Something.Create);
```

The compiler will take care of the T21Something life cycle (because it is managed as an interface) and will destroy it at an appropriate time (when the TBaseClass instance data is destroyed).

Alternatively, we can define a simple derived class, T42Class and use it in our code. We only have to re-implement the constructor, which takes care of passing the appropriate ISomething implementation to the base class, as shown here:

```
type
  T42Class = class(TBaseClass)
  public
    constructor Create;
  end;

constructor T42Class.Create;
begin
  inherited Create(T21Something.Create);
end;
```

Abstract factory

The abstract factory pattern is closely related to the factory method pattern. Sometimes, the problem requires the creation of multiple distinct objects that are somehow related. In such a case, we could introduce multiple factory methods, but then we have to manage them separately, which increases the possibility of implementations becoming out of sync. This approach also makes it hard to share common logic and state between those factory methods. A better way is to introduce an abstract factory, which functions as a factory for factories.

 If a factory method is a kid with a cookie cutter, an abstract factory is a kitchen chef. Give them a set of cooking tools and they'll make you a great dish. Give them access to a baking set and they'll make you a perfect pie.

We can implement abstract factory in the same object-oriented way that was used in the factory method pattern. We have to create a base abstract factory class that defines factory methods and a base class for the object that uses this factory. Then, we derive from the abstract factory to create specific implementations. We also have to create an overridden class to instantiate the concrete factory. The following code fragment sketches this approach:

```
type
  TBaseTool1 = class
    procedure UseTool; virtual;
  end;

  TBaseTool2 = class
    procedure UseTool; virtual;
  end;

  TBaseFactory = class
    function MakeTool1: TBaseTool1; virtual; abstract;
    function MakeTool2: TBaseTool2; virtual; abstract;
  end;

  TBaseClass = class
    function MakeFactory: TBaseFactory;
  end;

  TRealTool1 = class(TBaseTool1)
    procedure UseTool; override;
  end;

  TRealTool2 = class(TBaseTool2)
```

```
    procedure UseTool; override;
  end;

  TRealFactory = class(TBaseFactory)
    function MakeTool1: TBaseTool1; override;
    function MakeTool2: TBaseTool2; override;
  end;

  TRealClass = class(TBaseClass)
    function MakeFactory: TBaseFactory;
  end;

procedure TRealTool1.UseTool;
begin
  // do the work
end;

procedure TRealTool2.UseTool;
begin
  // do the work
end;

function TRealFactory.MakeTool1: TBaseTool1;
begin
  Result := TRealTool1.Create;
end;

function TRealFactory.MakeTool2: TBaseTool2;
begin
  Result := TRealTool2.Create;
end;

function TRealClass.MakeFactory: TBaseFactory;
begin
  Result := TRealFactory.Create;
end;
```

This approach works, but exhibits all the problems of the classical object-oriented factory method implementation. It is cumbersome, requires us to define and implement a bunch of classes, and restricts us in many ways. A much better way, which I'll explore in this section, is to use modern tools, such as **interfaces** and **injection**.

Finding a good topic to demonstrate abstract factories is not simple. A typical example in literature uses this pattern to dynamically create a user interface. This topic was important in the time when the Gang of Four book was created. A typical application with a graphical user interface in that time was running on Unix using X Windows Server with some specific toolkit to create the UI. An abstract factory provided a way to create multiple interface implementations that used multiple toolkits in one application.

In modern times, we approach such problems in a different way. A typical way would be to extract all business functionality into a model and then build a separate Model-View-Whatever application for each user interface. Still, writing a generic UI interface provides a good example, so I built a demonstration of the abstract factory pattern around that concept.

In the `Abstract factory` folder, you'll find the `AbstractUI` project group which contains two projects: `UIHostVCL` and `UIHostFMX`. Both create a minimal main form with one button. Clicking that button creates a secondary form by using a generic form-creation class and two factories: one to create a VCL form and another to create a FireMonkey form. Both applications are shown side-by-side in the following screenshot:

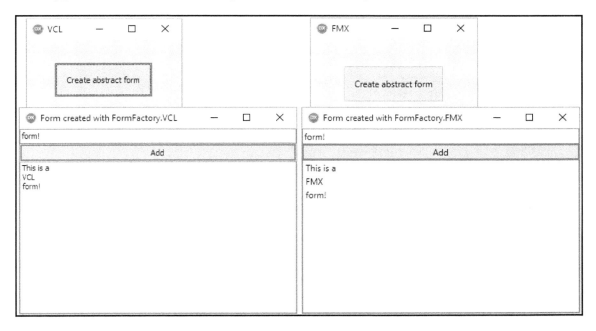

VLC and FMX forms, created with an abstract factory.

The form in this example is created and managed by the `TAbstractEBLForm` class, which is stored in the `AbstractEBLForm` unit. This class knows nothing about VCL or FMX; it creates the form through an abstract factory interface `IFormFactory`. The implementation of this class is shown here in full:

```
uses
  FormFactory.Intf;

type
  TAbstractEBLForm = class
  strict private
    FFactory: IFormFactory;
    FForm: IForm;
    FButton: IButton;
    FEdit: IEdit;
    FListbox: IListBox;
  public
    constructor Create(const factory: IFormFactory);
    procedure Make;
    procedure Show;
  end;

constructor TAbstractEBLForm.Create(const factory: IFormFactory);
begin
  inherited Create;
  FFactory := factory;
end;

procedure TAbstractEBLForm.Make;
begin
  FForm := FFactory.CreateForm;
  FEdit := FFactory.CreateEdit(FForm);
  FButton := FFactory.CreateButton(FForm);
  FButton.Caption := 'Add';
  FListbox := FFactory.CreateListbox(FForm);
  FButton.OnClick :=
    procedure
    begin
      FListbox.Add(FEdit.GetText);
    end;
end;

procedure TAbstractEBLForm.Show;
begin
  FForm.Show;
end;
```

The abstract factory is injected into the constructor from the code that creates the `TAbstractEBLForm` object. This way, we don't have to create a `TAbstractEBLForm` descendants that implements just a factory-creating function and nothing more. We will see soon how this constructor is called.

The `Make` method uses the abstract factory to create form, create and configure edit, button, and listbox components, and to define a button's `OnClick` handler. In short, this form implements the very first public Delphi 1 demo, an application with one `TEdit`, one `TButton`, and one `TListBox`, which appends text from the edit box to the listbox when the button is clicked.

The method `Show` simply calls the `IForm.Show` method to show the form. We will look into the implementation details later.

This code clearly uses no VCL or FMX concepts. It merely refers to interfaces defined in `FormFactory.Intf` without any knowledge about the specific implementation. In a way, this is an extreme implementation of the coding to the interface design principle.

Let's now examine how this abstract form is used. The VCL implementation in unit `UIHostVCLMain` uses concrete implementation of the abstract factory `TVCLFormFactory` from unit `FormFactory.VCL` to create a VCL form as shown next:

```
procedure TfrmVCLHost.Button1Click(Sender: TObject);
var
  form: TAbstractEBLForm;
begin
  form := TAbstractEBLForm.Create(TVCLFormFactory.Create);
  try
    form.Make;
    form.Show;
  finally
    FreeAndNil(form);
  end;
end;
```

A FireMonkey-targeting implementation in unit `UIHostFMXMain` is almost the same, except that it uses the factory `TFMXFormFactory` from the unit `FormFactory.FMX` to create the user interface components:

```
procedure TfrmFMXHost.Button1Click(Sender: TObject);
var
  form: TAbstractEBLForm;
begin
  form := TAbstractEBLForm.Create(TFMXFormFactory.Create);
  try
```

```
        form.Make;
        form.Show;
      finally
        FreeAndNil(form);
      end;
  end;
```

Let me now switch the focus from the top-level parts of the implementation to the platform-specific code. The full implementation is too long for the book, so I will only show selected parts here.

The factory interface `IFormFactory` is defined in the unit `FormFactory.Intf`. The next code fragment shows the factory interface and two of the four component interfaces: `IForm` and `IEdit`. The other two you can check in the source code:

```
  type
    IForm = interface ['{EB4D0921-F0FD-4044-80E8-80156C71D0E0}']
      procedure Show;
    end;

    IEdit = interface ['{39D02BD4-582A-4EBD-8119-2D6013E31287}']
      function GetText: string;
    end;

    IFormFactory = interface ['{776122CF-C014-4630-ACBF-8C639BEAE975}']
      function CreateForm: IForm;
      function CreateEdit(const form: IForm): IEdit;
      function CreateButton(const form: IForm): IButton;
      function CreateListbox(const form: IForm): IListbox;
    end;
```

We already saw how this factory is used. `CreateForm` creates a form, `CreateEdit` an edit box, and so on.

More interesting than that is the factory implementation. Let's start with the VCL factory, implemented in unit `FormFactory.VCL`. Again, I will only show the form and edit box implementations in full.

The factory implementation `TVCLFormFactory` is very simple. It just creates concrete objects that implement interfaces from `FormFactory.Intf`. The next code fragment shows the definition of the class and the implementation of functions that create the `IForm` and `IEdit` interfaces:

```
  type
    TVCLFormFactory = class(TInterfacedObject, IFormFactory)
    public
```

```
      function CreateForm: IForm;
      function CreateEdit(const form: IForm): IEdit;
      function CreateButton(const form: IForm): IButton;
      function CreateListbox(const form: IForm): IListbox;
   end;

function TVCLFormFactory.CreateForm: IForm;
begin
   Result := TVCLForm.Create;
end;

function TVCLFormFactory.CreateEdit(const form: IForm): IEdit;
begin
   Result := TVCLEdit.Create(form as IVCLForm);
end;
```

As the VCL implementation of virtual components needs access to the TForm object, the TVCLForm class implements a special interface IVCLForm. As shown next, this interface defines the method AsForm, which returns the base TForm object:

```
type
   IVCLForm = interface ['{8EC67205-31FD-4A40-B076-F572EF76CF0A}']
      function AsForm: TForm;
   end;

   TVCLForm = class(TInterfacedObject, IForm, IVCLForm)
   strict private
      FForm: TForm;
   public
      constructor Create;
      destructor Destroy; override;
      function AsForm: TForm;
      procedure Show;
   end;

constructor TVCLForm.Create;
begin
   inherited Create;
   FForm := TForm.CreateNew(nil);
   FForm.Position := poScreenCenter;
   FForm.Caption := 'Form created with FormFactory.VCL';
   FForm.Width := 400;
   FForm.Height := 300;
end;

destructor TVCLForm.Destroy;
begin
   FreeAndNil(FForm);
```

```
    inherited;
end;

function TVCLForm.AsForm: TForm;
begin
  Result := FForm;
end;

procedure TVCLForm.Show;
begin
  FForm.ShowModal;
end;
```

Form creation is simplified as much as possible to reduce the size of the example. Form size and position are hardcoded, and so is the caption. In a real-world GUI factory, such properties would have to be exposed through the IForm interface.

The edit box implementation TVCLEdit uses the TForm object so that it can correctly set the ownership and parenting of the TEdit component. The implementation of this class is shown next:

```
type
  TVCLEdit = class(TInterfacedObject, IEdit)
  strict private
    FEdit: TEdit;
  public
    constructor Create(owner: IVCLForm);
    function GetText: string;
  end;

constructor TVCLEdit.Create(owner: IVCLForm);
begin
  inherited Create;
  FEdit := TEdit.Create(owner.AsForm);
  FEdit.Parent := owner.AsForm;
  FEdit.Align := alTop;
end;

function TVCLEdit.GetText: string;
begin
  Result := FEdit.Text;
end;
```

For the implementation of the button and listbox components, you can check the code.

The other factory, `TFMXFormFactory` from unit `FormFactory.FMX` is almost line-for-line the same as the VCL factory. The used units differ, of course (for example, `FMX.StdCtrls` and `FMX.Forms` are used instead of `Vcl.StdCtrls` and `Vcl.Forms`), and some components have different names (`TButton.Text` instead of `TButton.Caption`), but all implementation logic follows the same principles. For example, `TFMXEdit` is defined and implemented as follows:

```
type
  TFMXEdit = class(TInterfacedObject, IEdit)
  strict private
    FEdit: TEdit;
  public
    constructor Create(owner: IFMXForm);
    function GetText: string;
  end;

constructor TFMXEdit.Create(owner: IFMXForm);
begin
  inherited Create;
  FEdit := TEdit.Create(owner.AsForm);
  FEdit.Parent := owner.AsForm;
  FEdit.Align := TAlignLayout.Top;
end;

function TFMXEdit.GetText: string;
begin
  Result := FEdit.Text;
end;
```

If you want to implement the user interface in this manner, be warned! You will have to write large amounts of code to implement all the needed components and their properties. The task, however, is not incredibly complicated, just tedious.

Prototype

The prototype pattern is very simple in concept. It describes a way for an object to make a copy of itself. In other words, we start with one object (prototype) and end with two indistinguishable copies.

We don't have to look far to find a real-life example of the prototype pattern. Life, as we know it, is based on cellular division, a process in which one cell divides into two identical copies of itself.

Every implementation of this pattern is very specific to the target environment. In Delphi, we can implement a prototype pattern by creating a new object and copying old contents to the new instance in some way. Creating a new object is simple, but copying data may not be. In this section, we'll mostly deal with the copy mechanism.

By implementing the prototype pattern (or cloning, as we also call this process), we bypass object initialization, which may be a lengthy operation. Sometimes, we even don't have access to the original data from which the object was initialized and the only possible way to create a copy of an object is to implement this pattern.

Although I am using the word object in this introduction, a prototype pattern equally applies to records. It's just that technical problems that we have to solve are different. As it turns out, cloning a Delphi record can be simpler than cloning an object.

Cloning records

Making copy of a record is simple, because records are value types in Delphi, similar to integers, floating-point numbers, and booleans. We can just assign one variable of a record type to another and the compiler will make a copy:

```
var
  a, b: TSomeRecord;

begin
  a.Initialize;
  b := a;
  // b now contains same data as a
end;
```

There are limitations to this approach, and they are best explained with an example. In the Prototype folder of this chapter's code, you'll find the project PrototypeRecord, which demonstrates simplicity, and problems, with record cloning.

In the unit `Prototype.Rec`, you'll find the definition of a record type `TCloneableRec` that contains fields of different types: string, integer, two kinds of arrays, interface, object, and nested record. The following code fragment shows all important parts of the record definition (internal fields, getters, and setters were removed for clarity):

```
type
  TNestedRecord = record
    ValueI: integer;
    ValueS: string;
  end;

  IInteger = interface ['{722BD9CC-BF41-4CDC-95C1-7EF17A28BF7B}']
    property Value: integer read GetValue write SetValue;
  end;

  TInteger = class(TInterfacedObject, IInteger)
    property Value: integer read GetValue write SetValue;
  end;

  TStaticArray = array [1..10] of integer;
  TDynamicArray = TArray<integer>;

  TCharacter = class
    property Value: char read FValue write FValue;
  end;

  TCloneableRec = record
    Str: string;
    Int: integer;
    Intf: IInteger;
    ArrS: TStaticArray;
    ArrD: TDynamicArray;
    Rec: TNestedRecord;
    Obj: TCharacter;
  end;
```

The code in the main unit `PrototypeRecordMain` creates and initializes a master record and logs its contents. Then it creates a clone and logs the contents of the copy. The code then modifies the original record and logs the clone again. The following screenshot shows the end result of this operation:

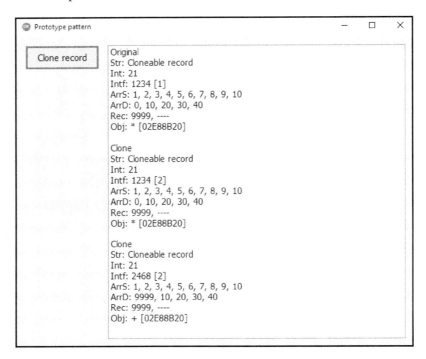

The end result of the PrototypeRecord program.

The first third of the output contains the content of the original record. There are two interesting parts of this output that I would like to point out.

Firstly, the text **Intf: 1234 [1]** means that the `Intf` field contains the value 1234 and that the reference count of this interface is 1. In other words, there is only one place in the code that refers to this interface, namely the `Intf` field.

Secondly, the text **Obj: * [02E88B20]** shows the content of the `Obj` object's value property and the address of the `Obj` object.

The middle part of the output contains the content of the cloned record. Mostly, it is the same as the output of the original record, but again there are two specifics that I'd like to mention.

The content of the Intf field now contains text [2]. When the copy of the original record was made, the compiler copied the address of the object implementing the IInteger interface from the original record's Intf field into the clone record's Intf field and incremented the interface's reference count to indicate that. Both records now share the same IInterface with a reference count of 2, indicating two owners.

Almost the same thing happens with the Obj field. It contains an address of the object, and this address is copied from the original record to the clone. The content of both Obj fields therefore contains the same address, and we cannot tell which record owns this object.

This only holds for classic Delphi platforms where objects are not reference-counted. On ARC-supporting platforms (Android, iOS, Linux), objects behave more-or-less the same as interfaces.

To facilitate this behavior, the example program maintains the TCharacter object globally. The main form creates one instance of this class and stores a reference to this instance (its address) in the original record. Making a copy of the record causes no problems, as both records are referring to the same master object, managed by the form. Only at the end, when the program is shutting down, is the object destroyed.

Before logging the last part, the code modifies the original record, as shown in the next fragment. A clone record is then logged:

```
source.Str := 'Changed';
source.Intf.Value := source.Intf.Value * 2;
source.ArrS[Low(source.ArrS)] := 9999;
source.ArrD[Low(source.ArrD)] := 9999;
source.Obj.Value := '+';
LogRecord('Clone', clone);
```

Although the source Str field was changed, the contents of the cloned Str were not modified. Most frequently used string types in Delphi (namely, AnsiString and UnicodeString, also known as string) are reference-counted, the same as interfaces, but they implement a copy-on- write mechanism that makes sure that changing one string variable doesn't cause any effect on shared copies.

Unlike this, the modified contents of `Intf.Value` (1234 originally, now 2468) in the original records are visible in the cloned record. Both records are just pointing to the same instance of the interface, and so a change in one place is reflected in the other. The same holds for the `Obj.Value` field.

Modifying an array results in two different results. The full content of a static array is stored inside an owner. Modifying a static array in the original therefore makes no change to the clone. A dynamic array, on the other hand, is a reference type, the same as objects, interfaces, and strings. Both records are therefore pointing to the same dynamic array instance, and modifying it in one place (in the original record) also makes it change in the clone.

 A full discussion about value and reference types, interface reference counting, and the copy-on-write mechanism is unfortunately too long to be included in this book. You can read more about such topics in my book *Delphi High Performance*, which was published by *Packt Publishing*.

When copying (cloning) records, you should always examine the type of data stored inside the record so that you can prevent unwanted data modification.

Cloning objects

Unlike records, objects in Delphi are reference types. When you create an object, memory is dynamically allocated and stored in the object variable. A variable that stores an object is actually just a pointer, pointing to the memory where the real object is stored.

The following code fragment therefore doesn't create a copy of an object:

```
var
  a, b: TSomeObject;

begin
  a := TSomeObject.Create;
  b := a;
  // a and b are now sharing the same object
  // they are both pointing to the same memory address
end;
```

To create a clone of an object, we have to *create* a new object and copy the content of the object from the original to the new object. There are three idiomatic ways to do that in Delphi and all are demonstrated in the prototype project.

The code in this project works with the class `TCloneable`, which is defined in the unit `Prototype.Cloneable`. The full class definition is shown next:

```
type
  TCloneable = class
  strict private
    FData: TStream;
    FIsBar: boolean;
    FName: string;
  public
    constructor Create;
    constructor CreateFrom(baseObj: TCloneable);
    destructor Destroy; override;
    procedure Assign(baseObj: TCloneable);
    function Clone: TCloneable;
    function FooBar: string;
    property Data: TStream read FData;
    property Name: string read FName write FName;
  end;
```

This class contains three fields: a boolean, a string, and a nested `TStream` class. To create a full clone, we have to copy all three.

The first idiomatic way to do this is to implement the function `Clone`, which creates and returns a new object. It is implemented as follows:

```
function TCloneable.Clone: TCloneable;
var
  dataPos: int64;
begin
  Result := TCloneable.Create;

  // make copy of published data
  Result.Name := Name;

  // clone state of owned objects
  // make sure not to destroy the state of owned objects
  // during the process!
  dataPos := Data.Position;
  Result.Data.CopyFrom(Data, 0);
  Data.Position := dataPos;
  Result.Data.Position := dataPos;

  // clone private state
  Result.FIsBar := FIsBar;
end;
```

We simply use the default constructor `Create` to create a new instance of the `TCloneable` class and then make a full copy of all the data. To create a completely identical object, we have to know how internally used classes (`TStream` in this case) are implemented so that we can correctly copy their properties. In our case, we have to not only copy the contents of the stream but correctly initialize the `Position` property in the clone.

To create a clone `FClone` of the original `FMaster`, we simply call the `Clone` method, as shown next:

```
FClone := FMaster.Clone;
```

Personally, I'm against this approach, as it makes for unreadable code. It differs enough from the standard way of creating Delphi objects that it's easy to ignore the this line creates new instance, meaning when you read it. That's why I prefer to use the second idiomatic approach: cloning with constructor.

A second way of doing the same thing works by implementing a constructor that accepts a `template` object: an object that is used as a master data source. In the example project, this functionality is implemented in `TCloneable.CreateFrom`, as shown next:

```
constructor TCloneable.CreateFrom(baseObj: TCloneable);
begin
  Create;
  Assign(baseObj);
end;

procedure TCloneable.Assign(baseObj: TCloneable);
var
  dataPos: int64;
begin
  // make copy of published data
  Name := baseObj.Name;

  // clone state of owned objects
  dataPos := baseObj.Data.Position;
  Data.CopyFrom(baseObj.Data, 0);
  baseObj.Data.Position := dataPos;
  Data.Position := dataPos;

  // clone private state
  FIsBar := baseObj.FIsBar;
end;
```

The code firstly calls the default constructor `Create`, which initializes the object and creates an internal `TStream` field. Then it calls the helper method `Assign`, which contains exactly the same code to copy the state from one object to another as it was implemented in the `Clone` function.

 I like to call this *cloning* constructor `CreateFrom`, but you can name it anything. It can simply be called `Create`, if that is more to your liking.

To create a clone in this way, you simply call `TCloneable.CreateFrom` as the next code fragment shows:

```
FClone := TCloneable.CreateFrom(FMaster);
```

I do believe that this approach more clearly indicates that an object is created at this point.

The third idiomatic way of cloning an object simply calls the default constructor `Create` and then explicitly calls `Assign` to copy the contents. The next code fragment shows how this can be done:

```
FClone := TCloneable.Create;
FClone.Assign(FMaster);
```

This way of doing things is undoubtedly the most flexible, as you can choose the constructor that will create the object, if there is more than one. It is also useful if you don't like using constructors with arguments.

If you are making the `Assign` method public, however, you should know that Delphi's run-time library overloads this method with a special meaning. When the users of your code see that it implements public `Assign`, they may have certain expectations, and it is proper that you anticipate this and meet them. The next few pages of the book deal with this topic.

Delphi idioms – Assign and AssignTo

The Delphi RTL class `TPersistent`, which is implemented in unit `System.Classes`, defines two methods: `Assign` and `AssignTo`. Relevant parts of this class are shown next:

```
type
  TPersistent = class(TObject)
  protected
    procedure AssignTo(Dest: TPersistent); virtual;
  public
```

```
      procedure Assign(Source: TPersistent); virtual;
   end;

procedure TPersistent.Assign(Source: TPersistent);
begin
   if Source <> nil then Source.AssignTo(Self) else AssignError(nil);
end;

procedure TPersistent.AssignTo(Dest: TPersistent);
begin
   Dest.AssignError(Self);
end;
```

Any descendent of the TPersistent class can override any or both of these methods. When you know how to copy data from some type into the object, you override Assign. When you know how to copy data from the object into some type, you override AssignTo. A typical implementation should follow the following pattern:

```
procedure TMyClass.Assign(Source: TPersistent);
begin
   if {we can handle Source} then
     // copy data from Source
   else
     inherited;
end;

procedure TMyClass.AssignTo(Dest: TPersistent);
begin
   if {we can handle Dest} then
     // copy data to Dest
   else
     inherited;
end;
```

When the program calls Assign method on an object, the following happens:

- If the object knows how to handle the source, it assigns the data and exits.
- If it doesn't, Assign from the parent class is called.
- This continues until a class is able to handle the source data or TPersistent is reached.
- TPersistent.Assign checks whether the input data is empty (nil) and simply calls Source.AssignTo(Self) otherwise. The reasoning behind this is as follows: Nobody in this chain of derived classes knows how to copy data from the source. Maybe somebody in the source's chain of derived classes knows how to copy data into our class.

- AssignTo from the `Source` class is called. If it knows how to handle our class, and it copies the data and exits.
- Otherwise, AssignTo from the parent class is called.
- This continues until a class is able to handle the destination data or TPersistent is reached.
- TPersistent.AssignTo simply raises an exception.

> You should always call Assign in your code to copy data between two objects. AssignTo is `protected`, anyway, and you cannot call it directly.

This chain of events results in a very flexible system for copying data that we can also exploit in creative ways. The example project PrototypePersisten shows how cloning can be implemented by using Assign.

The unit Prototype.CloneablePersistent implements two classes: a base class TCloneable, which derives from TPersistent, and a derived class TNewCloneable. Both implement the Assign method to implement the prototype pattern. The relevant parts of both classes are shown in the next code fragment:

```
type
  TCloneablePersistent = class(TPersistent)
  public
    procedure Assign(Source: TPersistent); override;
    function FooBar: string;
    property Data: TStream read FData;
    property Name: string read FName write FName;
  end;

  TNewCloneable = class(TCloneablePersistent)
  public
    procedure Assign(Source: TPersistent); override;
    property Value: integer read FValue write FValue;
  end;

procedure TCloneablePersistent.Assign(Source: TPersistent);
var
  baseObj: TCloneablePersistent;
  dataPos: int64;
begin
  if not (Source is TCloneablePersistent) then
    inherited
  else begin
    baseObj := TCloneablePersistent(Source);
```

```
      // make copy of published data
      Name := baseObj.Name;

      // clone state of owned objects
      dataPos := baseObj.Data.Position;
      Data.CopyFrom(baseObj.Data, 0);
      baseObj.Data.Position := dataPos;
      Data.Position := dataPos;

      // clone private state
      FIsBar := baseObj.FIsBar;
    end;
  end;

  procedure TNewCloneable.Assign(Source: TPersistent);
  begin
    if Source is TNewCloneable then
      Value := TNewCloneable(Source).Value;
    inherited;
  end;
```

The `TCloneablePersistent.Assign` method checks whether the `Source` is of type `TCloneablePersistent`. If so, it executes the already-well-known code to copy state from one object to another. If not, inherited is called so that the expected behavior of `Assign` is not broken.

The `TNewCloneable.Assign` checks whether the `Source` is of type `TNewCloneable` and if so, copies the `Value` property. Then, it always calls the inherited `Assign`. If the source is `TNewCloneable`, the inherited method will copy other data fields. Otherwise, it will pass execution to the parent of `TCloneablePersistent`.

As I said before, these functions (especially `AssignTo`) can be used in creative ways. We can, for example, use `AssignTo` to implement the logging functionality for our classes. Both classes in the example program use `AssignTo` to log their state into a `TStrings` object. The main program can then simply call `AssignTo` to log an object's state into a listbox, as the next code fragment shows:

```
  var
    lbLog: TListBox;

  lbLog.Items.Assign(FClone);
```

By implementing `AssignTo`, we can extend the functionality of a class that we cannot change. We cannot extend `TStrings.Assign` to handle our class, but we can easily handle `TStrings` in our `AssignTo` and the net result is the same.

You can check the implementation of `TCloneablePersistent.AssignTo` in the source code. `TNewCloneable.AssignTo`, which is simpler (as it only logs one value); it is implemented as follows:

```
procedure TNewCloneable.AssignTo(Dest: TPersistent);
begin
  inherited;

  if Dest is TStrings then
    TStrings(Dest).Add('Value: ' + Value.ToString);
end;
```

In this case, we are calling inherited first so that fields from the base class `TCloneablePersistent` are logged before fields from the derived class `TNewCloneable`.

Serialization

In addition to techniques discussed in this chapter, we can also use the *memento* pattern (also known as serialization) to clone objects. As an example, I have created a project `PrototypeJSON`, which converts an object into a JSON string and then creates a new object from that string. If you examine the project, you'll also notice that I had to remove the `TStream` internal field because it was not correctly handled. We will learn to deal with such problems in Chapter 7, *Iterator, Observer, Visitor, and Memento*.

Builder

The last pattern from this chapter, builder, helps with creating complex objects or their representations. The general idea behind the pattern is to separate such a process into two parts: one gives instructions to an abstract builder interface, and another converts the instructions into a concrete representation. This allows us to create multiple representations from the same construction process.

The builder pattern is similar to an automated coffee/tea machine that always follows the same build process: put a cup on the tray, insert the correct beverage into the system, flow hot water through the system into the cup, and beep at the end. While the build process is always the same, the end result depends on a concrete implementation of step two.

The builder pattern is very similar to the abstract factory pattern. In both cases, the shared class uses an abstract interface to execute a task. The difference is that the builder pattern is focused on step-by-step instructions that the builder object gives to the builder interface. These instructions can be hardcoded into the program, or can be generated according to some input.

There's a thin line between an abstract factory and a builder. For example, we could say that the VCL/FMX user interface generator example from the abstract factory pattern section is actually an example of a builder pattern. You can think of the abstract factory pattern as being a more generic mechanism that can be used to implement a builder pattern.

To demonstrate this, the *Builder* project from the builder folder implements a process that follows the step-by-step instructions paradigm even more closely. The implementation, however, matches the example from the abstract factory section.

The program implements a builder that creates an abstract structured data object that can be converted to an XML or a JSON representation. The builder interface `IDataBuilder` is defined in the unit `DataBuilder.Intf` and main program uses it as follows:

```
type
  IDataBuilder = interface ['{1BA8B314-4968-4209-AF1E-2496C7BEC390}']
    procedure BeginData;
    procedure BeginNode(const name: string);
    procedure AddField(const name, value: string);
    procedure EndNode;
    procedure EndData;
    function Make: string;
  end;

function TfrmBuilder.MakeData(const builder: IDataBuilder): string;
begin
  builder.BeginData;
  builder.BeginNode('Book');
  builder.AddField('Title', 'Hands-on Design Patterns');
  builder.AddField('Topic', 'design patterns, Delphi');
  builder.BeginNode('Author');
  builder.AddField('Name', 'Primoz Gabrijelcic');
  builder.AddField('Blog', 'thedelphigeek.com');
```

```
    builder.EndNode;
    builder.EndNode;
    builder.EndData;

    Result := builder.Make;
end;
```

The data object is constructed in a purely abstract manner. The `MakeData` method receives an implementation of the `IDataBuilder` interface and uses its methods to create an abstract object. In the last line, this representation is converted into a concrete representation. The result of both conversions, to JSON and to XML, is shown in the next screenshot:

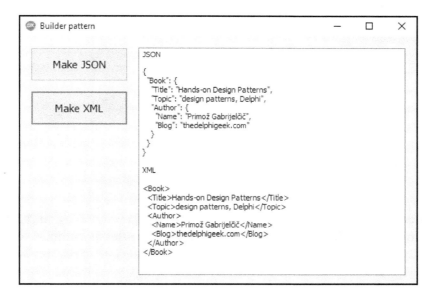

Abstract data structure converted to JSON and XML formats.

The data object from this example has the same internal structure as the following Delphi record:

```
Book = record
  Title: string;
  Topic: string;
  Author: record
    Name: string;
    Blog: string;
  end;
end;
```

The actual implementations of the `IDataBuilder` interface are found in units `DataBuilder.JSON` and `DataBuilder.XML`. Both are very similar in nature: representation is created line by line and is appropriately indented. To simplify the code, the shared functionality is implemented within another builder class: `TIndentedBuilder` from the unit `IndentedBuilder`. This class uses an internal field `FData: TStringList` to store data, and implements only four public functions, shown next:

```
procedure TIndentedBuilder.Indent;
begin
  Inc(FIndent, 2);
end;

procedure TIndentedBuilder.IndentLine(const line: string);
begin
  FData.Add(StringOfChar(' ', FIndent) + line);
end;

function TIndentedBuilder.ToString: string;
begin
  Result := FData.Text;
end;

procedure TIndentedBuilder.Unindent;
begin
  Dec(FIndent, 2);
end;
```

The XML builder `TXMLBuilder` then uses this class by *composition*. We could also inherit both builders from the indented builder, but that would needlessly complicate the code and introduce dependencies. Remember what `Chapter 1`, *Introduction to patterns* said: Favor object composition over class inheritance.

Besides the internal `TIndentedBuilder` field, XML builder also uses a stack of open (active) nodes. When we close a node, the builder has to end an element by inserting a `</node>` string. The name of that node has to be remembered somewhere, and so the `BeginNode` puts it on a stack and `EndNode` takes it off the stack.

The following code fragment shows the full implementation of the XML builder class:

```
type
  TXMLBuilder = class(TInterfacedObject, IDataBuilder)
  strict private
    FBuilder: TIndentedBuilder;
    FNodes: TStack<string>;
  public
    procedure AfterConstruction; override;
```

```
    procedure BeforeDestruction; override;
    procedure AddField(const name, value: string);
    procedure BeginNode(const name: string);
    procedure BeginData;
    procedure EndData;
    procedure EndNode;
    function Make: string;
  end;

procedure TXMLBuilder.AddField(const name, value: string);
begin
  FBuilder.IndentLine('<' + name + '>' + value + '</' + name + '>');
end;

procedure TXMLBuilder.AfterConstruction;
begin
  inherited;
  FBuilder := TIndentedBuilder.Create;
  FNodes := TStack<string>.Create;
end;

procedure TXMLBuilder.BeforeDestruction;
begin
  FreeAndNil(FNodes);
  FreeAndNil(FBuilder);
  inherited;
end;

procedure TXMLBuilder.BeginData;
begin
  // do nothing
end;

procedure TXMLBuilder.BeginNode(const name: string);
begin
  FBuilder.IndentLine('<' + name + '>');
  FBuilder.Indent;
  FNodes.Push(name);
end;

procedure TXMLBuilder.EndData;
begin
  // do nothing
end;

procedure TXMLBuilder.EndNode;
begin
  FBuilder.Unindent;
```

```
    FBuilder.IndentLine('</' + FNodes.Pop + '>');
end;

function TXMLBuilder.Make: string;
begin
  Result := FBuilder.ToString;
end;
```

The JSON builder is implemented in a similar manner. For details, see the source code.

I must point out that this implementation is very simple and should not be used in production. Input data is not checked, invalid XML/JSON characters (such as < and ") are not converted into appropriate representations, and so on. Both builders should be treated as a demonstration only.

Idioms – Fluent interfaces

A concept of a builder is often used together with a concept of fluent interfaces. When an interface or a class is written in a fluent manner, its every method (or at least most of the methods) returns the implementing object itself. To put this in Delphi terms: each method returns `Self`.

 This idiom is not specific to Delphi. Fluent interfaces are programmed in all kinds of languages, from C# to JavaScript.

Fluent interfaces allow us to chain method calls. For example, given an initialized object sb of type `TStringBuilder` (from unit `System.SysUtils`), we can create a simple string by using the following four commands:

```
sb.Append('The answer: ');
sb.Append(42);
sb.AppendLine;
ShowMessage(sb.ToString);
```

As both `Append` and `AppendLine` are actually functions returning `TStringBuilder`, we can simplify this code as follows:

```
ShowMessage(sb.Append('The answer: ').Append(42).AppendLine.ToString);
```

This approach simplifies the code but slightly complicates the debugging. If you use it and the code doesn't work correctly, you should rewrite it in a classical way so it will be simpler to debug.

Another great example of fluent interface are string helpers from the `System.SysUtils` unit. They allow us to write code such as this:

```
data := stringValue.TrimLeft.ToLower.Split([', '],
  TStringSplitOptions.ExcludeEmpty));
```

Or, you can use fluent interfaces to construct SQL statement in code. My open source `GpSQLBuilder` project (`https://github.com/gabr42/GpSQLBuilder`) allows you to construct SQL commands, as shown in the next example:

```
ExecuteQuery(CreateGpSQLBuilder
  .Select
    .Column(['DISTINCT', DBPLY_DBField_ID])
    .&Case
      .When([DBSBF_DBField_CreatedTime, '< ''2010-01-01'''])
        .&Then('*')
      .&Else('')
    .&End
  .From(DBT_PLY)
  .LeftJoin(DBT_SBF)
    .&On([DBSBF_PLY_ID, '=', DBPLY_DBField_ID])
  .OrderBy(DBPLY_DBField_ID)
  .AsString);
```

The last example comes from my multithreading library `OmniThreadLibrary` (`https://github.com/gabr42/OmniThreadLibrary`). It uses a fluent approach to construct parallel tasks. You can, for example, use the following code fragment to create a timed task that periodically executes some code in a background thread:

```
FTimedTask :=
  Parallel.TimedTask
  .Every(1000)
  .TaskConfig(Parallel.TaskConfig.OnMessage(Self))
  .Execute(SendRequest_asy);
```

Let me now return to the example from the beginning of this section. We can rewrite it in a fluent manner by changing interface methods to return the interface itself. We only cannot change the `Make` function, as it already returns a string. The new interface `IDataBuilderFluent` is defined in unit `DataBuilderFluent.Intf` as follows:

```
type
  IDataBuilderFluent = interface ['{1BA8B314-4968-4209-AF1E-2496C7BEC390}']
    function BeginData: IDataBuilderFluent;
    function BeginNode(const name: string): IDataBuilderFluent;
    function AddField(const name, value: string): IDataBuilderFluent;
    function EndNode: IDataBuilderFluent;
    function EndData: IDataBuilderFluent;
    function Make: string;
  end;
```

The project `BuilderFluent` shows how to use the fluent version of the builder interface. All builder functions have had to be modified in the same manner: they must return `Self` at the end, for example: `TXMLBuilder.BeginNode` is now implemented as follows:

```
function TXMLBuilder.BeginNode(const name: string): IDataBuilderFluent;
begin
  FBuilder.IndentLine('<' + name + '>');
  FBuilder.Indent;
  FNodes.Push(name);
  Result := Self;
end;
```

The new builder implementations can be found in units `DataBuilderFluent.JSON` and `DataBuilderFluent.XML`.

To simplify the comparison, I will repeat the original `MakeData` method here:

```
function TfrmBuilder.MakeData(
  const builder: IDataBuilder): string;
begin
  builder.BeginData;
  builder.BeginNode('Book');
  builder.AddField('Title', 'Hands-on Design Patterns');
  builder.AddField('Topic', 'design patterns, Delphi');
  builder.BeginNode('Author');
  builder.AddField('Name', 'Primož Gabrijelčič');
  builder.AddField('Blog', 'thedelphigeek.com');
  builder.EndNode;
  builder.EndNode;
  builder.EndData;
```

```
    Result := builder.Make;
end;
```

In the fluent version, it is implemented as follows:

```
function TfrmBuilderFluent.MakeData(
    const builder: IDataBuilderFluent): string;
begin
    builder
        .BeginData
        .BeginNode('Book')
            .AddField('Title', 'Hands-on Design Patterns')
            .AddField('Topic', 'design patterns, Delphi')
            .BeginNode('Author')
                .AddField('Name', 'Primoz Gabrijelcic')
                .AddField('Blog', 'thedelphigeek.com')
            .EndNode
        .EndNode
        .EndData;

    Result := builder.Make;
end;
```

Besides a bit less typing (we don't have to repeat the builder part all over), this approach allows us to get creative with indentation. The code indentation now resembles the structure of the generated data, which improves readability.

Summary

In this chapter, I have explored four more creational patterns.

The first pattern was a factory method. This pattern simplifies the creation of objects that depend on one another. We can implement it by following the classical object-oriented approach or in a modernized way by using interfaces and dependency injection.

From there, we moved to an abstract factory pattern. Abstract factory is a factory for factories. This pattern defines how abstract interfaces should be used to create collections of dependent objects.

The third pattern, prototype, is about making perfect copies of objects. In Delphi, we have to do this manually, and this section mostly explored the different ways of implementing the data-copying mechanism.

The last pattern in this chapter, builder, is closely related to an abstract factory pattern. It is used to split the creation of complex objects into two parts: one issues instructions to the abstract builder, which then generates a concrete representation.

In the next chapter, we will move to the new pattern group: structural patterns. We will explore the Composite pattern, Flyweight, Marker, and Bridge.

Section 3: Structural Patterns 3

In this chapter, the reader will learn the most important patterns from the structural patterns group. These patterns relate to class and object composition.

This section will comprise the following chapters:

Chapter 4, *Composite, Flyweight, Marker Interface, and Bridge*

Chapter 5, *Adapter, Proxy, Decorator, and Façade*

4
Composite, Flyweight, Marker Interface, and Bridge

Managing complex objects and collections of objects can quickly turn into a mess. **Structural patterns** were designed to help you think about object composition and to change disorder into order.

Structural patterns come in different shapes and sizes. Some consume one interface and expose the same or a slightly modified version of that interface to the user. Others consume multiple objects, or enhance their behavior in aspects that are completely unrelated to the functionality of consumed objects.

In this chapter, we'll firstly look into three unrelated structural patterns that cover different use cases. At the end, the bridge pattern will introduce us to the area of patterns that consume only one interface and mostly leave it unchanged, which will be the main topic of the next chapter. In this chapter, you will learn about the following:

- A composite pattern, which allows clients to ignore the difference between simple and complex objects
- A flyweight pattern, which minimizes memory consumption with data sharing
- A marker interface pattern, which introduces metadata programming
- A bridge pattern, which helps us to separate an abstract interface from its implementation

Composite

Sometimes, we have to work with data that is organized into a tree structure. There is an entry point, an object of some class *N*, which owns other objects of the same class *N* or objects of class *L*. We call this entry point a root, class *N*, an inner node, and *L*, a leaf.

When we perform some operation on such compound data, it is helpful if we can treat all objects the same. In other words, we don't want to distinguish between a root, an inner node, and a leaf. The composite pattern allows us to treat all types of components the same.

 Imagine an irrigation system. At some point, it is connected to a water supply. The irrigation system can then split into multiple branches that end in different kinds of water dispensers. We don't care much about that complicated structure, as all components of the system implement the same interface: you put the water in and it flows out the other end.

As specified in the Gang of Four book, a composite pattern works with two types of objects. Compound objects can own other objects, while leaf objects represent endpoints of the structure: they can only hold data but not other compounds or leaf objects.

To make sure that both kinds of objects implement the same interface, we derive both from the abstract class, which specifies these interfaces. For example, the following Delphi code fragment defines a very simple collection of classes implementing the composite pattern:

```
type
  TBaseClass = class
  public
    procedure Operation; virtual; abstract;
  end;

  TCompoundClass = class(TBaseClass)
  public
    procedure Operation; override;
  end;

  TLeafClass = class(TBaseClass)
  public
   procedure Operation; override;
  end;
```

It should be noted that, when we are discussing the composite pattern, the word interface does not mean `interface` as we know it in Delphi. The Gang of Four design patterns are purely object-oriented, and in this context, an interface means just a set of methods that a class exposes publicly.

In modern times, we mostly stay away from the composite pattern. In the case of a tree data structure, for example, we would work with just one data type: node. Each node can have multiple children of the same type. If it doesn't have any children, it represents a leaf node—simple and effective.

In other situations, when we need different classes to expose the same interface, we can do that by using Delphi interfaces. For example, we could easily rewrite the previous example as follows:

```
type
  ICommonInterface = interface
    procedure Operation;
  end;

  TCompoundClass = class(TInterfacedObject, ICommonInterface)
  public
    procedure Operation;
  end;

  TLeafClass = class(TInterfacedObject, ICommonInterface)
  public
    procedure Operation;
  end;
```

Still, this requires us to work with interfaces instead of objects, and sometimes that would require a significant rewrite of the existing code. In such cases, the composite pattern still represents a powerful tool.

Child management

While the composite pattern tries to equalize different kinds of objects in a data structure, there is still a significant difference between compound and leaf nodes, namely that compound nodes own other objects. To use this functionality in the code, compound nodes must implement child management operations. In other words, they must implement operations for adding, removing, and accessing child objects. It is, however, not clear in which place the class hierarchy we should implement these methods.

We can approach this in two different ways. One possibility is to define these operations in the interface class (TBaseClass in our example). This is called **design for uniformity** and enables the clients to treat leaf and composite objects completely uniformly. This approach, however, loses type safety, as the code can perform child management operations on leaf objects, and that doesn't make much sense. To prevent such errors, we have to override child management operations in the leaf class (TLeafClass) to raise an exception if they are called.

Another possibility is to implement child management operations in the composite class (TCompoundClass). This approach is called **design for type safety**. We gain type safety, child management is now simply not implemented for leaf objects, but we lose uniformity.

In my opinion, it is better to design for type safety as, in this case, the compiler can catch most of our errors. Still, it is good to understand both approaches so the next example will demonstrate both techniques.

The composite project in the composite folder implements a simple structure that can be used to define a modular system, for example, a personal computer. Two parallel implementations are made, one designed for uniformity and another for type safety. The designed-for-uniformity version is implemented in the CompositeUniformity unit, as shown here:

```
type
  TComponentU = class
  public
    constructor Create(const AName: string; const APrice: real);
    procedure Add(component: TComponentU); virtual;
    function Components: TArray<TComponentU>; virtual;
    function TotalPrice: real; virtual;
    property Name: string read FName;
    property Price: real read FPrice;
  end;

  TConfigurableComponentU = class(TComponentU)
  public
    procedure AfterConstruction; override;
    procedure BeforeDestruction; override;
    procedure Add(component: TComponentU); override;
    function Components: TArray<TComponentU>; override;
    function TotalPrice: real; override;
  end;

  TBasicComponentU = class(TComponentU)
  end;
```

The TComponentU class provides a common interface. Each component has a name (Name) and price (Price), and can return the price for itself and all subcomponents (TotalPrice). It also provides access to subcomponents (Components) and a method to add a new component (Add). To simplify the example, removing components is not supported. This class also provides some basic implementation for handling the name and price.

A composite object, TConfigurableComponentU implements child storage and management. It also overrides the TotalPrice method to take subcomponents into account. The code is trivial, and you can look it up in the CompositeUniformity unit. The most complicated method in the whole unit is the calculation of the total price for a composite object, which is shown next:

```
function TConfigurableComponentU.TotalPrice: real;
var
  comp: TComponentU;
begin
  Result := Price;
  for comp in FComponents do
    Result := Result + comp.TotalPrice;
end;
```

As we can see, this method doesn't care whether each child object is TConfigurableComponentU or TBasicComponentU. It simply calls the TotalPrice method, which is guaranteed to work uniformly in all types of components.

When you click the Composite [Uniformity] button, the following code creates a sample computer configuration and displays all components and the total price:

```
procedure TfrmComposite.LogComponentsU(component: TComponentU;
  indent: string);
var
  comp: TComponentU;
begin
  lbLog.Items.Add(Format('%s%s: %.1f',
    [indent, component.Name, component.Price]));
  indent := indent + ' ';
  for comp in component.Components do
    LogComponentsU(comp, indent);
 end;

procedure TfrmComposite.btnCompUniformClick(Sender: TObject);
var
  computer: TComponentU;
  motherboard: TComponentU;
begin
  computer := TConfigurableComponentU.Create('chassis', 37.9);
```

```
    computer.Add(TBasicComponentU.Create('PSU', 34.6));
    motherboard := TConfigurableComponentU.Create('motherboard', 96.5);
    motherboard.Add(TBasicComponentU.Create('CPU', 121.1));
    motherboard.Add(TBasicComponentU.Create('memory', 88.2));
    motherboard.Add(TBasicComponentU.Create('memory', 88.2));
    motherboard.Add(TBasicComponentU.Create('graphics', 179));
    computer.Add(motherboard);

    LogComponentsU(computer, '');
    lbLog.Items.Add('Total cost: ' +
      Format('%.1f', [computer.TotalPrice]));
    lbLog.Items.Add('');

    FreeAndNil(computer);
  end;
```

As in the `TotalPrice` method implementation, `LogComponentsU` treats all components the same. It doesn't matter whether the component parameter is actually a `TConfigurableComponentU` or `TBasicComponentU`, as they all implement the same interface.

The problem with the uniformity approach is that we can compile the following code without a problem:

```
    cpu := TBasicComponentU.Create('CPU', 121.1);
    cpu.Add(TBasicComponentU.Create('memory', 88.2));
```

As the `cpu` is a basic component, it makes no sense to add another component to it. The code, however, compiles and only reports a problem (by raising an exception) when executed.

An alternative implementation designed for type safety is implemented in the `CompositeSafety` unit. As shown here, it is mostly the same as the uniformity implementation, except that the child management functions appear only in the `TConfigurableComponentS` class:

```
    type
      TComponentS = class
      public
        constructor Create(const AName: string; const APrice: real);
        function Components: TArray<TComponentS>; virtual;
        function TotalPrice: real; virtual;
        property Name: string read FName;
        property Price: real read FPrice;
      end;

      TConfigurableComponentS = class(TComponentS)
```

```
public
  procedure AfterConstruction; override;
  procedure BeforeDestruction; override;
  procedure Add(component: TComponentS);
  function Components: TArray<TComponentS>; override;
  function TotalPrice: real; override;
end;

TBasicComponentS = class(TComponentS)
end;
```

Unlike in the previous example, the following code doesn't even compile:

```
cpu := TBasicComponentS.Create('CPU', 121.1);
cpu.Add(TBasicComponentS.Create('memory', 88.2));
```

Both versions are functionally identical and, as expected, provide the same output when used in the demonstration program. The following screenshot shows the program after each button was clicked once:

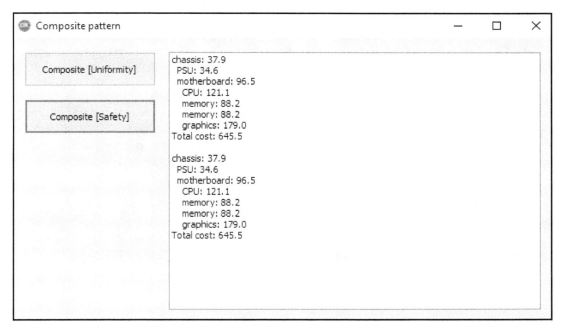

The result of running both uniformity and type safety versions

Flyweight

Structural patterns tell us how to put objects together. Their focus is mostly on organizing software components. They help us to maintain order in our code. That, however, is not true for each and every one of them. A case in point, for example, is the **flyweight pattern**.

The flyweight pattern helps us to reduce memory usage. As such, it is less and less important in modern times, where we are dealing with gigabyte memories. Sometimes, however, we will still significantly decrease memory usage by implementing it. Also, sometimes, it will help speed up the program.

This pattern works best when part of each object contains data that is also used in other objects. Instead of duplicating that data in every object, we can extract shared data into another object. We can then replace original data in an object with a pointer to the shared data. This allows multiple objects to share one copy of the data, hence reducing memory usage.

 In the past, libraries stored book indexes on index cards (small pieces of paper). They had different indexes: by title, by author, by topic... and in every index, the index card for a book contained only basic info (title and author) and its location in the library (a pointer to the shared data object: the book).

In terms of flyweight patterns, we divide each flyweight object into two parts: the normal object data (intrinsic part) and the shared data (extrinsic part). The intrinsic part is stored in the object, while the extrinsic part is stored in an external, shared object. We must take care not to accidentally modify the extrinsic part, as that would change external parts for all objects that are referencing it. In other words, the extrinsic part must be immutable.

In games, moving objects are frequently represented as sprites. A sprite is an image that can be displayed multiple times at different locations on a screen. An intrinsic part of a sprite object is its location and some kind of identifier (pointer or unique ID) that can be used to locate a sprite image bitmap (extrinsic part). If we have multiple copies of the same sprite displayed on the screen, they all point to the same extrinsic part (image bitmap).

String interning

If we examine a typical business application, we would frequently find that some string constants are used more than once in the source code. For example, we would probably find the ID, name, and similar strings all around the program.

This doesn't represent a big waste of memory. Compilers, however, sometimes look at that in a different manner and (correctly) notice that we don't really need multiple copies of such strings. Each (distinct) string constant can only be stored once in a complied program, and the code can then reference this shared data. By this, the compiler uses a flyweight design pattern to implement a concept called `string interning`.

We can find this behavior in various programming languages. It is, for example, implemented in Java. A Delphi compiler works in the same way.

A small program, `StringInterning` in the `Flyweight` folder demonstrates this behavior. It is shown in full here:

```
program StringInterning;

{$APPTYPE CONSOLE}

{$R *.res}

var
  a: string;

begin
  a := 'Name';
  Writeln(a);
  Writeln('Name');
  Readln;
end.
```

To actually prove that both name strings are represented by one shared instance, we have to look into the compiled code. The simplest way to do that is to press *F8* to step into debugger and then switch to CPU view with View, Debug Windows, CPU Windows, and Entire CPU. Continue pressing *F8* in the CPU view, until you arrive to a similar code, as shown in the next screenshot:

```
StringInterning.dpr.11:  a := 'Name';
⇨  0040B10E B888054100        mov eax,$00410588
   0040B113 BA88B14000        mov edx,$0040b188
   0040B118 E82FBDFFFF        call @UStrAsg
StringInterning.dpr.12:  Writeln(a);
   0040B11D A130C84000        mov eax,[$0040c830]
   0040B122 8B1588054100      mov edx,[$00410588]
   0040B128 E8B39DFFFF        call @Write0UString
   0040B12D E8AE9EFFFF        call @WriteLn
   0040B132 E8F58DFFFF        call @_IOTest
StringInterning.dpr.13:  Writeln('Name');
   0040B137 A130C84000        mov eax,[$0040c830]
⇨  0040B13C BA88B14000        mov edx,$0040b188
   0040B141 E89A9DFFFF        call @Write0UString
   0040B146 E8959EFFFF        call @WriteLn
   0040B14B E8DC8DFFFF        call @_IOTest
StringInterning.dpr.14:  Readln;
```

```
0040B188 4E 00 61 00 6D 00 65 00  N.a.m.e.
0040B190 00 00 00 00 00 00 00 00  ........
0040B198 00 00 00 00 00 00 00 00  ........
```

Example of string interning in Delphi code.

The address moved into the `edx` register points to the string name. It is possible that in your Delphi this string will be compiled to a different address, but still the same address should be used in both places marked in the screenshot.

If we examine the memory at that address, we'll find the string name. It is a Unicode string, and hence every second byte has a value of 0.

I must point out that the compiler implements string interning only for string constants. If the strings are constructed in code, testing whether a same string is already in use would be entirely too CPU- intensive.

If you would like to know more about how Delphi strings function, I would recommend *Chapter 3, Fine Tuning the Code*, from my book *Delphi High Performance* (https://www.amazon.com/dp/1788625455), published by Packt Publishing.

A practical example

To demonstrate the practical aspects of implementing a flyweight pattern, I have put together a simple application that stores and displays information about customers. It is implemented as the `Flyweight` and is stored in the `Flyweight` folder.

A customer is represented by an `ICustomer` interface, defined in the Customer unit as shown here:

```
type
  TPersonalInfo = record
  public
    ID: integer;
    Name: string;
    Address : string;
    constructor Create(const AName, AAddress: string);
  end;

  ICustomer = interface ['{1AE32361-788E-4974-9366-94E62D980234}']
    function GetCompanyInfo: TCompanyInfo;
    function GetPersonalInfo: TPersonalInfo;
    property CompanyInfo: TCompanyInfo read GetCompanyInfo;
    property PersonalInfo: TPersonalInfo read GetPersonalInfo;
  end;
```

The information about a customer is split into two parts. The personal data is stored inside the customer interface as a `TPersonalInfo` record. This represents the intrinsic part of a `Flyweight` object.

The information about the company may be the same for many customers and is therefore stored in an extrinsic record: `TCompanyInfo`. This record is defined in the company unit as follows:

```
type
  TCompanyInfo = record
  public
    ID: integer;
    Name: string;
    Address: string;
    constructor Create(const AName, AAddress: string);
  end;
```

Both `TPersonalInfo` and `TCompanyInfo` store just a name and an address. You can add other fields for an exercise. The `ID` field is not necessary for flyweight implementation. Is is just here to improve logging into the main application.

In the actual implementation of the `ICustomer` interface, `TCustomer`, the intrinsic part is stored directly as a field. The extrinsic part, however, is represented by a field of the `ICompany` type. The following code fragment shows the definition of the `TCustomer` class:

```
type
  TCustomer = class(TInterfacedObject, ICustomer)
  strict private
    FCompanyData: ICompany;
    FPersonalInfo: TPersonalInfo;
  strict protected
    function GetCompanyInfo: TCompanyInfo;
    function GetPersonalInfo: TPersonalInfo;
  public
    constructor Create(const personalInfo: TPersonalInfo;
      const companyInfo: TCompanyInfo;
      companyFactory: TCompanyFactory);
    property CompanyInfo: TCompanyInfo read GetCompanyInfo;
    property PersonalInfo: TPersonalInfo read GetPersonalInfo;
  end;
```

The `ICompany` interface is very simple. It is defined in the `Company` unit and just returns the company info:

```
type
  ICompany = interface ['{36C754FD-2C32-49CA-920E-2FED39121E79}']
    function GetInfo: TCompanyInfo;
    property Info: TCompanyInfo read GetInfo;
  end;
```

To create shared data (`ICustomer`), we have to implement a **factory method** pattern. For more information about this design pattern, see `Chapter 3`, *Factory Method, Abstract Factory, Prototype, and Builder*. In this example, the factory is implemented as the `CreateCompany` method from the `Company` unit. This factory takes the company data record and returns a shared data interface, as shown here:

```
function CreateCompany(const companyInfo: TCompanyInfo): ICompany;
```

We'll look into implementation of this factory method later. For now, let's see how all of these classes, records, and interfaces are used in the code.

When you click **Add customer data** on the main form, the following code creates a new `ICustomer` interface:

```
var
  customer: ICustomer;

customer := CreateCustomer(
  TPersonalInfo.Create(inpPersName.Text, inpPersAddr.Text),
  TCompanyInfo.Create(inpCompName.Text, inpCompAddr.Text),
  Company.CreateCompany);
```

This code uses a **dependency injection** pattern (namely, constructor injection) to inject the factory method, `CreateCompany` into the `TCustomer.Create` constructor. (For more information about the dependency injection, see Chapter 2, *Singleton, Dependency Injection, Lazy Initialization, and Object Pool*.) This constructor uses the injected factory function to convert `TCompanyInfo` into `ICompany` as shown next:

```
constructor TCustomer.Create(
  const personalInfo: TPersonalInfo;
  const companyInfo: TCompanyInfo;
  companyFactory: TCompanyFactory);
begin
  inherited Create;
  FPersonalInfo := personalInfo;
  FCompanyData := companyFactory(companyInfo);
end;
```

When the main program needs to access the company info, the code reads from the `ICustomer.CompanyInfo` property. This maps to a call to the `GetCompanyInfo` function, which uses `ICompany.Info` property to map the `ICompany` back into `TCompanyInfo`. `GetCompanyInfo` is shown in the next code fragment:

```
function TCustomer.GetCompanyInfo: TCompanyInfo;
begin
  Result := FCompanyData.Info;
end;
```

The last piece of the puzzle is implemented in the singleton class, `TCompanyStorage` from the unit `Company`. For more information about the singleton pattern, see Chapter 2, *Singleton, Dependency Injection, Lazy Initialization, and Object Pool*. The definition of this class is shown next:

```
type
  TCompanyStorage = class // singleton
  strict private
  class var
    FCompanyHash: TDictionary<TCompanyInfo, ICompany>;
    FCompanyComparer: IEqualityComparer<TCompanyInfo>;
    FDefaultComparer: IEqualityComparer<TCompanyInfo>;
  strict protected
    class function CompareInfoNoID(
      const left, right: TCompanyInfo): boolean;
    class function HashInfo(const value: TCompanyInfo): integer;
  public
    class constructor Create;
    class destructor Destroy;
    class function CreateCompany(
      const companyInfo: TCompanyInfo): ICompany;
  end;
```

This singleton implements the mapping function, `CreateCompany`, which is called directly from the factory function `CreateCompany`. It uses a dictionary `FCompanyHash` to store created instances of the `ICompany` interface.

As the next code fragment shows, `CreateCompany` firstly looks into the dictionary to see whether there already exists a shared instance of the company data. If `TryGetValue` fails, such data is not yet stored in the dictionary. In this case, the code creates a new `ICompany` object, sets it as a result, and stores it in the dictionary:

```
class function TCompanyStorage.CreateCompany(
  const companyInfo: TCompanyInfo): ICompany;
begin
  if FCompanyHash.TryGetValue(companyInfo, Result) then
    Exit;

  Result := TCompany.Create(companyInfo);
  FCompanyHash.Add(companyInfo, Result);
end;
```

To test the implementation, we can start the application and enter some data. The following screenshot, for example, shows data for two contacts from Embarcadero, and one from Microsoft:

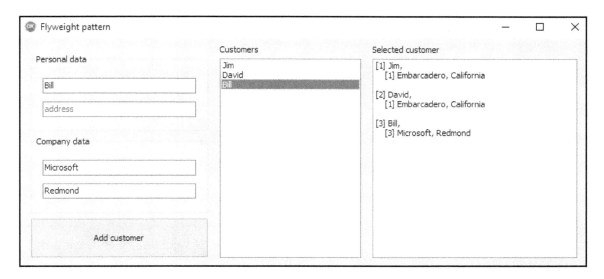

Sample program displaying customer contacts.

We can see from this log that each customer has a unique ID assigned (the number in square brackets before the customer's name). The company info assigned to the first two customers is, however, shared between them; both are referring to the company info record with ID 1.

Delphi idioms – comparers and hashers

The actual implementation of the TCompanyStorage contains some advanced Delphi techniques that come in handy when you are trying to push the most out of the TDictionary.

Delphi's dictionary implementation TDictionary<K, V> is a generic class, operating on two data types (key K and value V) that are specified when we create a concrete instance of that class. For example, in the Flyweight program, the data is stored in the dictionary class TDictionary<TCompanyInfo, ICompany>, so K is TCompanyInfo and V is ICompany.

The algorithm on which `TDictionary` is based needs two functions that operate on the `K` type. One takes two values of that type and compares them for equality, returning `Boolean`. The other takes one value of type `K` and creates a hash of that value: a smaller integer number calculated from the original value in some way. The former function is called an **equality comparer** and the latter a **hasher**. As they must operate on a generic type, `K`, they are declared as generic anonymous methods, as shown next:

```
type
   TEqualityComparison<T> = reference to function(const Left, Right: T):
Boolean;
   THasher<T> = reference to function(const Value: T): Integer;
```

You can find these definitions in the unit `System.Generics.Defaults`.

Besides these two methods, unit `System.Generics.Defaults` also defines the comparison function, `TComparison<T>`, which is used for sorting data.

The problem with equality comparers and hashers is that the `TDictionary` code cannot refer to some concrete implementation of them. When `System.Generics.Collections` (the unit containing `TDictionary` implementation) is compiled, `K` and `V` are not yet known. To circumvent this problem, the implementation contains some logic that examines the concrete instances of type `K` at runtime and then selects the appropriate functions.

This works great in simple cases, but fails when we have more complicated requirements. For example, it fails when `K` is a record containing a string. Another problematic situation occurs if we don't want to use the full record `K` for hashing and comparison.

The problem with hashing records containing strings lies in the implementation of a default record hasher and an equality comparer. They treat strings simply as pointers and not as string data. Two records can contain the same string value that is stored in a different location in memory. In such a case, the default functions won't function correctly. You can see this in action in the `DictionaryProblem`.

In our example program, we run into both problems at the same time. The `TCompanyInfo` record contains two string fields. It also has a field `ID`, which we don't want to use for hashing/comparison.

To fix this problem, we have to write our own `IEqualityComparer<K>`. We can then pass this interface to the `TDictionary` constructor. The correct way to construct this interface is to call `TEqualityComparer<K>.Construct` and pass in two anonymous methods: the equality comparer of type `TEqualityComparison<K>`, and the hasher of type `THasher<K>`. In the example program, this is done in the `TCompanyStorage` constructor, as shown next:

```
class constructor TCompanyStorage.Create;
begin
  FCompanyComparer := TEqualityComparer<TCompanyInfo>.Construct(
    CompareInfoNoID, HashInfo);
  FCompanyHash := TDictionary<TCompanyInfo, ICompany>.Create(
    FCompanyComparer);
end;
```

The equality comparer, `CompareInfoNoID` simply compares the name and address part. The code ignores case sensitivity (the words Canada and canada are treated equal), because that is usually what we want in such situations:

```
class function TCompanyStorage.CompareInfoNoID(
  const left, right: TCompanyInfo): boolean;
begin
  Result := SameText(left.Name, right.Name)
          and SameText(left.Address, right.Address);
end;
```

The hashing function `HashInfo` uses the fast hashing class `THashBobJenkins` from the `System.Hash` unit to generate a hash of both the name and the address. As we want to ignore the difference between uppercase and lowercase letters, all data is converted into uppercase before hashing:

```
class function TCompanyStorage.HashInfo(
  const value: TCompanyInfo): integer;
var
  hasher: THashBobJenkins;
begin
  hasher := THashBobJenkins.Create;
  hasher.Update(value.Name.ToUpperInvariant);
  hasher.Update(value.Address.ToUpperInvariant);
  Result := hasher.HashAsInteger;
end;
```

The `System.Hash` unit contains implementations of multiple hashing functions. You can use it to calculate MD5 (`THashMD5`), SHA1 (`THashSHA1`), and SHA2 (`THashSHA2`) hashes.

Marker interface

The **marker interface pattern** has its origin in the Java world. It is used to provide metadata capabilities in a language that doesn't have explicit support for that. The marker interface concept was largely replaced with the use of attributes or a similar code annotation tool in modern languages.

In programming, metadata provides a way of adding code-describing tags to the program. Unlike normal data variables and fields, which store information required to run the program and to process user data, metadata provides data about classes (and variables and fields) themselves.

 Metadata is a label attached to a product. It is a note on a car dashboard saying, "*Change oil at 150.000 km,*" or a message on a sandwich in a communal kitchen stating, "*This belongs to me!*"

A marker interface pattern provides a way of adding metadata descriptions to a class without changing its layout. For example, let's say that we have a customer information class, such as `TCustomer`, from the project `Marker` in the folder `Marker` interface. The following code fragment shows the public interface of this class. Private fields and all getters and setters are not shown:

```
type
  ICustomer = interface ['{A736226E-B177-4E3A-9CCD-39AE71FB4E1B}']
    property Address: string read GetAddress write SetAddress;
    property Email: string read GetEmail write SetEmail;
    property Name: string read GetName write SetName;
  end;

  TCustomer = class(TInterfacedObject, ICustomer)
  public
    property Address: string read GetAddress write SetAddress;
    property Email: string read GetEmail write SetEmail;
    property Name: string read GetName write SetName;
  end;
```

For some reason, we want to create a subclass that will contain information about important customers, but we must not add any fields to it. (Both an original and a new class must have the same memory layout.) The only way to do that is to decorate this subclass with metadata information. The unit `Customer.Interfaces` demonstrates how we can do this by using a marker interface pattern:

```
type
  IImportantCustomer = interface ['{E32D6AE5-FB60-4414-B7BF-3E5BDFECDE64}']
```

```
end;

    TImportantCustomer = class(TCustomer, IImportantCustomer)
    end;
```

Firstly, we define a `marker` interface, `IImportantCustomer`. A marker interface is nothing more than an interface definition that does not contain any methods.

Secondly, we derive a new subclass from `TCustomer`. This derived class implements the marker interface, but it doesn't add any data fields or methods. This, of course, requires that the original class is always used through the interface paradigm. In the demonstration program, for example, the code always uses `ICustomer` and not `TCustomer`.

The main program uses the following code to test the marker interface support:

```
procedure TfrmMarker.btnCustomerCheckIntfClick(Sender: TObject);
var
  cust1: ICustomer;
  cust2: ICustomer;
begin
  cust1 := TCustomer.Create;
  cust1.Name := 'Joe Schmoe';

  cust2 := TImportantCustomer.Create;
  cust2.Name := 'Mr. Big';

  LogCustomerIntf(cust1);
  LogCustomerIntf(cust2);
end;
```

This method simply creates two `ICustomer` interfaces: one implemented by the `TCustomer` object and another by `TImportantCustomer` object. Both interfaces are then passed to a logging function `LogCustomerIntf`, which is shown here:

```
procedure TfrmMarker.LogCustomerIntf(customer: ICustomer);
begin
  lbLog.Items.Add(customer.Name + ' is ' +
    IfThen(Supports(customer, IImportantCustomer),
      'very important client!',
      'just a regular guy'));
end;
```

From the viewpoint of the logging function, the code always passes in a `ICustomer` interface. The logging code then checks for the presence of the marker interface by calling `Supports(customer, IImportantCustomer)`. This function returns `True` if the `customer` interface also supports an `IImportantCustomer` interface.

As the following screenshot shows, the code correctly detects that Joe Schmoe is a regular guy, while Mr. Big is a very important client.

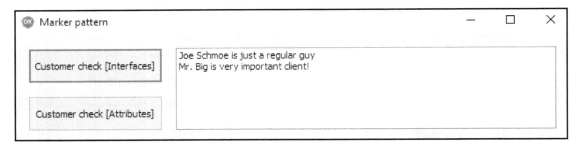

Logging metadata with a marker interface.

The big problem with this approach is that it is very limited. We can only apply marker interfaces to a class. It can also only be used when we are working with interfaces and as such can be hard to apply to a legacy code.

A better way of annotating code with metadata is to use attributes, a concept that was added to Delphi in the 2010 version.

Delphi idioms – attributes

Before we can use an attribute, we have to declare it. To declare an attribute, we have to derive it from a special class, `TCustomAttribute`:

```
type
  SpecialClassAttribute = class(TCustomAttribute)
  end;
```

To use this attribute, we annotate a Delphi entity (for example a class) by enclosing the attribute name in square brackets:

```
type
  [SpecialClassAttribute]
  TThisIsMySpecialClass = class
  end;
```

The Delphi compiler allows us to shorten the attribute name if it ends with `Attribute`:

```
type
  [SpecialClass]
  TThisIsAnotherSpecialClass = class
  end;
```

 By a commonly accepted convention, attribute names end with `Attribute` and don't start with a `T` prefix (even though they are technically classes).

A code can only use an attribute if the attribute class is visible at that point. In other words, the attribute must be declared in the same unit before the point of use, or it must be declared in the interface section of another unit that is listed in the `uses` section. If you forget to include the unit declaring the attribute or if you mistype the attribute name, you'll get a rather cryptic warning: `W1025 Unsupported language feature: custom attribute`.

Delphi allows you to annotate all kinds of entities, not just classes. Attributes work equally well on records, interfaces, fields, properties, methods, and even method parameters. The following interface definition (which has no relation to the code examples for this chapter) shows some of the places where attribute annotation is valid:

```
type
  [UriPath('{cardNumber}/{action}')]
  APIAdminHT = interface ['{54E1D5F5-EE4B-4F69-8025-55ED83960C0E}']
    [Accept('json')]
    function Info(cardNumber: integer;
      [Content] out htInfo: THTInfo): TRestResponse;
  end;
```

As this example shows, we can pass arguments to an attribute. To support this, the attribute must accept parameters in a constructor and store it in an internal field. For example, the `UriPath` attribute is declared as follows:

```
type
  URIPathAttribute = class(TCustomAttribute)
  strict private
    FValue: string;
  public
    constructor Create(const apiPath: string);
    property Value: string read FValue write FValue;
  end;
```

To check whether an entity is annotated with an attribute, we must search through the **run-time type information** (**RTTI**). This will be explored in more detail in the next section.

Markers and attributes

Armed with this information, we can now re-implement the marker interface by using attributes.

The `Customer.Attributes` unit defines a normal customer class as shown here in full:

```
type
  TNormalCustomer = class
  strict protected
    FAddress: string;
    FEmail: string;
    FName: string;
  public
    property Address: string read FAddress write FAddress;
    property Email: string read FEmail write FEmail;
    property Name: string read FName write FName;
  end;
```

As we are no longer using interfaces, we can implement a customer as a normal class, and properties can access storage fields directly, without using getters and setters. This allows for much shorter implementation and simplifies compatibility with a legacy code.

The same unit implements an `ImportantCustomer` attribute. While the marker interface is not configurable (we can only test for its presence), an attribute can accept parameters. In our case, we can pass any number of stars to an attribute to indicate the importance of this customer. The `ImportantCustomerAttribute` definition and implementation is shown next:

```
type
  ImportantCustomerAttribute = class(TCustomAttribute)
  strict private
    FStarred: string;
  public
    constructor Create(const AStarred: string);
    property Starred: string read FStarred;
  end;

constructor ImportantCustomerAttribute.Create(
  const AStarred: string);
begin
  inherited Create;
```

```
    FStarred := AStarred;
  end;
```

Now that we have an attribute defined, we can add multiple subclasses, each with its own star factor:

```
type
  [ImportantCustomer('***')]
  TVIPCustomer = class(TNormalCustomer)
  end;

  [ImportantCustomer('*****')]
  TStarCustomer = class(TNormalCustomer)
  end;
```

The same unit also implements a global function `IsImportantCustomer` that checks whether a customer is important and returns the number of stars, as shown next:

```
function IsImportantCustomer(customer: TNormalCustomer;
  var starred: string): boolean;
var
  a: TCustomAttribute;
  ctx: TRttiContext;
  t: TRttiType;
begin
  Result := false;
  starred := '';

  ctx := TRttiContext.Create;
  try
    t := ctx.GetType(customer.ClassType);
    for a in t.GetAttributes do
      if a is ImportantCustomerAttribute then
      begin
        starred := ImportantCustomerAttribute(a).Starred;
        Exit(true);
      end;
  finally
    ctx.Free;
  end;
end;
```

This function firstly accesses the RTTI by calling `TRTTIContext.Create`. Next, it finds the information about the actual type of the `customer` variable by calling `ctx.GetType`. The code then enumerates all attributes of that class by calling the `GetAttribute` function. This function returns `TArray<TCustomAttribute>` so we can use it directly in a `for..in` iterator.

For each attribute `a` the code checks whether it is actually an `ImportantCustomerAttribute`. If so, the code casts `a` to that type so that it can read the number of stars stored in the attribute.

The main program tests this implementation by creating three customers of a different level and passes each to a logging function. As we are no longer working with interfaces, we must also remember to destroy these three customers at the end:

```
procedure TfrmMarker.btnCustomerCheckAttrClick(Sender: TObject);
var
  cust1: TNormalCustomer;
  cust2: TNormalCustomer;
  cust3: TNormalCustomer;
begin
  cust1 := TNormalCustomer.Create;
  cust1.Name := 'Joe Schmoe';

  cust2 := TVIPCustomer.Create;
  cust2.Name := 'Mr. Big';

  cust3 := TStarCustomer.Create;
  cust3.Name := 'Mars ambassador';

  LogCustomerAttr(cust1);
  LogCustomerAttr(cust2);
  LogCustomerAttr(cust3);

  FreeAndNil(cust1);
  FreeAndNil(cust2);
  FreeAndNil(cust3);
end;
```

The logging function `LogCustomerAttr` looks very much the same as the `LogCustomerIntf`. As shown next, a call to `Supports` was replaced with a call to `IsImportantCustomer` and the number of stars is logged:

```
procedure TfrmMarker.LogCustomerAttr(customer: TNormalCustomer);
var
  descr: string;
  stars: string;
```

```
begin
  if IsImportantCustomer(customer, stars) then
    descr := 'very important client with rating ' + stars
  else
    descr := 'just a regular guy';
  lbLog.Items.Add(customer.Name + ' is ' + descr);
end;
```

The next screenshot proves that the status of customers is correctly identified by this code:

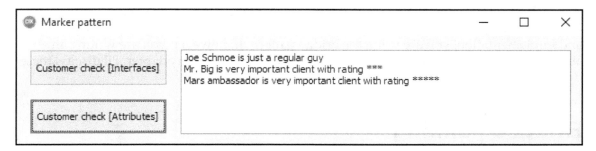

Logging metadata with attributes.

Bridge

An important aspect of a good object-oriented design is strong separation between an abstraction and its implementation. Multiple structural patterns deal specifically with this area. so the next part of the book is dedicated to them. I'll start with the **bridge** pattern and then dedicate the next chapter to other patterns of this kind.

The bridge pattern introduces a strong separation between an interface and its implementation. By this approach, we define the abstraction part as one inheritance hierarchy (a group of derived classes) and the implementation part as another hierarchy. The main point is that the abstraction and implementation hierarchies have nothing in common. The only connection between them is that the abstraction part is using implementation classes through composition.

In modern cars, most controls (steering wheel, throttle, brake...) don't access hardware directly. Instead, signals from controls go to a computer that then controls the electrical motors that drive the actual hardware. With this approach, we can change the implementation (car parts under the hood) without redesigning the interior of the car.

The bridge pattern allows switching different implementations on the fly. It is, however, perfectly valid to only have one implementation. The main idea behind a bridge is separation, not providing support for multiple implementations.

In C++, bridge decomposition with only one implementation frequently surfaces as a **PIMPL** idiom (**pointer to implementation**).

As you'll see in the next chapter, the bridge and adapter patterns look very much the same. The difference between them springs from the use case. If you are writing both abstraction and implementation, you are using the bridge pattern. If, however, you are writing an abstract layer over an existing implementation, you're creating an adapter. I'll discuss these differences in more detail at the beginning of the next chapter.

Bridged painting

For a demonstration of the bridge pattern, let's look at a simple hierarchy of shape objects. The project is called *Bridge* and you'll find it in the folder *Bridge*. The unit `Shapes.Abstraction` contains the following hierarchy of classes:

```
type
  TShape = class
  end;

  TRectangle = class(TShape)
  end;

  TTriangle = class(TShape)
  end;
```

For demonstration purposes, we want to implement support for two very different display types: a **Graphical User Interface** (GUI) and a console text mode (ASCII). If we don't use the bridge interface, we need to implement four more classes:

```
type
  TGUIRectangle = class(TRectangle)
  end;

  TASCIIRectangle = class(TRectangle)
  end;

  TGUITriangle = class(TTriangle)
  end;
```

```
TASCIITriangle = class(TTriangle)
end;
```

Such exploding hierarchy is usually sign of bad object decomposition. A bridge pattern will greatly improve the situation.

Instead of creating subclasses that are linked to a specific display type, we will move the whole rendering subsystem into the implementation. On the abstraction side, we only need the initial set of three classes. On the implementation side, however, we'll prepare two different implementations (GUI and ASCII) of the rendering subsystem.

To connect implementation to the abstraction, we can use **dependency injection** (for more information see Chapter 2, *Singleton, Dependency Injection, Lazy Initialization, and Object Pool*). All concrete rendering subsystems will derive from the abstract class TPainter, which is declared in the unit Shapes.Implementor as follows:

```
type
  TPainter = class
  public
    procedure DrawRectangle(bounds: TRect); virtual; abstract;
    procedure DrawTriangle(bounds: TRect); virtual; abstract;
  end;
```

A concrete instance of this class is injected into the TShape constructor. A full definition and implementation of shape classes is shown next:

```
type
  TShape = class
  strict private
    FPainter: TPainter;
  public
    constructor Create(painter: TPainter);
    destructor Destroy; override;
    property Painter: TPainter read FPainter;
  end;

  TRectangle = class(TShape)
  strict protected
    FBounds: TRect;
  public
    procedure Draw;
    property Bounds: TRect read FBounds write FBounds;
  end;

  TTriangle = class(TShape)
  strict protected
    FBounds: TRect;
```

```
public
  procedure Draw;
  property Bounds: TRect read FBounds write FBounds;
end;

constructor TShape.Create(painter: TPainter);
begin
  inherited Create;
  FPainter := painter;
end;

destructor TShape.Destroy;
begin
  FreeAndNil(FPainter);
  inherited;
end;

procedure TRectangle.Draw;
begin
  Painter.DrawRectangle(Bounds);
end;

procedure TTriangle.Draw;
begin
  Painter.DrawTriangle(Bounds);
end;
```

The main program can then use following two functions to draw a GUI and an ASCII rectangle, respectively:

```
procedure TfrmBridge.btnRectGUIClick(Sender: TObject);
var
  rect: TRectangle;
begin
  rect := TRectangle.Create(TPainterGUI.Create(outGUI.Canvas));
  rect.Bounds := TRect.Create(20, 60, 220, 200);
  rect.Draw;
  rect.Free;
end;

procedure TfrmBridge.btnRectASCIIClick(Sender: TObject);
var
  rect: TRectangle;
begin
  rect := TRectangle.Create(TPainterASCII.Create(outASCII.Lines));
  rect.Bounds := TRect.Create(5, 5, 35, 15);
  rect.Draw;
  rect.Free;
```

```
end;
```

All we need now are the GUI and ASCII rendering classes. The GUI version (unit `Shapes.Implementor.GUI`) is very simple, as it only calls appropriate canvas functions. The implementation of `TPainterGUI` is shown here in full:

```
type
  TPainterGUI = class(TPainter)
  strict private
    FCanvas: TCanvas;
  public
    constructor Create(canvas: TCanvas);
    procedure DrawRectangle(bounds: TRect); override;
    procedure DrawTriangle(bounds: TRect); override;
  end;

constructor TPainterGUI.Create(canvas: TCanvas);
begin
  inherited Create;
  FCanvas := canvas;
end;

procedure TPainterGUI.DrawRectangle(bounds: TRect);
begin
  FCanvas.Rectangle(bounds);
end;

procedure TPainterGUI.DrawTriangle(bounds: TRect);
var
  corners: TArray<TPoint>;
begin
  SetLength(corners, 3);
  corners[0] := Point(bounds.Left, bounds.Bottom);
  corners[1] := Point(bounds.Right, bounds.Bottom);
  corners[2] := Point((bounds.Left + bounds.Right) div 2, bounds.Top);
  FCanvas.Polygon(corners);
end;
```

The implementation of the ASCII renderer is much messier. If you'd like to examine it, open the `Shapes.Implementor.ASCII` unit. As a short sample, this is how an ugly triangle is painted:

```
procedure TPainterASCII.InternalDrawTriangle(bounds: TRect);
var
  leftX: integer;
  midX: integer;
  s: string;
  step: real;
```

```
  y: integer;
begin
  for y := 1 to bounds.Top - 1 do
    FCanvas.Add('');

  midX := (bounds.Left + bounds.Right) div 2;
  step := bounds.Width / bounds.Height / 2;

  for y := bounds.Top + 1 to bounds.Bottom - 1 do
  begin
    s := StringOfChar(' ', bounds.Right);
    s[Round(midX - (y - bounds.Top) * step)] := '/';
    s[Round(midX + (y - bounds.Top) * step)] := '\';
    FCanvas.Add(s);
  end;

  FCanvas.Add(StringOfChar(' ', bounds.Left - 1) + '/' +
  StringOfChar('-', bounds.Width - 2) + '\');
end;
```

In the following screenshot, you can compare both renderers:

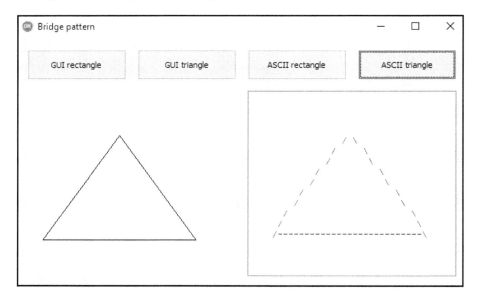

A comparison of the GUI and ASCII rendering of a triangle.

Summary

This chapter provided an overview of structural patterns.

This chapter opened with a composite pattern. This pattern describes how to create an interface that doesn't make a distinction between a basic object and a composite object that is composed of more basic or composite objects. It is especially appropriate when we are operating on tree structures.

The next pattern was flyweight. It is different than other structural patterns because of its focus on memory usage. The flyweight pattern tells us how to share static data between multiple objects to reduce memory usage. This chapter also discussed a practical implementation of this pattern: a string interning, and explored Delphi concepts of equality comparers and hashers.

Next on the list was marker interfaces. This pattern enables metadata annotation in languages that don't provide specific metadata features. In later years, it was mostly replaced with language-specific approaches. In Delphi, we can use attributes to annotate metadata, and so this chapter described this concept in short.

Lastly, we came to the bridge pattern. Its purpose is to put a strong separation between abstraction and implementation layers and enable the switching of different implementations. The bridge pattern is similar to the adapter and other patterns, which I'll explore next.

So, in the next chapter, we'll look into four more structural patterns: Adapter, Decorator, Facade, and Proxy.

Adapter, Proxy, Decorator, and Facade

5

Organizing objects in a clear and easy-to-understand way is an important part of good object design. To facilitate that, structural patterns offer multiple patterns, from composite and bridge, which were discussed in the previous chapter, to four more patterns that are the topic of this chapter.

Finding the correct design pattern to apply to your problem is not always easy. This is even more the case for the four structural patterns from this chapter. To help you find the appropriate solution, this chapter opens with a short discussion on the similarities and distinctions among these four patterns and the bridge pattern from the previous chapter.

This chapter will teach you how to do the following:

- Find out how to recognize a structural pattern that matches your problem
- Learn about the adapter, which helps when adapting old code to new use cases
- Explore the proxy pattern, which wraps an object and provides an identical interface to facilitate remoting, caching, or access control
- See how the decorator pattern allows the expanding functionality of existing objects
- Find out how facade provides a simplified view of a complex system

Selecting an appropriate structural pattern

Distinguishing between the Bridge, adapter, proxy, decorator, and the facade is not always easy. At first glance, both the bridge and the adapter look almost the same, and there is just a small step from a proxy to a decorator, which sometimes looks almost like a facade. To help you select the appropriate pattern, I have put together a few guidelines.

Both the bridge and the adapter design patterns look completely the same. They implement one interface and map it into another. The difference lies in the motivation for using the pattern.

When you define both the abstraction (the public interface) and the implementation (the actual worker object) at the same time, you are creating a bridge. If, however, you already have an existing object that implements an interface and you have to use it in an environment with different expectations, you will write an adapter.

The proxy pattern also looks very similar to both the bridge and the adapter. It, however, exposes the same interface as implemented by the wrapped object. Both the bridge and the adapter wrap an interface and expose a different one.

The decorator is similar to a proxy in the sense that it provides the same interface as a wrapped object. It, however, also defines a new functionality that is available for consumption.

The facade pattern wraps multiple objects and uses them to solve a particular problem. It then exposes a simplified interface that's specific to this problem.

So, bear in mind the following:

- Bridge, adapter, proxy, and decorator wrap one class. Facade wraps multiple classes.
- Bridge and Adapter modify the object's interface. Proxy exposes the same interface. Decorator adds functions to object's interface. Facade exposes a simplified interface.
- With bridge, we define both the abstract interface and the implementation. With adapter, the implementation exists in advance.

Adapter

Reusing existing components (objects, subsystems) is a common part of software development. Usually, it is better to reuse an existing solution than rewriting it from scratch, as the latter will inevitably take longer and introduce new bugs.

Using old components in new code, however, brings its own set of problems. Quite frequently, the newer code works against an abstract interface that does not exactly match the existing functionality. We have to write an intermediate object, a kind of translator from the new interface to the old one. This object is called an **adapter**.

Adapters are used in everyday life. For example, a cable with a USB type A connector on one side and a USB micro connector on the other is an adapter that allows us to plug a mobile phone into a personal computer. Another kind of adapter allows you to plug a device with a German power plug into a UK wall socket, or a device that uses 110 V power into a socket that provides 230 V.

Keep in mind that adapters should not be used when designing code. If parts of the design don't fit together, either change the design or use the bridge pattern. (See `Chapter 4`, *Composite, Flyweight, Marker Interface, and Bridge,* for more information.)

An adapter can do some internal processing. For example, Delphi's VCL library functions mostly as an adapter for existing Windows components. Take a `TCustomListBox` from the `Vcl.StdCtrls` unit as an example; the code mostly sends and processes Windows messages, but still contains some internal fields and does some processing.

An adapter can be implemented by using composition or inheritance. Although composition is usually a better solution, I will show both approaches in the following example. The implementation also differs depending on how the original API is exposed, as a bunch of virtual methods or as an interface.

The `Adapter` project in the `Adapter` folder demonstrates both approaches. The `Adapter.Example` unit defines the `TConsumer` class that implements two functions. The `Process` function uses an interface parameter called `IProducer` to do some processing, while the `FindTheAnswer` function uses an instance of a `TProblemSolver` class. They are declared as follows:

```
type
  IProducer = interface ['{8E4001F9-11EC-4C9C-BAD9-97C9601699FF}']
    function NextData: TValue;
  end;

  TProblemSolver = class
  public
    function SolveProblem(const problem: string): string;
      virtual; abstract;
  end;

  TConsumer = class
  public
    function Process(const intf: IProducer): integer;
    function FindTheAnswer(const solver: TProblemSolver): string;
  end;
```

How the `Process` and `FindTheAnswer` are implemented is not our concern. (If you want to know, check the code.) We are here to deal with a different problem.

Wrapping a class

We have inherited a problem-solver class called `TDeepThough` that we would like to pass to the `FindTheAnswer` function. This class is defined in the `Adapter.Example.Inheritance` unit as follows:

```
type
  TDeepThought = class
  public
    function FindTheAnswer: string;
  end;
```

We cannot use it directly, as it does not descend from the `TProblemSolver` class. Instead, we have to create an adapter. This adapter must inherit from the `TProblemSolver` class (otherwise, we would not be able to pass it to the `FindTheAnswer` function) and must somehow access an instance of a `TDeepThought` class that will do the real work. The following code fragment extracted from the `Adapter.Example.Inheritance` unit shows how this adapter is defined:

```
type
  TProblemAdapter = class(TProblemSolver)
  public
    function SolveProblem(const problem: string): string; override;
  end;
```

We could have created an instance of a `TDeepThough` externally and *injected* it into the `TProblemAdapter` in the constructor. (For more information on dependency injection, see *Chapter 2*, *Singleton, Dependency Injection, Lazy Initialization, and Object Pool*.) This approach will be used in the following example, but for this one, I decided on a simple version. The `TProblemAdapter` creates an instance of `TDeepThought` internally, as shown here:

```
function TProblemAdapter.SolveProblem(const problem: string): string;
var
  dt: TDeepThought;
begin
  dt := TDeepThought.Create;
  try
    Result := dt.FindTheAnswer;
  finally
    FreeAndNil(dt);
```

```
    end;
  end;
```

TIP

This approach tightly bonds adapter to the implementation. Most of the time, it is better to create such as implementation externally and inject it into the adapter, but sometimes such a simple solution is exactly what you need.

To use the adapter, we have to create an instance of the `TProblemAdapter` class and pass it to the `FindTheAnswer` call. The following code fragment from the main unit `AdapterMain` shows how this is implemented in the example program:

```
procedure TfrmAdapter.btnObjectAdapterClick(Sender: TObject);
var
  answer: string;
  consumer: TConsumer;
  problemAdapter: TProblemAdapter;
begin
  consumer := TConsumer.Create;
  try
    problemAdapter := TProblemAdapter.Create;
    try
      answer := consumer.FindTheAnswer(problemAdapter);
    finally
      FreeAndNil(problemAdapter);
    end;
    lbLog.Items.Add('The answer is: ' + answer);
  finally
    FreeAndNil(consumer);
  end;
end;
```

Wrapping an interface

The second part of the solution creates an adapter that can be used with the `Process` function that expects a `IProducer` interface. The existing code, which can be found in the `Adapter.Example.Composition` unit, however, implements an `IIncompatible` interface. Both the original interface and the adapter are shown here:

```
type
  IIncompatible = interface ['{4422CF75-2CBE-4F7D-9C14-89DC160CD3C7}']
    function NextElement: integer;
  end;

  TIncompatible = class(TInterfacedObject, IIncompatible)
```

```
    function NextElement: integer;
  end;

  TProducerAdapter = class(TInterfacedObject, IProducer)
  strict private
    FWrapped: IIncompatible;
  public
    constructor Create(const wrapped: IIncompatible);
    function NextData: TValue;
  end;
```

In this solution, the adapter must implement the IProducer interface so that we are able to pass it to the Process function. This adapter is also more flexible than the TProblemAdapter, as it does not create the wrapped interface internally. An instance of the IIncompatible class is injected into the constructor instead.

 I would like to make clear that the choice of creating an implementation internally versus injecting it has nothing to do with the implementation of the original component (object versus interface). We could equally well inject an existing object or create an interface inside the adapter.

In this case, implementation of the adapter is trivial. The constructor must store the implementation in an internal field and the NextData function must forward the call to the old implementation. The full implementation is shown here:

```
constructor TProducerAdapter.Create(const wrapped: IIncompatible);
begin
  inherited Create;
  FWrapped := wrapped;
end;

function TProducerAdapter.NextData: TValue;
begin
  Result := FWrapped.NextElement;
end;
```

To use this adapter, we must first create an instance of the IIncompatible class, inject it into the TProducerAdapter constructor, and send IProducer to the Process function. The code for this (from the AdapterMain unit) is as follows:

```
procedure TfrmAdapter.btnInterfaceAdapterClick(Sender: TObject);
var
  consumer: TConsumer;
  oldProducer: IIncompatible;
  producerAdapter: IProducer;
  value: integer;
```

```
begin
  consumer := TConsumer.Create;
  try
    oldProducer := TIncompatible.Create;
    producerAdapter := TProducerAdapter.Create(oldProducer);
    value := consumer.Process(producerAdapter);
    lbLog.Items.Add('Result: ' + value.ToString);
  finally
    FreeAndNil(consumer);
  end;
end;
```

Implementing a queue with a list

For a more meaningful example, we can see how we can adapt code that expects to operate on a double-ended queue when we don't have an implementation of such a structure ready.

 A double-ended queue, or **deque**, is a queue that allows you to add and remove elements both at the front and at the back of the queue.

The `AdapterMain` unit implements two methods, `RotateLeft` and `RotateRight`, as follows:

```
procedure TfrmAdapter.RotateLeft(const deque: IDeque<integer>);
begin
  deque.PushBack(deque.PopFront);
end;

procedure TfrmAdapter.RotateRight(const deque: IDeque<integer>);
begin
  deque.PushFront(deque.PopBack);
end;
```

Both are using the following double-ended queue interface from `Deque.Intf`:

```
type
  IDeque<T> = interface
    function IsEmpty: boolean;
    procedure PushBack(const element: T);
    procedure PushFront(const element: T);
    function PopBack: T;
    function PopFront: T;
  end;
```

As we don't have a double-ended queue implementation handy, we would like to use a `TList<T>` for storage, so we have to write an adapter. It is called `TDequeList<T>` and is defined in the `Deque.Adapter` unit as follows:

```
type
  TDequeList<T> = class(TInterfacedObject, IDeque<T>)
  strict private
    FStorage: TList<T>;
  public
    constructor Create(storage: TList<T>);
    function IsEmpty: boolean;
    procedure PushBack(const element: T);
    procedure PushFront(const element: T);
    function PopBack: T;
    function PopFront: T;
  end;
```

The code uses an already-seen approach to wrapping an interface around an injected implementation. The implementation is simple and treats the list element `[0]` as deque's front and the list element `[Count-1]` as deque's back:

```
constructor TDequeList<T>.Create(storage: TList<T>);
begin
  inherited Create;
  FStorage := storage;
end;

function TDequeList<T>.IsEmpty: boolean;
begin
  Result := FStorage.Count = 0;
end;

function TDequeList<T>.PopBack: T;
begin
  if IsEmpty then
    raise Exception.Create('TDequeList<T>.PopBack: List is empty')
  else
  begin
    Result := FStorage[FStorage.Count - 1];
    FStorage.Delete(FStorage.Count - 1);
  end;
end;

function TDequeList<T>.PopFront: T;
begin
  if IsEmpty then
    raise Exception.Create('TDequeList<T>.PopFront: List is empty')
```

```
  else
  begin
    Result := FStorage[0];
    FStorage.Delete(0);
  end;
end;

procedure TDequeList<T>.PushBack(const element: T);
begin
  FStorage.Add(element);
end;

procedure TDequeList<T>.PushFront(const element: T);
begin
  FStorage.Insert(0, element);
end;
```

The code creates `TList<integer>` storage in the main form's `OnCreate` event and fills it with numbers from `0` to `9`. It then injects this list into the `TDequeList<integer>` adapter and passes the result into `ResultLeft` or `ResultRight`. The relevant parts of the code are shown here:

```
procedure TfrmAdapter.FormCreate(Sender: TObject);
var
  i: integer;
begin
  FData := TList<integer>.Create;
  for i := 0 to 9 do
    FData.Add(i);
end;

procedure TfrmAdapter.btnRotateLeftClick(Sender: TObject);
begin
  RotateLeft(TDequeList<integer>.Create(FData));
  Log(FData);
end;

procedure TfrmAdapter.btnRotateRightClick(Sender: TObject);
begin
  RotateRight(TDequeList<integer>.Create(FData));
  Log(FData);
end;
```

The output after pressing **Rotate left** nine times followed by pressing **Rotate right** nine times is shown in the following screenshot:

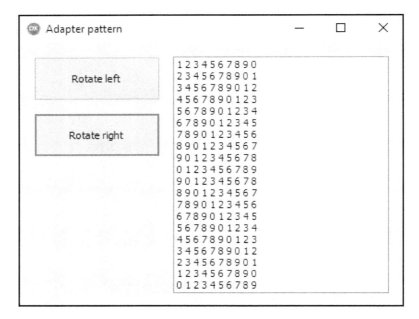

Rotating a list wrapped in an adapter

Proxy

A proxy is a component that wraps another component and exposes the wrapped interface. This definition doesn't make much sense. Why would anyone want to add another layer of indirection (another wrapper) and expose the same wrapped interface? They would do this simply because a proxy doesn't guarantee that each call of that interface will be forwarded to the wrapped object. It is entirely possible that the proxy will generate the result internally or execute something else (introduce a side effect) before or after calling the wrapped interface.

When you are accessing the web from inside a business environment, the traffic usually flows through a http filtering and caching proxy. This software catches all http requests generated in browsers and other applications and then decides whether it will forward a request to the target site, return the result from the cache, or deny the request if the site is on the blocked list.

In that example, an http proxy checks whether the access is allowed and then allows or blocks access to the remote web server. A proxy of that kind, one that checks credentials and acts accordingly, is called a **protection proxy**.

Another kind of proxy, a **remoting proxy**, forwards interface calls over the network to another location, where they are executed. Remote execution frameworks, such as DCOM, RPC, and CORBA, are examples of such a proxy class.

A proxy can delay the creation of a wrapped object until it is required. For example, a remoting proxy may open the connection not when the proxy is created, but when the first wrapped interface function is called. This can save time when a proxy is created by default till the time they are used.

A proxy can work as a caching proxy and return results of some functions from the cache. An extreme example of this kind is a virtual proxy that never creates the wrapped object but rather generates all responses internally. This kind of proxy is especially useful for unit testing, where we call it a **mock object**.

Another interesting possibility is a proxy that logs the parameters and results of wrapped interface functions. This **logging proxy** is especially useful when debugging a hard problem.

Sometimes, we want to use an existing component that was not written with parallel processing in mind in a multithreaded environment. In such a case, we have to protect each call to the existing component's interface with locking. The simplest way to do that is to implement a **locking proxy** that acquires a lock just before the wrapped function is called and releases it immediately after it returns.

In the next part of this chapter, I'll look into three quite different proxy use-cases. I'll implement a logging proxy that logs calls to VCL library, show how smart pointers can simplify object life cycle management, and explore a simple unit-testing scenario.

Delphi idioms – replacing components in runtime

The `LoggingProxy` program from the `Proxy` folder shows how we can catch and log calls to VCL methods, such as `TButton.Click`. It uses an interesting trick that allows our code to insert a proxy class without changing the original code. The only downfall of this method is that it can only replace `virtual` methods, and in the VCL many interesting methods are not marked as such.

The main unit, LoggingProxyMain, implements a simple form containing one button and one listbox. When the button is clicked, a message is displayed. The whole form is implemented as follows:

```
type
  TfrmProxy = class(TForm)
    btnLoggingProxy: TButton;
    lbLog: TListBox;
    procedure btnLoggingProxyClick(Sender: TObject);
  public
    procedure Log(const msg: string);
  end;

procedure TfrmProxy.btnLoggingProxyClick(Sender: TObject);
begin
  Log('Click!');
end;

procedure TfrmProxy.Log(const msg: string);
begin
  lbLog.Items.Add(msg);
end;
```

When the Delphi program is started, it loads the form definition from a resource. A binary representation of the .dfm form file is stored in the .exe file. The code reads this binary representation, walks its structure, and creates controls.

When, for example, the btnLoggingProxy definition is found in the resource, a TButton object is created, initialized, and placed on the form. We can explore a less-known implementation detail when the TButton class is located (so that the object can be created), and the first visible definition of that class is used.

In other words, if we define a TButton class inside the LoggingProxyMain unit before the TfrmProxy is defined, the form-loader will create an instance of *this* class and not of a TButton from unit, Vcl.StdCtrls.

We can use that fact to insert a proxy for TButton into the LoggingProxyMain unit. We just have to define a new class with the name TButton and derive it from Vcl.StdCtrls.TButton. In this class, we can override any virtual method to catch its execution.

The demonstration program uses this trick to log every button-click. An injected TButton class defines the Click method, which overrides the original method. The overridden method writes to the log and calls the inherited method (which in turn executes the OnClick handler) and writes to the log again. The full implementation of the injected TButton is shown here:

```
type
  TButton = class(Vcl.StdCtrls.TButton)
  public
    procedure Click; override;
  end;

procedure TButton.Click;
begin
  frmProxy.Log('Button ' + Self.Name + ' will be clicked!');
  inherited;
  frmProxy.Log('Button ' + Self.Name + ' was clicked!');
end;
```

The following screenshot shows how the execution is logged:

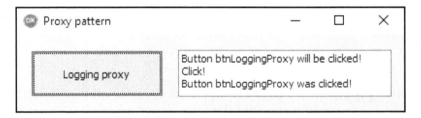

Logging a click on a button control

This component injection method allows for some interesting tricks, as the injected TButton could also be defined in a different unit. We only have to make sure that this unit is listed in the uses list after the Vcl.StdCtrls unit.

Smart pointers

Handling an object's life cycle in Delphi can be a pain. Each object that was created in code must also be destroyed; otherwise, the program will be losing memory. An attempt to solve this was the introduction of **Automatic Reference Counting** (**ARC**), which treats objects the same as interfaces. This experiment, however, is losing tract. It was recently announced that the Linux compiler will stop using ARC and that both mobile compilers (Android and iOS) will also be moved back to normal object implementation in the future.

We can simplify object life cycle management by using smart pointers. As in ARC, a smart pointer is reference counted, so the code knows when it should be destroyed and does that for us.

Delphi doesn't support smart pointers yet. Currently, the best implementation that I know of can be found in the Spring4D library (https://bitbucket.org/sglienke/spring4d). The SpringProxy demo shows how Spring4D smart pointers are used.

Why am I talking about smart pointers in the section on the proxy design pattern? Because smart pointers are an implementation of a proxy pattern. A smart pointer wraps certain objects, stores an object in a reference-counted wrapper, and makes sure that we can work with that wrapper, as if it were the original object.

The SpringProxy demo requires a Spring4D library to function. To run the program, you'll have to install this library and then add its folders, Source and Source\Base, to Delphi's Library path or to the project's search path. If you unpack the library into the folder, Chapter 5\Spring4D project's search path will already be correctly configured, and you can simply press *F9* to run the program.

If you have git installed, you can execute the following command in the Chapter 5 folder to install Spring4D: git clone https://bitbucket.org/sglienke/spring4d.

The demonstration program uses the technique from the previous section to inject custom TButton and TListBox components into the code. The implementation overrides the Click method in the TButton class and the DoEnter and DoExit methods in the TListBox class, as shown here:

```
type
  TButton = class(Vcl.StdCtrls.TButton)
  public
    procedure Click; override;
  end;

  TListBox = class(Vcl.StdCtrls.TListBox)
  protected
    procedure DoEnter; override;
    procedure DoExit; override;
  end;
```

As in the previous example, these methods will do some logging. This time, however, we would like to log more information. To facilitate that, each method creates an instance of a `TLogInfo` class, initializes it with the appropriate information, and sends it to the main form so that it can be logged. The implementation of this class is shown here:

```
type
  TLogInfo = class
  strict private
    FClassName: string;
    FComponentName: string;
    FMethodName: string;
  public
    constructor Create(AComponent: TComponent; const AMethod: string);
    property ClassName: string read FClassName write FClassName;
    property ComponentName: string
      read FComponentName write FComponentName;
    property MethodName: string read FMethodName write FMethodName;
  end;

constructor TLogInfo.Create(AComponent: TComponent; const AMethod: string);
begin
  inherited Create;
  ComponentName := AComponent.Name;
  ClassName := AComponent.ClassName;
  MethodName := AMethod;
end;
```

After the main form logs the information, it would have to destroy the `TLogInfo` instance. This, however, is a good way to introduce problems. If a piece of code implements object creation and destruction at two completely unrelated points, it is just too easy to forget to destroy something. A better way is to use a **reference-counted object** (aka a **smart pointer**), which is destroyed automatically.

We could also rewrite the code to use an interface approach. `TLogInfo` would implement `ILogInfo`, and we would send the interface around. Sometimes, however, we cannot change the object definition and introduce interfaces at will.

In Spring4D, smart pointers are called **shared pointers**. They are created by calling `Shared.New<T>`, which returns a `IShared<T>` proxy. I'll return to the implementation in a moment, but first let's take a look at how we can use this in practice.

To create a smart pointer, we have to create the actual `TLogInfo` object and then pass it to the `Shared.New<TLogInfo>` function, which returns `IShared<TLogInfo>`. The following code fragment shows how this is implemented in `TButton.Click`:

```
procedure TButton.Click;
var
  info: TLogInfo;
begin
  inherited;
  info := TLogInfo.Create(Self, 'Click');
  frmProxy.Log(Shared.New<TLogInfo>(info));
end;
```

Delphi allows us to simplify the code, as in this case, the `T` parameter of `New<T>` can be deduced automatically. The code in overridden `TListBox` methods shows this approach:

```
procedure TListBox.DoEnter;
begin
  inherited;
  frmProxy.Log(Shared.New(
  TLogInfo.Create(Self, 'DoEnter')));
end;

procedure TListBox.DoExit;
begin
  inherited;
  frmProxy.Log(Shared.New(
  TLogInfo.Create(Self, 'DoExit')));
end;
```

When we want to treat the data as a smart pointer, we can simply assign this `IShared<TLogInfo>` to another variable (or parameter) of the same type, and it will be managed correctly. When we want to treat it as a `TLogInfo`, we can also do that automatically. For example, the logging function `TfrmProxy.Log` is implemented as follows:

```
procedure TfrmProxy.Log(const logInfo: IShared<TLogInfo>);
begin
  lbLog.Items.Add(Format( 'Executed %s.%s on %s',
    [logInfo.ClassName, logInfo.MethodName, logInfo.ComponentName]));
end;
```

This function accepts a smart pointer, but then accesses the `ClassName`, `MethodName`, and `ComponentName` of the `TLogInfo` class simply by accessing the `logInfo` proxy.

The magic behind the scenes is hidden in the `IShared<T>` implementation (and partially in the Delphi compiler). The relevant parts of the smart pointers implementation are shown here:

```
type
  IShared<T> = reference to function: T;

  Shared = record
  public
    class function New<T>(const value: T): IShared<T>; overload; static;
  end;
```

`Shared.New<T>` creates a `IShared<T>`, but we already know that. The tricky part lies in `IShared<T>` being defined as an anonymous function returning `T`.

In Delphi, anonymous functions are actually interfaces, so they are reference-counted. If we assign one variable of that type to another of the same type, the compiler will treat them as an interface and update reference counts accordingly. In all other cases, the compiler calls the anonymous function that returns the wrapped object. That allows us to call the methods of this object directly. The compiler inserts a call to the anonymous function behind the scenes, but that is not apparent from the code, which merely accesses `logInfo.ClassName` (for example).

That all helps destroy the `IShared<T>` instance when it is no longer in use, but who destroys the original `T` (or `TLogInfo`, in our case)? The answer lies in another implementation trick.

In Delphi, an anonymous function that returns `T` is equivalent to an interface that implements `function Invoke: T`. The `New<T>` function actually creates and returns an instance of an internal `TObjectFinalizer` class that implements `IShared<TObject>`, and is defined as follows:

```
type
  Shared = record
  private type
    TObjectFinalizer = class(TInterfacedObject, IShared<TObject>)
    private
      fValue: TObject;
      function Invoke: TObject;
    public
      constructor Create(typeInfo: PTypeInfo); overload;
      constructor Create(const value: TObject); overload;
      destructor Destroy; override;
    end;
    . . .
```

This instance manages the life cyle of the original object. When `IShared<T>` is no longer in use, `TObjectFinalizer` is destroyed, and its destructor destroys the wrapped object.

The smart pointer implementation in Spring also handles records in addition to objects. Records are managed by the `TRecordFinalizer` internal class (not shown here). The `New<T>` function is the final piece of magic that brings all of this together:

```
class function Shared.New<T>(const value: T): IShared<T>;
begin
  case TType.Kind<T> of
    tkClass: IShared<TObject>(Result) :=
      Shared.TObjectFinalizer.Create(PObject(@value)^);
    tkPointer: IShared<Pointer>(Result) :=
      Shared.TRecordFinalizer.Create(PPointer(@value)^, TypeInfo(T));
  end;
end;
```

The only downside of smart pointers is that they require additional memory (used for `TObjectFinalizer` or `TRecordFinalizer`) and that they are slightly slower than accessing the object directly.

Unit testing with mock objects

I mentioned before that proxy objects can be used for unit testing. In unit testing, we frequently encounter a situation when the tested unit uses some interface from another (and therefore not tested) unit and that second interface pulls in whole lots of code, accesses database, runs a lengthy calculation, or in other ways disturbs the testing process. In such cases, we can replace that interface with a mock object that functions as a virtual proxy.

Creating mock objects is a broad topic, and multiple Delphi libraries exist to help with that job. In this example, I will use the Spring4D library (`https://bitbucket.org/sglienke/spring4d`) and its `Mock<T>` record.

A short demonstration of Spring4D mocking, which barely scratches the surface, is given in the `MockingProxy` program. To run the program, you'll have to install the Spring4D library and then add its folders (`Source`, `Source\Base`, `Source\Base\Collections`, `Source\Core\Interception`, and `Source\Core\Mocking`) to Delphi's Library path or to, the project's Search path. If you unpack the library into the folder `Chapter 5\Spring4D` project's Search path will already be correctly configured, and you can simply press *F9* to run the program.

If you have `git` installed, you can execute the following command in folder `Chapter 5` to install Spring4D: `git clone https://bitbucket.org/sglienke/spring4d`.

The demonstration program doesn't run any real unit tests. For a simple demo, it defines an interface called `ICalculation`, which is used in a form function called `DoSomething`. Both are shown here:

```
type
  {$TYPEINFO ON}
  ICalculation = interface ['{E0040339-325F-4CA8-96D9-12524F58CBAE}']
    function GetTheAnswer: integer;
    function AddTwo(value: integer): integer;
  end;
  {$TYPEINFO OFF}

procedure TfrmMocking.DoSomething(const calc: ICalculation);
begin
  lbLog.Items.Add(Format('ICalculation.GetTheAnswer = %d',
    [calc.GetTheAnswer]));
  lbLog.Items.Add(Format('AddTwo(2) = %d', [calc.AddTwo(2)]));
  lbLog.Items.Add(Format('AddTwo(3) = %d', [calc.AddTwo(3)]));
end;
```

We don't have an implementation of `ICalculation` handy, so we will use mocking to create it. Spring4D's mocking support uses **run-time type information** (**RTTI**) to get information about the wrapped interface, and that requires the interface to be compiled in the `TYPEINFO ON` state.

Another way to force RTTI generation for an interface is to inherit it from `IInvokable` or from another interface that is compiled with the switch `TYPEINFO ON`.

Instead of `{$TYPEINFO ON}` and `{$TYPEINFO OFF}`, you can also use `{$M+}` and `{$M-}`.

The whole process of setting up the mock object is implemented in the button's `OnClick` handler, as follows:

```
procedure TfrmMocking.btnMockClick(Sender: TObject);
var
  mockCalc: Mock<ICalculation>;
begin
  mockCalc := Mock<ICalculation>.Create(TMockBehavior.Strict);
```

```
    mockCalc.Setup.Returns(42).When.GetTheAnswer;

    mockCalc.Setup.Executes(
      function(const callInfo: TCallInfo): TValue
      begin
        lbLog.Items.Add(Format('%s(%d) is not supported',
          [callInfo.Method.Name, callInfo.Args[0].AsInteger]));
      end).When.AddTwo(TArg.IsAny<integer>);

    mockCalc.Setup.Returns(4).When.AddTwo(2);

    DoSomething(mockCalc);
  end;
```

The first line creates our mock object, `Mock<ICalculation>`. It is implemented as a record, but nevertheless I'll use the accepted convention and call it a mock object. This record that functions as a virtual proxy is created in `Strict` mode. In that mode, the code fails if it calls an interface method that is not explicitly set up.

The second line, `mockCalc.Setup.Returns(42).When.GetTheAnswer;`, sets up the proxy so that it returns number 42 whenever the `GetTheAnswer` method is called.

The next block of lines configures the code to log an error whenever the `AddTwo` function is called. The syntax `AddTwo(TArg.IsAny<integer>)` allows us to execute the same code for all possible integer parameters.

Near the end, the line `mockCalc.Setup.Returns(4).When.AddTwo(2);` overrides this behavior and returns 4 if and only if the parameter is 2. You should keep in mind that more generic variations of a call should always be set up first, and more specific variations later.

At the end, the code calls the `DoSomething` method. Although the code expects an `ICalculation` parameter, we can pass in a `Mock<ICalculation>` record. The `Mock<T>.Implicit` operator will convert it into `ICalculation`.

A click on the **Mock** button shows that all the methods are indeed executing as expected. `GetTheAnswer` returns 42, `AddTwo(2)` returns 4, and `AddTwo(3)` logs an error and returns 0, which is the default value for integer results:

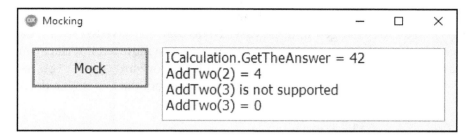

Mock object in action

Decorator

The **decorator** pattern is an incredibly useful tool that helps you enhance existing interfaces with an additional functionality and without changing the original implementation. In addition to that, we can apply this additional functionality to any subclass of the original implementation. As such, the decorator is a useful tool for enhancing existing behavior.

A Christmas tree by itself doesn't do much. It stands in one place and looks nice. We can, however, enhance its value by adding decorations, such as colorful lights. This decoration doesn't change the original interface of the tree—it just improves it. Furthermore, we can apply the same decoration to many different kinds of trees, not just a specific sort.

Every decorator operates on an existing interface, which is used in two different places. As it has to support original functionality, it must somehow wrap the original interface. Typically, we use an injection to pass the original component to the decorator's constructor. On the other side, the decorator must also expose the original functionality so it either has to implement the original interface, or it must inherit from the original class.

A short example will help clarify that complicated explanation. Let's say we have an original class, TLegacy, that exposes an interface, as follows:

```
type
  TLegacy = class
  public
    function Operation: string; virtual;
  end;
```

We want to enhance this functionality with another method, `OperationUC`, that returns the result of the `Operation` changed to uppercase. To do that, we have to create a decorator that both inherits from the `TLegacy` (so that it supports the required interface) and consumes an instance of the `TLegacy` class (so that it can forward `Operation` requests to it). The following code fragment shows a possible implementation of such a decorator:

```
type
  TUCDecorator = class(TLegacy)
  private
    FWrapped: TLegacy;
  public
    constructor Create(wrapped: TLegacy);
    destructor Destroy; override;
    function Operation: string; override;
    function OperationUC: string; virtual;
    property Wrapped: TLegacy read FWrapped;
  end;

constructor TUCDecorator.Create(wrapped: TLegacy);
begin
  inherited Create;
  FWrapped := wrapped;
end;

function TUCDecorator.Operation: string;
begin
  Result := FWrapped.Operation;
end;

function TUCDecorator.OperationUC: string;
begin
  Result := Operation.ToUpper;
end;

destructor TUCDecorator.Destroy;
begin
  FreeAndNil(FWrapped);
  inherited;
end;
```

This code (which can be found in the `Example` in the `Decorator` project folder) demonstrates two important points. Firstly, a decorator typically takes over the ownership of the wrapped object. When a decorator is destroyed, the wrapped object is also destroyed. This simplifies life cycle management in the code that uses the decorator.

The decorator pattern illustrates the open/closed principle (part *O* of the SOLID principle). It keeps the original implementation closed (the implementation is not modified), yet it makes it open for extensions.

Secondly, operations implemented by the original interface (such as `Operation`) are passed to the wrapped object and not to the `inherited` parent. Always keep in mind that you are wrapping the injected object and not the parent class!

This allows us to decorate any class derived from `TLegacy`. For example, the following code decorates the derived class, `TSubLegacy`:

```
type
  TSubLegacy = class(TLegacy)
  public
    procedure DoSomething(const s: string); virtual;
  end;

var
  decorator: TUCDecorator;

begin
  decorator := TUCDecorator.Create(TSubLegacy.Create);
  TSubLegacy(decorator.Wrapped).DoSomething(decorator.OperationUC);
  decorator.Free;
end;
```

This code fragment shows how we can pass any subclass of `TLegacy` to the decorator. The only problem here is that the decorator loses information about the wrapped object's type, and we have to use casting to access the operations of the `TSubLegacy` class.

One way out of this conundrum is to keep the original reference handy. We could store the `TSubLegacy` object in a separate variable, as shown here:

```
var
  decorator: TUCDecorator;
  subLegacy: TSubLegacy;

begin
  subLegacy := TSubLegacy.Create;
  decorator := TUCDecorator.Create(subLegacy);
  subLegacy.DoSomething(decorator.OperationUC);
  decorator.Free;
  // at this point, subLegacy points to already released memory block
  subLegacy := nil;
end;
```

This approach can cause problems, because now we have two references to the same memory location (the `TSubLegacy` instance), one in the `subLegacy` variable , and another in `decorator.FWrapped`. When we destroy the decorator, the wrapped `TSubLegacy` object is also destroyed and the `subLegacy` variable now points to the memory location that is no longer in use. Other parts of the program may overwrite this memory soon (this holds especially true for multithreaded programs), and in such cases, accessing `subLegacy` after this point may have unexpected consequences. The previous example solves that by setting `subLegacy` to `nil`, but such a step is easy to overlook.

Another solution is to use generics to define the correct type of wrapped objects. The following class definition shows how we could adapt `TUCDecorator` in that direction:

```
type
  TUCDecorator<T: TLegacy> = class(TLegacy)
  private
    FWrapped: T;
  public
    constructor Create(wrapped: T);
    destructor Destroy; override;
    function Operation: string; override;
    function OperationUC: string; virtual;
    property Wrapped: T read FWrapped;
  end;
```

The implementation of `TUCDecorator<T>` looks exactly the same as the implementation of `TUCDecorator` (and you can verify that in the example program). This version, however, allows us to remove casting from the code, as shown here:

```
decoratorT := TUCDecorator<TSubLegacy>.Create(TSubLegacy.Create);
decoratorT.Wrapped.DoSomething(decoratorT.OperationUC);
decoratorT.Free;
```

Decorating streams

To better illustrate the power and problems of writing decorators, the `StreamDecorator` project from the folder folder implements a decorator for the `TStream` class. The `DecoratedStream` unit implements a decorator that extends the `TStream` class (and its subclasses) with eight new functions.

The problem with decorating rich classes such as `TStream` arises from the fact that the decorator must implement complete `TStream` interface. In the case of `TStream`, that means writing lots and lots of functions. Just the declaration of the decorator is a whopping one hundred and eighty-five lines long! The following code fragment shows just a few parts of that declaration:

```
type
  TDecoratedStream = class(TStream)
  strict private
    FWrapped: TStream;
  private
    function GetPosition: Int64;
    procedure SetPosition(const Pos: Int64);
    procedure SetSize64(const NewSize: Int64);
  protected
   function GetSize: Int64; override;
  public
    constructor Create(wrappedStream: TStream);
    destructor Destroy; override;
    // new functionality
    procedure Advance(delta: int64);
    procedure Append(source: TStream);
    function AtEnd: boolean;
    function BytesLeft: int64;
    procedure Clear;
    procedure GoToStart;
    procedure GoToEnd;
    procedure Truncate;

    // TStream
    function Read(var Buffer; Count: Longint): Longint; overload; override;
    function Write(const Buffer; Count: Longint): Longint; overload;
      override;
    // ...
    property Position: Int64 read GetPosition write SetPosition;
    property Size: Int64 read GetSize write SetSize64;
  end;
```

While the implementation of new functions is trivial, the majority of the work lies in writing (equally trivial) implementations for functions from the `TStream` interface. The following code fragment shows the implementation of the new functionality and two examples of how `TStream` methods are implemented:

```
procedure TDecoratedStream.Advance(delta: int64);
begin
  Position := Position + delta;
end;
```

```
procedure TDecoratedStream.Append(source: TStream);
begin
  Position := Size;
  FWrapped.CopyFrom(source, 0);
end;

function TDecoratedStream.AtEnd: boolean;
begin
  Result := (BytesLeft = 0);
end;

function TDecoratedStream.BytesLeft: int64;
begin
  Result := (Size - Position);
end;

procedure TDecoratedStream.Clear;
begin
  Size := 0;
end;

procedure TDecoratedStream.GoToEnd;
begin
  Position := Size;
end;

procedure TDecoratedStream.GoToStart;
begin
  Position := 0;
end;

procedure TDecoratedStream.Truncate;
begin
  Size := Position;
end;

function TDecoratedStream.Read(var Buffer: TBytes; Count: Longint):
Longint;
begin
  Result := FWrapped.Read(Buffer, Count);
end;

procedure TDecoratedStream.ReadBuffer(var Buffer; Count: NativeInt);
begin
  FWrapped.ReadBuffer(Buffer, Count);
end;
```

The main unit uses the new functionality to implement the very simple task of deleting the last 12 characters from a string:

```
procedure TfrmDecorator.btnStreamClick(Sender: TObject);
var
  stream: TDecoratedStream;
begin
  stream := TDecoratedStream.Create(TStringStream.Create(
    'Hands-On Design Patterns with Delphi'));
  try
    stream.GoToStart;
    while stream.BytesLeft > 12 do
      stream.Advance(1);
    stream.Truncate;

    lbLog.Items.Add(TStringStream(stream.Wrapped).DataString);
  finally
    FreeAndNil(stream);
  end;
end;
```

As `TDecoratedStream` doesn't implement typed access to the wrapped object (as was implemented in the `TUCDecorator<T>` example), we have to cast the wrapped object to `TStringStream` if we want to access methods specific to that class.

Delphi idioms – helpers

As you can see, writing decorators can result in lots of very tedious work. If you check the DecoratedStream unit, you'll see more than 900 very boring lines. Is there a better way?

The answer to that is both *yes* and *no*. It's *no* if we want to stick to traditional decorator implementation, but it's *yes* if we are a bit more pragmatic than that and we use a Delphi-specific concept of helpers.

Delphi helpers give us a way to extend existing classes, records, and even simple data types with new methods. They work in the same open/closed way as decorators. The original class, record, or data type stays the same (is closed), but as far as the other parts of code are concerned, it is extended with the new functionality (is open).

The definition of a class helper looks just the same as a normal class definition, except that it is introduced with `class helper for T`, where `T` is the class that we want to extend (or with `record helper for T` if we are extending a record or a simple data type). For example, we could extend the `TLegacy` class with the following helper:

```
type
  TLegacyHelper = class helper for TLegacy
  public
    function UCOperation: string;
  end;

function TLegacyHelper.UCOperation: string;
begin
  Result := Operation.ToUpper;
end;
```

Inside the helper, we can access all parts of the extended class, with the exception of the `strict private` section. We can even refer to the extended class with the identifier `Self` if we have to disambiguate a symbol.

 The `ToUpper` function in `UCOperation` is part of a `TStringHelper` helper that extends the `string` data type. It is defined in the `System.SysUtils` unit.

You should keep in mind that helpers are not decorators. With decorators, we can use an object bare (without any additions), or we can decorate it with a decorator (or even with one of many decorators). We can even do that in runtime, during the execution of the program.

Helpers are more fixed in their ways. Once a helper is visible at some point (either by being declared in the same unit or in an interface section of a used unit), it will be available to the program.

Another problem with helpers is the so-called **Highlander problem**. At any point in the program, there can be only one active helper for a class, record, or data types. If the code declares two helpers for the same type, only the second helper will be active, and the first will be ignored.

Nevertheless, helpers are useful. If nothing else, we can create one with a very small amount of code. The helpers project shows how we can create a `TStream` helper with the same functionality as was implemented in the `TDecoratedStream` decorator. The definition of the helper is shown here, while you can check the `StreamHelper` unit to see the implementation (which is almost the same as the equivalent part of `TDecoratedStream`):

```
type
  TStreamHelper = class helper for TStream
  public
    procedure Advance(delta: int64);
    procedure Append(source: TStream);
    function AtEnd: boolean;
    function BytesLeft: int64;
    procedure Clear;
    procedure GoToStart;
    procedure GoToEnd;
    procedure Truncate;
  end;
```

Helpers extend the class directly. There is no need to access the wrapped instance via the `Wrapped` property in the decorator. This simplifies the code in the demo, which can now directly access the `DataString` property of the `TStringStream`, as shown here:

```
procedure TfrmHelpers.btnStreamClick(Sender: TObject);
var
  stream: TStringStream;
begin
  stream := TStringStream.Create('Hands-On Design Patterns with Delphi');
  try
    stream.GoToStart;
    while stream.BytesLeft > 12 do
      stream.Advance(1);
    stream.Truncate;

    lbLog.Items.Add(stream.DataString);
  finally
    FreeAndNil(stream);
  end;
end;
```

The same example also implements a simple extension for the `string` type that implements the `MixedCase` function, as follows:

```
type
  TStringHelper = record helper for string
    function MixedCase: string;
  end;

function TStringHelper.MixedCase: string;
var
  i: Integer;
begin
  Result := Self;
  for i := 1 to Length(Result) do
    if Odd(i) then
      Result[i] := UpCase(Result[i])
    else if CharInSet(Result[i], ['A'..'Z']) then
      Result[i] := char(Ord(Result[i]) + (Ord('a') - Ord('A')));
end;
```

The code in the main form uses this helper to write out a string converted to the mixed case, as shown here:

```
procedure TfrmHelpers.btnStringClick(Sender: TObject);
begin
  lbLog.Items.Add('Hands-On Design Patterns with Delphi'.MixedCase);
  // Will not work as StringHelper.TStringHelper overrides
  // SysUtils.TStringHelper
  // lbLog.Items.Add('Hands-On Design Patterns with Delphi'.ToUpper);
end;
```

This part of code also demonstrates how the introduction of a string helper disables all functionality of the string helper that's implemented in the `System.SysUtils` unit. If you remove the comment before the last line of the method, the code will not compile, as the compiler will not be able to find the helper function `ToUpper`.

The following screenshot shows both helpers in action:

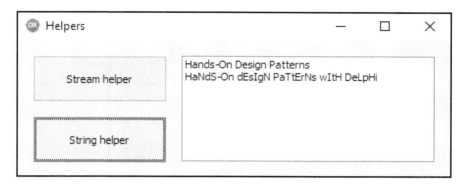

Example implementation of TStream and string helpers

Facade

The last pattern we described in this chapter is a bit different than the three we described before. The previous patterns were all wrapping one and only one component, while the facade pattern wraps multiple components and subsystems. In addition to that, facade is the only pattern from this chapter that provides a reduced interface and not a full feature set of wrapped components.

As such, a facade represents a front for a complex subsystem. Besides connecting subsystems together, it also provides a problem-specific interface. In fact, if we follow the single responsibility principle, we can implement multiple facades for the same set of subsystems, each providing a very specific interface to solve one specific problem.

When you ask your smart device *OK, <insert name>, will it rain today?*, you are accessing a Facade for an incredibly complex system. Your words are first converted to text, and then another subsystem tries to understand your question. The third one provides information about your location, and the fourth one gives a weather forecast, and at the end a text-to-speech module reads the answer to you. All that complexity is hidden behind very simple user interface.

A facade may provide some additional functionality that is not implemented by the wrapped components. It can also preprocess data before it is sent to wrapped components and postprocess the result. That, however, should not be the focus of a facade. If you need complex additional functionality, implement it in a separate component, and then use it in the facade.

The biggest trap with facades is that sometimes they try to do too much. A facade should not wrap everything, and it must not become a *god object*. Always keep the single responsibility principle in mind and design facades that are simple and dedicated to a specific case.

For example, the `Facade` project in the `Facade` folder provides a very simple RSS reader. It can read RSS content from the web or from a file, parse it, and display it in a very primitive user interface.

 RSS is a type of web feed that allows organized access to web resources. It is typically used in news and blog concentrators. The data in an RSS feed is stored in a standarized XML file.

The following screenshot shows the facade project in action:

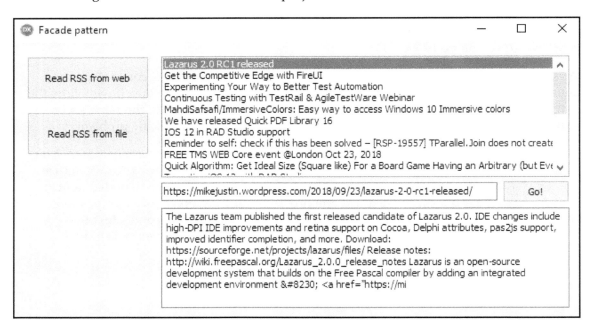

A simple RSS browser

Clicking on the **Read RSS from web** button loads the RSS feed of the popular Delphi blog concentrator site at http://beginend.net. A list of posts is displayed at the top. After you click on a post, its URL is shown in the TEdit control in the middle, and a short description is shown at the bottom. The description may contain some HTML, as no postprocessing and cleanup is done.

As a side effect, the code asks where to save the downloaded RSS file so you can use it to test the second part of the functionality: loading RSS file from a file. The **Read RSS from file** button does that.

The code behind the web downloader, file reader, and the RSS parser is mildly complicated. It uses the internal class TRSSParser, Delphi's classes THttpClient and TStreamReader, and Delphi's XML subsystem.

To simplify the code, and to wrap all multi-purpose classes into a problem-specific interface, the unit RSSReader implements the facade TRSSReader. The declaration part of this facade is shown here:

```
type
  TRSSReader = class
  strict private
    FItems: TList<TRSSItem>;
    FRSS: string;
  strict protected
    function Parse(const sRss: string): TRSSError;
  public
    constructor Create;
    destructor Destroy; override;
    function ReadFromURL(const url: string): TRSSError;
    function ReadFromFile(const fileName: string): TRSSError;
    property Items: TList<TRSSItem> read FItems;
    property RSS: string read FRSS;
  end;
```

This gives us enough information to implement the main form. The **Read RSS from web** executes the following code:

```
procedure TfrmFacade.btnReadRSSWebClick(Sender: TObject);
var
  reader: TRSSReader;
begin
  reader := TRSSReader.Create;
  try
    if ShowResult(reader.ReadFromURL(CBeginEndURL), reader) then
      if FileSaveDialog1.Execute then
        SaveToFile(FileSaveDialog1.FileName, reader.RSS);
  finally
    FreeAndNil(reader);
  end;
end;
```

The reader method `ReadFromURL` is called, and its output is passed to the `ShowResult` method, which displays errors and updates the user interface. If the reader was successful, the user is asked for a file name, and the RSS file is saved.

The method activated by clicking the **Read RSS from file** button is equally as simple, as shown here:

```
procedure TfrmFacade.btnReadRSSFileClick(Sender: TObject);
var
  reader: TRSSReader;
begin
  if not FileOpenDialog1.Execute then
    Exit;

  reader := TRSSReader.Create;
  try
    ShowResult(reader.ReadFromFile(FileOpenDialog1.FileName), reader);
  finally
    FreeAndNil(reader);
  end;
end;
```

Firstly, the user is asked for a file name. After that, `ReadFromFile` is called, and the user interface is updated.

The `ShowResult` method clears the UI and then either displays an error or loads the result into the UI controls by calling the `LoadItems` function. Both are shown here:

```
function TfrmFacade.ShowResult(rssResult: TRSSError; reader: TRSSReader):
boolean;
begin
  Result := false;
  lbTitles.Items.Clear;
  inpLink.Clear;
  inpDescription.Clear;
  FItems.Clear;

  case rssResult of
    TRSSerror.OK:
      begin
        FItems.Clear;
        FItems.AddRange(reader.Items);
        LoadItems;
        Result := true;
      end;
    TRSSerror.GetFailed: ShowMessage('GET failed');
    TRSSerror.CantReadFile: ShowMessage('Failed to read from file');
    TRSSerror.InvalidFormat: ShowMessage('Invalid RSS format');
    else raise Exception.Create('Unexpected result!');
  end;
end;

procedure TfrmFacade.LoadItems;
var
  i: integer;
begin
  lbTitles.Items.BeginUpdate;
  try
  for i := 0 to FItems.Count - 1 do
    lbTitles.Items.Add(FItems[i].Title);
  finally
    lbTitles.Items.EndUpdate;
  end;
end;
```

When a user clicks on a post, information is simply updated from the internal `FItems` structure, as shown here:

```
procedure TfrmFacade.lbTitlesClick(Sender: TObject);
begin
  inpLink.Text := FItems[lbTitles.ItemIndex].Link;
  inpDescription.Text := FItems[lbTitles.ItemIndex].Description;
end;
```

This clearly demonstrates how a facade can provide a simple interface over a set of multipurpose classes. Still, we can take a look at how the `ReadFromURL` and `ReadFromFile` are implemented.

The `ReadFromURL` function uses a built-in `THttpClient` to read the contents of the RSS URL for the `BeginEnd` concentrator. As shown here, a helper function called `Parse` is executed on successful read:

```
function TRSSReader.ReadFromURL(const url: string): TRSSError;
var
  httpClient: THttpClient;
  response: IHTTPResponse;
begin
  Result := TRSSError.OK;
  FItems.Clear;

  httpClient := THttpClient.Create;
  try
    response := httpClient.Get(
      'https://www.beginend.net/api/recent.rss.dws');
    if response.StatusCode <> 200 then
      Exit(TRSSError.GetFailed);
    Result := Parse(response.ContentAsString);
  finally
    FreeAndNil(httpClient);
  end;
end;
```

Similarly, `ReadFromFile` reads contents of a file by using Delphi's `TStreamReader`. If the file cannot be read, an exception is converted to a result. Otherwise, the helper `Parse` function is called as in `ReadFromURL`. This function is implemented as follows:

```
function TRSSReader.ReadFromFile(const fileName: string): TRSSError;
var
  reader: TStreamReader;
begin
  Result := TRSSError.OK;
  FItems.Clear;
```

```
try
  reader := TStreamReader.Create(fileName, true);
except
  on EFOpenError do begin
    Result := TRSSError.CantReadFile;
    Exit;
  end;
end;

try
  Result := Parse(reader.ReadToEnd);
finally
  FreeAndNil(reader);
end;
end;
```

As shown in the following code, the `Parse` function uses the internal `TRSSParser` class from the RSSParser unit to parse the RSS file:

```
function TRSSReader.Parse(const sRss: string): TRSSError;
var
  parser: TRSSParser;
begin
  Result := TRSSError.OK;
  FRSS := sRss;
  parser := TRSSParser.Create;
  try
    if not parser.ParseRSS(FRSS, FItems) then
      Result := TRSSError.InvalidFormat;
  finally
    FreeAndNil(parser);
  end;
end;
```

The `TRSSParser` class uses Delphi's built-in XML processing capabilities to parse the XML file. For details, see the RSSParser unit.

Now, let me restate that a very useful, and often overlooked, use case for facades lies not just in hiding a complex functionality behind the curtain, but to implement a single-purpose interface over a set of multi-purpose tools.

Summary

In this chapter, we have explored four more structural patterns. As they look quite similar to one another, this chapter opened with a discussion about how to select the proper design pattern for your needs.

The first pattern that was described in this chapter was the adapter pattern. Although it is very similar to the bridge pattern from the previous chapters, it occupies a different niche. Bridge is used to connect two parts of a new design, while the adapter helps us reuse old code in a new environment.

After that, I moved to the proxy pattern. It can appear in many different disguises: protection proxy, remoting proxy, virtual proxy, caching proxy, and more. In all cases, the proxy wraps an interface and then exposes the same interface, possibly by changing the operation of some (or even all) methods of that interface.

Next on the list was the decorator pattern. Although similar to the proxy, it works in a completely different way. A decorator wraps an interface and enhances it with a new functionality. As a side effect of the implementation, a decorator can operate on all subclasses of a wrapped class. A similar functionality to decorators is offered by Delphi's helper mechanism, and this chapter explored the similarities and differences between the two.

At the end of this chapter, we covered the facade pattern. It is designed to hide complexities and bind together functionality from multiple classes and subsystems. A very important aspect of this pattern is that it can create a problem-specific interface over a set of multi-purpose classes, which results in code that better conforms to the single responsibility principle (the *S* part in the SOLID principle), which we briefly covered in `Chapter 1`, *Introduction to Patterns*.

In the next chapter, we'll move away from structural patterns and start talking about **behavioral patterns**, a big group of patterns that focuses on defining communications paths and messages among a group of cooperating objects.

Section 4: Behavioral Patterns 4

In this chapter, the reader will learn the most important patterns from the last of the three Gang of Four categories—behavioral patterns.

This section will comprise the following chapters:

6
Nullable Value, Template Method, Command, and State

Every moderately complex program is a collection of many interlocked parts. In Delphi, as in other object—oriented languages, these parts are represented by objects that can cooperate in different ways. They can be tightly connected one object can own others, or they may just cooperate for a short time.

As with every complex system, there's a big chance that it will evolve into a big mess of parts that are connected in random ways without any order and reason. (Sometimes, we affectionately call such a mess a big ball of mud. It is not a pleasant sight.) The patterns in the behavioral group help us to organize objects so that they are tightly coupled where they have to be, can cooperate with each other when the need occurs, and ignore each other in almost all other instances.

In this chapter, you will learn about the following topics:

- The null object pattern, which can reduce the need for frequent if statements in the code
- The Template method pattern, which helps to create adaptable algorithms
- The Command pattern, which treats actions as objects
- The State pattern, which allows an object to change its behavior on demand

Null object

In object-oriented programming, code sometimes refers to an optional object. The absence of an object doesn't represent an error; it is just an obstacle to writing clean code. Sometimes, we can replace such a missing object (a nil value) with a null object. A null object implements the same interface as a real object, but replaces each method with a do nothing implementation.

Most modern operating systems know about the concept of a null device. For example, NUL on Windows and /dev/null on Unix and similar systems are devices that are empty if we read from them. They will also happily store any file you copy onto them, no matter what the size. You'll never be able to retrieve that file, though, as the null device will stay empty no matter what you do with it.

The null object pattern is a relatively recent addition to the object-oriented programmer's arsenal. It was first introduced in 1996 in a paper by Bobby Woolf, which is still available on the internet at http://www.cs.oberlin.edu/~jwalker/refs/woolf.ps.

If you have trouble viewing the PostScript (.ps) file, convert it into a PDF file by using any free online converter.

To give a practical example, a null object helps simplify code that looks something like the following:

```
type
  TSomeObject = class
  public
    procedure DoSomething; virtual;
  end;

procedure Process(obj: TSomeObject);
begin
  if assigned(obj) then
    obj.DoSomething;
end;

Process(nil);
```

Instead of testing whether an object is defined and then branching the code, we can introduce a null object that implements the same interface as TSomeObject. Instead of passing a nil value to the Process method, we can use this null object, as demonstrated in the following code fragment:

```
type
  TNullObject = class(TSomeObject)
  public
    procedure DoSomething; override;
  end;

procedure TNullObject.DoSomething;
begin
```

```
end;

procedure Process(obj: TSomeObject);
begin
  obj.DoSomething;
end;

null := TNullObject.Create;
Process(null);
FreeAndNil(null);
```

In a strict object-oriented world, the base object must be ready for an extension its public functions and procedures must be marked as `virtual`. This allows us to derive the null object from the base object and `override` all public methods.

If we are programming with interfaces, there's no need for subclassing. A null object must implement the same interface as the base object, and that's it. The following code fragment shows the previous example, but translated into the language of interfaces:

```
type
  IDoSomething = interface
    procedure DoSomething;
  end;

  TSomeObject = class(TInterfacedObject, IDoSomething)
  public
    procedure DoSomething;
  end;

  TNullObject = class(TInterfacedObject, IDoSomething)
  public
    procedure DoSomething;
  end;

procedure TNullObject.DoSomething;
begin
end;

procedure Process(const something: IDoSomething);
begin
  something.DoSomething;
end;

Process(TNullObject.Create);
```

If the code frequently uses the null object, we can save some memory and CPU cycles and implement it as a singleton. (For more information about singletons, see `Chapter 2, Singleton, Dependency Injection, Lazy Initialization, and Object Pool`.)

Writing replacement procedures is simple. As the previous code examples show, the null procedure simply doesn't do anything. When implementing a `null` function, however, we have to return a result. Deciding on what to return is not always easy. We must know how the returned value is used in the algorithm before we can decide what should be returned.

Let's illustrate this with a short example. The following code shows a simple class with two functions and a method that consumes an instance of this class:

```
type
  TBaseClass = class
  public
    function Value1: integer; virtual;
    function Value2: integer; virtual;
  end;

function Process(input: integer; params: TBaseClass): integer;
begin
  if not assigned(params) then
    Result := input
  else
    Result := input * params.Value1 + params.Value2;
end;
```

To write a null object version of `TBaseClass`, we need to return correct the values from `Value1` and `Value2` so that they will not modify the `input` parameter. The following code shows the solution to this:

```
type
  TNullClass = class(TBaseClass)
  public
    function Value1: integer; override;
    function Value2: integer; override;
  end;

function TNullClass.Value1: integer;
begin
  Result := 1;
end;

function TNullClass.Value2: integer;
begin
  Result := 0;
end;
```

```
function Process(input: integer; params: TBaseClass): integer;
begin
  Result := input * params.Value1 + params.Value2;
end;
```

Multiplying by one and adding zero will not change the input, so this code will work.

In some cases, you will not be able write a null version of a function because a single value won't exist that represents a do nothing operation in all places that call the function. If that happens, you still have to use the if..then code in such places.

A null object is functionally equal to a do nothing virtual proxy. (For more information about the proxy pattern, see Chapter 5, *Adapter, Proxy, Decorator, and Facade*.) The purpose of both patterns is, however, different. A virtual proxy (a mock object) is used when we need to pass a simple version of an object to a piece of code so that we can test that code. A null object is passed a piece of code so that we can remove conditional statements and simplify the program.

A null object can also be considered a special case of the *strategy* pattern or a special case of the *state* pattern. (For more information on the state pattern, see Chapter 7, *Iterator, Observer, Visitor, Memento*. The strategy pattern is not covered in this book.)

 Keep in mind that the null and nullable objects represent two completely different ideas. The former is a version of the object with a do nothing implementation and the latter is a normal functioning version that can be set to a special, null state (which is not equal to a nil value).

To end this section, I have prepared two very simple (but functional) examples. The first implements a null version of a TStream class. It is implemented in the NullStreamPattern project and is stored in the Null object folder.

A null stream should behave the same as the null device that we described at the beginning of this chapter. It should appear empty when the code tries to read from it and it should accept (and throw away) any data that is being written into it.

Interestingly, a `TStream` class itself almost perfectly satisfies these conditions. It is empty and it will throw away any data that's written to it, but it raises an exception if the code queries the current position or size. To fix this, we only have to write one small function, as shown in the following code:

```
type
  TNullStream = class(TStream)
  public
    function Seek(const Offset: Int64;
      Origin: TSeekOrigin): Int64; overload; override;
  end;

function TNullStream.Seek(const Offset: Int64; Origin: TSeekOrigin): Int64;
begin
  if Offset <> 0 then
    raise Exception.Create('Cannot seek in null stream');
  Result := 0;
end;
```

This code that's stored in the `NullStream` unit implements a `Seek` method, which can only move to offset 0. As the code simulates a stream that is always empty, this seems more appropriate than simply returning 0 in all cases.

The second project, `NullLogger`, demonstrates the use of null objects for logging. The `Logger.Intf` unit defines a simple logging interface called `ILogger`, as follows:

```
type
  ILogger = interface ['{738C066A-0777-4BA8-ACB6-2DE68A3968AD}']
    function Initialize: boolean;
    procedure Log(const msg: string); overload;
    procedure Log(const msg: string; const params: array of const);
      overload;
    procedure Close;
  end;
```

The main unit uses the `ILogger` interface in a simple piece of code. Instead of using the if assigned logger then pattern a lot, it depends on the caller providing an initialized `logger` parameter:

```
procedure TfrmNullLogger.Test(const logger: ILogger);
var
  i: Integer;
begin
  logger.Log('Starting test');
  for i := 1 to 10 do
    logger.Log('Step: %d', [i]);
  logger.Log('Test completed');
```

```
end;

procedure TfrmNullLogger.TestWithLogger(const logger: ILogger);
begin
  if not logger.Initialize then
    raise Exception.Create('Failed to initialize logger');
  Test(logger);
  logger.Close;
end;
```

To demonstrate this, the main form provides three buttons. One logs to a file, another logs to a listbox, and the third uses a null object implementation.

Implementations can be found in units, such as Logger.TextFile (file logger), Logger.ListBox (listbox logger), and Logger.Null (null logger). The implementation of the null logger is shown here:

```
uses
  Logger.Intf;

type
  TNullLogger = class(TInterfacedObject, ILogger)
  public
    function Initialize: boolean;
    procedure Log(const msg: string); overload;
    procedure Log(const msg: string; const params: array of const);
      overload;
    procedure Close;
  end;

procedure TNullLogger.Close;
begin
end;

function TNullLogger.Initialize: boolean;
begin
  Result := true;
end;

procedure TNullLogger.Log(const msg: string);
begin
end;

procedure TNullLogger.Log(const msg: string; const params: array of const);
begin
end;
```

In this case, it was not hard to decide what the `Initialize` function should return. The null logger should always be able to initialize itself, so this function must return `True`.

Template method

A template method (sometimes just called a template) is a design pattern that defines a template for an algorithm. Instead of coding a full, working solution, a template method implements just the important parts and leaves some details unfinished. It is up to the derived subclasses to implement the missing parts and through that, provide a working algorithm.

 A recipe in a cookbook represents a template method. It may say something like take three cups of flour (without specifying where exactly you should get this flour from), put into the oven (without specifying exactly which of your baking tins you should use and what specific mark of oven that should be), serve when cold (without providing any detail about serving plates and table setting), and so on.

As defined by the Gang of Four, the template method implements the important part of the algorithm (the business logic) and leaves concrete details unfinished. Usually, they are implemented as a set of abstract methods that are called from the **template** method.

To fully implement an algorithm, you have to implement a derived class that implements these abstract methods (but leaves the template method untouched!). This allows for the development of multiple specialized classes that implement different versions of the algorithm.

Separating important parts of the algorithm from customizable parts and especially writing an algorithm so that it is complete but still open for extensions is not an easy task. It takes some experience to do this correctly, especially if you only have to code one concrete implementation at the moment.

 Your task will be simpler if you have to write two or more concrete implementations together with the template method. This allows you to better anticipate potential problems when writing future specializations. If you only need one concrete implementation, you can write another one simply for testing purposes.

In a strictly object-oriented approach, the base class implements the template method as a normal method (it is not marked as `virtual`) so that it cannot be changed in a derived class. All customizable parts are implemented as a method that's marked as `virtual; abstract;`. The `virtual` part allows us to `override` (replace) this method in a derived class (a subclass) and the `abstract` specifier tells the compiler that the method is not implemented and that any code that calls this method directly (instead of calling the method from the derived class) will raise an exception.

An example from Delphi's VCL framework shows such a pattern. In the `Vcl.Graphics` unit, the `TCustomCanvas` class defines (besides lots of other methods) two functions, as we can see in the following code:

```
type
  TCustomCanvas = class(TPersistent)
    // lots and lots of definitions
    function TextExtent(const Text: string): TSize; virtual; abstract;
    function TextWidth(const Text: string): Integer;
  end;
```

Out of these two functions, only `TextWidth` is implemented, as shown in the following code:

```
function TCustomCanvas.TextWidth(const Text: string): Integer;
begin
  Result := TextExtent(Text).cX;
end;
```

In this example, `TextWidth` is a template method (a very simple one) and `TextExtent` is the customizable part. It is implemented in two derived classes a normal canvas called `TCanvas` (the `Vcl.Graphics` unit) and a Direct2D canvas called `TDirect2DCanvas` (the `Vcl.Direct2D` unit).

Technically, we could also implement customizable parts through injection. (For more information on dependency injection, see `Chapter 2`, *Singleton, Dependency Injection, Lazy Initialization, and Object Pool*) For example, each customizable part could be injected into the constructor.

 Don't inject customizable parts through property injection. This approach should be used to inject optional code. Inject any required code with constructor injection.

The template method pattern is also useful when working with auto-generated code. A code generator may produce an unfinished template, which is then realized in a derived class. This is, for example, a common approach in lexical parsers and compiler generators.

Calculating the average value

As an example, the `TemplateMethod` project from the `Template method` folder implements two specialized versions of a shared template method. The complete definition of the base object and template method is shown here:

```
type
  TDataAggregatorTemplate = class
  protected
    procedure CloseDataSource; virtual; abstract;
    function GetNextValue(var value: integer): boolean; virtual; abstract;
    function OpenDataSource: boolean; virtual; abstract;
  public
    function CalculateAverage: real;
  end;

function TDataAggregatorTemplate.CalculateAverage: real;
var
  sum: integer;
  total: integer;
  value: integer;
begin
  if not OpenDataSource then
    raise Exception.Create('Failed!');
  try
    total := 0;
    sum := 0;
    while GetNextValue(value) do
    begin
      Inc(total);
      Inc(sum, value);
    end;
    if total = 0 then
      raise Exception.Create(
        'Cannot calculate average of empty data set!');
    Result := sum/total;
  finally
    CloseDataSource;
  end;
end;
```

The template method, `CalculateAverage`, first opens a data source by calling an abstract method called `OpenDataSource`. We don't know what this data source is, and we don't care. It could be a file, an in-memory list, a database, and so on. The template method simply doesn't need to know the specifics.

If the data source cannot be opened, the code simply raises an exception. A better way to handle this error is left as an exercise for the reader.

After initializing a few internal variables, the code starts calling the abstract method, `GetNextValue`, which should return the next value from the data source. If there's no more data, the method must return `False`. The code in the template method adds all of the values together and counts the number of values. This allows it to calculate the average value with a simple division.

At the very end, the code calls the third abstract function, `CloseDataSource`, to close the data source.

A first concrete implementation of our data aggregator works with files. The `TFileDataAggregator` class from the `DataAggregator.TextFile` unit opens a file and reads it line by line. It expects to find exactly one integer number in each line.

An implementation, which is shown in the following code, uses Delphi's `TStreamReader` class from the `System.Classes` unit to read the file line by line:

```
type
  TFileDataAggregator = class(TDataAggregatorTemplate)
  strict private
    FFileName: string;
    FReader: TStreamReader;
  protected
    procedure CloseDataSource; override;
    function GetNextValue(var value: integer): boolean; override;
    function OpenDataSource: boolean; override;
  public
    constructor Create(const fileName: string);
    destructor Destroy; override;
  end;

constructor TFileDataAggregator.Create(const fileName: string);
begin
  inherited Create;
  FFileName := fileName;
end;

destructor TFileDataAggregator.Destroy;
begin
```

```
    CloseDataSource;
    inherited;
  end;

  procedure TFileDataAggregator.CloseDataSource;
  begin
    FreeAndNil(FReader);
  end;

  function TFileDataAggregator.GetNextValue(var value: integer): boolean;
  var
    line: string;
  begin
    while not FReader.EndOfStream do
    begin
      line := FReader.ReadLine;
      if TryStrToInt(line, value) then
        Exit(true);
    end;
    Result := false;
  end;

  function TFileDataAggregator.OpenDataSource: boolean;
  begin
    CloseDataSource;
    try
      FReader := TStreamReader.Create(FFileName);
    except
      on E: EFOpenError do
        Exit(false);
    end;
    Result := true;
  end;
```

Two parts of the code deserve a special mention. First, OpenDataSource catches the EFOpenError exception, which is raised if the file doesn't exist or cannot be opened and converts it into a False result.

Second, the GetNextValue function ignores all lines that don't contain an integer value (all lines that cannot be converted from a string to an integer with a call to the TryStrToInt function). This is an implementation detail that can be easily changed if it turns out that the customer expects a different behavior.

To calculate an average value with this aggregator, the main unit creates an instance of the `TFileDataAggregator` object and passes in the name of the data file, as shown here:

```
procedure TfrmTemplateMethod.btnFileAggregatorClick(Sender: TObject);
var
  aggregator: TFileDataAggregator;
begin
  aggregator := TFileDataAggregator.Create('..\..\data.txt');
  Log('Average value: %.4f', [aggregator.CalculateAverage]);
  aggregator.Free;
end;
```

The code then calls the `CalculateAverage` function and logs the result. With the data file that comes with the project, the result should be 4.7143 (rounded to four decimal places).

To simplify unit testing, the project also implements a data aggregator that works on dynamic arrays. It is implemented in the `DataAggregator.DynArray` unit as follows:

```
type
  TMockDataAggregator = class(TDataAggregatorTemplate)
  strict private
    FIndex: integer;
    FValues: TArray<integer>;
  protected
    procedure CloseDataSource; override;
    function GetNextValue(var value: integer): boolean; override;
    function OpenDataSource: boolean; override;
  public
    constructor Create(const values: TArray<integer>);
  end;

constructor TMockDataAggregator.Create(const values: TArray<integer>);
begin
  inherited Create;
  FValues := values;
end;

procedure TMockDataAggregator.CloseDataSource;
begin
end;

function TMockDataAggregator.GetNextValue(var value: integer): boolean;
begin
  Result := (FIndex <= High(FValues));
  if Result then
  begin
    value := FValues[FIndex];
    Inc(FIndex);
```

```
    end;
  end;

function TMockDataAggregator.OpenDataSource: boolean;
begin
  FIndex := 0;
  Result := true;
end;
```

The code is even simpler than the one in the file aggregator because it doesn't have to deal with errors. The input can always be opened and the data source cannot contain non-integer data.

To test the template method, the code in the main unit passes an array with the first seven Fibonacci numbers to `TMockDataAggregator` while also displaying a manually calculated result for comparison, as shown here:

```
procedure TfrmTemplateMethod.btnArrayAggregatorClick(Sender: TObject);
var
  aggregator: TMockDataAggregator;
begin
  aggregator := TMockDataAggregator.Create([1, 1, 2, 3, 5, 8, 13]);
  Log('Average value: %.4f, Expected value: %.4f',
    [aggregator.CalculateAverage, (1+1+2+3+5+8+13)/7]);
  aggregator.Free;
end;
```

 This template method is actually an implementation of an Iterator pattern. See `Chapter 7`, *Iterator, Observer, Visitor, Memento,* for more details on how to better approach such problems.

The following screenshot shows both versions of the template method in action:

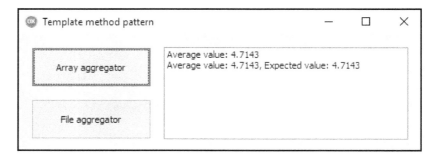

Calculating the average value of file- and memory-based data

Inversion of control

A template method is all well and good, but its use in modern times has greatly declined. This pattern was frequently used to virtualize access to a piece of data (or some other resource) just as in the example from this chapter, that is, the `TemplateMethod` project discussed earlier, but nowadays we know how to approach such problems in a more decoupled and manageable way.

In a way, a template method tells us that the code doesn't follow the single responsibility principle and that it tries to do too much. It wants to be business logic and something else (a data source, in our case).

Instead of writing subclasses that implement missing functionality, we can take a step back, look at the missing functionality as a whole, and try to define what that functionality represents in an abstract sense. Most of the time, we'll find out that it can be represented with one or few simple interfaces that (each by themselves) conform to the single responsibility principle.

In our case, the three missing functions clearly represent a way to access a data source. We can extract them from the `TDataAggregatorTemplate` class into a separate abstract class (a class that contains only an abstract function) or we can use an interface, as shown in the following code fragment:

```
type
  IDataSource = interface ['{63B8C863-E168-4204-9982-3E74D105FFF3}']
    procedure CloseDataSource;
    function GetNextValue(var value: integer): boolean;
    function OpenDataSource: boolean;
  end;
```

This interface, which is defined in the `DataSource.Intf` unit (which is itself part of the `AveragingIoC` project), is then injected into the calculation method. Since the `CalculateAverage` method doesn't depend on any data fields in the `TDataAggregatorTemplate` class, we can remove this class altogether. We only need a single method, implemented in the `DataAggregatorIoC` unit, as follows:

```
function CalculateAverage(const dataSource: IDataSource): real;
var
  sum: integer;
  total: integer;
  value: integer;
begin
  if not dataSource.OpenDataSource then
    raise Exception.Create('Failed!');
  try
```

```
      total := 0;
      sum := 0;
      while dataSource.GetNextValue(value) do
      begin
        Inc(total);
        Inc(sum, value);
      end;
      if total = 0 then
        raise Exception.Create('Cannot calculate average of empty data
set!');
      Result := sum/total;
    finally
      dataSource.CloseDataSource;
    end;
  end;
```

The new version of the code accepts the IDataSource interface and uses it to iterate over the data source. There's no need to change this source as all configurable functionality is now encompassed by the IDataSource interface.

A program implements two versions of this interface. TFileDataSource in the DataSource.TextFile unit knows how to iterate over a file. An implementation is line-to-line identical to the implementation in the TFileDataAggregator class, so I won't show it here. Another data source, TArrayDataSource, from the DataSource.DynArray unit, implements the data source working with a dynamic array. Again, the implementation is almost identical to the TArrayDataAggregator class, so I will only show the declaration of the TArrayDataSource class here:

```
type
  TArrayDataSource = class(TInterfacedObject, IDataSource)
  strict private
    FIndex: integer;
    FValues: TArray<integer>;
  public
    constructor Create(const values: TArray<integer>);
    procedure CloseDataSource;
    function GetNextValue(var value: integer): boolean;
    function OpenDataSource: boolean;
  end;
```

The code in the main unit uses both data sources to calculate the average value of numbers that are stored in an array and in a file. As there's no need to create the data averaging class anymore and as the interfaces are managed by the compiler and destroyed automatically the code is even simpler than before, as follows:

```
procedure TbtnAveraging.btnArrayAggregatorClick(Sender: TObject);
begin
  Log('Average value: %.4f, Expected value: %.4f',
    [CalculateAverage(TArrayDataSource.Create([1, 1, 2, 3, 5, 8, 13])),
    (1+1+2+3+5+8+13)/7]);
end;

procedure TbtnAveraging.btnFileAggregatorClick(Sender: TObject);
begin
  Log('Average value: %.4f',
    [CalculateAverage(TFileDataSource.Create('..\..\data.txt'))] );
end;
```

Command

All interactive programs are organized around actions. The user presses a key, moves or clicks a mouse, touches the screen, and so on, and the program reacts to that by performing an action. This action frequently has parameters attached to it. For example, a keypress action knows which key was pressed, the screen touch knows the coordinates of a person's touch, and so on. At some time at the very moment the action was triggered the action will result in some operation being executed on some object.

The command pattern helps with organizing such a system by converting actions into objects. Instead of treating the action as a bunch of loosely connected data, the code creates a special object (a command) and stores the action parameters inside this command object. A typical system will know about multiple command types, all of which are realized by subclassing the command object. For example, a keypress would create TKeypressCommand, a mouse move would create the TMouseMove command, and so on.

As defined in the *Design Patterns* book, written by Gang of Four, the command pattern is a complicated mechanism with multiple participants, each performing a specific part of the pattern. To discuss this pattern, we first have to define four important terms: command, client receiver, and invoker.

A command is an action, wrapped inside an object. It is created by the client object, for example, as an response to the user input. When a command is executed, it operates on a target object called a **receiver**. The receiver is determined by the client when the command is created and is stored in the command as a parameter.

The last part, invoker, is responsible for executing commands. A command is not directly executed by the client, but is passed to the invoker instead. The invoker may execute the command immediately, or it can queue the execution or use some other mechanism to execute the command in the appropriate context.

 When you send a package through a delivery agency, you are using a command pattern. A package (command) is delivered to the *receiver* by a delivery agency (issuer) and the whole action is triggered by the client (you).

In real-world applications, the invoker and even the receiver may not be represented by an object. A commonly-encountered variation of this pattern implements the invoker as a simple method or an event handler.

A command should be treated as a black box. The client creates the command object and initializes it with parameters, but after that point, the command object is just transferred around and no part of the code changes its content. The command object is also responsible for executing the command action. When the invoker decides that the command has to be executed, it will call the appropriate method inside the command object (typically, this is `Execute`) and the command object will do the rest.

This pattern allows us to do all kinds of interesting things. We can store a command in a list, which enables the creation of an undo/redo mechanism. We can group commands inside other commands and, with that, implement a macro recording mechanism.

We can even store a command in a file or a database to create a log of all executed commands. That enables the application to implement a journaling system that allows the user to start an application and re-apply all of the commands from the previous session (for example, after a program malfunction).

 For more information on preserving objects in external storage, see the *memento* pattern in `Chapter 7`, *Iterator, Visitor, Observer, and Memento*.

We can even implement a scripting system where commands are generated from a script that is executed in an internal interpreter and not as a result of user actions.

Command-based editor

A command pattern has many moving parts, so it is not a surprise that the example for this pattern is one of the more complicated ones in this book.

The `Editor` project in the `Command` folder implements a very simple text editor that internally uses the command pattern. Although it offers only primitive editing capabilities, the example implements both an undo system and a simple macro recorder.

The client part of the pattern is represented by the `TfrmCommand` form in the `EditorMain` unit. The command receiver is a `TMemo` field, which is for reasons of simplicity part of the main form. As we'll see later, the code actually implements two editors, each with its own memo component as a receiver.

The command hierarchy starts with the `TCommand` class. The system also knows what key was pressed via the `TKeyPressCommand` command, what character was deleted via the `TDeleteLeftCommand` command, and what macro was used via the `TMacroCommand` command. There's also a class called `TUndoableCommand` that serves as a basis for all commands that support the undo operation. All of these classes are implemented in the `Editor.Commands` unit.

The invoker is implemented as the `TEditor` class from the `Editor.Editor` unit. It implements both the method execution and the undo stack. As the program contains two memo fields and we want each one to have its own undo stack, the code also creates two invokers.

Creating commands

Instead of writing a full-fledged editor, the `Editor` project simulates just the bare minimum functionality of such a component. The text is displayed in a `TMemo` component with the `Readonly` property set to `True`. This prevents the user from typing directly into the memo field.

 The user can still click inside the memo field and move the caret around with the cursor keys. As an exercise, you can try extending the program so that this functionality will also be implemented with a command pattern.

Key press commands are created in the form's OnKeyPress event. To make sure that all of the keys are seen, even when the memo itself has focus, the KeyPreview property of the form should be set to True. The OnKeyPress is only interested in letters, digits, and whitespace, and converts all of these keys into TKeyPressCommand. Additionally, a key with code #8 (a backspace key) is converted into TDeleteLeftCommand, as shown in the following code:

```
procedure TfrmCommand.FormKeyPress(Sender: TObject; var Key: Char);
begin
  if key.IsLetterOrDigit or key.IsWhiteSpace then
  begin
    Execute(TKeyPressCommand.Create(ActiveMemo, key));
    Key := #0;
  end
  else if key = #8 then
  begin
    Execute(TDeleteLeftCommand.Create(ActiveMemo));
    Key := #0;
  end;
end;
```

In both cases, the resulting command receives the active memo component as a parameter. In the case of the key—pressed command, the key that's pressed is also passed to the command as a parameter.

ActiveMemo and ActiveEditor are very simple helper functions that return the currently active TMemo and TEditor components. To find the implementation for this, see the source code.

The Execute function passes a command to the invoker. We'll come back to this later.

The creation of the last supported command, TMacroCommand, will be explained later in the *Macros* section.

Commands

All commands are subclasses of the `TCommand` class, as shown in the following code:

```
type
  TCommand = class
  strict private
    FReceiver: TMemo;
  public
    constructor Create(receiver: TMemo);
    function Clone: TCommand; virtual;
    procedure Execute; virtual;
    procedure Undo; virtual;
    property Receiver: TMemo read FReceiver write FReceiver;
  end;
```

Each command knows about the intended receiver, which is injected into the constructor. The receiver can also be changed later this functionality is used when replaying macros.

Each command implements the `Execute` (executes the command) and `Undo` (undoes effects of command execution) methods. In the `TCommand` object, both are implemented as empty methods.

Each command also knows how to make a copy of itself. We'll look into the implementation of the `Clone` method later in the *Cloning* section.

The `TCommand` class has only one child class, `TUndoableCommand`. This class is used as a parent for commands that can undo their operations. To support that, its `Execute` method stores the current memo text and position, while the `Undo` method assigns stored text and its position in the memo component. The implementation with the exception of the `Clone` method is shown here:

```
type
  TUndoableCommand = class(TCommand)
  strict private
    FText: string;
    FPosition: Integer;
  strict protected
    procedure StoreState;
  public
    function Clone: TCommand; override;
    procedure Execute; override;
    procedure Undo; override;
  end;

procedure TUndoableCommand.Execute;
```

```
begin
  StoreState;
end;

procedure TUndoableCommand.StoreState;
begin
  FText := Receiver.Text;
  FPosition := Receiver.SelStart;
end;

procedure TUndoableCommand.Undo;
begin
  Receiver.Text := FText;
  Receiver.SelStart := FPosition;
end;
```

All other commands are derived from the `TUndoableCommand` class. They don't override the `Undo` command as the default behavior works fine for all of them. The implementation of `TKeyPressCommand` (again, with the exception of the `Clone` method) is shown here:

```
type
  TKeyPressCommand = class(TUndoableCommand)
  strict private
    FKey: char;
  public
    constructor Create(receiver: TMemo; key: char);
    function Clone: TCommand; override;
    procedure Execaute; override;
  end;

constructor TKeyPressCommand.Create(receiver: TMemo; key: char);
begin
  inherited Create(receiver);
  FKey := key;
end;

procedure TKeyPressCommand.Execute;
var
  pos: Integer;
  s: string;
begin
  inherited;
  s := Receiver.Text;
  pos := Receiver.SelStart;
  Insert(FKey, s, pos+1);
  Receiver.Text := s;
  Receiver.SelStart := pos + 1;
end;
```

For the implementation of `TDeleteLeftCommand`, see the source code. `TMacroCommand` will be examined later in the *Macros* section.

Invoker

The next part of the solution is the invoker, which is stored in the `Editor.Editor` unit. It is defined as a simple class that can execute and undo commands, as shown here:

```
type
  TEditor = class
  strict private
    FUndo: TStack<TCommand>;
  public
    constructor Create;
    destructor Destroy; override;
    procedure Execute(command: TCommand);
    procedure Undo(command: TCommand);
    function IsUndoEmpty: boolean;
    function PopLastCommand: TCommand;
  end;
```

Leaving the boring creation and destruction aside (for more details, see the source code), the interesting methods are implemented as follows:

```
procedure TEditor.Execute(command: TCommand);
begin
  command.Execute;
  FUndo.Push(command);
end;

function TEditor.IsUndoEmpty: boolean;
begin
  Result := FUndo.Count = 0;
end;

function TEditor.PopLastCommand: TCommand;
begin
  Result := FUndo.Pop;
end;

procedure TEditor.Undo(command: TCommand);
begin
  command.Undo;
  command.Free;
end;
```

The `Execute` method executes the command. As noted before, the command is treated as a black box. The invoker has no idea what the `command.Execute` will do. After that, the command object is pushed to the undo stack.

`IsUndoEmpty` and `PopLastCommand` are helper functions that are used by the client to correctly implement the user interface. We'll see them in action in a moment.

At the end, the `Undo` command executes the `Undo` method of the command and destroys the command object.

Client

All of this comes together in the client. Besides creating and dispatching commands, the client also provides a user interface for undoing last action and an interface for recording and playing macros, as shown in the following screenshot:

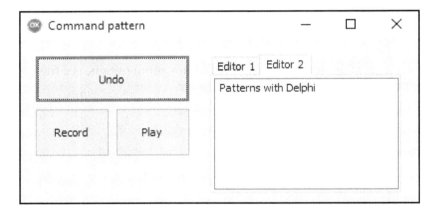

Command-driven editor

All of the user interfaces in this program are action-driven. Every button has a corresponding action with `Update` and `Execute` event handlers attached. This allows the program to enable/disable buttons according to the current program's state.

 Delphi's `TAction` object is in fact, an implementation of the command design pattern!

As we can see in the following code, the `actUndo` action is enabled when the active `TEditor` has at least one command on the undo stack. When executed (when the Undo button is clicked), the action pops the last command from the undo stack and passes it to the `TEditor.Undo` method:

```
procedure TfrmCommand.actUndoExecute(Sender: TObject);
begin
  ActiveEditor.Undo(ActiveEditor.PopLastCommand);
end;

procedure TfrmCommand.actUndoUpdate(Sender: TObject);
begin
  (Sender as TAction).Enabled := (not ActiveEditor.IsUndoEmpty);
end;
```

Macros

For the last part of the puzzle, I have to show you how macro recording is implemented. This is actually the most complicated part of the program.

Let's start with the command object. A macro is just a special kind of command, `TMacroCommand`. As we can see in the following code, it implements an `Add` command, which stores other commands in the internal list:

```
type
  TMacroCommand = class(TUndoableCommand)
  strict private
    FCommands: TObjectList<TCommand>;
  public
    procedure Add(command: TCommand);
    procedure AfterConstruction; override;
    procedure BeforeDestruction; override;
    function Clone: TCommand; override;
    procedure Execute; override;
  end;

procedure TMacroCommand.Add(command: TCommand);
begin
  FCommands.Add(command);
end;
```

When executed, the `Execute` method calls all of the `Execute` methods of all of the commands in the list. As commands can be recorded when one editor is active, and later replayed when the other editors are active, the `Execute` method also forces `Receiver` parameter of all commands in the list to point to the correct receiver, as follows:

```
procedure TMacroCommand.Execute;
var
  cmd: TCommand;
begin
  inherited;
  for cmd in FCommands do begin
    cmd.Receiver := Receiver;
    cmd.Execute;
  end;
end;
```

The call to `inherited` calls `TUndoableCommand.Execute`, which creates a snapshot of the current state of the `Receiver`, thereby allowing for a later undo operation.

The main program allows for only one macro, which is stored in the form field, `FMacro: TMacroCommand`. This field is (re)created whenever the `actRecord` action is executed. As the following code shows, clicking the `Record` button sets the internal where we are recording flag, sets the button action to `actStop` (so that it will display the text **Stop** instead of **Record**), and recreates the `FMacro` field:

```
procedure TfrmCommand.actRecordExecute(Sender: TObject);
begin
  FRecording := true;
  btnMacro.Action := actStop;
  FreeAndNil(FMacro);
  FMacro := TMacroCommand.Create(nil);
end;
```

The macro command has no dedicated receiver, so the `nil` parameter is passed to the constructor.

When the user clicks the **Stop** button, the internal recording flag is turned off and the action button is set back to `actRecord`, as follows:

```
procedure TfrmCommand.actStopExecute(Sender: TObject);
begin
  FRecording := false;
  btnMacro.Action := actRecord;
end;
```

The `actPlay` action is enabled only when the `FMacro` field is assigned and when the program is not recording a macro. When executed, `actPlay` sets the receiver of the `FMacro` command to the currently active memo and then calls the invoker's `Execute` method to execute the macro, as shown in the following code:

```
procedure TfrmCommand.actPlayExecute(Sender: TObject);
begin
  FMacro.Receiver := ActiveMemo;
  ActiveEditor.Execute(FMacro.Clone);
end;

procedure TfrmCommand.actPlayUpdate(Sender: TObject);
begin
  (Sender as TAction).Enabled := (not FRecording) and assigned(FMacro);
end;
```

The macro command is just like every other command stored on the undo stack. If its operation is undone at a later time, the command that's stored on the stack is destroyed. This would also invalidate the `FMacro` field (it would point to an unallocated area of memory), which could cause all kinds of problems. To prevent that, the code creates a copy of the command by calling its `Clone` function. I'll return to the cloning implementation in a moment, but first I have to show you one last missing piece of the macro implementation.

You now know how macros are stored and replayed, but nowhere have I shown you how commands are added to the `FMacro` command. This is done in the `Execute` method of the main form, which can optionally make a copy of the command being executed and store this copy in the `FMacro` command, as shown in the following code:

```
procedure TfrmCommand.Execute(command: TCommand);
begin
  if FRecording then
    FMacro.Add(command.Clone);
  ActiveEditor.Execute(command);
end;
```

Again, the cloning mechanism is used to create a copy of the command.

There are three `Execute` methods inside the `TfrmCommand` form, the `TEditor` invoker, and all of the commands based on `TCommand`. This is slightly confusing, so be careful when you read or modify the program.

Cloning

The last unexplored part of the program is the mechanism for creating copies of command objects (cloning). In this program, I went for a simple solution where each class implements the virtual function known as `Clone`, which knows how to create a perfect copy of the object. The following code fragment shows the implementation of this for four command classes:

```
function TCommand.Clone: TCommand;
begin
  Result := TCommand.Create(Receiver);
end;

function TUndoableCommand.Clone: TCommand;
begin
  Result := TUndoableCommand.Create(Receiver);
end;

function TKeyPressCommand.Clone: TCommand;
begin
  Result := TKeyPressCommand.Create(Receiver, FKey);
end;

function TDeleteLeftCommand.Clone: TCommand;
begin
  Result := TDeleteLeftCommand.Create(Receiver);
end;
```

In each class, the `Clone` function creates an object of the same type and sets its parameters.

Only the more complicated cloning method creates a copy of the `TMacroCommand` object. As we can see in the following code, it must create a copy of the command itself and then fill the command list of the new command with copies of all of the commands that are stored inside the current macro object:

```
function TMacroCommand.Clone: TCommand;
var
  cmd: TCommand;
begin
  Result := TMacroCommand.Create(Receiver);
  for cmd in FCommands do
    TMacroCommand(Result).Add(cmd.Clone);
end;
```

State

The last pattern in this chapter, state, allows an object to change its behavior on demand. This is especially useful when an object implements an algorithm that goes through different execution states. If the object's internal behavior changes when its state is changed, you've got an excellent candidate for a state pattern.

 Any vending machine follows the state pattern. The behavior of a machine when the customer presses the buttons to select a certain product depends on the current state. If the customer has already paid for the product, the machine will deliver the merchandise. Otherwise, it will only display the cost of the product.

This Gang of Four pattern can only be used in rare occasions. A typical candidate for the introduction of this pattern is an object that implements some kind of state machine. Standard examples include TCP socket management, line encryption, text file parsers, and the implementation of painting tools.

 For more information about state machines, see the Finite-state machine entry in Wikipedia (`https://en.wikipedia.org/wiki/Finite-state_machine`).

The last example is particularly interesting because, at first glance, it doesn't seem to include a changing state. There is, however, a behavior change connected to clicking the mouse buttons. If the user just moves the mouse around, nothing happens (besides the mouse cursor moving around the screen, of course). If, however, the user first clicks and holds the mouse button, the painting application enters a different state and starts drawing on the screen.

To implement a state pattern, we have to move all state-specific functions out of a class into a state object. Then, we implement multiple state objects, one for each possible state of the object. The main object then delegates state-specific functions to the current state object and recreates the state object on each state change.

The main motivation behind the state pattern lies in code organization. Without this pattern, the main object contains all state-specific behavior and uses lots of `case` or `if` statements to execute the appropriate behavior for the current state. After the introduction of this pattern, each state object contains only the code specific to one state and no `case` or `if` statements are needed to select the appropriate behavior.

Unquoting a string

The following example shows two implementations of some code that *unquotes* a string a classical implementation and an implementation with a state pattern.

A quoted string starts and ends with a double-quote character ("). Any occurrence of a double-quote character in a string is represented by two occurrences of that character. The following table shows a few examples of strings that have been converted into a quoted form:

String	Quoted string
Delphi	"Delphi"
Delphi and patterns	"Delphi and patterns"
Delphi "ROCKS!"	"Delphi ""Rocks!"""

An unquoting algorithm takes the quoted string (for example, `"quoted ""quoted"""`) and converts it into its original form (`quoted "quoted"`). Its behavior can be represented with the following state diagram:

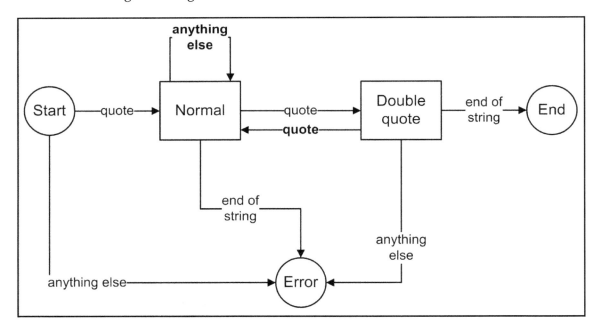

State diagram for unquoting a string

The object always starts in a Start state. A character is then read from the input. If the character is a quote character, the object changes to a Normal state. Otherwise, the input does not represent a quoted string and the converter should report an error.

While in the Normal state, the object reads the next character. If an end of string is encountered, the string is not terminated with a double quote and an error is reported. If the character is not a double quote, the object stays in the same state and copies the character to the output. If the character **is** a double quote, then the code doesn't know what to do. It could have reached the end of the string or a " " combination in the middle of the string. To resolve this, the state is changed to a double quote.

In the double quote state, the next character is read. If an end of string is reached, the state is changed to End and conversion is completed. If the character is a double quote, the code has found a " " combination, a single " character is written to the output and the state changes back to Normal. In all other cases, the input string is invalid. For example, the `Delphi Pattern` string should cause such an error because the middle " character is not duplicated.

The `State` project from the `State` folder implements this algorithm in two different ways. The `UnqoteString.Classical` unit, which I'll explore first, uses a classical parser mess to parse the string. This unit exposes the following public function:

```
function Unquote(const s: string): string;
var
  reader: TStringStream;
  writer: TStringStream;
begin
  reader := TStringStream.Create(s);
  try
    writer := TStringStream.Create('');
    try
      UnquoteStr(reader, writer);
      Result := writer.DataString;
    finally
      FreeAndNil(writer);
    end;
  finally
    FreeAndNil(reader);
  end;
end;
```

The Unquote function merely represents a wrapper that allows the parser to treat the input and output string as a stream. The real work is done in the UnquoteStr function, as shown in the following code:

```
procedure UnquoteStr(reader, writer: TStringStream);
type
  TState = (stStart, stNormal, stQuote, stEnd);
var
  next : string;
  state: TState;
begin
  state := stStart;
  while state <> stEnd do
  begin
    next := reader.ReadString(1);
    case state of
      stStart:
        begin
          if next = '"' then
            state := stNormal
          else
            InvalidString;
        end;
      stNormal:
        begin
          if next = '"' then
            state := stQuote
          else if next <> '' then
            writer.WriteString(next)
          else
            InvalidString;
        end;
      stQuote:
        begin
          if next = '' then
            state := stEnd
          else if next = '"' then
          begin
            writer.WriteString('"');
            state := stNormal;
          end
          else
            InvalidString;
        end;
      stEnd:
        begin
          raise Exception.Create('UnqouteStr: Internal error');
        end;
```

```
    end; //case state
  end; // while
end;
```

The code works exactly how we described it. It starts in the `stState` state, reads characters, and moves to the appropriate state according to the input. To understand the code, you only have to know that the `ReadString(1)` function returns one character from the input stream or an empty string when the end of the stream is reached.

 The helper function, `InvalidString` merely raises an exception.

Even in this simple example, the `UnquoteStr` method looks like a mess. The `If` and `case` statements are all interlocked into unreadable code. Truth be told, we could separate the behavior for each separate state into its own method, but that would only solve one half of the problem. The true order comes from the implementation of the state pattern, as in the `UnquoteString.State` unit.

In this version, the unquoting functionality is implemented in the `TUnquoter` class, which is defined as follows:

```
type
  TUnquoter = class
  strict private
    FState: TUnquoteState;
  strict protected
    function GetState: TState;
    procedure Update(const input: string; var output: string;
      var newState: TState);
    procedure SetState(const value: TState);
    property State: TState read GetState write SetState;
  public
    destructor Destroy; override;
    procedure Unquote(reader, writer: TStringStream);
  end;
```

The input and output streams are again prepared in the `Unquote` function, which you can check in the code.

All state-specific behavior is moved to descendants of the base state class, `TUnquoteState`, which is implemented as follows:

```
type
  TState = (stStart, stNormal, stQuote, stEnd);

  TUnquoteState = class
  strict private
    FState: TState;
  protected
    procedure RaiseInvalidString;
  public
    constructor Create(const state: TState);
    procedure Update(const input: string; var output: string;
      var newState: TState); virtual;
    property State: TState read FState;
  end;

constructor TUnquoteState.Create(const state: TState);
begin
  inherited Create;
  FState := state;
end;

procedure TUnquoteState.RaiseInvalidString;
begin
  raise Exception.Create('Invalid quoted string');
end;

procedure TUnquoteState.Update(const input: string; var output: string;
  var newState: TState);
begin
  output := '';
  newState := State;
end;
```

Each state class knows which state it represents (the `State` property) and can process an input in the `Update` procedure. This procedure also optionally produces `output` (which will be copied to the output stream) and tells the caller what the next state should be (`newState`).

Leaving the implementation of state objects aside for a moment, we can now look into the implementation of the unquoting process in the `TUnquoter` class. As we can see in the following code, the `Unquote` procedure is extremely simple if we compare it to the previously shown `UnquoteStr`:

```
procedure TUnquoter.Unquote(reader, writer: TStringStream);
var
  emit: string;
  newState: TState;
begin
  State := stStart;
  while State <> stEnd do
  begin
    FState.Update(reader.ReadString(1), emit, newState);
    if emit <> '' then
      writer.WriteString(emit);
    State := newState;
  end;
end;
```

The code starts in the `stState` state. Then, for each character from the input stream, it calls the `Update` method on the current state object. If this method produces any data, it is written to the output stream. State is then changed to the new state. Simple, effective, and to the point!

The state-changing magic happens inside the setter for the `State` property. When `State` is written to, the `SetState` setter is called. In this setter, the state object is recreated if the state is changed, as follows:

```
procedure TUnquoter.SetState(const value: TState);
begin
  if assigned(FState) and (FState.State = value) then
    Exit;
  FreeAndNil(FState);
  case value of
    stStart: FState := TStartState.Create(value);
    stNormal: FState := TNormalState.Create(value);
    stQuote: FState := TQuoteState.Create(value);
    stEnd: FState := TEndState.Create(value);
  end;
end;
```

The state-handling logic is now split into four classes. Each handles one possible state. The class definitions are shown in the following code:

```
type
  TStartState = class(TUnquoteState)
  public
    procedure Update(const input: string; var output: string;
      var newState: TState); override;
  end;

  TNormalState = class(TUnquoteState)
  public
    procedure Update(const input: string; var output: string;
      var newState: TState); override;
  end;

  TQuoteState = class(TUnquoteState)
  public
    procedure Update(const input: string; var output: string;
      var newState: TState); override;
  end;

  TEndState = class(TUnquoteState)
  public
    procedure Update(const input: string; var output: string;
      var newState: TState); override;
  end;
```

Implementation of the Update method inside each state object is now easy for understand. The stState state can only move to the stNormal state or raise an error, as shown here:

```
procedure TStartState.Update(const input: string; var output: string;
  var newState: TState);
begin
  inherited;
  if input = '"' then
    newState := stNormal
  else
    RaiseInvalidString;
end;
```

The call to inherited initializes output to an empty string and newState to the current state.

A `stNormal` state can either move to the `stQuote` state, output a character, or raise an exception, as follows:

```
procedure TNormalState.Update(const input: string; var output: string;
  var newState: TState);
begin
  inherited;
  if input = '"' then
    newState := stQuote
  else if input <> '' then
    output := input
  else
    RaiseInvalidString;
end;
```

The `stQuote` state can either move to the `stEnd` state, output a double quote **and** move to the `stNormal` state, or raise an exception, as shown in the following code:

```
procedure TQuoteState.Update(const input: string; var output: string;
  var newState: TState);
begin
  inherited;
  if input = '' then
    newState := stEnd
  else if input = '"' then
  begin
    output := '"';
    newState := stNormal;
  end
  else
    RaiseInvalidString;
end;
```

The `Update` method of the `stEnd` state should never be called. Any activation of this method indicates a programming error and the code reflects that, as shown in the following code:

```
procedure TEndState.Update(const input: string; var output: string;
  var newState: TState);
begin
  raise Exception.Create('TEndState.Update: Internal error');
end;
```

This results in a program that is easy to understand and simple to maintain.

Summary

This chapter provided an overview of four behavioral patterns. All of the patterns in this group help you to organize complex systems into well-behaved maintainable structures.

We opened up with a null object pattern. This simple pattern allows us to remove `if assigned(object)` tests from the code and replace them with a special do-nothing null version of the object. Although the concept behind this pattern is simple, the pattern itself can be very useful.

Next, we looked at the template method pattern. This pattern explains how to use object-oriented programming to design extensible and adaptable algorithms. We also demonstrated how we can solve such problems by using the concepts that were developed after the Gang of Four times.

The command pattern helps with organizing action-based programming. It tells us how to systematically convert actions into objects and how to separate the client code from the code that executes the action object. This flexible approach can be a base for the undo/redo mechanism, macro recording, scripting, and more.

Finally, we described the state pattern. This pattern explains how to organize objects that can change functionality according to an internal state. If your object implements a state machine, this is the pattern that you should use.

In the next chapter, we will stay on topic and look into four more behavioral patterns, which are Iterator, Visitor, Observer, and Memento.

Iterator, Visitor, Observer, and Memento

7

When your task is writing code that is simple to maintain and test, you strive away from tightly connected parts that know too much about each other. The four patterns that will be described in this chapter will help you write complex code that interacts in different ways but is not interconnected in all possible—and impossible—ways in an unmanageable mess.

Two patterns from this chapter, iterator and observer, are, in my opinion, the two most important patterns from the Gang of Four collection. If you incorporate only two patterns into your code, let them be these two! They both help with decoupling parts of code and programming to the interface, not the implementation; two guidelines that will help you write maintainable code.

That doesn't mean that you should ignore other patterns from this chapter, or from this book! All patterns can be important—you just have to know when and how they should be used. Visitor and Memento are certainly no exception.

In this chapter, you will learn about the following:

- How to effectively access all data structures and how to write generic, structure-independent algorithms with the iterator pattern
- How to extend classes in accordance with the Open/Closed principle with the visitor pattern
- How to use the observer pattern to write loosely-coupled programs that react to changes in the business model
- How to store a state of a complex object in a separate container with the memento pattern

Iterator

An iterator pattern is used to traverse a container and access its elements. The power of this pattern is that it decouples algorithms from the container implementation. We can then write an algorithm that is coded to the iterator interface and not to the actual implementation of the container.

Let's say we have two completely different data structures, an array and a linked *list*. If we need to implement the same algorithm operating on both structures, we have to write two versions of the code. You would access an array with direct addressing and the other would walk the linked list.

On the other hand, if both the array and linked list implement the same interface that allows the algorithm to walk over the data and access all elements, we can write only one version of the algorithm. Instead of working with data structures directly, the algorithm would work with that interface.

 An *interface* in this context means any public interface (a set of methods). It doesn't have to be implemented with a Delphi interface mechanism.

Even if the code has no such needs and it always works with only one kind of a data structure, using an iterator pattern has its advantages. Using this pattern instead of accessing data elements directly leads to a cleaner code. A code that uses an iterator has no need to hardcode implementation details. A typical example in Delphi is code that iterates over some list, which usually starts as follows:

```
for i := 0 to list.Count - 1 do
```

This `for` loop depends on the fact that the first element in the list has index 0. Of course, that will never change in future Delphi versions, but it still seems wrong that we have to iterate *from* zero to count minus one instead of over all elements. As we'll see in this chapter, an iterator pattern helps with that.

 If you browse through TV channels by clicking the next channel button on a remote, you are using an iterator pattern.

An iterator can be external to the object or it can be implemented internally, inside the object. When we are creating a new data structure and we know what iteration interface we want to expose, it is best to implement it inside the data structure object. On the other hand, when adapting existing code, we typically write an interface as an external piece of code.

Special kinds of iterators, called **robust iterators**, allow the underlying data structure to change while an iterator is in use. As a rule of thumb, a typical iterator doesn't support such behavior and it is safer simply not to change the data structure while using an iterator. As far as I know, none of Delphi's built-in iterators are robust.

A special kind of iterator always returns no elements. It is called a **null iterator** and can, in some circumstances, be used to simplify the code.

 Besides being an *iterator*, a null iterator is also an example of a *null object* pattern, as covered in Chapter 6, *Nullable Object, Template Method, Command, State*.

Implementing an iterator pattern in code is not complicated. The example project HandMadeIterators in the Iterator folder shows two possible approaches, while the last section of this chapter, *Memento*, explores a third option.

The HandMadeIterators project defines the TDataContainer class, which is just a wrapper around a dynamic array of integers. This class, which is shown as follows, implements two different ways to enumerate its pattern:

```
type
  TDataContainer = class
  public type
    TIterateAction = reference to procedure (value: integer);
  strict private
    FData: TArray<integer>;
    FIndex: integer;
  public
    constructor Create(const data: TArray<integer>);
    procedure Iterate(action: TIterateAction);
    function GetFirst(var value: integer): boolean;
    function GetNext(var value: integer): boolean;
  end;
```

The first iterator is implemented as a method called `Iterate`, which accepts an anonymous method parameter. This anonymous method is called for each element in the data container, as shown here:

```
procedure TDataContainer.Iterate(action: TIterateAction);
var
  i: integer;
begin
  for i := Low(FData) to High(FData) do
    action(FData[i]);
end;
```

The caller of the Iterate method can actually work inside this anonymous method. The following code shows such an example:

```
procedure TfrmHandMade.btnIterateClick(Sender: TObject);
var
  data: TDataContainer;
begin
  data := TDataContainer.Create([1, 2, 3, 4, 5]);
  try
    data.Iterate(
      procedure (value: integer)
      begin
        lbLog.Items.Add(value.ToString);
      end);
  finally
    FreeAndNil(data);
  end;
end;
```

The second implementation uses two functions: `GetFirst` and `GetNext`. Both functions return `False` if there's no more data in the container and `True` (plus an element from the container) otherwise. The difference between them is that `GetFirst` starts iteration from the beginning and `GetNext` resumes from the last element. They are implemented as follows:

```
function TDataContainer.GetFirst(var value: integer): boolean;
begin
  FIndex := 0;
  Result := GetNext(value);
end;

function TDataContainer.GetNext(var value: integer): boolean;
begin
  Result := FIndex <= High(FData);
  if Result then begin
```

```
      value := FData[FIndex];
      Inc(FIndex);
    end;
  end;
```

The `HandMadeMain` unit contains an example of how such code can be used, as follows:

```
procedure TfrmHandMade.btnGetFirstClick(Sender: TObject);
var
  data: TDataContainer;
  element: Integer;
begin
  data := TDataContainer.Create([6, 7, 8, 9, 10]);
  try
    if data.GetFirst(element) then
      repeat
        lbLog.Items.Add(element.ToString)
      until not data.GetNext(element);
  finally
    FreeAndNil(data);
  end;
end;
```

Before using homegrown approaches, you should explore the idiomatic way that's built into Delphi—the `for..in` statement.

Delphi idioms – iterating with for..in

Since version 2005, Delphi supports a concept of iteration over containers. In this version, a classical `for..to` statement was extended with a `for..in` counterpart. It allows us to iterate over arrays, strings, sets, and any other data structure without referring to the implementation details. For example, the `for i := 0 to list.Count - 1 do` statement from the beginning of this chapter can be rewritten as follows:

```
for el in list do
  Process(el);
```

This code will execute the body of the `for` loop once for each element in the `list`. In each iteration, the `el` variable will be set to that element. This `for..in` loop is functionally equivalent to the following code:

```
for i := 0 to list.Count - 1 do
begin
  el := list[i];
  Process(el);
end;
```

The built-in Delphi iterators will always iterate from the lowest to highest index (such as in the previous example). This, however, doesn't need to be the case. An iterator could implement a different traversal order. For example, we could have an iterator that returns elements in order from the last to the first (although such an iterator is not part of Delphi RTL). It would be functionally equivalent to the following code:

```
for i := list.Count - 1 downto 0 do
begin
  el := list[i];
  Process(el);
end;
```

 When iterating over a binary tree data structure, we can usually select from (at least) three possible traversal orders: inorder (left subtree of a node is visited first, followed by the node itself and then the right subtree), preorder (parent node is visited first, left subtree next, and right subtree last), and postorder (left subtree is visited first, followed by the right subtree, and the parent node).

The `BuiltInIterators` project from the `Iterator` folder shows how we can use iterator patterns on some built-in data structures, namely arrays, strings, and sets.

This project shows two ways to iterate over an array. We can either use the implementation-specific knowledge and know that we can get the lowest and highest index of a dynamic array with a call to built-in `Low` and `High` functions, or we can use the `for..in` iteration, as in the following code:

```
procedure TfrmIterator.btnArrayClick(Sender: TObject);
var
  el: Integer;
  fib: TArray<Integer>;
  i: Integer;
begin
  fib := TArray<integer>.Create(1, 1, 2, 3, 5, 8, 13);

  Log('"Standard" array access');
```

```
  for i := Low(fib) to High(fib) do
    Log(fib[i].ToString);

  Log('Iterating over an array');
  for el in fib do
    Log(el.ToString);
end;
```

We can use this approach to iterate over static and dynamic arrays. The syntax is the same in both cases.

Similarly, we can iterate over all characters in a string. The following code shows how to do that with a standard `for` statement and with a `for..in` version:

```
procedure TfrmIterator.btnStringClick(Sender: TObject);
var
  ch: Char;
  s: string;
  i: Integer;
begin
  s := 'Delphi!';

  Log('"Standard" string access');
  for i := 1 to Length(s) do
    Log(s[i]);

  Log('Iterating over a string');
  for ch in s do
    Log(ch);
end;
```

In this case, using a standard `for` statement is even more bound to the implementation as strings in Delphi can start from 1 or from 0! (This weird design choice is controlled with the `{$ZEROBASEDSTRINGS}` compiler directive.)

The previous example shows how to iterate over a set. In this case, the `for..in` statement again simplifies the code a lot. As shown in the following, the standard `for` statement has to iterate over all elements in the TAlign enumeration and only display ones that are also present in the set. The `for..in` construct does all that internally, as follows:

```
procedure TfrmIterator.btnSetClick(Sender: TObject);
var
  align: TAlign;
  alignSet: TAlignSet;
begin
  alignSet := [alLeft, alRight, alTop, alBottom];
```

```
      Log('"Standard" set access');
      for align := Low(TAlign) to High(TAlign) do
        if align in alignSet then
          Log(AlignName(align));

      Log('Iteration over a set');
      for align in alignSet do
        Log(AlignName(align));
    end;
```

The enumeration over the three types of built-in data that I have just shown are implemented by the compiler. We can, however, add iterator support to any data structure. We only have to implement a few simple functions.

Implementing custom enumerators

If we want to add iterator support to a data structure, we have to implement a **public** method called GetEnumerator. This method must return either a class, interface, or a record. Let's call this returned value an enumerator.

The enumerator must implement one function and one property. Both must be declared **public**. The function must be named MoveNext and it must return a boolean result. The for..in loop uses this method to move to the next element in the container and to check whether there are more elements in the container.

The enumerator property must be called Current and it must return the current element in the container (however, the enumerator defines what current is). Usually it is implemented by calling the GetCurrent method (which you also have to write), but that is not a requirement.

 All iterators for Delphi RTL data structures (except the three we have already shown) are implemented in this way.

With this infrastructure in place, the compiler converts the `for..in` statement into a simple while loop. If we have data structure called `collection`, which contains an element of type `T`, the compiler-generated code will be equivalent to the following code fragment:

```
var
  element: T;

enumerator := collection.GetEnumerator;
try
  while enumerator.MoveNext do
  begin
    element := enumerator.Current;
    // process 'element' in the body of the for..in loop
  end
finally
  enumerator.Free;
end
```

The last part, `enumerator.Free`, is only generated if the enumerator is implemented as a class.

An important point that we can derive from this template, and which determines how an enumerator is implemented, is that `MoveNext` is called once before the first data element is accessed. In the following examples, we'll see how this affects the implementation.

 There is also another, even simpler way to add iterator support to a data container. Implement a function (`ToArray`, for example) that returns a dynamic array containing all elements from the data container. As Delphi knows how to iterate over arrays, you can then use a fragment like this to iterate over your container: `for el in container.ToArray do`. This is a perfectly valid solution if the container always stores only a small number of elements.

Using an iterator interface

If we want to write a generic version of an algorithm, one that is not bound to a data structure but to an iterator pattern, we have to somehow pass the iterator pattern to the algorithm.

In the 2005 release, Delphi defined interfaces `IEnumerable` and `IEnumerator`. They can be found in the System unit and are defined as follows:

```
type
  IEnumerator = interface(IInterface)
    function GetCurrent: TObject;
    function MoveNext: Boolean;
    procedure Reset;
    property Current: TObject read GetCurrent;
  end;

  IEnumerable = interface(IInterface)
    function GetEnumerator: IEnumerator;
  end;
```

We can write an algorithm that uses either `IEnumerable` or `IEnumerator`, but then we always have to convert the `Current` property to appropriate data type. This is clumsy, so with the introduction of generics, we also got the generic versions of these interfaces, which are shown as follows:

```
type
  IEnumerator<T> = interface(IEnumerator)
    function GetCurrent: T;
    property Current: T read GetCurrent;
  end;

  IEnumerable<T> = interface(IEnumerable)
    function GetEnumerator: IEnumerator<T>;
  end;
```

At first glance this looks perfect, but as soon as we try to implement `IEnumerator<T>`, we also have to implement `IEnumerator`. To do that, we have to write two `GetCurrent` functions and we cannot use the overloading mechanism (the `overload` keyword) for that because they both have same parameters (none). So, what can we do to resolve this conundrum?

The `CustomIterators.TextFile.IEnumerable` unit from the `CustomIterators` project shows one possible solution. This unit implements an iterator that walks over a text file and returns lines of text, one by one. The only public part of that unit, function `TextFileContentI`, takes a file name and returns an `IEnumerable<string>`, as follows:

```
function TextFileContentI(const fileName: string): IEnumerable<string>;
```

As IEnumerable<string> implements a GetEnumerator function, we can use this result in a for..in loop. The main unit executes the following code if you click the File IEnumerable button:

```
procedure TfrmIterator.btnFileInterfaceClick(Sender: TObject);
var
  line: string;
begin
  Log('Content of "CustomIterators.dpr":');
  for line in TextFileContentI('..\..\CustomIterators.dpr') do
    Log(line);
end;
```

The IEnumerable<string> interface is implemented in the TTextFileEnumerator class, which is defined as follows:

```
type
  TTextFileEnumeratorBase = class(TInterfacedObject, IEnumerable,
                                                     IEnumerator)
  public
    function GetEnumerator: IEnumerator; virtual; abstract;
    function GetCurrent: TObject; virtual; abstract;
    function MoveNext: Boolean; virtual; abstract;
    procedure Reset; virtual; abstract;
    property Current: TObject read GetCurrent;
  end;

  TTextFileEnumerator = class(TTextFileEnumeratorBase, IEnumerable<string>,
                                                       IEnumerator<string>)
  strict private
    FReader: TStreamReader;
    FLine: string;
  public
    constructor Create(const fileName: string);
    destructor Destroy; override;
    function GetEnumerator: IEnumerator<string>;
    function GetCurrent: string; reintroduce;
    function MoveNext: boolean; override;
    procedure Reset; override;
    property Current: string read GetCurrent;
  end;
```

The implementations of the IEnumerator and IEnumerable methods and properties (we'll see soon why we need both) were put into the TTextFileEnumeratorBase class. As they are actually never used, they are marked as virtual; abstract; so that we don't have to implement them. All actual code is implemented in the TTextFileEnumerator class, which is derived from TTextFileEnumeratorBase.

Let's start with the GetEnumerator function. It simply returns Self, as shown here:

```
function TTextFileEnumerator.GetEnumerator: IEnumerator<string>;
begin
  Result := Self;
end;
```

In this example, one class implements both parts of iterator support: the GetEnumerator function and actual enumerator. We can do that because both are implemented as an interface. If we were to implement the iterator support with classes (as we will in the following example), this trick would not work.

The actual enumeration work is done in the MoveNext method. It uses an internal TStreamReader class to read data from the input line by line and stores each line read in the internal FLine field. The GetCurrent method then simply returns the contents of the FLine field. The important parts of the code are shown as follows:

```
constructor TTextFileEnumerator.Create(const fileName: string);
begin
  inherited Create;
  FReader := TStreamReader.Create(fileName, true);
end;

function TTextFileEnumerator.GetCurrent: string;
begin
  Result := FLine;
end;

function TTextFileEnumerator.MoveNext: boolean;
begin
  Result := not FReader.EndOfStream;
  if Result then
    FLine := FReader.ReadLine;
end;
```

As we have seen before, the compiler guarantees that MoveNext will be called once before the Current property is accessed so that we always have the correct initial state in the FLine field.

TIP Keep in mind that the code can access the `Current` property multiple times for one element, so `GetCurrent` should never change the internal state of the enumerator. The safe way is to always do all the work in the `MoveNext` method and just read data from the internal field in the `GetCurrent` function.

Since Delphi 2009, when generics were introduced, we got a better and simpler way of working with generic iterators. The `TEnumerable<T>` and `TEnumerator<T>` classes are defined in the `System.Generics.Collections` unit as follows:

```
type
  TEnumerator<T> = class abstract
  protected
    function DoGetCurrent: T; virtual; abstract;
    function DoMoveNext: Boolean; virtual; abstract;
  public
    property Current: T read DoGetCurrent;
    function MoveNext: Boolean;
  end;

  TEnumerable<T> = class abstract
  private
    function ToArrayImpl(Count: Integer): TArray<T>; // used by descendants
  protected
    function DoGetEnumerator: TEnumerator<T>; virtual; abstract;
  public
    destructor Destroy; override;
    function GetEnumerator: TEnumerator<T>;
    function ToArray: TArray<T>; virtual;
  end;
```

The implementation in `CustomIterators.TextFile.TEnumerable` allows us to iterate over text file lines with the following code:

```
procedure TfrmIterator.btnFileObjectClick(Sender: TObject);
var
  line: string;
begin
  Log('Content of "CustomIterators.dpr":');
  for line in TextFileContentO('..\..\CustomIterators.dpr') do
    Log(line);
end;
```

As you can see, it is completely the same as the previous example, which used the `TextFileContentI` function. The implementation is, however, quite different. As the following code fragment shows, `TextFileContentO` returns a record that implements a `GetEnumerator` function:

```
type
  TTextFileContentO = record
  private
    FFileName: string;
  public
    constructor Create(fileName: string);
    function GetEnumerator: TEnumerator<string>;
  end;

function TextFileContentO(fileName: string): TTextFileContentO;
```

The `for line in TextFileContentO(...)` statement works like this:

1. The `TextFileContentO` function is evaluated. It returns a record. Records are a static data type (they are stored on the stack) and therefore we don't have to care about their life cycle (we don't have to explicitly destroy them).
2. The compiler sees the returned `TTextFileContentO` record and implements a `GetEnumerator` function, so it calls that function and uses the resulting object for enumeration.
3. At the end of enumeration, the object is destroyed.

Instead of showing the rest of the code here, which would be pretty much uninteresting as the code is almost the same as in the `IEnumerator<T>` example, I'll instead show you how to construct an iterator over a built-in data type.

If we want to use a built-in data type (for example, an array) in a generic algorithm, we have to write our own iterator. The array itself doesn't implement either an `IEnumerable` interface or a `TEnumerable` class. (The code that is generated by the compiler when we use `for..in` with an array does not follow the enumeration template that I showed previously.) We have to implement such an iterator ourselves.

The demonstration program shows how to add `TEnumerator<T>` support to a dynamic array, `TArray<T>`. We can then use this enumerator (instead of the built-in version) with the following code:

```
procedure TfrmIterator.btnArrayClick(Sender: TObject);
var
  dynArray: TArray<integer>;
  el: Integer;
```

```
begin
  dynArray := [1, 1, 2, 3, 5, 8, 13];

  Log('Content of a dynamic array:');
  for el in ArrayEnum.Enum<integer>(dynArray) do
    Log(el.ToString);
end;
```

This doesn't make sense by itself, of course, as we could simply write `for el in dynArray do`, but it will be useful later when we pass an array to a generic algorithm.

To implement this support, the `CustomIterators.DynArray` unit implements a record called `ArrayEnum` with one function, `Enum<T>`, as follows:

```
type
  ArrayEnum = record
  public
    class function Enum<T>(const data: TArray<T>): TArrayEnumerable<T>;
      static;
  end;
```

This complication is required because Delphi doesn't allow us to write a generic global function. The `Enum<T>` function simply creates a `TArrayEnumerable<T>` record, as follows:

```
type
  TArrayEnumerable<T> = record
  private
    FData: TArray<T>;
  public
    constructor Create(const data: TArray<T>);
    function GetEnumerator: TEnumerator<T>;
  end;

class function ArrayEnum.Enum<T>(const data: TArray<T>):
  TArrayEnumerable<T>;
begin
  Result := TArrayEnumerable<T>.Create(data);
end;
```

The `TArrayEnumerable<T>` record simply stores away the input data in the constructor and creates an instance of the `TArrayEnumerator<T>` object in `GetEnumerator`, as follows:

```
type
  TArrayEnumerator<T> = class(TEnumerator<T>)
  private
    FData: TArray<T>;
    FCurrent: integer;
  protected
    function DoGetCurrent: T; override;
    function DoMoveNext: Boolean; override;
  public
    constructor Create(const data: TArray<T>);
  end;

constructor TArrayEnumerable<T>.Create(const data: TArray<T>);
begin
  FData := data;
end;

function TArrayEnumerable<T>.GetEnumerator: TEnumerator<T>;
begin
  Result := TArrayEnumerator<T>.Create(FData);
end;
```

The actual enumeration support is implemented partially in the built-in `TEnumerator<T>` and partially in the derived class, `TArrayEnumerable<T>`, as shown here:

```
constructor TArrayEnumerator<T>.Create(const data: TArray<T>);
begin
  inherited Create;
  FData := data;
  FCurrent := -1;
end;

function TArrayEnumerator<T>.DoGetCurrent: T;
begin
  Result := FData[FCurrent];
end;

function TArrayEnumerator<T>.DoMoveNext: Boolean;
begin
  Result := FCurrent < High(FData);
  if Result then
    Inc(FCurrent);
end;
```

We don't have to implement a `Current` property and a `MoveNext` function as they are already defined in the `TEnumerator<T>` class. Instead of that, we have to implement `DoGetCurrent` and `DoMoveNext`, which are called from `TEnumerator<T>`, as shown here:

```
type
  TEnumerator<T> = class abstract
  protected
    function DoGetCurrent: T; virtual; abstract;
    function DoMoveNext: Boolean; virtual; abstract;
  public
    property Current: T read DoGetCurrent;
    function MoveNext: Boolean;
  end;

function TEnumerator<T>.MoveNext: Boolean;
begin
  Result := DoMoveNext;
end;
```

Again, we took into account that `DoMoveNext` (called from `TEnumerator<T>.MoveNext`) is called once before the first element is accessed. That's why `FCurrent` is initialized to -1.

When we want to use this enumerator in code, we can accept `TEnumerable<T>` or `TEnumerator<T>`. The choice in this example was simple, as the code in `CustomIterators.DynArray` doesn't implement `TEnumerable<T>`, just `TEnumerator<T>`.

The main unit `CustomIteratorsMain` implements a method, `GenericEnum`, that walks over a `TEnumerator<string>` supporting data structure. This method skips every second element and logs the rest to the screen, as follows:

```
procedure TfrmIterator.GenericEnum(enumerator: TEnumerator<string>);
begin
  while enumerator.MoveNext do
  begin
    Log(enumerator.Current);

    // skip every second line
    if not enumerator.MoveNext then
      break; //while
  end;
end;
```

When you click the `Generic TEnumerable` button, this code is called twice. The first time it iterates over a file and the second time over a dynamic array. The code is shown here:

```
procedure TfrmIterator.btnGenericClick(Sender: TObject);
var
  dynArray: TArray<string>;
  enumerator: TEnumerator<string>;
begin
  enumerator := TextFileContentO('..\..\CustomIterators.dpr')
                  .GetEnumerator;
  try
    GenericEnum(enumerator);
  finally
    FreeAndNil(enumerator);
  end;

  dynArray := ['D', 'e', 'l', 'p', 'h', 'i', '!'];
  enumerator := ArrayEnum.Enum<string>(dynArray).GetEnumerator;
  try
    GenericEnum(enumerator);
  finally
    FreeAndNil(enumerator);
  end;
end;
```

The result of executing this code is shown in the following screenshot:

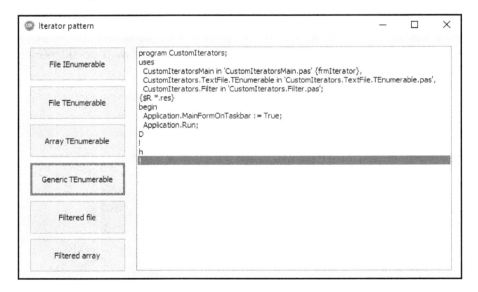

Logging every second line of a file and every second element of an array

This example program also implements a filter enumerator. This type of enumerator wraps around another enumerator (a source) and only returns some elements from the source enumerator. In other words, it acts as a filter.

A `Filter` record in the `CustomIterators.Filter` unit accepts any enumerator and a filtering function, and returns a `TEnumerable<T>` that only returns elements for which the `filter` function returns `True`, as follows:

```
type
  Filter = record
    class function Process<T>(source: TEnumerator<T>;
      const filter: TFilterFunc<T>): TFilterEnumerable<T>; static;
  end;
```

The main program demonstrates how to use this enumerator to display every second line from a file, as follows:

```
procedure TfrmIterator.btnFilterFileClick(Sender: TObject);
var
  line: string;
  enumerator: TEnumerator<string>;
  oddFilter: TFilterFunc<string>;
begin
  // allow even-indexed elements; first element has index = 0
  oddFilter :=
    function (index: integer; const item: string): boolean
    begin
      Result := not Odd(index);
    end;

  enumerator := TextFileContentO('..\..\CustomIterators.dpr')
              .GetEnumerator;
  try
    Log('Filtered content of a file:');
    for line in Filter.Process<string>(enumerator, oddFilter) do
      Log(line);
  finally
    FreeAndNil(enumerator);
  end;
end;
```

The code uses the already familiar function `TextFileContentO` to create an enumerable record and then calls its `GetEnumerator` function to create the actual enumerator. As the enumerator is implemented as a normal Delphi class, we also have to destroy it later, in the `finally` statement. This enumerator is then passed to the `Filter.Process<string>` function together with an anonymous method that filters out odd-numbered lines.

The implementation of the filter enumerator closely follows the pattern from `CustomFilters.DynArray`, so it is not included in this book. I will only point out one method, namely `DoMoveNext`, which is shown here:

```
function TFilterEnumerator<T>.DoMoveNext: Boolean;
begin
  repeat
    Result := FSource.MoveNext;
    if not Result then
      break;
    Inc(FIndex);
  until FFilter(FIndex, Current);
end;
```

In this example, `DoMoveNext` calls the `MoveNext` function of the enumerator that was passed to the `Filter.Process<T>` function (for example, `FSource`). As we don't want to return all elements, the code must loop until there is no more data in the source enumerator or until the `FFilter` filtering function returns `True`.

Visitor

The iterator pattern shows us how to separate the internal structure of a data container from the code that operates on it. A visitor pattern is similar in topic, but applies not so much to composite data as to composite objects. It shows how to implement an algorithm/object separation, which allows us to add new operations to existing objects without modifying their structure. As such, it represents a good example of the Open/Closed principle in practice.

In classical object-oriented code, a part of code (an algorithm) would take an object, inspect its internal structure, and operate on its parts. If we use the visitor pattern, this approach is turned on its head. The algorithm merely passes a method to the object and kindly asks it to execute that method on its constituent parts.

 After you enter a city sightseeing bus, you have no longer control over your transportation. The bus driver drives you from one attraction to another and on each stop allows you to perform an action (take some photos).

To implement this pattern, the composite object implements a method (typically called `Accept`), which accepts a visitor object. The code then calls a special method of the visitor object (typically called `Visit`) on each part of the composite object.

While the visitor pattern doesn't work without the proper implementation of the `Accept` method, we only have to implement it once. If we need to add new functionality, we just create a new visitor class and put new functionality there. We only have to update the `Accept` method if internal implementation of the composite model is changed.

If the composite object contains only a list of child objects, the visitor pattern functions pretty much as an iterator in disguise. With an iterator, we would write code like so:

```
for element in DataStructure do
  Process(element);
```

With the visitor pattern, we create a new visitor, which implements a `Visit` method, similar to the following code fragment:

```
procedure TVisitor.Visit(element: T);
begin
  Process(element);
end;
```

Next, we pass this visitor to the composite object, as shown here:

```
var
  visitor: TVisitor;

visitor := TVisitor.Create;
DataStructure.Accept(visitor);
```

This looks like a complicated way to traverse a data structure—and in a way it is. The visitor pattern was designed to iterate over composite objects that contain children objects of many different types. When traversing such hierarchies with a classical iterator, we would have to write code similar to the following:

```
for element in DataStructure do
  if element is ChildType1 then
    DoSomething(ChildType1(element))
  else if element is ChildType2 then
    DoSomethingElse(ChildType2(element))
  else
    . . .
```

As we've seen in the section on the *command* pattern in `Chapter 6`, *Nullable Object, Template Method, Command, State*, such if ladders are hard to understand and maintain. A visitor pattern simplifies such code in a manner similar to the command pattern. We only have write a specific `Visit` method for each data type and the `Accept` method does the rest. If we reimplement the previous example with a visitor, the result would look like this:

```
procedure TVisitor.Visit(element: ChildType1);
begin
  DoSomething(element);
end;

procedure TVisitor.Visit(element: ChildType2);
begin
  DoSomethingElse(element);
end;
```

This makes the visitor pattern the perfect tool when we work with a complex model. A typical example of such a pattern is implementing an export of internal rich text representation into multiple formats, for example, HTML, RTF, plain text, and so on. Another use can be found in drawing programs, which can use this pattern to export the drawing into any of supported file formats.

To demonstrate the use of the visitor pattern, I have revisited the *Composite* project from `Chapter 4`, *Composite, Flyweight, Marker Interface, Bridge*. In this example program, I have implemented a simple object model that handles configurable computer configuration. We used it to build a model of a computer with chassis, motherboard, CPU, memory, and a few other parts.

From that model, I borrowed the `CompositeSafety` unit, renamed it to `ComponentModel`, and improved it with a visitor pattern support. The demonstration project is named `Visitor` and is stored in the `Visitor` folder.

The `ComponentModel` unit implements a model for a configurable configuration. Each hardware component is represented with a subclass of the base class `TComponent`. The base class is never created. Instead, the code creates objects of the `TBasicComponent` and `TConfigurableComponent` classes.

The former represents a fixed component that cannot be configured with subcomponents, while the latter represents a configurable component that can contain any number of subcomponents of the TComponent type. The full declaration of all three classes is shown as follows:

```
type
  IVisitor = interface;

  TComponent = class
  strict private
    FName: string;
    FPrice: real;
  public
    constructor Create(const AName: string; const APrice: real);
    procedure Accept(const visitor: IVisitor); virtual; abstract;
    function Components: TArray<TComponent>; virtual;
    function TotalPrice: real; virtual;
    property Name: string read FName write FName;
    property Price: real read FPrice write FPrice;
  end;

  TConfigurableComponent = class(TComponent)
  strict private
    FComponents: TObjectList<TComponent>;
  public
    procedure Accept(const visitor: IVisitor); override;
    procedure AfterConstruction; override;
    procedure BeforeDestruction; override;
    procedure Add(component: TComponent);
    function Components: TArray<TComponent>; override;
    function TotalPrice: real; override;
  end;

  TBasicComponent = class(TComponent)
  public
    procedure Accept(const visitor: IVisitor); override;
  end;
```

The base class implements properties that allow the naming of the component (Name) and the setting of a price for the component (Price). We can also get the total price for the component with all subcomponents (TotalPrice) and access all subcomponents (Components). In addition, TConfigurableComponent allows for the addtion of new subcomponents (Add).

All of this allows us to create a computer configuration in code, as in the following example:

```
procedure TfrmVisitor.FormCreate(Sender: TObject);
var
  motherboard: TConfigurableComponent;
begin
  FComputer := TConfigurableComponent.Create('chassis', 37.9);
  FComputer.Add(TBasicComponent.Create('PSU', 34.6));

  motherboard := TConfigurableComponent.Create('motherboard', 96.5);
  motherboard.Add(TBasicComponent.Create('CPU', 121.1));
  motherboard.Add(TBasicComponent.Create('memory', 88.2));
  motherboard.Add(TBasicComponent.Create('memory', 88.2));
  motherboard.Add(TBasicComponent.Create('graphics', 179));

  FComputer.Add(motherboard);
end;
```

To support the visitor pattern, all three classes implement the `Accept` method. As the instances of the base class are never created, `TComponent.Accept` is marked as `abstract`. That saves us from writing a method that is never used and also helps to catch programming errors. If the code somehow manages to call `TComponent.Accept`, an `EAbstractError` exception is raised.

The `Accept` method accepts a visitor parameter of type `IVisitor`. As this visitor has to be able to work with two different subclasses, it needs two overridden `Visit`, methods as shown here:

```
type
  IVisitor = interface ['{147411D4-2555-4174-9923-5AD6B0D91F5D}']
    procedure Visit(component: TConfigurableComponent); overload;
    procedure Visit(component: TBasicComponent); overload;
  end;
```

As I have said before, we don't have to follow Gang of Four definitions to the letter. Although the original visitor pattern specifies that a visitor is an object, a Delphi implementation will frequently be simpler if we implement it as an interface.

The implementation of both `Accept` methods is very simple. The `TBasicComponent` cannot contain any subcomponents and therefore just calls the `visitor` parameter, providing itself as an object, as follows:

```
procedure TBasicComponent.Accept(const visitor: IVisitor);
begin
  visitor.Visit(Self);
end;
```

The `TConfigurableComponent` has a more complex job. Firstly, it visits itself and then recursively calls the `Accept` method on all subcomponents, passing the same visitor as a parameter. The code is shown here:

```
procedure TConfigurableComponent.Accept(const visitor: IVisitor);
var
  component: TComponent;
begin
  visitor.Visit(Self);
  for component in Components do
    component.Accept(visitor);
end;
```

With this implementation, `Accept` recursively walks over the object structure and calls `visitor.Visit` for each object.

The demonstration program contains two buttons. The `Apply discount` button applies 5% discount to basic components and 10% to configurable components, while the Raise prices button raises all prices by 10 units. As shown in the following code, both buttons also log the updated configuration:

```
procedure TfrmVisitor.btnDiscountClick(Sender: TObject);
begin
  FComputer.Accept(TDiscountVisitor.Create(5, 10));

  lbLog.Items.Add(
    'Applied 5% discount to basic and 10% to configurable components');
  LogConfiguration;
end;

procedure TfrmVisitor.btnRaiseClick(Sender: TObject);
begin
  FComputer.Accept(TRaiseVisitor.Create(10));

  lbLog.Items.Add(
    'Raising prices of components by 10 units');
  LogConfiguration;
end;
```

The real job is done in both visitors, `TDiscountVisitor` and `TRaiseVisitor`. As the `Accept` method expects an `IVisitor` parameter, we can just create a visitor object on the fly and pass it to the method. Delphi will treat it as an interface and destroy it when the `OnClick` event handler exits.

Both visitors are implemented in a similar manner. The constructor stores the configuration parameters while the `Visit` methods operate on the composite object. The implementation for `TDiscountVisitor` is as follows:

```
type
  TDiscountVisitor = class(TInterfacedObject, IVisitor)
  strict private
    FDiscountBasic: integer;
    FDiscountConfig: integer;
  public
    constructor Create(discountBasic, discountConfigurable: integer);
    procedure Visit(component: TConfigurableComponent); overload;
    procedure Visit(component: TBasicComponent); overload;
  end;

constructor TDiscountVisitor.Create(discountBasic,
  discountConfigurable: integer);
begin
  inherited Create;
  FDiscountBasic := discountBasic;
  FDiscountConfig := discountConfigurable;
end;

procedure TDiscountVisitor.Visit(component: TBasicComponent);
begin
  component.Price := component.Price * (1 - FDiscountBasic/100);
end;

procedure TDiscountVisitor.Visit(component: TConfigurableComponent);
begin
  component.Price := component.Price * (1 - FDiscountConfig/100);
end;
```

The TRaiseVisitor is implemented in the same way, except that it applies different changes to the composite model. As you can see in the following code, both Visit methods raise the price, while the visitor for TConfigurableComponent also prefixes the component name with the string NEW to justify the raised price:

```
type
  TRaiseVisitor = class(TInterfacedObject, IVisitor)
  strict private
    FRaiseBy: real;
  public
    constructor Create(raiseBy: real);
    procedure Visit(component: TConfigurableComponent); overload;
    procedure Visit(component: TBasicComponent); overload;
  end;

constructor TRaiseVisitor.Create(raiseBy: real);
begin
  inherited Create;
  FRaiseBy := raiseBy;
end;

procedure TRaiseVisitor.Visit(component: TConfigurableComponent);
begin
  component.Price := component.Price + FRaiseBy;
  component.Name := 'NEW ' + component.Name;
end;

procedure TRaiseVisitor.Visit(component: TBasicComponent);
begin
  component.Price := component.Price + FRaiseBy;
end;
```

The following screenshot shows the result of applying the discount and then raising the prices:

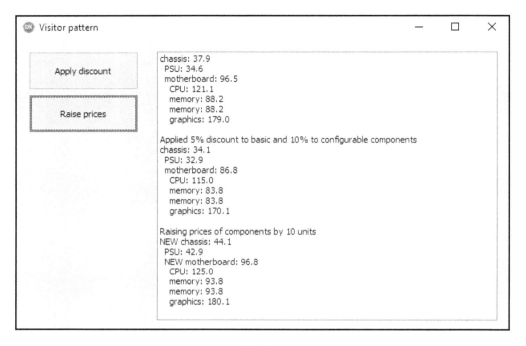

A discount followed by a price raise

Observer

The observer pattern regulates communication between an object (called a **subject**) and other objects (**observers**) that want to react to changes in the subject. Instead of checking periodically for changes, observers register their interest with the subject and are notified about the changes with some callback or messaging mechanism.

If you subscribe to a magazine, you don't go to the publisher every day to check if a new edition is ready. Rather, you wait until the publisher sends you each issue.

This Gang of Four pattern is a basic part in distributed event handling systems. For example, a Model-View-Controller architectural pattern is always implemented with some application of the observer pattern.

The Live Binding mechanism that's in Delphi is also based on the observer model. It uses the observer mechanism built into the component library (the `TComponent.Observers` property).

Any implementation of the observer pattern follows the following steps:

1. The observer registers its interest with the subject
2. Whenever the subject is modified, it calls a callback method in all registered observers
3. The observer unregisters its interest from the subject

This results in a very tight coupling between the subject and the observers. A variation of the observer pattern called *publish-subscribe* introduces a small change in the notification mechanism, which results in more loose coupling, as follows:

1. The subscriber registers its interest with the publisher
2. Whenever the publisher is modified, it sends a message to all registered subscribers
3. The subscriber unregisters its interest from the publisher

This approach to the observer pattern allows us to split an application into multiple processes, which can (with proper implementation) even run on multiple computers.

The biggest problem with the observer pattern is that it can result in large amounts of updates. If a code modifies multiple properties of the subject, each modification ends in notifying all observers that something has changed. For this reason, the subject sometimes implements a mechanism that temporarily prevents updates to be triggered. We'll see later in this chapter how such functionality can be implemented.

Another problem is that observers have no idea which part of the subject was changed. We can extend the callback mechanism so that the notification method also provides information about the changed parts. We can also change the registration mechanism so that observers specify their area of interest during registration. The subject then notifies only observers that have specified interest in the changed area.

Instead of implementing such modifications, however, you should inspect the actual subject. In many cases, a need for a more granular notification mechanism simply tells us that the subject is too complex and is trying to do too many things. Maybe it is best to split it into multiple subcomponents, where each implements its own observer pattern.

To demonstrate the implementation of observer support from scratch, I have prepared a demonstration project, `Observer`, which is stored in the `Observer` folder.

The subject implements an interface, ISubject. This interface allows observers to register (Attach) and unregister (Detach) their interest with the observer. Each observer must implement the IObserver interface containing one method, Update. The subject will call this method whenever its content is modified. Both interfaces are defined in the ObserverModel unit and are shown as follows:

```
type
  IObserver = interface ['{966246BE-5DE8-431E-BB95-BEB5A1A9C1B8}']
    procedure Update(Subject: TObject);
  end;

  ISubject = interface ['{C9D55859-6009-4AA4-8E8F-B94DE5009D56}']
    procedure Attach(Observer: IObserver);
    procedure Detach(Observer: IObserver);
  end;
```

The subject class, TObservableModel, is defined in the same unit. To separate responsibilities, observer functionality was moved to a class called TObservable, while the business code is implemented in the TObservableModel class. This class also implements the mechanism that can temporarily pause notifications, namely pair of methods called BeginUpdate/EndUpdate. The following code fragment shows the definition of both classes:

```
type
  TObservable = class(TInterfacedObject, ISubject)
  strict private
    FObservers: TList<IObserver>;
  strict protected
    procedure Notify;
  public
    constructor Create;
    destructor Destroy; override;
    procedure Attach(Observer: IObserver);
    procedure Detach(Observer: IObserver);
  end;

  TObservableModel = class(TObservable, ISubject)
  strict private
    FBasePrice: real;
    FDiscount: integer;
    FUpdateCount: integer;
    FModified: boolean;
  strict protected
    function GetEndPrice: real;
    procedure Notify;
    procedure SetBasePrice(const value: real);
```

```
    procedure SetDiscount(const value: integer);
  public
    procedure BeginUpdate;
    procedure EndUpdate;
    property BasePrice: real read FBasePrice write SetBasePrice;
    property Discount: integer read FDiscount write SetDiscount;
    property EndPrice: real read GetEndPrice;
  end;
```

Alternatively, we could use composition instead of inheritance, and use TObservable as a component inside the TObservableModel class.

This approach enables us to reuse code that handles observers (TObservable). Later in this chapter, we'll see how we can use observer support implemented in the Spring library instead of writing our own TObservable.

The TObserver class is just a very basic wrapper around a list of IObserver interfaces. The only interesting part, which is shown in the following code, is the Notify method:

```
procedure TObservable.Notify;
var
  observer: IObserver;
begin
  for observer in FObservers do
    observer.Update(Self);
end;
```

This method walks the list of registered observers and calls the Update method on each of them. The subject (Self) is passed as a parameter. The Notify method is declared in the strict protected section as it should only be called from the TObservableModel code.

The TObservableModel contains three properties. External code can set the BasePrice (price for a product) and Discount (applied discount), and then read the EndPrice property to get the discounted price. Both BasePrice and Discount implement setters that change the value and then trigger the notification mechanism, as follows:

```
procedure TObservableModel.SetBasePrice(const value: real);
begin
  FBasePrice := value;
  Notify;
end;

procedure TObservableModel.SetDiscount(const value: integer);
begin
```

```
    Assert((value >= 0) and (value <= 100), 'Discount must be between 0 and
  100 percent.');
    FDiscount := value;
    Notify;
  end;
```

The `BeginUpdate`, `EndUpdate,` and `Notify` methods work together. They are implemented as follows:

```
procedure TObservableModel.BeginUpdate;
begin
  Inc(FUpdateCount);
end;

procedure TObservableModel.EndUpdate;
begin
  Assert(FUpdateCount > 0);
  Dec(FUpdateCount);
  if (FUpdateCount = 0) and FModified then
  begin
    Notify;
    FModified := false;
  end;
end;

procedure TObservableModel.Notify;
begin
  if FUpdateCount = 0 then
    inherited Notify
  else
    FModified := true;
end;
```

The `Notify` method checks whether the `BeginUpdate` has been called. If not (`FUpdateCount = 0`), it will simply forward the call to the base implementation in `TObserver.Notify`, which will notify all observers. Otherwise, an internal flag called `FModified` is set to `True`.

The `BeginUpdate` method simply increments the `FUpdateCount` count. This counter is decremented in the `EndUpdate` method. If the new value is 0, the code has matched every `BeginUpdate` with an `EndUpdate`, and notifications are no longer suspended. If the `FModified` flag is set (meaning that `Notify` was called after `BeginUpdate`), `Notify` is called again so that it can notify all observers.

This implementation allows us to nest BeginUpdate/EndUpdate calls inside other BeginUpdate/EndUpdate calls, which can greatly simplify the main program. Delphi RTL implements such BeginUpdate/EndUpdate functionality in many places.

The main form contains two spinedit inputs. inpPrice specifies the price for the product and inpDiscount specifies the applied discount. The subject is stored in the FModel field, which is created in the OnCreate handler, as follows:

```
procedure TfrmObserver.FormCreate(Sender: TObject);
begin
  FModel := TObservableModel.Create;
  FModel.BasePrice := inpPrice.Value;
  FModel.Discount  := inpDiscount.Value;

  FEditObserver := TModelObserver.Create(
    procedure (model: TObservableModel)
    begin
      inpEndPrice.Text := Format('%.1f', [model.EndPrice]);
    end);
  FModel.Attach(FEditObserver);

  FListBoxObserver := TModelObserver.Create(
    procedure (model: TObservableModel)
    begin
      lbLog.ItemIndex := lbLog.Items.Add(
        Format('New price: %.1f (%.1f * %d%%)',
          [model.EndPrice, model.BasePrice, 100 - model.Discount]));
    end);
  FModel.Attach(FListBoxObserver);
end;
```

This event also attaches two observers to the subject. The helper class TModelObserver implements the IObserver interface and the Update method calls an anonymous function, which was passed to the constructor as parameter. This allows for the simple creation of customized observers.

The OnCreate handler creates two observers. The FEditObserver displays every change in a TEdit field and the FListBoxObserver logs changes to a listbox.

The full implementation of TModelObserver is shown here:

```
type
  TModelObserver = class(TInterfacedObject, IObserver)
  strict private
    FNotifier: TProc<TObservableModel>;
  public
    constructor Create(notifier: TProc<TObservableModel>);
    procedure Update(Subject: TObject);
  end;

constructor TModelObserver.Create(notifier: TProc<TObservableModel>);
begin
  inherited Create;
  FNotifier := notifier;
end;

procedure TModelObserver.Update(Subject: TObject);
begin
  FNotifier(Subject as TObservableModel);
end;
```

The OnDestroy event handler unregisters both observers and destroys the subject, as shown here:

```
procedure TfrmObserver.FormDestroy(Sender: TObject);
begin
  FModel.Detach(FEditObserver);
  FModel.Detach(FListBoxObserver);
  FreeAndNil(FModel);
end;
```

To finish the implementation, OnChange handlers for both input fields such as inpDiscount and inpPrice change FModel properties, as shown here:

```
procedure TfrmObserver.inpDiscountChange(Sender: TObject);
begin
  FModel.Discount := inpDiscount.Value;
end;

procedure TfrmObserver.inpPriceChange(Sender: TObject);
begin
  FModel.BasePrice := inpPrice.Value;
end;
```

Each change causes the Update method in both observers to be triggered and that executes both anonymous methods, which results in both editbox and listbox being updated.

The user interface also contains the **BeginUpdate** and **EndUpdate** buttons, which call the `BeginUpdate` and `EndUpdate` methods of the `FModel`, respectively(not shown here).

If you play with the program, you'll see that each change of the input fields results in the output being updated, that is unless the **BeginUpdate** button was clicked more times than the **EndUpdate** button. In such cases, updates are suspended until **EndUpdate** is clicked enough times. The following screenshot shows one such interaction:

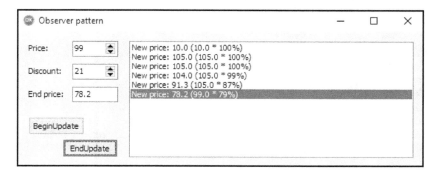

Interacting with an observed business model

Observing with Spring

The next two examples show how we can simplify our code by using support for the observer pattern that is built into the wonderful Spring4D library (`https://bitbucket.org/sglienke/spring4d`).

Both programs that I'll present—SpringObserver and SpringMulticast—require the Spring4D library to function. To run any of them, you'll have to install this library and then add its folders, `Source` and `Source\Base`, to Delphi's Library path or to the project's Search path. If you unpack the library into the `Chapter 7\Spring4D` folder, the project's Search path will already be correctly configured and you can simply press *F9* to run the program.

> If you have `git` installed, you can execute the following command in the `Chapter 7` folder to install Spring4D: `git clone https://bitbucket.org/sglienke/spring4d`.

Spring4D implements observer support in the `Spring.DesignPatterns` unit. The `IObservable<T>` interface defines support for managing and notifying observers of type `T`. This interface is implemented in `TObservable<T>`, which we can use as a base class for our subject. The following code fragment shows both the interface and the class definition:

```
type
  IObservable<T> = interface(IInvokable)
    procedure Attach(const observer: T);
    procedure Detach(const observer: T);
    procedure Notify;
  end;

  TObservable<T> = class(TInterfacedObject, IObservable<T>)
  private
    fLock: TMREWSync;
    fObservers: IList<T>;
  protected
    procedure DoNotify(const observer: T); virtual; abstract;
    property Observers: IList<T> read fObservers;
  public
    constructor Create;
    destructor Destroy; override;

    procedure Attach(const observer: T);
    procedure Detach(const observer: T);
    procedure Notify;
  end;
```

How `TObservable<T>` is implemented is not really our concern. We just want to use it. Still, if you look into the code, you'll see that the implementation is very similar to `TObservable` from the previous example, with the additional bonus of support for multithreaded programs.

There is, in fact, a small implementation detail that we should be aware of. `TObservable<T>.Notify` doesn't directly call the observers' `Update` method. This class doesn't know in advance what `T` will represent and which methods it will implement. Instead of that, `Notify` calls the virtual `DoNotify` method for each observer. Our subject must override this method and use it to call the appropriate notification mechanism.

The subject implementation in `SpringObserverModel` (part of
the `SpringObserver` project) is similar to previous implementations of
`TObservableModel`, except that this time it is derived from
the `TObservable<IObserver>` class. As shown in the following code, this version doesn't
support `BeginUpdate/EndUpdate` functionality:

```
type
  IObserver = interface ['{966246BE-5DE8-431E-BB95-BEB5A1A9C1B8}']
    procedure Update(Subject: TObject);
  end;

  TObservableModel = class(TObservable<IObserver>)
  strict private
    FBasePrice: real;
    FDiscount: integer;
  strict protected
   procedure DoNotify(const observer: IObserver); override;
    function GetEndPrice: real;
    procedure SetBasePrice(const value: real);
    procedure SetDiscount(const value: integer);
  public
    property BasePrice: real read FBasePrice write SetBasePrice;
    property Discount: integer read FDiscount write SetDiscount;
    property EndPrice: real read GetEndPrice;
  end;
```

 You can add `BeginUpdate/EndUpdate` support to this implementation
as an exercise.

The implementation of `TObservableModel` in this program is almost the same as the one
we have already seen. The biggest difference lies in the `DoNotify` method, which serves as
a mapper from a purely abstract implementation in `TObservable<T>` into our custom
`IObserver`, as follows:

```
procedure TObservableModel.DoNotify(const observer: IObserver);
begin
  observer.Update(Self);
end;
```

The main program is almost the same as in the previous example. You can try it out on your own.

Another approach that we can use to implement observer support is *multicast events*.

An event handler in Delphi is similar to an observer callback (the `Update` method in our observers), except that it only supports one observer at a time. This limitation can be bypassed with a different event implementation. Each multicast event must be backed by a list of currently attached (registered) event handlers (observers). We can implement such support ourselves or use the already made `Event<T>` record from Spring.

This feature is demonstrated in the `SpringMulticast` project. The `SpringMulticastModel` unit reimplements the already well-known observable model, as follows:

```
type
  TObservableModel = class
  strict private
    FBasePrice: real;
    FDiscount: integer;
    FEndPriceChanged: Event<TNotifyEvent>;
  strict protected
    function GetEndPrice: real;
    procedure SetBasePrice(const value: real);
    procedure SetDiscount(const value: integer);
  public
    property BasePrice: real read FBasePrice write SetBasePrice;
    property Discount: integer read FDiscount write SetDiscount;
    property EndPrice: real read GetEndPrice;
    property EndPriceChanged: Event<TNotifyEvent> read FEndPriceChanged;
  end;
```

Instead of adding support for multiple observers, `TObservableModel` implements the multicast event `EndPriceChanged`. As this event is backed by a record type, `Event<T>`, no special creation or destruction of `FEndPriceChanged` is required.

The code calls `EndPriceChanged.Invoke(Self)` to invoke all event handlers that are currently attached, as shown here:

```
procedure TObservableModel.SetBasePrice(const value: real);
begin
  FBasePrice := value;
  EndPriceChanged.Invoke(Self);
end;

procedure TObservableModel.SetDiscount(const value: integer);
```

```
begin
  Assert((value >= 0) and (value <= 100), 'Discount must be between 0 and
100 percent.');
  FDiscount := value;
  EndPriceChanged.Invoke(Self);
end;
```

The Self parameter will be passed to all event handlers as the Sender parameter. In other words, all TNotifyEvent handlers will be triggered as we expect them to be in Delphi.

The main unit defines two methods with the TNotifyEvent signature. As shown in the following code, these two methods are added to the event handler inside the OnCreate event and removed in the OnDestroy event:

```
type
  TfrmSpringMulticast = class(TForm)
    ...
    procedure PriceChangedEdit(Sender: TObject);
    procedure PriceChangedListBox(Sender: TObject);
  end;

procedure TfrmSpringMulticast.FormCreate(Sender: TObject);
begin
  FModel := TObservableModel.Create;
  FModel.BasePrice := inpPrice.Value;
  FModel.Discount := inpDiscount.Value;

  FModel.EndPriceChanged.Add(PriceChangedEdit);
  FModel.EndPriceChanged.Add(PriceChangedListBox);
end;

procedure TfrmSpringMulticast.FormDestroy(Sender: TObject);
begin
  FModel.EndPriceChanged.Remove(PriceChangedEdit);
  FModel.EndPriceChanged.Remove(PriceChangedListBox);
  FreeAndNil(FModel);
end;
```

The implementation of these two event handlers is the same as the code in the two anonymous methods that were used for the observer action in the previous example. The following fragment shows both event handlers:

```
procedure TfrmSpringMulticast.PriceChangedEdit(Sender: TObject);
begin
  inpEndPrice.Text := Format('%.1f', [(Sender as
TObservableModel).EndPrice]);
end;

procedure TfrmSpringMulticast.PriceChangedListBox(Sender: TObject);
var
  model: TObservableModel;
begin
  model := Sender as TObservableModel;
  lbLog.ItemIndex := lbLog.Items.Add(
    Format('New price: %.1f (%.1f * %d%%)',
      [model.EndPrice, model.BasePrice, 100 - model.Discount]));
end;
```

If you play with the program, you'll see that it behaves exactly the same as the previous example.

It may be tempting to always implement observers, as in the previous example. It required the least amount of code and was the simplest to write. There is, however, a big difference between multicast events and proper observer mechanisms. The client in both observer-based implementations was coded strictly to an interface and was therefore not dependent on an implementation. The multicast event approach forces a client that is fixed to a specific implementation and is therefore harder to test and maintain.

Memento

The last pattern in this chapter, memento, helps us save and restore a state of a complex object. It was originally introduced by the Gang of Four.

When you want to store and restore a current state of a complex object, you can easily run into problems with encapsulation. There may, for example, exist an internal state that is important for the correct functioning of the object, but is not accessible to the public. In such a case, we may not be able to access this state from the code that is not part of the object.

Even if all internal fields are accessible by the public, accessing internal state from external code is a bad practice. The internal representation of an object may change unexpectedly (for example, with a software update), and if a maintainer of such external code is not aware of that, the program would break.

The memento pattern prescribes how a complex object (called originator) saves its internal state into a simpler object (memento). An external object (caretaker) can manage memento objects but cannot inspect their internal structure. In other words, memento objects are opaque to the code outside of the originator and memento objects.

 A memento behaves the same as a save point in a computer game. When you save your state in a game, a representation of your current progress is saved. Later, you can restore the game from this representation to the previous state.

The memento pattern is often used to implement an undo capability in a program. Whenever a new state is stored, a new memento object is created and pushed to the undo stack. When an operation is undone, a memento object is taken from the stack and the state of the program is reloaded from that memento.

Another use of a memento pattern is to implement an iteration mechanism. In this context, a memento object is frequently called a **bookmark**. For example, the following code fragment shows a class called `TDataCollection<T>`, which implements some kind of data storage mechanism for class `T`:

```
type
  TBookmark = record
    //...
  end;

  TDataCollection<T> = class
  //...
  public
    function First: TBookmark;
    function Current(const bookmark: TBookmark): T;
    procedure Next(var bookmark: TBookmark);
    function AtEnd(const bookmark: TBookmark): boolean;
  end;
```

To allow external code to travel this data collection, a memento called `TBookmark` is created in the `First` method. The `Current` method returns a value of type `T`, corresponding to the given bookmark. The `Next` method takes a bookmark, moves to the next value, and updates the bookmark. The last method, `AtEnd`, returns `True` if the current bookmark lies after the last element in the collection.

Together, these methods allows external code to travel the collection, as shown here:

```
var
  data: TDataCollection;
  state: TBookmark;
begin
  state := data.First;
  while not data.AtEnd(state) do
  begin
    Process(data.Current);
    data.Next(bookmark);
  end;
end;
```

As the iteration state is not internal to the `TDataCollection` but external (stored in the caller code), this approach allows multiple iterations to occur in parallel. Of course, if concurrent iterations occur in multiple threads, you have to take special care to protect simultaneous access to `TDataCollection` internals. We'll talk about that in detail in the next chapter, `Chapter 8`, *Locking Patterns*.

A memento can also be used to implement a `for..in` iteration internally.

Let's take a look at a short example, taken from the *MementoEditor* project in the *Memento* folder. The *MementoExample* unit implements a very simple originator object, `TComplexObject`, as follows:

```
type
  TComplexObject = class
  private
    FValue: integer;
  public
    procedure Increment;
    function CreateMemento: TMemento;
    procedure RestoreMemento(const memento: TMemento);
    property Value: integer read FValue;
  end;
```

This object contains an internal state field, `FValue`, which can be read from external code via the `Value` property. There is, however, no functionality exposed by the `TComplexObject` to set `FValue` to a specific value. This prevents us from implementing a save/restore mechanism by accessing FValue directly.

To fix that, `TComplexObject` implements a function called `CreateMemento`, which creates a *memento* object called `TMemento`, and a procedure called `RestoreMemento`, which takes a memento object and restores its internal state from it.

In this case, a memento object is actually a record. This simplifies life cycle management of memento objects in the caretaker code. It is, of course, perfectly valid to implement a memento as an object or as an interface.

The following code shows how a memento record is created and consumed in the `TComplexObject` code:

```
function TComplexObject.CreateMemento: TMemento;
begin
  Result.FValue := FValue;
end;

procedure TComplexObject.RestoreMemento(const memento: TMemento);
begin
  FValue := memento.FValue;
end;
```

A memento object can also be used for serialization/deserialization of a complex problem, although that at least partially breaks the pattern. We have to either allow (de)serialization code to access the internal state of the memento object, (which breaks the memento is opaque assumption), or implement the (de)serialization code inside the memento code (which breaks the single responsibility principle).

For a more complex example, I have revisited the *command* pattern demo from Chapter 6, *Nullable Object, Template Method, Command, State*. In that chapter, I implemented a simple editor with an undo capability.

The undo mechanism in the Editor demo from that chapter manages a state of a `TMemo` editor inside the `TUndoableCommand` object as a set of fields (`FText` and `FPosition`), as follows:

```
type
  TUndoableCommand = class(TCommand)
  strict private
    FText: string;
    FPosition: Integer;
  strict protected
    procedure StoreState;
  public
```

```
    function Clone: TCommand; override;
    procedure Execute; override;
    procedure Undo; override;
  end;
```

The MementoEditor project in the Memento folder contains an improved version of the Editor demo from the previous chapter.

Instead of accessing the TMemo object directly and storing state as a set of fields, the new TUndoableCommand uses a memento called TMemoMemento, as shown in the following code (the implementation of the Clone and Execute methods is not shown as it is not relevant for the memento pattern):

```
type
  TUndoableCommand = class(TCommand)
  strict private
    FMemoMemento: TMemoMemento;
  strict protected
    procedure StoreState;
  public
    function Clone: TCommand; override;
    procedure Execute; override;
    procedure Undo; override;
  end;

procedure TUndoableCommand.StoreState;
begin
  FMemoMemento := Receiver.CreateMemento;
end;

procedure TUndoableCommand.Undo;
begin
  Receiver.RestoreMemento(FMemoMemento);
end;
```

This code fully follows the memento opaque approach. The TUndoableCommand only creates, stores, and uses a memento. It doesn't access its internal implementation.

The memento itself is implemented in Memo.Memento unit. TMemoMemento is a memento object (although implemented as a record) for a TMemo object. It only stores four TMemo properties that interest us, as shown here:

```
type
  TMemoMemento = record
  private
    FCaretPos: TPoint;
    FSelLength: Integer;
```

```
    FSelStart: Integer;
    FText: string;
  end;
```

A memento doesn't have to store the full internal state of an originator object. It may only store a partial state, as shown in this example.

As we cannot implement methods to create and restore a memento inside the originator object, they are implemented as a class helper. This allows the code in the TUndoableCommand (as shown before) to directly call CreateMemento and RestoreMemento on the TMemo object. The following code fragment shows the definition and implementation of the memo helper TMemoHelper:

```
type
  TMemoHelper = class helper for TMemo
  public
    function CreateMemento: TMemoMemento;
    procedure RestoreMemento(const memento: TMemoMemento);
  end;

function TMemoHelper.CreateMemento: TMemoMemento;
begin
  Result.FCaretPos := CaretPos;
  Result.FSelStart := SelStart;
  Result.FSelLength := SelLength;
  Result.FText := Text;
end;

procedure TMemoHelper.RestoreMemento(const memento: TMemoMemento);
begin
  CaretPos := memento.FCaretPos;
  SelStart := memento.FSelStart;
  SelLength := memento.FSelLength;
  Text := memento.FText;
end;
```

The rest of the example project is left unchanged from the previous chapter.

Summary

In this chapter, we have examined four more behavioral patterns. They are a bit more complex than the patterns from the previous chapter, but they also help a lot with organizing the code and are well worth your consideration.

The iterator pattern is well-known to Delphi programmers. Most of you know how to write a `for..in` loop, even though the implementation details hiding behind this construct may not be your biggest concern. In this chapter, we have also explored the other part of iterators, namely, how to use them as a tool for writing generic algorithms.

This chapter continued with the *visitor* pattern, which is in some aspects iterator's counterpart. Unlike the iterator, this pattern wasn't designed to walk over data structures, but to iterate over complex object structures. With a proper implementation, it allows us to open a small window into object internals and use it to write extensions that enhance existing objects.

The observer pattern, also know as publish-subscribe, is a basic tool behind event-driven systems, such as the Model-View-Controller architecture or Delphi's own LiveBindings. In this chapter, I looked into multiple implementations based on custom code and on the popular open source Spring4D library.

The last behavioral pattern covered in this book, memento, is one of the simplest ones. In fact, it looks so trivial that it's easy to overlook and ignore. Nevertheless, the concept of memento is something that you should have in mind when you work with systems that need to capture and restore the state of complex objects.

In the next chapter, we'll move away from Gang of Four patterns and step into the modern world of multithreaded programming, where even the simplest tasks require special care and consideration.

Section 5: Concurrency Patterns

5

In this part, the reader will learn about modern approaches to patterns used in parallel programming. This part will also cover relevant Delphi run—time library support.

This section will comprise the following chapters:

Chapter 8, *Locking Patterns,*

Chapter 9, *Thread pool, Messaging, Future, and Pipeline*

8
Locking patterns

Very modern programmer should know something about parallel programming, and we Delphi programmers are no exception. The programs we write and maintain are getting more and more complex, while our customers expect them to keep performing swiftly and without blocking the user interface. A lot of times, we can only satisfy such requirements by introducing parallelism into our software.

Getting parallel, however, is far from simple. When we introduce multiple threads of execution into our programs, we also introduce a big source of potential problems. Writing good parallel code means writing very ordered code that follows established patterns—even more so than that in a standard, single-threaded application.

The most important concept of multithreaded programs is data sharing. After all, no thread is an island and we must somehow make sure that all code in the program is cooperating instead of fighting with each other. That is why this chapter is dedicated to different variations of a locking pattern, which regulates access to shared resources.

In this chapter, you will do the following:

- Learn the basics of multithreaded programming with Delphi
- Find out everything about the locking pattern
- Explore lock striping to see how locking can be even more granular
- Learn how to optimize the creation of shared resources with double-checked locking
- Make resource initialization even faster with optimistic locking
- Learn how to make data readers and data writers work in perfect harmony with readers-writer lock

Delphi idioms – parallel programming

Delphi offers many tools to write multithreaded programs. As this is a book about patterns, not about parallel programming, I will not be able to go into much detail on that topic. Still, it is good to know which tools you have available so that you can do additional research in your own time.

In this introductory section, I will walk you through the Delphi tools that facilitate the writing of multithreaded applications. The `DelphiThreading` project from the `Parallel programming in Delphi` folder provides a simple example for every one of them.

 For more details, you can refer to Chapters *6 and* Chapter *7* of my book, *Delphi High Performance* (`https://www.amazon.com/dp/1788625455`), published by Packt Publishing.

A standard platform-independent way to create a new thread in Delphi is to create a descendant of a `TThread` class (implemented in the `System.Classes` unit) and override its `Execute` method. Delphi will use operating system functions to create a new thread and start the `Execute` method inside that thread. This functionality has been available since Delphi 2, which was the first Delphi version to support 32-bit Windows (16-bit Windows did not support threaded programming at all).

The demonstration project implements a `TStandardThread` object, which posts a message to the main window every second until the thread is destroyed. It is implemented as follows:

```
type
  TStandardThread = class(TThread)
  protected
    procedure Execute; override;
  end;

procedure TStandardThread.Execute;
begin
  while not Terminated do
  begin
    PostMessage(frmDelphiThreading.Handle, WM_LOG, ThreadID, 0);
    Sleep(1000);
  end;
end;
```

To create this thread, the code simply creates a new `TStandardThread` object. The code also sets an `OnTerminate` event, which is called once the thread has terminated, as shown here:

```
procedure TfrmDelphiThreading.btnThreadClick(Sender: TObject);
begin
  FThread := TStandardThread.Create;
  FThread.OnTerminate := ReportThreadTerminated;
  btnThread.OnClick := btnStopThreadClick;
  btnThread.Caption := 'Stop';
end;
```

To destroy the thread, the code calls its `Terminate` method, which sets the `Terminated` property of the `TThread` class. A thread will sooner or later (at most, in one second) see that `Terminated` has been set and will exit. The `WaitFor` call waits for the thread to exit from the `Execute` method. After that, the code can destroy the thread object. The whole process is shown here:

```
procedure TfrmDelphiThreading.btnStopThreadClick(Sender: TObject);
begin
  FThread.Terminate;
  FThread.WaitFor;
  FreeAndNil(FThread);
  btnThread.OnClick := btnThreadClick;
  btnThread.Caption := 'TThread';
end;
```

The code can also create a thread that automatically destroys its object when it is no longer used by setting the `FreeOnTerminate` property, as shown here:

```
procedure TfrmDelphiThreading.btnFreeOnTermClick(Sender: TObject);
begin
  FThreadFoT := TFreeOnTerminateThread.Create(True);
  FThreadFoT.FreeOnTerminate := true;
  FThreadFoT.OnTerminate := ReportThreadTerminated;
  FThreadFoT.Start;
end;
```

When a thread object requires some configuration (as in this case), it is good practice to create it in a suspended (non-running) state by passing `True` to the constructor. After that, you can configure everything, knowing that the thread is not running yet. At the end, you must call `Start` to actually start the thread.

The first approach of manually stopping the thread is more appropriate when we have a long-running thread providing some service. The main program starts the thread when it needs that service and stops it when the service is no longer needed. If, however, the background thread just runs some operation and then stops, it is simpler to allow the thread to terminate itself.

Delphi also allows us to use an anonymous method instead of a `TThread` descendant for code that is to be run in a thread. This approach is suitable for small tasks that require just a few lines of code.

In Delphi XE7, a new unit, `System.Threading`, was introduced, which moved multi-threaded programming from the thread-based approach to modern task-based code. Instead of having to deal with threads (starting, stopping, and managing them), the new approach automates all of these processes. We merely create a task (for example, a piece of code that we want to run in a thread) and the infrastructure from `System.Threading` will do the rest.

The following code example creates a new task interface, `FTask: ITask`, that executes the `Asy_TaskWorker` method in a new thread:

```
procedure TfrmDelphiThreading.btnITaskClick(Sender: TObject);
begin
  FTask := TTask.Create(Asy_TaskWorker);
  FTask.Start;
end;
```

Instead of calling `Create` followed by `Start`, you can also call the helper `Run` function, as follows:

```
procedure TfrmDelphiThreading.btnITaskClick(Sender: TObject);
begin
  FTask := TTask.Run(Asy_TaskWorker);
end;
```

The `Asy_TaskWorker` method does some work (simulated with a `Sleep` function) and then uses `TThread.Queue` to execute an anonymous method in a main thread. This anonymous method logs the status to the listbox and destroys the `FTask` interface, as follows:

```
procedure TfrmDelphiThreading.Asy_TaskWorker;
var
  i: Integer;
  threadID: TThreadID;
begin
  threadID := GetCurrentThreadID;
```

```
    Sleep(5000);

    TThread.Queue(nil,
      procedure
      begin
        lbLog.Items.Add('Task in thread ' + threadID.ToString +
          ' has stopped');
        FTask := nil;
      end);
end;
```

When writing multithreaded code in Delphi, always keep in mind that you should only access VCL from the main thread!

This code is equivalent to the `FreeOnTerminate` version of `TThread` based code. We could also write the task in a service-like way, so that it runs in a loop until the main thread stops it. In both cases, we can use the `Wait` method of the `ITask` interface to wait until the task finishes execution.

The approach of using tasks in combination with explicit waiting is used in all examples in this chapter.

The task approach is used to create wrappers that operate on an even higher level of abstraction. Delphi XE7 introduced three such abstractions: join, future, and parallel for.

Join allows us to start any number of tasks in parallel. The following call creates two tasks, each running the same method, `Asy_TaskWorker`:

```
    TParallel.Join(Asy_TaskWorker, Asy_TaskWorker);
```

`TParallel.Join` returns an `ITask` interface that we can use to control execution. We can, for example, call its `Wait` method to wait on all parallel tasks to complete their work.

`Join` should use multiple threads to execute the tasks, but this doesn't work correctly in all Delphi versions. Delphi 10.1 Berlin introduced a bug that was only fixed in Delphi 10.3 Rio, which caused the `Join` method to sometimes execute the first two tasks in the same thread.

If you start the DelphiThreading program and click on the `Join` button, you'll see messages from two threads if you are using Delphi without this bug, and messages that come only from one thread if you are using Delphi 10.1 or 10.2.

As a workaround, you can insert a null task as a first parameter to the `Join` call, as in the following example:

```
TParallel.Join([procedure begin end, Asy_TaskWorker, Asy_TaskWorker]);
```

The second abstraction, future, creates a function that executes in a thread and returns a result. This kind of execution is initialized by calling the `ITask.Future<T>` function, which returns a future interface called `IFuture<T>`. The `Future` button in the demonstration program creates such a background calculation, as follows:

```
procedure TfrmDelphiThreading.btnFutureClick(Sender: TObject);
begin
  FFuture := TTask.Future<integer>(
    function: Integer
    begin
      Sleep(2000);
      Result := 42;
      TThread.Queue(nil, ReportFuture);
    end);
end;

procedure TfrmDelphiThreading.ReportFuture;
begin
  lbLog.Items.Add('Result = ' + FFuture.Value.ToString);
  FFuture := nil;
end;
```

The last high-level abstraction included with Delphi is a parallel for. It allows us to very simply replace a normal `for` loop with a parallel version. Unlike join and future, parallel for stops the main thread until the loop is completed. This simplifies the programming while still allowing you to run a parallel loop inside a task if you don't want to block the main thread.

The following code shows how to implement a parallel for loop:

```
procedure TfrmDelphiThreading.btnParallelForClick(Sender: TObject);
begin
  TParallel.For(1, 16,
    procedure (i: integer)
    begin
      PostMessage(frmDelphiThreading.Handle, WM_LOG,
        TThread.Current.ThreadID, i);
      Sleep(100);
    end);
end;
```

If you are only programming for Windows and you are not using the FireMonkey framework, you can also use my parallel programming library, OmniThreadLibrary (`www.omnithreadlibrary.com`). It offers superior support for communication between threads and many other high-level abstractions, such as pipeline, timed task, background worker, and more.

Lock

The big power of multithreaded programming lies in the fact that all threads can access all the memory in the program. When we create a new thread that will process some program data, we don't need any special preparations. We just create the thread and that data will be available to it.

This, however, is also the biggest weakness of multithreaded programming. If multiple threads are accessing the same data, they can easily interfere with each other. One thread can overwrite the data of another thread or it can modify the structure that another thread is using. This results in all kinds of problems, including random crashes at unexpected locations.

As an example, imagine this situation. A first thread is walking some list and processing elements with the following code:

```
for i := 0 to FList.Count - 1 do
  DoSomethingWith(FList[i]);
```

FList is a global object and while this `for` loop is running, the second thread deletes an element from the list with `FList.Delete(0)`.

Let's say that the FList initially contains 1,000 elements with indices from 0 to 999. Before the `for` loop starts, the Delphi compiler calculates `FList.Count - 1` and stores the result (999) in a temporary variable. This expression is only calculated on the beginning and not on each repetition of the `for` loop!

While the `for` loop is executing, the second thread deletes the first element from the list, which now contains only 999 elements with indices from 0 to 998. The first thread has no knowledge of that and at the end of the `for` loop, it tries to access element 999, which results in a range check exception.

This problem can potentially occur every time multiple threads are operating on the same data and at least one thread modifies that data. As we will soon see, we don't need a complicated structure, such as a list, to exhibit the problem. It can occur even when threads are accessing one simple `integer` field.

Such problems will also appear if you try to work with the user interface (manipulate VCL controls) from a background thread. All Delphi programmers that want to use multithreaded code should always keep the prime directive in mind: never access VCL from a background thread!

We can fix such a situation in two ways. One is to re-architect the application so that multiple threads never share the data. This is hard to do and in some situations almost impossible. I will discuss potential approaches for changing the code that way in the next chapter.

The other approach is to introduce the lock pattern. For this pattern to function, we must wrap each access to shared data in this pattern. That can again be hard work, especially if we are adapting existing code that uses the shared data object all over the place. The pattern is effective only if all code that accesses the data uses the pattern! Miss one place and the code can still run into problems.

The lock pattern protects the shared resource in the same way as a normal lock does. Before the program uses the shared resource, it must acquire the lock. This locks the door for any other thread. If another thread tries to acquire the same lock, it will have to stop and wait for the resource to be unlocked (we also say that the thread is blocked).

When the first thread doesn't need the shared resource anymore, it *releases* the lock. This unlocks the resource and allows another thread to acquire the lock. If a thread is already waiting for the lock, the operating system will automatically re-lock the resource and allow that thread to continue execution.

Of course, there are cases when multiple threads may be waiting on the same lock. In such cases, the operating system will wake only one of the threads at a time and keep the others waiting.

In real life, a lock corresponds to a latch on the inner side of a changing room door. While locked, it prevents other users from accessing the changing room that is already in use.

Before we look into the different ways we can implement this pattern, let us write some pseudocode. If we are using some fictional `lock` object with the `Acquire` and `Release` methods we can rewrite the previous example as follows:

```
procedure Thread1;
begin
  lock.Acquire;
  try
    for i := 0 to FList.Count - 1 do
      DoSomethingWith(FList[i]);
  finally
    lock.Release;
  end;
end;

procedure Thread2;
begin
  lock.Acquire;
  try
    FList.Delete(0);
  finally
    lock.Release;
  end;
end;
```

In this example, one thread is executing the `Thread1` procedure and another is executing `Thread2`. As access to the `FList` is now protected, its contents cannot be modified while the `for` loop is being executed and the problems cannot occur.

If, however, we forget to fix just one place in code and `FList.Delete(0)` is called there without being wrapped in a lock, the program can still crash! That one piece of code is enough to corrupt the data while another thread is thinking that it can safely iterate over the list.

Locks should be inserted so that they wrap the smallest amount of code that uses the shared resource. We could, for example, acquire the lock when a thread is created, and release it when it is destroyed, but that would completely negate the purpose of multithreaded programming, as we would only be able to run one thread at a time.

It is also possible to lock too small an area of code. For example, the following code would not operate properly:

```
lock.Acquire;
try
  count := FList.Count;
finally
  lock.Release;
end;

for i := 0 to count - 1 do
begin
  lock.Acquire;
  try
    DoSomethingWith(FList[i]);
  finally
    lock.Release;
  end;
end;
```

This implementation still locks every access to the shared resource but does so on a too-local level. With this implementation, the content of the list can still be modified while the `for` loop is running.

You may have noticed that I am using the `try..finally` statement to ensure that the lock is always released in case of an exception. This is important, as some other part of the program (for example, code that tries to save data to disk in case of an exception) may need to use the same lock. If we didn't unlock at the place of exception, that other part would get stuck in its *acquire* call and the whole program would lock up.

Another decision that awaits you, as a programmer in the multithreaded world, is how many locks to introduce into code. Technically, we can fix everything with only one lock, but then one part of the code would wait for object A while another thread would work on object B, even when they are completely unrelated. Introducing a master lock is a great way to make multithreaded program slow down to a crawl.

Usually, you will want to protect each shared resource with a separate lock. Sometimes, however, this is not the best idea and we need to introduce locks that protect multiple objects. Unfortunately, there is no solution that will apply to all cases. You will have to think about what your program is doing and then protect the appropriate areas.

Before I show you how the lock pattern can be implemented in Delphi code, I would like to show another example of bad code: two threads fighting to access the same integer-sized data. The example project, `Lock`, in the `Lock` folder, contains all the code that will be used in the continuation of this chapter.

The Unsafe data access button starts very simple code that uses two threads. The `btnUnsafeClick` method initializes the shared data field `FSharedData: integer` to 0, starts two threads, waits on both to finish work, and logs the execution time and final value of `FSharedData`, as follows:

```
procedure TfrmLock.btnUnsafeClick(Sender: TObject);
var
  decTask: ITask;
  incTask: ITask;
  timer: TStopwatch;
begin
  FSharedData := 0;
  timer := TStopwatch.StartNew;
  incTask := TTask.Run(IncrementValue);
  decTask := TTask.Run(DecrementValue);
  incTask.Wait;
  decTask.Wait;
  timer.Stop;
  Log('Unsafe value: %d; time: %d ms',
    [FSharedData, timer.ElapsedMilliseconds]);
end;
```

The first thread runs the `IncrementValue` method, as follows:

```
const
  CNumRepeats = 1000000;

procedure TfrmLock.IncrementValue;
var
  i: integer;
begin
  for i := 1 to CNumRepeats do
    Inc(FSharedData);
end;
```

This code simply increments the shared value by a million times.

The other thread runs the `DecrementValue` method, which decrements the shared value by a million times, as follows:

```
procedure TfrmLock.DecrementValue;
var
  i: integer;
begin
  for i := 1 to CNumRepeats do
    Dec(FSharedData);
end;
```

If we execute one method after another, the result would be obvious. The shared value would be incremented a million times and then decremented a million times, so at the end it would reach the starting value of zero. Running both operations in parallel, though, has unexpected consequences. We can never know what the end value will be, and the following screenshot proves that:

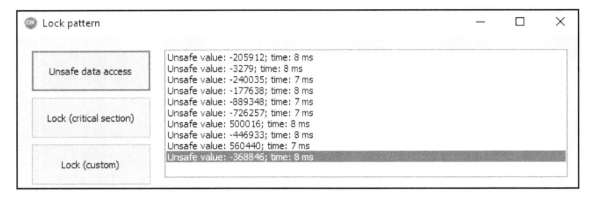

Modifying the shared value from multiple threads ends in an unpredictable result

The problem here is that the `Inc` and `Dec` instructions are not atomic (they don't execute in one indivisible step). Rather, `Inc` is implemented on the CPU as the following sequence of operations:

1. Load the data from memory.
2. Increment the value.
3. Store the data back to memory.

`Dec` is very similar, except that it decrements the value.

Because of that, the following can happen. Let's assume that `FSharedValue` contains the value 42. The two threads (let's call them I and D) then execute the following operations:

- Thread I loads value 42 from `FSharedValue`.
- Thread D loads value 42 from `FSharedValue`.
- Thread I increments the value and gets 43.
- Thread D decrements the value and gets 41.
- Thread I saves value 43 to `FSharedValue`.
- Thread D saves value 41 to `FSharedValue`.

The starting value, 42, was incremented and decremented once, so ideally it should stay the same. However, the value is now 41. As this will happen many times during the execution of a program, we will get a completely unpredictable result.

To fix the code, we have to introduce locking, and a common approach to that is to use a concept called a critical section. This concept is implemented on all major operating systems and it will work equally well on all platforms that Delphi can compile for. As the implementation is different on each operating system, Delphi nicely hides the specifics from us in a platform-independent class called TCriticalSection. It is implemented in the System.SyncObjs unit.

As it is a class, we have to create it before its first use and destroy it when we don't need it anymore. The Lock program does that in the OnClick handler for the **Lock** (critical section) button, as shown here:

```
procedure TfrmLock.btnCriticalSectionClick(Sender: TObject);
var
  decTask: ITask;
  incTask: ITask;
  timer: TStopwatch;
begin
  FLock := TCriticalSection.Create;
  try
    FSharedData := 0;
    timer := TStopwatch.StartNew;
    incTask := TTask.Run(LockIncrementValue);
    decTask := TTask.Run(LockDecrementValue);
    incTask.Wait;
    decTask.Wait;
    timer.Stop;
    Log('Lock value: %d; time: %d ms',
      [FSharedData, timer.ElapsedMilliseconds]);
  finally
    FreeAndNil(FLock);
  end;
end;
```

The rest of the code is very similar to that of the previously seen btnUnsafeClick, except that now, the following two methods are executed in separate threads:

```
procedure TfrmLock.LockDecrementValue;
var
  i: integer;
begin
  for i := 1 to CNumRepeats do
  begin
```

```
      FLock.Acquire;
      try
        Dec(FSharedData);
      finally
        FLock.Release;
      end;
    end;
  end;

  procedure TfrmLock.LockIncrementValue;
  var
    i: integer;
  begin
    for i := 1 to CNumRepeats do
    begin
      FLock.Acquire;
      try
        Inc(FSharedData);
      finally
        FLock.Release;
      end;
    end;
  end;
```

Each `Inc` and `Dec` is now protected with a critical section so that both `Inc` and `Dec` can never be executed at the same time. As the `for` loop doesn't depend on the `FSharedData` value, we are locking each increment/decrement. That allows the threads to run in parallel. The following screenshot shows the result of the fixed code:

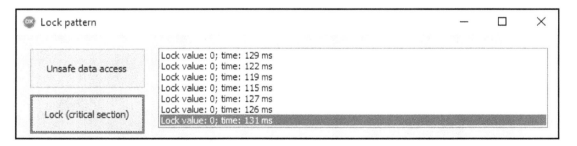

Locking with a critical section

We can immediately notice two things. First, the result is always correct! Second, the code now needs around 120 milliseconds to execute. Before the change, it needed only 8! Using critical sections will fix your program, but it will also make it run slower.

One way to improve the code is to use interlocked instructions, namely `TInterlocked.Increment` and `TInterlocked.Decrement`. They implement locking at the CPU level. As they can only be used in very specific circumstances, I will not discuss them in this book.

We are, however, not limited to using `TCriticalSection`. Operating systems support other synchronization concepts, such as mutexes and semaphores, which I will not explore in this book. I will instead show how to use the `TMonitor` class, which was introduced in Delphi 2009.

The chapter *Getting Started with the Parallel World,* of my book *Delphi High Performance* (`https://www.amazon.com/dp/1788625455`), published by Packt Publishing, covers locking with different synchronization primitives and interlocked instructions in painstaking detail.

The `TMonitor` class is implemented in *System* and allows us (besides other functionality) to lock any Delphi object without the need to maintain a separate lock. This represents a big improvement over a critical section where we have to maintain a separate lock object.

To lock an object, `obj`, we simply call `TMonitor.Enter(obj)` and to unlock, we call `TMonitor.Exit(obj)`. As the name `TMonitor` (unfortunately) conflicts with the `TMonitor` class from the `Vcl.Forms` unit, we can also use the helper functions `MonitorEnter` and `MonitorExit`.

The **Lock (monitor)** button starts the `MonitorIncrementValue` and `MonitorDecrementValue` methods, which it uses to protect access to the shared `FSharedData`. They are implemented as follows:

```
procedure TfrmLock.MonitorIncrementValue;
var
  i: integer;
begin
  for i := 1 to CNumRepeats do
  begin
    System.TMonitor.Enter(Self);
    try
      Inc(FSharedData);
    finally
      System.TMonitor.Exit(Self);
    end;
  end;
end;

procedure TfrmLock.MonitorDecrementValue;
var
```

```
     i: integer;
   begin
     for i := 1 to CNumRepeats do
     begin
       MonitorEnter(Self);
       try
         Dec(FSharedData);
       finally
         MonitorExit(Self);
       end;
     end;
   end;
```

To demonstrate two possible ways of locking/unlocking an object, each method uses one approach. In practice, of course, you will decide on one. I'm always using MonitorEnter/MonitorExit as it requires less typing.

The code also uses a non-obvious trick. TMonitor can only be used to lock objects and our shared data is not an object. To simplify the code, the program simply locks the form object itself (Self). This would be a bad habit in a complex program and should be reserved for testing and trivial examples.

Let's see how TMonitor fares in practice. The following screenshot shows the results of a few consecutive runs:

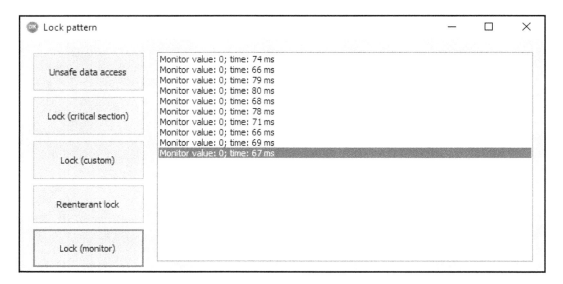

Locking with TMonitor

Not only is the result correct, but the code is now much faster! This gives us another good reason (besides not requiring a separate lock object) to use it for locking.

Custom locking mechanism

It is actually not that hard to implement a lock pattern in our code without using any external implementation. We only need a little help in the form of the `TInterlocked` class that I mentioned previously. The **Lock (custom)** button on the demonstration program activates two methods that use this approach.

The code uses an integer field called `FCustomLock: integer` as a lock. The logic is very simple; when this field contains a value of 0, access is granted. If the value is 1, access is locked.

The main program creates two threads, one executing `CustomLockIncrementValue` and another executing `CustomLockDecrementingValue`. The former is shown here:

```
procedure TfrmLock.CustomLockIncrementValue;
var
  i: integer;
begin
  for i := 1 to CNumRepeats do
  begin
    CustomAcquire(FCustomLock);
    try
      Inc(FSharedData);
    finally
      CustomRelease(FCustomLock);
    end;
  end;
end;
```

As with the previous examples, the pattern is lock-use-unlock. The `CustomRelease` method is very simple. It just stores a zero into the lock field, as shown here:

```
procedure TfrmLock.CustomRelease(var lock: integer);
begin
  lock := 0;
end;
```

The `CustomAcquire` method, however, is not so simple. It executes code that functions like this:

```
procedure CustomAcquireBad(var lock: integer);
begin
  while lock <> 0 do
    ;
  lock := 1;
end;
```

This code waits for the lock to become unlocked and then sets it to 1 to lock the access. This implementation, however, would fail in a multithreaded environment. Imagine the following scenario:

- The lock is unlocked
- Thread A reaches the `while` statement. As the lock is unlocked, `while` does not execute
- Thread B reaches the `while` statement. The lock is still unlocked, so `while` does not execute
- Thread A locks the lock
- Thread B locks the lock

The lock is now locked, but both threads think that they own the lock and both threads continue operation.

We need to execute this loop *and* set operation atomically, that is, in one indivisible step, and the correct way to do that is to use the appropriate CPU instructions. Instead of supporting each platform separately, however, it is better to use the platform-independent class `TInterlocked` from the `System.SyncObjs` unit. We can then rewrite the code as follows:

```
procedure TfrmLock.CustomAcquire(var lock: integer);
begin
  while TInterlocked.CompareExchange(lock, 1, 0) <> 0 do
    ;
end;
```

This code uses the very helpful `CompareExchange` method, which works as follows:

- It compares the first parameter (lock) with the third parameter (0)
- If both are the same, it sets the first parameter to the second parameter (1)
- In both cases, the code returns the original value of the first parameter

All three steps are executed as one indivisible unit.

The CustomAcquire method calls CompareExchange. If the old value of lock is 0, it will set it to 1 and return 0. The while loop will then exit. If the old value of lock is 1, CompareExchange will not change it and will return 1 (old value). The while loop will then repeat the CompareExchange call.

If two threads call this code at the same time, only one CompareExchange will win. It will see the lock value as 0 and will set it to 1 and exit. The other one will see it as 1 and will wait until it is set to 0.

If you run the code and test this lock, you will see that it a) works and b) runs slower than a critical section, which brings forth the question: why would we want to use such a custom solution if it is slower and more complicated?

In most cases, the answer is simple—we wouldn't. It is better and much safer to use an existing solution. In some cases, however, we could use such tricks to conserve memory usage. The *Lock striping pattern* section, later in this chapter will extend this approach to a more meaningful solution.

This custom lock also demonstrates one aspect of locks that I have not yet mentioned. Locks can be reentrant or non-reentrant. A reentrant lock can be acquired again in the same thread (after which we also need an additional release call to unlock it). Simply put, a reentrant lock allows us to run the following code:

```
lock.Acquire;
lock.Acquire;
ModifySharedValue;
lock.Release;
// lock is still owned by this thread
lock.Release
// lock is now unlocked
```

A non-reentrant lock does not support such usage. The previous example would stop forever in the second Acquire call if the lock is a non-reentrant lock.

This code looks stupid, but in practice, and especially when adapting legacy code, this second lock may be hidden in some other code that is called from ModifySharedValue. The Reentrant lock button on the demonstration program shows how such a situation may be reached. One thread, for example, executes the LockReenterIncrementValue method, which is shown here:

```
procedure TfrmLock.ChangeValue(var value: integer; delta: integer);
begin
  FLock.Acquire;
  try
    value := value + delta;
```

```
    finally
      FLock.Release;
    end;
end;

procedure TfrmLock.LockReenterIncrementValue;
var
  i: integer;
begin
  for i := 1 to CNumRepeats do
  begin
    FLock.Acquire;
    try
      ChangeValue(FSharedData, +1);
    finally
      FLock.Release;
    end;
  end;
end;
```

This method locks access to `FSharedData` and then calls `ChangeValue`, which locks/unlocks access again. This is only possible because a `TCriticalSection` implements a reentrant lock.

> `TMonitor` also implements a reentrant lock. Our custom solution, however, is non-reentrant.

Before I end this discussion on locking, I must mention another problem that locks introduce (besides slowing the program down). If we want to put together multiple parts of code that use locking, we must understand how locks are used in the original code if we want to write a correct program.

Imagine the following situation. A banking system uses the `Deposit` method that uses locking to guarantee that an account is not modified by anyone else while the method is operating. It also uses a `Withdraw` method that locks the account for the same reason. Let's say that they are implemented with the following pseudocode:

```
procedure Deposit(money, account);
begin
  lock(account);
  put money into account;
  unlock(account);
end;
```

```
procedure Withdraw(money, account);
begin
  lock(account);
  take money from account;
  unlock(account);
end;
```

This locking, however, doesn't help us when we want to transfer money from one account to another. So, the following approach doesn't work:

```
procedure Transfer(money, from, to);
begin
  Withdraw(money, from);
  Deposit(money, to);
end;
```

After `Withdraw` has executed but before `Deposit` starts, both accounts are unlocked and in a consistent state, but money cannot be found in any of them!

This is not acceptable, and to fix it we need to know how both `Deposit` and `Withdraw` are implemented internally and how they use locks. We can then write the fixed implementation, as follows:

```
procedure Transfer(money, from, to);
begin
  lock(from); lock(to);
  Withdraw(money, from);
  Deposit(money, to);
  unlock(to); unlock(from);
end;
```

We, therefore, cannot just put operations that use locking together to create more complicated operations. We can also say that locks don't compose.

Such an approach of locking multiple locks before executing the critical code can also bring the program into deadlock. Let's say that the following two calls are executed at exactly the same time in two threads:

```
Transfer(100, accA, accB);
Transfer(100, accB, accA);
```

In other words, we want to transfer the same amount of money from one account to another and back, at exactly the same time. The code will then run like so:

- The first thread locks the accA account (`lock(from)`).
- The second thread locks the accB account (`lock(from)`).
- The first thread tries to lock the accB account (`lock(to)`). As it is already locked, the thread starts waiting.
- The second thread tries to lock the accA account (`lock(to)`). As it is already locked, the thread starts waiting.
- The threads wait until the heat death of the universe or until someone kills the program.

In practice, this occurs when the code uses multiple locks but doesn't always lock them in the same order. For example, the demonstration program uses the following two methods to demonstrate a deadlock:

```
procedure TfrmLock.Lock12;
var
  i: integer;
begin
  for i := 1 to CNumRepeats do
  begin
    FLock.Acquire;
    FLock2.Acquire;

    FLock2.Release;
    FLock.Release;
  end;
end;

procedure TfrmLock.Lock21;
var
  i: integer;
begin
  for i := 1 to CNumRepeats do
  begin
    FLock2.Acquire;
    FLock.Acquire;

    FLock.Release;
    FLock2.Release;
  end;
end;
```

The first method locks `FLock` first and `FLock2` second. The second method has this order reversed.

If you click the Deadlock button, nothing will happen because both threads will block. If you click the pause button in the IDE (or select Run, Program Pause from the menu), the program will break into the debugger. At that moment, the Thread Status window will tell you that our two worker threads are waiting for each other, as shown in the following screenshot:

Thread Id	State	Wait Chain
Lock.exe (22704)		
816	Stopped	
21228	Stopped	
24228	Stopped	
23036	Stopped	
Worker Thread - TThreadPool.TQueueWorkerThread #1 ...	Stopped	Blocked on Critical Section owned by Thread Worker Thread - TThreadPool.TQueueWorkerThread #2 ...
Worker Thread - TThreadPool.TQueueWorkerThread #2 ...	Stopped	Blocked on Critical Section owned by Thread Worker Thread - TThreadPool.TQueueWorkerThread #1 ...

Two deadlocked threads

The solution is to always lock in the same order. If you, for example, change `Lock21` to acquire `FLock` first and `FLock2` second, the code will work correctly.

> The order of `Release` calls is not important.

In practice, this situation is frequently hard to find because both `Acquire` calls will not appear next to each other, but will be scattered around the code. The simplest solution is to use a helper function that locks all required locks and calls that function when entering any area of code that requires these locks. If you are using a reentrant lock, the original code can then acquire locks again in any order. That will work because all locks will already be acquired.

Lock striping

In the previous section, I recommended using one lock per shared resource. We also saw that sometimes we cannot do such fine-grained locking and that we have to implement locks that protect more than one resource at the same time.

The lock striping pattern covers the opposite case. Sometimes, one lock per resource is not enough. On some occasions, we may want to implement multiple locks for one shared resource. We could, for example, add a lock to each element in an array or list.

 Imagine the fitting rooms in a clothing store. They are not protected with one master lock as that would prevent multiple customers from trying out clothes at the same time. Rather, each room has its own lock.

This pattern can only be applied when the size of the shared resource is not modified during the execution. It does not help us if we lock two elements in an array and then another thread ignores these locks and removes one element between them, shifting the data around.

It can also be expensive (in terms of time and memory usage) to maintain all these additional locks. Later in this section, I'll show you how we can implement a custom locking mechanism that only uses one additional bit. If we can find one bit of data that is not used in the program, we can use it as a lock. Such an implementation needs no additional memory and doesn't have to manage additional locks.

To demonstrate the lock striping pattern, the `LockStriping` program in the `Lock striping` folder shuffles a deck of cards with four parallel threads.

For simplicity, the cards are represented by a number from 0 to 51. They are stored in a dynamic integer array called `TArray<integer>` and are generated with the following method:

```
function TfrmLockStriping.GenerateData: TArray<integer>;
var
  i: integer;
begin
  SetLength(Result, 52);
  for i := 0 to 51 do
    Result[i] := i + 1;
end;
```

 The program ignores the actual names of the cards. You can write your own function that maps from the integer range 0–51 to card names for practice. For example, numbers from 0 to 12 could represent one suite, numbers from 13 to 25 another, and so on.

To shuffle the deck, the program starts four parallel threads, which all repeat the following two steps 100,000 times:

- Select two cards
- Exchange these two cards

The following code is used to select two cards. It simply calculates two random numbers from 0 to 51 and returns them in two `var` parameters, as follows:

```
procedure TfrmLockStriping.PickTwo(dataLen: integer; var idx1, idx2:
integer);
var
  temp: integer;
begin
  idx1 := Random(dataLen);
  idx2 := Random(dataLen);
  if idx1 > idx2 then
  begin
    temp := idx1;
    idx1 := idx2;
    idx2 := temp;
  end;
end;
```

The code guarantees that `idx2` is always equal to or greater than `idx1`. This will become important once we implement the lock striping pattern.

The selection algorithm doesn't access any shared resource (the process just creates two random numbers). That is not true for the code that exchanges two cards as it must modify the shared resource—the deck of cards. One possible solution is to simply use a lock pattern to get exclusive access to the deck before two cards are switched.

The following method generates a deck, starts shuffling threads, waits for them to finish, and logs the state of the shuffled deck, all with a master lock we'll call, well, `lock`:

```
procedure TfrmLockStriping.btnMasterLockClick(Sender: TObject);
var
  data: TArray<integer>;
  lock: TCriticalSection;
  time_ms: int64;
begin
  data := GenerateData;
  lock := TCriticalSection.Create;
  try
    time_ms := RunTasks(
      procedure
```

```
      var
        iShuffle: integer;
      begin
        for iShuffle := 1 to CNumShuffles do
          ExchangeTwoMaster(lock, data);
      end);
    LogData('Master lock', time_ms, data);
    VerifyData(data);
  finally
    FreeAndNil(lock);
  end;
end;
```

Threads are started in the `RunTasks` method, which is not important for this discussion. You can look it up in the source code.

The actual shuffling is implemented in the `ExchangeTwoMaster` method, which takes two parameters, a master lock and a dynamic array that is to be shuffled. The code selects two cards, locks the master lock, exchanges the cards, and unlocks the master lock, as follows:

```
procedure TfrmLockStriping.ExchangeTwoMaster(lock: TCriticalSection;
  const data: TArray<integer>);
var
  idx1: Integer;
  idx2: Integer;
  temp: Integer;
begin
  PickTwo(Length(data), idx1, idx2);
  if idx1 = idx2 then
    Exit;

  lock.Acquire;
  try
    temp := data[idx1];
    data[idx1] := data[idx2];
    data[idx2] := temp;
  finally
    lock.Release;
  end;
end;
```

As an optimization step, the code also immediately exits (without locking) if the `PickTwo` method has picked the same card twice.

To verify that locking is indeed required in this case, just comment out the `Acquire` and `Release` calls and run the program. You will see that shuffling now generates an invalid deck in which some numbers (some cards) are repeating.

This code works and you can immediately test it by running the demonstration program and clicking on the Master lock button. But we can do better than that. Let's look at the card switching code again:

```
temp := data[idx1];
data[idx1] := data[idx2];
data[idx2] := temp;
```

This code actually doesn't have to protect the whole deck of cards. It only requires access to elements with indices `idx1` and `idx2`, so we only need to protect access to these two elements. Other threads can do whatever they want with the rest of the deck while this exchange is in progress.

Instead of using a master lock, we can implement the lock striping pattern by generating 52 critical sections. Each critical section protects one element of the card deck array.

The `btnSeparateLocksClick` method generates such an array of locks, then runs the testing code, and at the end, cleans up all additional locks. The rest of the code is mostly the same as before, except that an `ExchangeTwoSeparate` method is called to exchange two cards, as follows:

```
procedure TfrmLockStriping.btnSeparateLocksClick(Sender: TObject);
var
  data: TArray<integer>;
  locks: TArray<TCriticalSection>;
  time_ms: int64;
  i: Integer;
begin
  data := GenerateData;
  SetLength(locks, Length(data));
  for i := Low(locks) to High(locks) do
    locks[i] := TCriticalSection.Create;
  try
    time_ms := RunTasks(
      procedure
      var
        iShuffle: integer;
      begin
        for iShuffle := 1 to CNumShuffles do
          ExchangeTwoSeparate(locks, data);
      end);
```

```
    LogData('Separate locks', time_ms, data);
    VerifyData(data);
  finally
    for i := Low(locks) to High(locks) do
    locks[i].Free;
  end;
end;
```

The card-exchanging method again receives two parameters, but this time the first parameter represents the whole array of additional locks. As shown in the following code, the code selects two cards, locks both cards, exchanges them, unlocks, and exits:

```
procedure TfrmLockStriping.ExchangeTwoSeparate(
  const locks: TArray<TCriticalSection>; const data: TArray<integer>);
var
  idx1: Integer;
  idx2: Integer;
  temp: Integer;
begin
  PickTwo(Length(data), idx1, idx2);
  if idx1 = idx2 then
    Exit;

  locks[idx1].Acquire;
  try
    locks[idx2].Acquire;
    try
      temp := data[idx1];
      data[idx1] := data[idx2];
      data[idx2] := temp;
    finally
      locks[idx2].Release;
    end;
  finally
    locks[idx1].Release;
  end;
end;
```

We can now see why `PickTwo` returns an ordered pair of cards. As we are locking two critical sections, we must always lock them in the same order, otherwise the code can deadlock. The simplest way to enforce the order is to always lock the critical section with smaller index first.

The following screenshot shows the program after the cards were shuffled five times with a **Master lock** algorithm and five times with a lock striping algorithm:

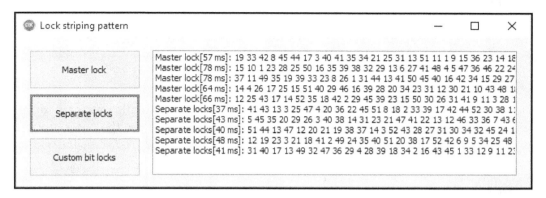

Comparing master lock with lock striping

We can see that both algorithms shuffle the deck (no surprise here) and that a lock striping approach is indeed faster. The pattern, therefore, works at least in this case, but it is quite awkward to implement with all the additional locks that we have to maintain. We can fix this problem by implementing a custom locking method that reuses one bit of data for locking purposes.

Single bit locks

Getting one bit of data is not as hard as you may think. In our case, for example, most of the `integer` data type that's used to store a card number is unused. We only need 6 bits to represent numbers from 0 to 51, which means that the other 24 bits are unused. In most cases, you'll be able to find one such spare bit in existing data (if not, you can still implement lock striping by introducing additional locks).

To make the code clearer, I have extracted the logic that maintains the lock-striped array of cards into a separate record of type `TLockStripingArray`. It is defined in the `LockStripingArray` unit, as follows:

```
type
  TLockStripingArray = record
  private const
    CMaskBit = 31;
    CBitMask = 1 SHL CMaskBit;
  var
    FData: TArray<integer>;
```

```
      function GetItem(idx: integer): integer; inline;
      procedure SetItem(idx: integer; const value: integer); inline;
    public
      procedure Acquire(idx: integer); inline;
      procedure Release(idx: integer); inline;
      property Data: TArray<integer> read FData write FData;
      property Items[idx: integer]: integer read GetItem write SetItem;
        default;
    end;
```

This record stores a dynamic integer array in its Data property and allows access to individual items through the Items property. The application can use the Data property to initialize the record, but after that, it should use the Items property to access individual items.

The record also implements the Acquire and Release methods, which lock and unlock a specific item. All of this is used in the main program, as follows:

```
procedure TfrmLockStriping.btnCustomLocksClick(Sender: TObject);
var
  data: TLockStripingArray;
  time_ms: int64;
begin
  data.Data := GenerateData;
  time_ms := RunTasks(
    procedure
    var
      iShuffle: integer;
    begin
      for iShuffle := 1 to CNumShuffles do
        ExchangeTwoCustom(data);
    end);
  LogData('Custom bit lock', time_ms, data.Data);
  VerifyData(data.Data);
end;
```

This code is the simplest of all three approaches as it doesn't have to maintain any locks at all. The item exchanging method ExchangeTwoCustom, shown in the following code, still has to lock and unlock array elements and is almost identical to the lock striping implementation ExchangeTwoSeparate:

```
procedure TfrmLockStriping.ExchangeTwoCustom(
  const data: TLockStripingArray);
var
  idx1: Integer;
  idx2: Integer;
  temp: Integer;
```

```
begin
  PickTwo(Length(data.Data), idx1, idx2);
  if idx1 = idx2 then
    Exit;

  data.Acquire(idx1);
  try
    data.Acquire(idx2);
    try
      temp := data.Data[idx1];
      data.Data[idx1] := data.Data[idx2];
      data.Data[idx2] := temp;
    finally
      data.Release(idx2);
    end;
  finally
    data.Release(idx1);
  end;
end;
```

The locking implementation is very similar to the custom solution from the section on the lock pattern from the *Lock* section.It uses the highest integer bit- bit 31-to represent a lock. If the bit is 0, the integer is not locked. Setting the bit to 1 acquires a lock.

As with the previous custom implementation, releasing a lock is simple. We merely have to clear bit 31, as follows:

```
procedure TLockStripingArray.Release(idx: integer);
begin
  FData[idx] := FData[idx] AND NOT CBitMask;
end;
```

If you are not familiar with Delphi bitwise operations (AND NOT CBitMask), don't worry. I will explain this concept later in this chapter.

To acquire a lock, we must again implement an atomic compare and set operation. If bit 31 is zero, we would like to set it to 1 and exit. If bit 31 is 1, we would like to wait until it becomes zero. The Acquire method implements this logic, as shown here:

```
procedure TLockStripingArray.Acquire(idx: integer);
var
  el: Integer;
begin
  while TInterlocked.BitTestAndSet(FData[idx], 31) do
    ;
end;
```

The `BitTestAndSet` method of the `TInterlocked` class does the heavy work. Similar to `CompareExchange`, which we have used before, it returns the previous state of the bit (`False` or `True` for 0 and 1) and sets the bit to 1. The `Acquire` method works as follows:

- If the bit 31 is 0, it is set to 1 and `False` is returned. The `While` loop then exits.
- If the bit 31 is 1, it is not changed and `True` is returned. The `While` loop then repeats.

As this is done atomically, the code works correctly in a multithreaded environment.

This covers the locking, but we must still do some additional work to correctly implement the `Items` properly. If, for example, we lock an element containing value 42, the bit 31 of that value gets set, turning 42 (or $2A) into $8000002A, or -2147483606. If we read the value at that time, we would get an invalid result (this is the reason why the `Data` property must not be used directly while the program is running). The `GetItem` function, therefore, strips bit 31 away and returns bits from 0 to 30, as follows:

```
function TLockStripingArray.GetItem(idx: integer): integer;
begin
  Result := FData[idx] AND NOT CBitMask;
end;
```

A reverse operation happens when the code is assigned to the `Items` property. The original bit 31 of the `FData` array must be preserved (as it indicates the lock state), and only other value bits must be modified. The `SetItem` implements this logic as follows:

```
procedure TLockStripingArray.SetItem(idx: integer; const value: integer);
begin
  FData[idx] := (value AND NOT CBitMask) OR (FData[idx] AND CBitMask);
end;
```

The following screenshot shows a comparison between an implementation with a critical section and a custom implementation with a lock bit:

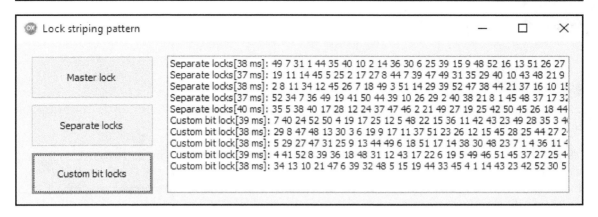

Comparing critical sections with custom bit locks

We can see that neither outperforms the other. The final choice, that is, using separate locks or stealing a data bit somewhere, is yours. Use whatever fits best into the architecture of your program.

Delphi idioms – bitwise operators

The standard logical operators and, or, xor, and not have an additional hidden side in Delphi. We can also use them to perform operations on individual bits of a number. Besides being logical operators, they also function as bitwise (bit by bit) operators.

The meaning of an operator, for example, and, is automatically detected from the context. When the compiler encounters a code like a and b and both a and b are Boolean variables (or expressions), and is compiled to a logical operator. If a and b are both an integer (or word or NativeUInt, or any other integer type), and is compiled to a bitwise operator. If a is an integer and b is a boolean, the compiler reports an error.

 To improve readability of code, I write logical operators in lower case (and, or, ...) and bitwise operators in upper case (AND, OR, ...).

Bitwise operators work exactly the same as logical operators, except that the operation is performed on each bit pair (taking into account that 0 is the same as False and 1 is the same as True). The operator combines bit 0 of both operands into bit 0 of the result, bit 1 of both operands into bit 0 of the result, and so on.

Let's explore how these operators work on examples from the custom bit locking code. The `TLockStripingArray` record defines the following two constants:

```
CMaskBit = 31;
 CBitMask = 1 SHL CMaskBit;
```

The `1 SHL CMaskBit` operation shifts bit 1 to the left 31 times. In other words, it multiplies it by two 31 times to get the result of 2^{31} or $80000000.

To get the reverse mask (where zeros are ones and ones are zeros), the code uses the expression `NOT CBitMask`. The `CBitMask` starts with binary `1000 0000`, which `NOT` turns into `0111 1111` or $7F. Other bytes are all 0, or `0000 0000`, and `NOT` turns them into `1111 1111` or $FF. `NOT CBitMask` is therefore equal to $7FFFFFFF.

To remove the lock bit from value, the code uses `AND NOT CBitMask`, which is the same as `AND $7FFFFFFF`. If, for example, the original value has a lock bit set, it must be in the form of $800000xy (the last two places are enough to represent all values from 0 to 51). The initial byte is calculated as `1000 0000 AND 0111 1111 = 0000 0000` (as with Boolean values, `0 AND 1 = 0` and `1 AND 1 = 1`). The highest bit is therefore removed. All middle bytes stay at zero because `0000 0000 AND 1111 1111 = 0000 0000`.

The last byte, which holds the actual card number, can be written as `00ab cdef`, where each letter represents one bit. When we `AND` it with `1111 1111`, we get the original value back. If a (or any other bit) is 0, `0 AND 1 = 0` and the result is 0. If a is 1, `1 AND 1 = 1` and the result is 1. `AND 1`, therefore, leaves the original bit unchanged.

To merge a value and the lock bit, the code executes the following expression:

```
(value AND NOT CBitMask) OR (FData[idx] AND CBitMask)
```

As we are using bit 31 to represent a lock, it must not be used for data; therefore, we must remove it with `value AND NOT CBitMask` (we have already seen how that works). The code then extracts the state of the current lock bit with `FData[idx] AND CBitMask`. This will give us either $00000000 (if the value is not locked) or $80000000 (if it is).

Both values are then combined with `OR`. When we `OR` with 0, the result will be the same as the original bit (`0 OR 0 = 0, 1 OR 0 = 1`). All `value` bits (from 0 to 30) will, therefore, be left unchanged. The highest bit, which is 0 in `value AND NOT CBitMask`, is OR-ed with the current lock bit (0 or 1). That leaves the lock bit unchanged (`0 OR 0 = 0, 0 OR 1 = 1`).

The result, therefore, takes the highest bit from `FData[idx]` and all other bits from `value`, which is exactly what we need.

The following table will help you write such bitwise expressions:

Expression	Result
NOT 0	1
NOT 1	0
x OR 0	x
x OR 1	1
x OR y	y OR x
x AND 0	0
x AND 1	x
x AND y	y AND x

Double-checked locking

When we are writing code that sometimes requires some object to be created, and sometimes not, we can save some execution time by only creating this object when it is needed. This process-lazy initialization is explained in Chapter 2, *Singleton, Dependency Injection, Lazy Initialization, and Object Pool*. That chapter, however, only covered single-threaded applications.

To do lazy initialization properly in a multithreaded world, we need locking. And to do it correctly and fast, we need a double-checked locking pattern. This pattern can speed up any lock that is only acquired if some condition is met. It is also called *test, lock, and test again*.

For instance, when you are changing lanes in a car, you check the traffic around you first, then turn on your indicator, check the traffic again, and then change lane.

In the demonstration program `DoubleCheckedLocking` from the `Double-checked locking` folder, the `TLazyOwner` class functions as an owner that can create a field called `FLazy: TLazyObject` on demand. Both classes are defined as follows:

```
type
  TLazyObject = class
  public
    constructor Create;
    destructor Destroy; override;
```

```
  end;

  TLazyOwner = class
  strict private
    FLazy: TLazyObject;
    FLock: TCriticalSection;
  public
    function DoubleChecked: TLazyObject;
    function LazySingleThreaded: TLazyObject;
    function LockAndCheck: TLazyObject;
    function TestAndLock: TLazyObject;
    constructor Create;
    destructor Destroy; override;
  end;
```

The code uses a standard test and create pattern to create the `FLazy` object in single-threaded code, as shown here:

```
function TLazyOwner.LazySingleThreaded: TLazyObject;
begin
  if not assigned(FLazy) then
    FLazy := TLazyObject.Create;
  Result := FLazy;
end;
```

The demonstration program then creates a `TLazyOwner` object, logs some information, accesses the lazily created objects, logs some more, and exits, as follows:

```
procedure TfrmDoubleChecked.btnLazyInitClick(Sender: TObject);
var
  lazy: TLazyObject;
  owner: TLazyOwner;
begin
  owner := TLazyOwner.Create;
  try
    Log('Execute some code ...');
    Log('Access lazy object...');
    lazy := owner.LazySingleThreaded;
    Log('Use lazy object ...');
    Log('Destroy lazy object ...');
  finally FreeAndNil(owner); end;
end;
```

If you run the program and click on the Lazy initialization button, you'll see in the log when the `TLazyObject` object is created and destroyed.

The problems occur when we want to lazily create a shared object in a multithreaded application. Multiple threads cannot just use a simple test and create algorithm, as it can result in lost objects, as shown here:

```
if not assigned(FLazy) then
  FLazy := TLazyObject.Create;
```

If two threads execute this at the same time, they would both decide that `FLazy` doesn't exist yet, they would both create a new `TLazyObject`, and they would both store it in the `FLazy` property. One would do that slightly before the other and its `FLazy` object will be lost because `FLazy` will be overwritten with the value generated in the second thread. The first object will stay lost in memory until the program is closed.

The simplest solution to this problem is to use a *lock* pattern. A lock and test algorithm in the function `LockAndCheck` enters a critical section, tests whether the object has already been created, and creates it if required. It is shown here:

```
function TLazyOwner.LockAndCheck: TLazyObject;
begin
  FLock.Acquire;
  try
    if not assigned(FLazy) then
      FLazy := TLazyObject.Create;
  finally
    FLock.Release;
  end;
  Result := FLazy;
end;
```

You already know that any introduction of locking slows down the program. Programmers that don't yet know the double-checked locking pattern frequently try to speed up the code by introducing a test and lock anti-pattern. The `TestAndLock` function shows how lazy creation should never be performed in the multithreaded environment, as follows:

```
function TLazyOwner.TestAndLock: TLazyObject;
begin
  // Bad implementation, do not use!
  if not assigned(FLazy) then
  begin
    FLock.Acquire;
    try
      FLazy := TLazyObject.Create;
    finally
```

```
      FLock.Release;
    end;
  end;
  Result := FLazy;
end;
```

The code tests whether `FLazy` exists. If not, it enters a critical section, creates the object, and exits the critical section. This, however, doesn't fix anything. It is quite possible that `FLazy` was created in another thread after the `if` test passed and before the critical section was acquired which, again, results in a lost object!

A proper solution is to implement double-checked locking, or the test, lock, and test again pattern. The following `DoubleChecked` function shows how the test should be performed:

```
function TLazyOwner.DoubleChecked: TLazyObject;
begin
  if not assigned(FLazy) then
  begin
    FLock.Acquire;
    try
      if not assigned(FLazy) then
        FLazy := TLazyObject.Create;
    finally
      FLock.Release;
    end;
  end;
  Result := FLazy;
end;
```

The code first tests whether `FLazy` is assigned. If not, it enters the critical section and performs the same test again. In a way, the whole initialization is still executed inside the critical section. The initial `if` statement is just an optimization step that prevents the critical section from being unnecessarily acquired once the object is created.

We could rewrite the function as follows and it would perform the same action:

```
function TLazyOwner.DoubleChecked: TLazyObject;
begin
  if not assigned(FLazy) then
    Result := LockAndCheck;
end;
```

It can still happen that two threads execute the `if` statement at the same time and both enter the `LockAndCheck` method, but as this method does both (test and create) in one atomic step, only one object would be created.

The test code runs two threads and inside each calls the object creation method one million times. The following screenshot shows a comparison of the three initialization methods:

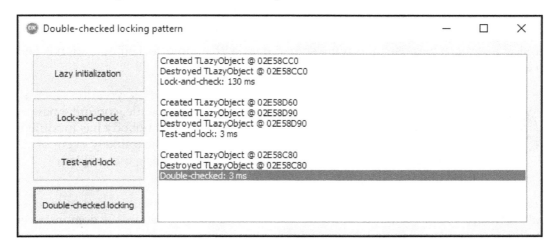

Comparing the "lock and test", "test and lock", and "test, lock, and test again" algorithms

The initial approach of locking and testing does the job in 130 milliseconds. Bad test and lock implementation is much faster. It runs in 3 milliseconds, but it creates two `TLazyObject` objects. The double-checked locking approach takes the best aspects from both, and as a result, the code is correct and fast.

Optimistic locking

We saw before that locks can sometimes be replaced with interlocked operations and we also used such operations to implement custom-made locking. Interlocked operations are also the basis for the optimistic locking pattern, which can be used to implement changes in shared data without using a classical locking mechanism.

Optimistic locking works when a chance of conflict between threads is very low. Like a database transaction mechanism, optimistic locking assumes that there will be no problem and applies required modifications on its own copy of the data (creates a new object, for example). In the second step, optimistic locking tries to commit the change. With one atomic step (usually implemented with an interlocked instruction), the current state is replaced with a new value.

This atomic replacement can, however, fail (if the state was modified by another thread in the meantime). In such a case, optimistic locking must revert the change (roll back a transaction). As such, this locking may result in duplicate work.

Even though it may sometimes do something twice, optimistic locking can work faster than a classical approach because modifying shared data with an interlocked operation is faster than acquiring and releasing a lock.

 In modern version control systems, such as SVN and git, you don't lock a file that you want to change. Instead, you modify the file, commit a new version to the version control system, and hope that nobody has modified the same lines of the same file in the meantime. In the unlikely event of a conflict, you have to spend some additional time fixing the problem (merging the changes).

We can use optimistic locking to implement lazy initialization without any additional lock. We already know how to do it with the double-checked locking pattern, as demonstrated in the following pseudocode:

```
if object is not yet created then
begin
  acquire lock;
  if object is not yet created then
    shared object := create object;
  release lock;
  return shared object;
end;
```

With optimistic locking, this algorithm changes to the following:

```
if object is not yet created then
begin
  temp object := create object;
  if not atomically store temp object into shared object then
    destroy temp object;
  return shared object;
end;
```

The `OptimisticLocking` project from the `Optimistic locking` folder implements this pattern to lazily initialize an object. The program has the same structure as the `DoubleCheckedLocking` program from the previous section and implements the same double-checked locking algorithm. This allows us to compare the results of both techniques.

Optimistic lazy initialization is implemented in the Optimistic method, as follows:

```
function TLazyOwner.Optimistic: TLazyObject;
var
  tempLazy: TLazyObject;
begin
  if not assigned(FLazy) then
  begin
    tempLazy := TLazyObject.Create;
    if TInterlocked.CompareExchange(pointer(FLazy), tempLazy, nil) <> nil
then
      FreeAndNil(tempLazy);
  end;
  Result := FLazy;
end;
```

The code first checks whether the FLazy field has already been created. If not, it assumes that there will be no problems and creates a new TLazyObject. As we cannot write into the shared FLazy field without special care, we have to store the newly-created object in a temporary variable.

After that, the code uses the interlocked CompareExchange instruction to store a new object in the FLazy field if FLazy is still nil. If FLazy has been modified between the if and CompareExchange, the latter will return a non-nil value (an object that was created in another thread), which is a signal for the Optimistic method to throw the temporary object away.

If you run the program, you'll see that both approaches, double-checked locking and optimistic locking, need the same time to execute the code. This is not surprising as both methods create the object only once. Most of the time, they just test the if not assigned(FLazy) condition and then do nothing. The following screenshot proves that:

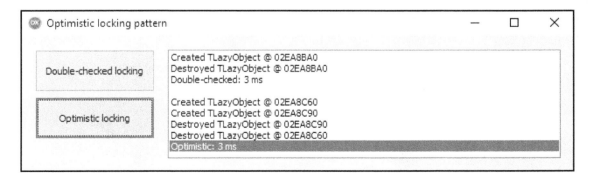

Comparing double-checked locking and optimistic locking

This screenshot also shows that in optimistic locking, one object too many was created and thrown away.

To really compare the execution speed, I had to create a version of the program that repeats the test 100,000 times (you can find it in the `OptimisticLockingSpeedTest` project). This results in the lazy object also being created 100,000 times, and that gives us a measurable result. The following screenshot shows the result of this modified program:

Comparing 100,000 executions of double-checked and optimistic locking

As I mentioned in `Chapter 2`, *Singleton, Dependency Injection, Lazy Initialization, and Object Pool,* we can use the Spring4D library to lazily initialize objects. As Spring4D implementation supports multithreading, let's take a look at the technique used in the library. The following method can be found in the Spring unit:

```
class function TLazyInitializer.EnsureInitialized<T>(var target: T): T;
var
  value: T;
begin
  if target = nil then
  begin
    value := T.Create;
    if AtomicCmpExchange(PPointer(@target)^, PPointer(@value)^, nil) <> nil
then
      value.Free;
  end;
  Result := target;
end;
```

As we can see, it is almost the same as the `Optimistic` method except that it uses `AtomicCmpExchange` and not `TInterlocked.CompareExchange`. The latter (which lives in the `System.SyncObjs` unit) is actually implemented as an `inline` function, which directly calls the `AtomicCmpExchange` function (from the *System* unit) as follows:

```
class function TInterlocked.CompareExchange(var Target: Pointer;
  Value: Pointer; Comparand: Pointer): Pointer;
begin
  Result := AtomicCmpExchange(Target, Value, Comparand);
end;
```

In most cases, both will compile to the same code because of the `inline` directive. The difference between the two is that `AtomicCmpExchange` doesn't require us to list the SyncObjs unit in the `uses` clause. You can use whichever you want.

Readers-writer lock

All the locking mechanisms that I have discussed so far were designed for *symmetric* scenarios. In all examples, they were synchronizing multiple threads that were all doing (more or less) the same work. This is, however, not the only type of shared data access we can encounter.

Another frequent situation that occurs in multithreaded applications is when multiple threads are just reading from the shared data without doing any modifications. That by itself would not require any locking at all, except that from time to time, the data has to be modified. To do that, we somehow have to stop the reading threads. We must also, as before, prevent two writers from working on the data at the same time.

In such a situation, we need a synchronization mechanism that allows multiple *readers* to *share* the resource while also allowing one *writer* to acquire *exclusive* access to the resource when necessary. We call such a synchronization mechanism a *readers-writer* or *shared-exclusive* lock (other names are also used in the literature and on the internet, including **multiple readers, single writer (MRSW)**, **multiple readers, exclusive writer (MREW)**, **single writer, multiple readers (SWMR)**, and more).

This design allows readers who are the most frequent users of the resource to work at the same time. Where there's a need to modify the resource, the writer requests exclusive access, which blocks all readers, modifies the resource, and unlocks it.

A road is a resource that was designed for sharing. Multiple cars are using it at the same time. When there's a need to modify the road (paint new road marks, fix the pavement, and so on), they have to close down the traffic so that the road is exclusively available to the maintenance crew.

Readers-writer lock is a complicated mechanism that can be implemented in many different ways. As with normal locks, it can be reentrant or non-reentrant. A reentrant lock can be acquired again for the same level of access after it has been acquired once.

A reentrant lock allows a read (shared) lock to be acquired again for the read (shared) access but not for a write (exclusive) access. Turning a reader into a writer without dropping the lock in the meantime is only possible if the locking mechanism supports that. A lock that enables such a promotion is called **upgradeable** or **promotable**. A lock may also allow a writer to be changed into a reader, in which case we call it **downgradeable**.

Readers-writer lock implementations also differ in how they handle requests for write access. If at least one reader is active, a writer cannot get access immediately. It has to wait for that reader to release the lock. If in the meantime, another thread requests read access, the lock can respond in two ways.

A read-biased or read-preferring lock will immediately grant read access to the new thread. Such an implementation is faster, but can lead to writer starvation. If at least one reader exists at all times, a writer can never get access to the resource.

An alternative approach implemented by a writer-biased or write-preferring lock would, in such an event, block the new reader. With such an implementation, a reader can never get access to the shared resource while at least one writer is waiting its turn. This prevents writer starvation, but requires a more complicated implementation, which makes the lock perform slower.

 The name *readers-writer* may suggest that you can only have one writer thread. That is not true. You most certainly *can* have more than one, but they can only get write access one at a time.

Delphi comes with a custom implementation of a readers-writer lock in the form of a `TMultiReadExclusiveWriteSynchronizer` class, which can be found in the `System.SysUtils` unit. As typing that long name is not good for your fingers, the same unit also defines a shorter alias: `TMREWSync`.

This synchronize is only available on Windows. On other supported platforms, TMultiReadExclusiveWriteSynchronizer is just an alias for the TSimpleRWSync class. They both implement the same interface, IReadWriteSync, which exposes readers-writer functionality. The following code fragment will help you understand the relationship between these classes on different platforms:

```
type
  IReadWriteSync = interface ['{7B108C52-1D8F-4CDB-9CDF-57E071193D3F}']
    procedure BeginRead;
    procedure EndRead;
    function BeginWrite: Boolean;
    procedure EndWrite;
  end;

  TSimpleRWSync = class(TInterfacedObject, IReadWriteSync)
    ...
  end;

{$IFDEF MSWINDOWS}
  TMultiReadExclusiveWriteSynchronizer = class(TInterfacedObject,
IReadWriteSync)
    ...
  end;
{$ELSE}
  TMultiReadExclusiveWriteSynchronizer = TSimpleRWSync;
{$ENDIF}

  TMREWSync = TMultiReadExclusiveWriteSynchronizer;
```

The big difference between TSimpleRWSync and Windows-only TMultiReadExclusiveWriteSynchronizer is that the latter is a true readers-writer lock, while the former simply functions as a wrapper around a TMonitor lock. By using TSimpleRWSync, the code will only support one simultaneous reader.

This approach allows multiplatform programs to use TMREWSync on all platforms. On Windows, the code will benefit from multiple readers working in parallel, while on other platforms it will not work as fast, but at least it will still work.

Another possibility is to use the Slim Reader/Writer synchronisation mechanism, which has been part of the Windows operating system since Windows Vista. To help you use this implementation, I have written a simple class called `TSlimReaderWriter`, which wraps the Windows API and exposes it through the `IReadWriteSync` interface. It is implemented in the `SlimReaderWriter` unit and is defined as follows:

```
type
  IReadWriteSyncEx = interface ['{21BDDB51-29B4-44A4-B80A-1E5D72FB43DA}']
    function TryBeginRead: Boolean;
    function TryBeginWrite: Boolean;
  end;

  TSlimReaderWriter = class(TInterfacedObject, IReadWriteSync,
IReadWriteSyncEx)
  public
    constructor Create;
    procedure BeginRead;
    function BeginWrite: Boolean;
    procedure EndRead;
    procedure EndWrite;
    function TryBeginRead: Boolean;
    function TryBeginWrite: Boolean;
  end;
```

Comparing reader-writer implementations

To compare different implementations, I have prepared a test program called `ReadersWriterLock` stored in the `Readers-writer lock` folder. This program starts six reader threads that process a shared list and one writer thread that modifies this list ten times per second.

A method, `RunTests`, which you can look up in the code, accepts a `IReadWriteSync` interface and runs the tests on it. The form contains three buttons, each one to run tests on a specific implementation, as follows:

```
procedure TfrmReadersWriter.btnMREWClick(Sender: TObject);
begin
  RunTests('TMREWSync', TMREWSync.Create);
end;

procedure TfrmReadersWriter.btnSimpleRWClick(Sender: TObject);
begin
  RunTests('TSimpleRWSync', TSimpleRWSync.Create);
end;
```

```
procedure TfrmReadersWriter.btnSRWClick(Sender: TObject);
begin
  RunTests('TSlimReaderWriter', TSlimReaderWriter.Create);
end;
```

The reader thread runs the `TestReader` method, which accepts a shared resource called `list` and a readers-writer lock called `mrew`, as follows:

```
function TfrmReadersWriter.TestReader(list: TList<integer>;
  const mrew: IReadWriteSync): integer;
var
  a: real;
  el: Integer;
  timer: TStopwatch;
  i: Integer;
begin
  Result := 0;
  timer := TStopwatch.StartNew;
  while timer.ElapsedMilliseconds < (CTestDuration_sec * 1000) do
  begin
    mrew.BeginRead;
    try
      for el in list do
      begin
        a := 1/el;
        // simulate workload
        for i := 1 to 1000 do
          a := Cos(a);
      end;
    finally
      mrew.EndRead;
    end;
    Inc(Result);
    Sleep(1);
  end;
end;
```

The code runs for 3 seconds and tries to process the list as many times as possible. To prevent a total starvation of the writer thread, the code sleeps for 1 millisecond after each processing cycle.

The writer thread `TestWriter` adds 1,000 elements to the shared list, waits for 100 milliseconds, and repeats, as follows:

```
function TfrmReadersWriter.TestWriter(list: TList<integer>;
  const mrew: IReadWriteSync): Integer;
var
  nextEl: Integer;
```

```
    timer: TStopwatch;
    i: Integer;
begin
  Result := 0;
  timer := TStopwatch.StartNew;
  nextEl := 1;
  while timer.ElapsedMilliseconds < (CTestDuration_sec * 1000) do
  begin
    mrew.BeginWrite;
    try
      for i := 1 to 1000 do
      begin
        list.Add(nextEl);
        Inc(nextEl);
      end;
    finally
      mrew.EndWrite;
    end;
    Inc(Result);
    Sleep(100);
  end;
end;
```

The testing code displays how many times the writer was able to update the data in 3 seconds and how many times each reader thread did the same. The following screenshot shows the comparison of three locking implementations:

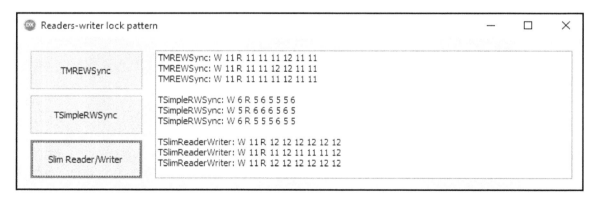

Comparing TMREWSync, TSimpleRWSync, and TSlimReaderWriter

As expected, the lock-based `TSimpleRWSync` is the slowest of the three. As it doesn't allow multiple readers to execute in parallel, the program runs only at about 50% speed.

The other two implementations run at approximately the same speed. A writer did 11 updates in both cases, while each reader managed to do between 11 and 12 cycles. The Windows implementation seems just a tad faster, though.

This is not surprising given the fact that the Delphi and Windows implementations are very different in design. The TMREWSync is reentrant, upgradeable, and write-biased. The Slim Reader/Writer, on the other hand, is non-reentrant, non-upgradeable, and read-biased.

In this program, the raw speed of the Delphi and Windows implementation doesn't matter much because the program doesn't access the locks that much. If we were locking smaller parts of code with greater frequency, however, the speed of particular implementation would come into play.

To measure the raw speed of each readers-writer implementation, the ReadersWriterLock program uses another test, SpeedTest, which measures the time required to get a read lock 1 million times, and then does the same for the write lock. It is implemented as follows:

```
procedure TfrmReadersWriter.SpeedTest(const name: string;
  const mrew: IReadWriteSync);
var
  i: Integer;
  readTime: int64;
  timer: TStopwatch;
begin
  timer := TStopwatch.StartNew;
  for i := 1 to CSpeedTestRepeats do
  begin
    mrew.BeginRead;
    mrew.EndRead;
  end;
  readTime := timer.ElapsedMilliseconds;
  timer := TStopwatch.StartNew;
  for i := 1 to CSpeedTestRepeats do
  begin
    mrew.BeginWrite;
    mrew.EndWrite;
  end;
  timer.Stop;
  lbLog.Items.Add(Format('%s: W %d R %d',
    [name, timer.ElapsedMilliseconds, readtime]));
end;
```

This method gives us an entirely different view of the three implementations. The following screenshot shows the execution speed being measured on my test computer:

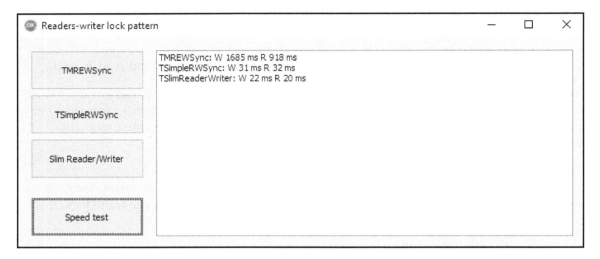

Comparing the raw speed of TMREWSync, TSimpleRWSync, and TSlimReaderWriter

We can see that the `TMREWSync` implementation is really, really slow. While the `TMonitor` implementation needs 30 milliseconds to execute 1 million readers or writers and the Windows implementation is even faster than that, `TMREWSync` needs 18x more time to acquire a read lock and 37x more time to get a write lock!

If you need a readers-writer lock in your program, you should not use the Delphi implementation, but the Windows one instead. If, however, you are writing a multiplatform program, you should code against the `IReadWriteSync` interface and then use a `TSlimReaderWriter` implementation on Windows and a `TSimpleRWSync` implementation on other operating systems.

Summary

This chapter opened with the topic of *Concurrency* patterns by exploring five different patterns related to managing access to shared data from multiple threads.

We learned that the lock pattern ensures that two threads are not trying to modify shared data or an object at the same time. It is also useful when one thread is reading from a shared object while another wants to modify it. We explored three different implementations of this pattern and compared their advantages and disadvantages.

We also learned that the lock pattern can be improved by introducing lock striping—a pattern that further fragments data inside one object and protects it with multiple locks instead of one. This approach is useful when we manipulate data in a list or array and don't add or remove existing elements. We explored two use possibilities, adding an array of locks or using one unused bit of existing data in combination with a custom locking solution.

After that, we spent some time exploring the lazy creation of objects in a multithreaded environment. As we always want programs to run as fast as possible, we cannot use the normal locking approach for this. Rather, we must introduce a specialized pattern of double-checked locking. Under some conditions, we can replace it with an even faster optimistic locking, which we covered as well.

Finally, we ended this chapter with a discussion of asymmetric data access. When we have multiple reader threads working on data that is only rarely modified, standard locking doesn't give us good enough performance. Instead, we should use a *readers-writer lock*. We discussed two implementations: a built-in Delphi version and the Slim Reader/Writer synchronization mechanism, which is part of the Windows operating system.

In the next chapter, we will explore four more concurrency patterns: thread pools, messaging, future, and pipeline.

9
Thread pool, Messaging, Future and Pipeline

Multithreaded programming is complicated. I hope that the previous chapter has sufficiently demonstrated how hard it is to coordinate multiple threads that work on shared data. There are just so many possibilities for writing code that doesn't always work correctly or to implement a fix that slows a program down so much that the new and improved parallel solution is actually slower than the original single-threaded code.

In this chapter, I will continue exploring design patterns (with a bit of architectural thinking thrown in) in a completely different direction. Instead of working on shared data, the patterns from this chapter will be used to write parallel tasks that are independent of each other. To achieve that, they use multiple copies of data and communicate with messages.

Introducing such patterns, however, often requires a redesign of the program architecture, which may be an impossible task in some situations. To help with such situations, this chapter also introduces two patterns that can be simply plugged into existing code – thread pool and future.

In this chapter, you will do the following:

- See how to speed up thread creation by introducing a thread pool pattern
- Learn how the locking architecture can be replaced with messaging
- Find out about different messaging solutions that can be used in your programs
- Learn how to speed up programs with minimal complications by introducing the future pattern into your code
- Learn about pipelines and how they can be used to speed up complicated tasks

Thread pool

A thread pool pattern can be simply described as a collection of threads. Some of them may be doing useful work, while others are sitting idle, waiting for you to run any job in them.

To the careful reader of this book, the thread pool pattern would seem like an old acquaintance. After all, it is nothing more than a variation on a object pool pattern, which was discussed in Chapter 2, *Singleton, Dependency Injection, Lazy Initialization, and Object Pool*.

 A thread pool is like a taxi service. When you need to travel somewhere, you call the dispatch and as soon as they have a taxi ready, they will send it to pick you up.

Using a thread pool minimizes the time a background task needs to start up. Creating a thread can take some time (up to ten milliseconds and more on older hardware), which can be a problem in highly optimized, heavily multi-threaded programs, for example, in a server handling many concurrent clients. Starting a job in a thread from a thread pool (provided that at least one thread is sitting idle), however, is a much faster operation.

A thread pool can also regulate your program thread consumption. Starting too many threads at the same time will just slow you down as the system will then spend too much time on thread switching and not enough on executing the program. A good thread pool will therefore limit the maximum number of concurrently running threads. When a thread pool is full (all threads are busy working), new jobs will enter a waiting queue. As the threads finish their current work, they take jobs from the waiting queue and process them.

Another advantage of thread pools is their capability of initializing some shared resource when a thread is created and freeing it up when the thread is destroyed. We can, for example, initialize a database connection when a thread is created and then reuse this connection for all operations that are executed in the context of this thread. This enables us to create a connection pool – a pool of threads that are connected to the database. Each time a database request has to be made, a thread from the connection pool can execute it without the overhead of connecting to the database.

Although you can write your own thread pool, this is a cumbersome and error-prone process. There were some attempts at providing Delphi programmers with a generic thread pool, but none were widespread. The first really useful thread pool appeared with the introduction of the OmniThreadLibrary open source library (www.omnithreadlibrary.com) in Delphi 2007, while we had to wait for the first built-in solution until Delphi XE7 when the System.Threading unit was introduced.

Traditionally, we used the TThread object to create new threads in Delphi. Calling TThread.Create creates a new thread and then executes your workload inside that thread. Using tasks, on the other hand, automatically uses a thread pool for server management. Calling TTask.Run, for example, runs your task in a thread that comes from the internal thread pool TThreadPool.Default.

 For more information on starting and managing threads. see the *Delphi idioms – parallel programming* section in Chapter 8, *Locking Patterns*.

The demonstration program ThreadPool from the Thread pool folder proves that allocating threads from a thread pool is indeed a faster operation than creating new threads. The program creates a number of threads or tasks (the number is settable in the user interface) and measures how long it takes until all threads are started up.

The thread example uses a worker thread called TWorkerThread. This simple object sets up an internal is started flag as soon as the thread's Execute method is invoked. Then, the code sleeps for two seconds (simulating hard work) and exits. The thread definition and implementation, which is part of the program's main unit, is shown here:

```
type
  TWorkerThread = class(TThread)
  strict private
    FIsStarted: boolean;
  public
    procedure Execute; override;
    property IsStarted: boolean read FIsStarted;
  end;

procedure TWorkerThread.Execute;
begin
  FIsStarted := true;
  Sleep(2000);
end;
```

A bit more work is needed to manage the threads. Clicking on the **Start threads** button calls the btnThreadsClick method which implements the test as follows:

```
procedure TfrmThreadPool.btnThreadsClick(Sender: TObject);
var
  i: Integer;
  sw: TStopwatch;
  threads: TArray<TWorkerThread>;
begin
```

```
    SetLength(threads, inpWorkers.Value);
    sw := TStopwatch.StartNew;
    for i := Low(threads) to High(threads) do
      threads[i] := TWorkerThread.Create;
    for i := Low(threads) to High(threads) do
      while not threads[i].IsStarted do
        ;
    sw.Stop;

    for i := Low(threads) to High(threads) do
    begin
      threads[i].WaitFor;
      lbLog.Items.Add('Thread ID: ' + threads[i].ThreadID.ToString);
      threads[i].Free;
    end;

    lbLog.ItemIndex := lbLog.Items.Add('Threads were created in ' +
    sw.ElapsedMilliseconds.ToString + ' ms');
  end;
```

The code stores all running threads in the internal `threads` array. The measurement part starts a stopwatch, creates all the threads (stores them in the array), and waits until all threads have set the `IsStarted` flag. Then, the code stops the stopwatch. The number of running threads is set by changing the Number of workers input field in the user interface.

After that, the code waits for each thread to finish execution by calling the `WaitFor` method, logs the unique ID of the executing thread (`ThreadID`), and destroys the thread. At the end, the time that's required to start the thread is reported.

 You should always run such code without the Delphi debugger. (Instead of *F9*, you should press *Ctrl-Shift-F9*.) The Delphi debugger interferes with thread creation and drastically slows it down. You can run this program with and without the debugger to see the difference the debugger makes.

If you run the program and start a larger amount of threads (sixty, for example), you'll notice that it takes a few milliseconds to start them up. Next time you click this button, the code will take approximately the same time to start the threads.

If you limit the number of running threads to a lower number (for example, four) and click the **Start threads** button a few times, you'll see that different thread IDs are displayed for each execution. This proves that new threads are created each time. (The operating system assigns each new thread a random thread ID.)

Testing with tasks is a bit trickier. The following example shows some slightly simplified code from the demonstration program:

```
procedure TfrmThreadPool.btnTasksClick(Sender: TObject);
var
  i: Integer;
  sw: TStopwatch;
  tasks: TArray<ITask>;
  taskID: TArray<TThreadID>;
  taskStarted: TArray<boolean>;

  function MakeTask(num: integer): TProc;
  begin
    Result :=
      procedure
      begin
        taskStarted[num] := true;
        taskID[num] := TThread.Current.ThreadID;
        Sleep(2000);
      end;
  end;

begin
  SetLength(tasks, inpWorkers.Value);
  SetLength(taskID, Length(tasks));
  SetLength(taskStarted, Length(tasks));

  sw := TStopwatch.StartNew;
  for i := Low(tasks) to High(tasks) do
    tasks[i] := TTask.Run(MakeTask(i));
  for i := Low(tasks) to High(tasks) do
    while not taskStarted[i] do
      ;
  sw.Stop;

  TTask.WaitForAll(tasks);
  for i := Low(tasks) to High(tasks) do
    lbLog.Items.Add('Thread ID: ' + taskID[i].ToString);

  lbLog.ItemIndex := lbLog.Items.Add('Tasks were created in ' +
    sw.ElapsedMilliseconds.ToString + ' ms');
end;
```

The worker tasks have been created as anonymous functions. This was done by calling the MakeTask function. The task stores its running flag in the internal array taskStarted and the thread ID of the executing thread in the internal array taskID. The logic of measuring the startup time and logging the information stays the same.

Before you click the **Start tasks** button, make sure that the **Min threads in pool** value is at least as large as the **Number of workers** and that the **Max threads in pool** value is larger than the **Min threads in pool**. The reasons for that will become clear soon.

If you run the test on sixty tasks, you'll notice that the program needs about the same time to run the tasks as it needed to start the threads. When you click this button for the second time, however, you'll see that the startup time drops to less than one millisecond.

If you repeat the test with four tasks, you'll also notice that the same thread IDs are displayed when you run the test multiple times. This proves that threads are not destroyed but reused.

The following screenshot shows four threads being created twice, followed by four tasks being also created twice. There's no significant difference in speed, but you can see that the second run of the four tasks uses the same thread IDs as the first run:

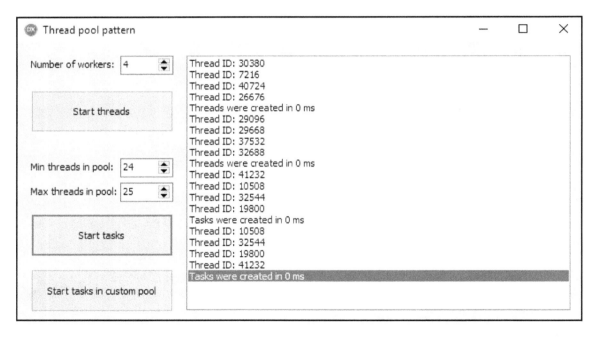

Comparing thread and task creation

Idiosyncrasies of Delphi's TThreadPool

As expected of a good thread pool, Delphi's implementation allows you to set the minimum and maximum number of executing threads. The maximum number of executing threads represents a hard limit of the maximum number of concurrently executing tasks. If you create more tasks than that, some of them will wait until the threads in the pool finish executing previous tasks.

The minimum number of executing threads sets the number of threads that are always waiting for new tasks. Setting this number to a high value preallocates a large number of threads, which allows a large number of tasks to quickly start when needed.

At least, that is the theory. The implementation, however, can be best described as weird.

The number of maximum threads is set by calling the `SetMaxWorkerThreads` method, while the number of minimum threads is set by calling the `SetMinWorkerThreads` method. The demonstration program contains the following two lines, which were not shown in the previous code example, and are used to adjust the thread pool limits before tasks are started:

```
TThreadPool.Default.SetMaxWorkerThreads(inpMaxThreads.Value);
TThreadPool.Default.SetMinWorkerThreads(inpMinThreads.Value);
```

The default values for these limits are initialized to very high numbers. The `TThreadPool.Create` constructor sets the defaults, as follows:

```
FMinLimitWorkerThreadCount := TThread.ProcessorCount;
FMaxLimitWorkerThreadCount := TThread.ProcessorCount * MaxThreadsPerCPU;
```

The `MaxThreadsPerCPU` constant is equal to twenty-five, so on a computer with six cores, the limits would be set to six and one-hundred and fifty, respectively. On a better workstation with twenty-four cores, the limits would be twenty-four and six-hundred. The value for the upper limit is, let me say, extremely high, and should only be used if your tasks spend most of their time waiting for something to happen. If, on the other hand, the tasks are CPU intensive, starting that many concurrent threads is a sure way to bring the system to a crawl.

If your process starts multiple CPU intensive tasks and uses a thread pool to limit them in number, make sure that you always call the `SetMaxWorkerThreads` method with a lower number (`TThread.ProcessorCount`, for example). Interestingly, you cannot set the maximum number of threads to a number lower than the number of CPU cores in the system as the `SetMaxWorkerThreads` implementation prevents that!

The second weird part comes from `SetMinWorkerThreads`, which makes sure that the minimum number of threads is always strictly smaller than the maximum number of threads. That's why I recommended that you test the program with **Max threads in pool** set to a higher value than **Min threads in pool**. You cannot have a thread pool where all of the threads are pre-allocated and cannot be created or destroyed. Or, again, that is the theory.

As it turns out, the minimum number of threads doesn't actually mean what you would assume. If you call `SetMinWorkerThreads(8)`, for example, the thread pool will not create eight threads. This is only documented in the source code, where a comment states the following:

> "*The actual number of pool threads could be less than this value depending on actual demand.*"

Even after taking all of that in account, the implementation has its quirks. For example, set the **Number of workers** to four, **Min threads in pool** to four, and **Max threads in pool** to nine. Start the tasks once.

Now, change both the **Number of workers** and **Min threads in pool** to eight. Click the **Start tasks** button. As we are now starting 8 tasks in a thread pool with at least eight threads (and at most nine or the number of cores in the system, whichever's larger), we would expect all of the tasks to be started in parallel – but no! As the following screenshot proves, only four threads are used and starting the tasks takes two seconds as the first set of four tasks must finish their job before the next set of four tasks is started:

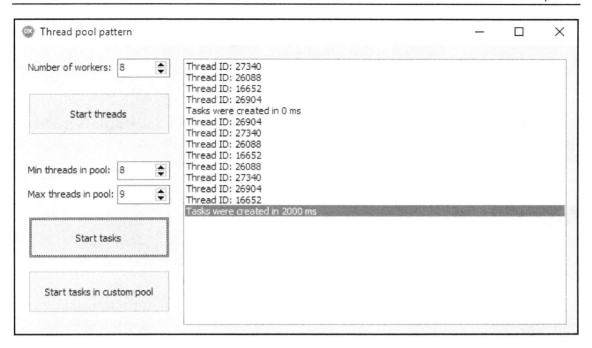

Running 8 tasks after running 4 tasks in Delphi's thread pool

This problem has only been fixed in Delphi 10.3 Rio, which was released during the production of this book. To prevent such problems in Delphi 10.2 and below, you can use the following workaround.

The `TTask.Create` and `TTask.Run` methods accept a `TThreadPool` parameter, which represents a thread pool that will be used to run the task. Instead of using the default thread pool, you can create a new one in the code by calling `ThreadPool.Create`. When a required minimum number of threads in the pool changes, the current thread pool can be destroyed (provided that no threads are running in it, of course) and recreated. The event handler `btnTasksCustomClick`, which is called by clicking the **Start tasks in custom pool** button, uses the following code to (re)create a custom pool and start a task in that pool:

```
TThreadPool.Default.SetMaxWorkerThreads(inpMaxThreads.Value);
if (not assigned(FCustomPool)) or (FCustomPool.MinWorkerThreads <>
inpMinThreads.Value) then begin
  FreeAndNil(FCustomPool);
  FCustomPool := TThreadPool.Create;
  FCustomPool.SetMinWorkerThreads(inpMinThreads.Value);
end;

sw := TStopwatch.StartNew;
```

```
for i := Low(tasks) to High(tasks) do
  tasks[i] := TTask.Run(MakeTask(i), FCustomPool);
for i := Low(tasks) to High(tasks) do
  while not taskStarted[i] do
    ;
sw.Stop;
```

While this hack alleviates some problems, it doesn't solve them all. You will do better by upgrading to fresh Delphi, which fixes some other glaring errors in the `System.Threading` unit.

Messaging

As we saw in the previous chapter, processing shared data from multiple threads introduces all sorts of problems that cannot be easily fixed especially if we want the program to executed faster than in a single—threaded version.

A common solution for this problem is to redesign the program. Instead of using the shared data access and locking pattern, we replace the shared data with multiple copies of the same and synchronize (lock) with the message pattern.

 If you play chess on the internet, you are not sharing a chessboard with your partner. Instead, each of you have your own copy of the chessboard and figures, and you synchronize the state between the two copies by sending messages (representing the piece moves) to each other.

Messaging is not a design but an architectural pattern. The implementation of messaging is, however, usually specific to a platform or a language and can be considered almost an idiom. As the messaging pattern is extremely important if you want to write parallel programs that are fast and relatively easy to debug, I decided to cover it in this book.

Messaging frequently takes an active role in the implementation of other patterns. It can, for example, be used to implement a publish-subscribe pattern (see the discussion of the Observer pattern in `Chapter 7`, *Iterator, Visitor, Observer, and Memento*). I will also use it later in this chapter to enhance the future pattern and to implement the pipeline pattern.

In the messaging pattern, one side (sender) creates a message and sends it to the other side (receiver). The message typically consists of an ID and data (although this is not a requirement, as we'll see later). The message ID tells the receiver what to do with the message data.

A message is delivered with help from some mechanism that is, in most cases, implemented in our code externally. It can be part of an operating system or a runtime library. We can also use custom messaging solutions, but that should be reserved for special cases where none of the pre-made messaging solutions fit.

The important point of the messaging pattern is that the message can easily travel from one thread to another. Support for that is usually built into the implementation of the message transfer mechanism. It can use normal queues combined with locking or some form of thread-safe queues, which typically use interlocked operations internally to deliver thread-safety.

To demonstrate different ways of messaging, I have built a Messaging project that's stored in the Messaging folder. This program shows four different ways that messages can be sent from a background thread to a main thread. (For sending messages from any thread to a background thread, see the implementation of the pipeline pattern later in this chapter.)

The Messaging project implements a simple thread called TFooBarThread, which plays the well-known FooBar game. The thread generates numbers from 1 to 100 but replaces each number that is divisible by three with a Foo, each number divisible by five with a Bar, and each number divisible by both three and five with a FooBar.

The implementation of this thread, which can be found in the ThreadedFooBar unit, is not complete. It implements the kernel of the algorithm that uses the abstract method SendMessage to send the current element (either a number, a Foo, Bar, or FooBar) to the main thread. This method is implemented in derived classes, which we'll explore later.

The implementation of the base thread TFooBarThread is as follows:

```
type
  TFooBarThread = class(TThread)
  strict protected
    procedure SendMessage(const msg: string); virtual; abstract;
  public
    procedure Execute; override;
  end;

procedure TFooBarThread.Execute;
var
  number: Integer;
begin
  for number := 1 to 100 do begin
    case number mod 15 of
      0: SendMessage('FooBar');
      3,6,9,12: SendMessage('Foo');
```

```
      5,10: SendMessage('Bar');
      else SendMessage(number.ToString);
    end;
    Sleep(100);
  end;
  SendMessage(#13#10);
end;
```

Messages are sent with a slight delay (hundred milliseconds) so that we can better see how they are processed and displayed in the form.

Windows messages

The first option we have available is to use the Windows messaging system to send messages to the main thread. (This messaging system can also be used to send messages to a background thread, which is a more complicated topic that I will not pursue in this book.)

One limitation of this approach is obvious. We can only use it if we compile our program for Windows. If you are targeting other operating systems, you must use one of the other available solutions.

Another limitation is that a Windows message consists of a message ID and two integer parameters that represent message data. We cannot attach an object or a string as message data – at least not directly. We'll see how to circumvent this limitation later.

The `ThreadedFooBar.WindowsMsg` unit contains an implementation of a `TWindowsMsgFooBarThread`, a descendant of `TFooBarThread` that uses windows messaging to send messages. This thread class is defined as follows:

```
type
  TWindowsMsgFooBarThread = class(TFoobarThread)
  strict private
    FMessage: cardinal;
    FReceiver: THandle;
  strict protected
    procedure SendMessage(const msg: string); override;
  public
    constructor Create(receiver: THandle; message: cardinal;
      createSuspended: boolean);
  end;
```

The constructor takes two additional parameters. Receiver specifies the window (form) that will receive the messages, while message contains the message ID that will be used for communication. As our thread has no idea how it will be integrated into the application and which messages will be sent to the receiving form from other components, it is best that the form injects this message ID into the thread.

As we cannot send string messages over the Windows messaging subsystem, the code in the SendMessage method wraps each message into an instance of the TFooBarMessage class. Each Delphi object is internally represented with a pointer to the memory block where the object resides. We can treat this pointer as an integer and send it as message data. The receiving side must then make sure to destroy the object when it is no longer needed. The following code fragment shows the string wrapper class and the SendMessage implementation:

```
type
  TFooBarMessage = class
  strict protected
    FValue: string;
  public
    constructor Create(const AValue: string);
    property Value: string read FValue write FValue;
  end;

constructor TFooBarMessage.Create(const AValue: string);
begin
  inherited Create;
  FValue := AValue;
end;

procedure TWindowsMsgFooBarThread.SendMessage(const msg: string);
begin
  PostMessage(FReceiver, FMessage, WParam(TFooBarMessage.Create(msg)), 0);
end;
```

In the main thread, we must define a custom message (WM_FOOBAR_MSG). Windows allows us to use values that are greater or equal to WM_USER (a constant defined in the Winapi.Messages unit) as custom messages. Next, we declare a message handler, MsgFooBar, which will be automatically called whenever the form receives this message. The following code shows relevant parts of form implementation:

```
const
  WM_FOOBAR_MSG = WM_USER;

type
  TfrmMessaging = class(TForm)
```

```
  ...
    procedure MsgFooBar(var msg: TMessage); message WM_FOOBAR_MSG;
  end;

procedure TfrmMessaging.MsgFooBar(var msg: TMessage);
var
  oMsg: TFooBarMessage;
begin
  oMsg := TFooBarMessage(msg.WParam);
  memoLog.Text := memoLog.Text + oMsg.Value + ' ';
  oMsg.Free;
end;
```

On the receiving side, the integer parameter is again treated as a TFooBarMessage object. The contents of that object are then logged and the object is destroyed.

To create the thread, the btnWindowsMsgClick event handler creates the TWindowsMsgFooBarThread object and passes it to the constructor of the Handle of the main form and the WM_FOOBAR_MSG message ID. The form is set to automatically destruct whenever the Execute method completes its job (FreeOnTerminate := true), as shown in the following code:

```
procedure TfrmMessaging.btnWindowsMsgClick(Sender: TObject);
var
  fooBar: TWindowsMsgFooBarThread;
begin
  fooBar := TWindowsMsgFooBarThread.Create(Handle, WM_FOOBAR_MSG, true);
  fooBar.FreeOnTerminate := true;
  fooBar.Start;
end;
```

If you run the program and click on the **Windows messages** button, you'll see that messages from the worker thread are displayed as they arrive.

Queue and Synchronize

The second (and third) messaging option provided by Delphi is to use TThread.Queue or TThread.Synchronize. As they are just variations of the same concept, I'll describe them together.

Unlike Windows messages, which can be sent from the main thread to a background thread if you write the background thread in an appropriate way, Queue and Synchronize don't provide any support for that. You can only use them to send messages to the main thread.

The beauty of Queue and Synchronize is that they are completely platform independent. Delphi's RTL makes sure that you can use them with VCL or FireMonkey on any of their supported platforms.

If you want to use Queue or Synchronize in a console application, your application must periodically call the CheckSynchronize method, which is defined in the System.Classes unit.

The Queue and Synchronize methods don't use the message ID/message data concept. Instead, you pass in an anonymous method that's captured on the sending side and executed in the main thread. To pass any data along the "message", you just use it in the anonymous method and Delphi's capturing mechanism will take care of the rest.

The ThreadedFooBar.Queue unit implements a TQueueFooBarThread that's derived from TFooBarThread and implements a Queue-based messaging mechanism. The following code fragment shows the definition and implementation of this thread in full:

```
type
  TQueueFooBarThread = class(TFooBarThread)
  strict private
    FOnNewValue: TProc<string>;
    FOnTerminated: TProc;
  strict protected
    procedure SendMessage(const msg: string); override;
  public
    procedure Execute; override;
    property OnNewValue: TProc<string> read FOnNewValue write FOnNewValue;
    property OnTerminated: TProc read FOnTerminated write FOnTerminated;
  end;

procedure TQueueFooBarThread.Execute;
begin
  inherited;
  OnTerminated();
end;

procedure TQueueFooBarThread.SendMessage(const msg: string);
begin
  TThread.Queue(nil,
    procedure
    begin
      OnNewValue(msg);
    end);
end;
```

As with the Windows message approach, the worker thread doesn't know what method of the main form it should execute when `SendMessage` is called. Instead of introducing hard-coded dependencies, the implementation defines the `OnNewValue` event, which is called from `SendMessage`. The application must take care of correctly initializing this event handler before the thread is started.

The `TThread.Queue` call takes two parameters – a `TThread` (which is `nil` in this example) and an anonymous method. `Queue` then inserts these two parameters in an internal queue and immediately exits. The thread can then continue with its execution.

At some later time, the main thread calls the `CheckSynchronize` method from `System.Classes` (this typically happens when the application is idle). `CheckSynchronize` checks the internal queue, fetches the anonymous method(s) from it, and executes them one by one.

The first parameter of the `TThread` type tells the system which thread produced the message. You can set it to `nil`, as in this code example. Alternatively, you can set it to `TThread.Current` – a function that returns the current `TThread` object.

If you use the second approach, you will be able to remove specific messages from the queue before they are executed by calling the `TThread.RemoveQueuedEvents` method. As this functionality is rarely required, you'll see that most examples simply use `nil` for the first parameter, which is a tad faster than calling `TThread.Current`.

If you use `TThread.Queue` with a thread that automatically destroys itself when `Execute` exits (`FreeOnTerminate := True`), you have to be very careful. Let's think about what can happen if `TQueueFooBarThread` were to automatically destroy itself:

- The thread calls `SendMessage`, which calls `TThread.Queue`.
- An anonymous method that refers the `OnNewValue` handler is inserted in the queue.
- The thread exits. As its `FreeOnTerminate` property is set to `True`, the thread object is destroyed. The `OnNewValue` handler does not exist anymore.
- The main form takes the anonymous method from the message queue and tries to execute it. With some luck, this ends in access violation when the anonymous method tries to call `OnNewValue`. If you are unlucky, some random code may execute and do something undefined.

This is a serious problem, but luckily Delphi RTL offers a way out of this trap. You just have to be aware of it and write your code accordingly. There are two ways to fix this problem, so you have to pick the one that applies to your specific situation.

If you are using a `FreeOnTerminate` thread, then you should never pass `nil` to `TThread.Queue`. Just before the thread is destroyed, the `TThread` destructor calls `RemoveQueuedEvents(Self)`, which removes all unprocessed messages that are sent by this thread from the queue.

If you want all messages to be received and processed in the main thread, however, you should never use the `FreeOnTerminate` approach. Instead of that, the code should signal the main thread to say that execution was completed, as in this example. As that will be the last message that's sent by the thread, all previous messages will be already processed when this last method is executed and so the thread can be safely destroyed.

Your thread may also work for a long time, in which case the main program will be the one that tells the thread to stop. In that case, the code should always use the idiomatic approach to stop the thread, as follows:

```
thread.Terminate;
thread.WaitFor;
FreeAndNil(thread);
```

The important step is a call to `WaitFor`. Inside this method, `CheckSynchronize` is called to clean the message queue. When `WaitFor` exits, you can be sure that there are no messages from that thread waiting in the queue, and you can safely destroy the thread object.

The following code shows how `TQueueFooBarThread` is created and destroyed in the main program:

```
procedure TfrmMessaging.btnQueueClick(Sender: TObject);
var
  fooBar: TQueueFooBarThread;
begin
  fooBar := TQueueFooBarThread.Create(true);
  fooBar.OnNewValue :=
    procedure (value: string)
    begin
      memoLog.Text := memoLog.Text + value + ' ';
    end;
  fooBar.OnTerminated :=
    procedure
    begin
      fooBar.Free;
    end;
  fooBar.Start;
end;
```

We must make sure that the thread doesn't run before event handlers are set so that the thread object is created in a suspended state (the `true` parameter of the constructor enforces that). After that, both event handlers are set and the thread is started. `btnQueueClick` then exits.

When a new message is posted via `SendMessage`, `OnNewValue` is eventually called. The code looks like it's part of `btnQueueClick`, but in reality `procedure (value: string)` ... is an independent entity that exists as long as the `OnNewValue` handler refers to it. (An anonymous method is implemented as an interfaced object that exists as long as some other part of the code is referring to it.)

To destroy the thread, we must keep the thread object (`fooBar`) active until the `OnTerminated` event handler is called. In traditional Delphi programming, we would have to define a form field, such as `FFooBar: TQueueFooBarThread`, and store the thread object in it.

If we use anonymous methods, as in this example, the local variable `fooBar` is captured by the compiler and exists somewhere (we don't really care where) while the `OnTerminated` anonymous method is alive. The anonymous method can therefore safely refer to the local variable (which is now not really a local variable, but we don't care about that) and destroy it by calling `fooBar.Free`.

 If you call `TThread.Queue` from a main thread, the anonymous method is executed directly from the `Queue` method and is not inserted in the internal queue. To put an anonymous method in an internal queue from a main thread, you should use the `ForceQueue` method, which is only available in Delphi 10.2 Tokyo and later.

The `Synchronize` method is used in exactly the same way as `Queue`. The differences only show up when the program is running.

While the `Queue` pushes the message into a queue and immediately exits so that the thread can do further work, `Synchronize` waits until the main thread **receives** and **processes** the message. Only after that will the code inside the thread continue execution. `Synchronize` therefore **blocks** the thread's execution, which slows the thread down. You should use it only when absolutely necessary, for example, when a background thread needs the main thread to provide a certain value. (Even then, using `Synchronize` indicates bad program architecture that should be rethought.)

The demonstration program implements `TSynchronizeFooBarThread` in the `ThreadedFooBar.Synchronize` unit. Both the implementation of the thread and thread management in the main form are almost the same as in the `Queue` example.

Polling

For the last approach, I will show a solution that doesn't require any support from an operating system or runtime library. You can implement it with standard tools, for example, with a timer, list, and critical section.

Unlike the previous solutions, which followed a push model (a message triggers some code in the main thread that can't do much to prevent that), this approach requires cooperation from code running in a main thread. This code will periodically check (poll) whether a message has arrived.

To implement this kind of messaging system, both the main thread and the background thread must share some structure that can store a list of messages and which is *thread-safe* (can be safely used in a multi-threaded environment). We can, for example, use a standard `TList` in combination with a *critical section* or `TMonitor` for locking or, as in the following example, a thread-safe queue, `TThreadedQueue<T>`. (For more information on locking with critical sections and `TMonitor`, see `Chapter 8`, *Locking Patterns*).

A thread sends a message by storing information in this shared structure. As we have the shared structure under our own control, we don't run into the same problem as with Windows messages where we could only send integer data.

The receiving thread must check the shared queue from time to time. This process is known as **polling**. If there's a message in the queue, the receiving thread removes the message from the queue and processes it.

The beauty of this approach is that we don't really care which thread is a background thread and which is the main thread. We can post messages (put them into the shared queue) from any thread. We can also poll the queue from a main thread (with a `TTimer` or in the `OnIdle` event) or from a background thread (with a simple loop). In this section, I will show you how to read from such a queue in a main thread. To see how you can receive messages in a background thread, check the discussion of the pipeline pattern later in this chapter.

This solution is also useful when you have multiple senders or even multiple receivers. This capability will also be used in the pipeline pattern.

The downside of the polling approach is that is typically uses a bit more CPU time than other solutions and messages are not processed as promptly as with other approaches. As we'll see later, we can make the polling more responsive, but for the price of a larger CPU usage.

A polling approach is implemented in TPollingFooBarThread, which is implemented in the ThreadedFooBar.Polling unit, as follows:

```
type
  TPollingFooBarThread = class(TFooBarThread)
  strict private
    FQueue: TThreadedQueue<string>;
  strict protected
    procedure SendMessage(const msg: string); override;
  public
    procedure AfterConstruction; override;
    procedure BeforeDestruction; override;
    property MessageQueue: TThreadedQueue<string> read FQueue;
  end;

procedure TPollingFooBarThread.AfterConstruction;
begin
  inherited;
  FQueue := TThreadedQueue<string>.Create(100);
end;

procedure TPollingFooBarThread.BeforeDestruction;
begin
  FreeAndNil(FQueue);
  inherited;
end;

procedure TPollingFooBarThread.SendMessage(const msg: string);
begin
  FQueue.PushItem(msg);
end;
```

As the thread is only sending string data, the shared message queue is implemented as a TThreadedQueue<string> object, which is managed by the thread. This class requires us to set the maximum number of stored entities (strings, in this example) when it is created. The code sets this value to 100, thus assuming that the main thread will have no problems reading messages from the queue.

To send a message, the code simply calls `FQueue.PushItem`. This will add a message to the queue in a thread-safe way. In other words, we don't care what the other threads are doing with this `TThreadedQueue` as the implementation of `PushItem` guarantees correctness in the multi-threaded world.

In the unlikely event of a queue being full, `PushItem` will simply wait until the main thread removes one message from the queue. Then, it will write the message into the queue and exit. In such a situation the execution of the background thread can be temporarily blocked. If that is a problem, you can increase the queue size or decrease the push timeout (which can be set by providing additional parameters to the `TThreadedQueue` constructor).

A bit more work than usual has to be done in the main thread. The code in `btnPollingClick` sets up the thread and event handlers, as follows:

```
procedure TfrmMessaging.btnPollingClick(Sender: TObject);
begin
  FPollingFooBar := TPollingFooBarThread.Create(true);
  FPollingFooBar.OnTerminate := PollingFooBarTerminated;
  FPollingFooBar.Start;
  btnPolling.Enabled := false;
  tmrPollThread.Enabled := true;
end;
```

This code also enables the timer that will read and process the messages and disables the button that created the polling thread. Unlike the previous approaches, where the implementation allowed us to create multiple worker threads, the simple polling implementation in the demonstration program allows for only one worker.

The timer method `tmrPollThreadTimer` checks whether there are messages in the shared queue and reads them one by one with `PopItem`, as shown here:

```
procedure TfrmMessaging.tmrPollThreadTimer(Sender: TObject);
begin
  while FPollingFooBar.MessageQueue.QueueSize > 0 do
    memoLog.Text := memoLog.Text + FPollingFooBar.MessageQueue.PopItem + '
';
end;
```

The thread termination handler `PollingFooBarTerminated` is called when `TPollingFooBarThread` terminates. It disables the timer and calls the timer message method `tmrPollThreadTimer` for the last time. That cleans potential unprocessed messages from the queue. After that, it destroys the thread and re-enables the button. This method is shown in the following code:

```
procedure TfrmMessaging.PollingFooBarTerminated(Sender: TObject);
begin
  tmrPollThread.Enabled := false;
  tmrPollThreadTimer(nil);
  FPollingFooBar.Terminate;
  FPollingFooBar := nil;
  btnPolling.Enabled := true;
end;
```

If you run the program, you'll notice that the messages from the polling thread appear in chunks, a few at a time. This happens because the timer interval is set to two hundred and fifty milliseconds, while the messages are produced one every one hundred milliseconds. You can improve the responsiveness of the program by decreasing the timer interval. This will, of course, increase the number of times the timer method is called, which will slightly increase the CPU usage. It is up to you to find a polling interval that works well in your situation.

Future

The future pattern, also known as a promise, can be simply described as a function that runs in the background thread. The basic usage pattern is intentionally very simple:

- The main thread creates a future (starts a calculation in another thread).
- The main thread does some other work.
- The main thread reads the result of the future (reads the result of the calculation). If the calculation is not finished yet, the main thread blocks until the result is available.

The future pattern allows the program to execute multiple tasks in parallel while it neatly encapsulates the background calculation in a separate function. It also provides a simple way of re-synchronization between two threads when the result of calculation is required.

In a kitchen, the chef asks their assistant to cut up a few onions. While the assistant peels, cuts, and cries, the chef continues preparing other meals. At a later time, when they need to use the onion, it will hopefully be already prepared and waiting.

This simple pattern is also equally simple to use in Delphi programs. We only have to call `TTask.Future<T>` to create a future, returning `T`, which is represented by a `IFuture<T>` interface. This automatically creates a new task that starts calculating the result.

When the program needs to use this result, the code accesses the `Value` property of the `IFuture<T>` interface. This returns the result of the calculation. If the calculation is not finished yet, the code will wait (block) inside the `Value` getter until the calculation is done and the result can be returned.

The `Future` program from the `Future` folder demonstrates this approach. The **Create Future** button executes the following code, which creates and starts the future:

```
procedure TfrmFuture.btnFutureClick(Sender: TObject);
begin
  FFuture := TTask.Future<integer>(CountPrimes);
end;
```

The `FFuture` is a form field of the `IFuture<integer>` type.

The `CountPrimes` function counts all prime numbers that are smaller than 5,000,000. On a typical personal computer, the code returns the results in a few seconds.

To read the result, the **Get value** button reads the `FFuture.Value` property. After the result is displayed, the code destroys the future interface by setting the `FFuture` field to `nil`, as shown in the following code:

```
procedure TfrmFuture.btnGetValueClick(Sender: TObject);
begin
  if not assigned(FFuture) then
    Exit;

  lbLog.Items.Add('Result = ' + FFuture.Value.ToString);
  FFuture := nil;
end;
```

If you run the program, click the **Create Future** button, wait a few seconds and click the **Get value** button, you'll immediately get the result. If, however, you click the **Get value** button immediately after clicking the **Create Future** button, the main thread will block for a few seconds inside the `FFuture.Value` getter. During that time, the program will be unresponsive. You will not, for example, be able to move the program window around the screen.

If this potential blocking is not acceptable, we can sometimes redesign the program to function asynchronously. We can start the future like we did previously, but instead of reading the result directly, we delay that until we know that the future has finished its job (has calculated the result). The simplest way to achieve this is to use the messaging pattern to send a message from the future back to the main thread when the result is ready.

The **Create Future** *2* button in the demonstration program starts a future that notifies the main program when the result is ready. The code is as follows:

```
procedure TfrmFuture.btnFuture2Click(Sender: TObject);
begin
  FFuture := TTask.Future<integer>(
    function: Integer
    begin
      Result := CountPrimes;
      TThread.Queue(nil, ReportFuture);
    end);
end;
```

The `ReportFuture` method simply reads the result of the calculation and destroys the `FFuture` interface. As the result is guaranteed to exist at this point, accessing the `Value` property will never block. The code for this is as follows:

```
procedure TfrmFuture.ReportFuture;
begin
  lbLog.Items.Add('Result = ' + FFuture.Value.ToString);
  FFuture := nil;
end;
```

Although with this approach the user interface can never block, we have to redesign the program, and sometimes this is not feasible. In such cases, we can still use the original pattern, which doesn't give perfect results but still speeds up the execution of the program.

Pipeline

To wrap up our discussion of concurrency patterns, I will present a very important concept – the pipeline pattern. This pattern, which is sometimes also called **staged processing**, is not strictly a design pattern, but more of an architectural one. It is, nevertheless, one of the most important patterns you can use in parallel programming, which is why it is covered in this book.

If we are to be able to apply the pipeline pattern to a process, two conditions must be applied. First, the process must be able to process parts of the input one by one. In other words, we must be able to split the input into smaller blocks (processing units), which are processed sequentially. Second, the process itself must be doing the processing in separate steps (stages) that are executed one after another.

The pipeline works by passing the first processing unit to the first stage. After the stage finishes its work, it passes the partially processed unit to the second stage. While the second stage does its work, the first stage can already work on the second processing unit. This process continues with as many stages as we need – the longer the processing pipeline, the more stages can be working at the same time and the better results we'll achieve.

A robotized assembly line builds a product in stages. Each robot takes a partially finished product, makes some modifications, and passes the product to the next robot. This allows multiple robots to work at the same time, which speeds up production.

The following simple example will help you understand the process of creating a pipeline from a normal, sequential process. Let's say we have a file encryption process, which works like so:

1. A file is read into memory.
2. Data is encrypted.
3. The encrypted data is written into another file.

Since we may be working with huge files that may not fit into our available memory, we have coded this algorithm like so:

```
while not EndOfSource do
begin
  ReadFromSource(buffer);
  Encrypt(buffer);
  WriteToDestination(buffer);
end;
```

This pseudocode reads data from input one buffer at a time. Each buffer is encrypted and then written to a destination file.

We can see that this process satisfies the conditions I stated previously. Data is processed in smaller units (buffer) and the process itself runs in three separate stages.

To show you how we can create a pipeline out of such a process, let's complicate this process a little and put a message queue between stages. The code would still execute at approximately the same speed, except the data would (seemingly without any reason) pass through a queue before it is used in the next stage. The pseudocode would look as follows:

```
while not EndOfSource do
begin
  ReadFromSource(buffer1);
  queue1.Write(buffer1);

  queue1.Read(buffer2);
  Encrypt(buffer2);
  queue2.Write(buffer2);

  queue2.Read(buffer3);
  WriteToDestination(buffer3);
end;
```

Now, the stages don't use the same `buffer` (shared data), but each work with their own copy of the data. We can now simply split up each process into a thread (or a task), as the following pseudocode shows:

```
// thread 1
while not EndOfSource do
begin
  ReadFromSource(buffer1);
  queue1.Write(buffer1);
end;
queue1.Close;

// thread 2
while not queue1.Closed do
begin
  queue1.Read(buffer2);
  Encrypt(buffer2);
  queue2.Write(buffer2);
end;
queue2.Close;

// thread 3
while not queue2.Closed do
begin
  queue2.Read(buffer3);
  WriteToDestination(buffer3);
end;
```

The only data shared between the threads are message queues, which are by nature designed with this application in mind. The data itself is never shared, so we don't need to implement any locking.

This example also shows how to stop a pipeline. Each stage must be able to somehow signal to the next stage that the work was done. We can implement this by sending a special message over the message queue or we can use support that's built into a messaging subsystem, as in this example.

In practice, we usually implement the pipeline so that all of the stages use two message queues; one for input and one for output. The first stage can then receive initial data (if any) from the main thread over the input queue and the last stage can return results (if any) to the main thread over its output queue.

If we don't care about the order in which the output is produced, we can run some stages in multiple parallel threads. By doing that, we add more workers to the slowest part of the problem. To do that, the messaging subsystem must support multiple simultaneous readers and writers.

The beauty of a pipeline is that it can be easily implemented with standard Delphi functionality. Each stage runs as a separate `TThread` or `ITask`, while the `TThreadedQueue` is used for interconnecting message queues.

The following template can be used for each stage in a pipeline:

```
procedure Stage(
  inQueue: TThreadedQueue<T1>;
  outQueue: TThreadedQueue<T2>);
var
  data: T1;
begin
  // initialize per-thread data
  try
    while inQueue.PopItem(url) = wrSignaled do
    begin
      if inQueue.ShutDown then
        break; //while

      outQueue.PushItem(ProcessInput(data));
    end;
    outQueue.DoShutDown;
  finally
    // cleanup per-thread data
  end;
end;
```

Each stage runs as a separate task, which receives data of type T1 over the TThreadedQueue<T1> queue and outputs data of type T2 into the TThreadedQueue<T2> queue. Both queues are *injected* as parameters.

Data structures that are used for the entire process can be initialized at the beginning and cleaned up at the end. There's no need to recreate them each time a processing unit is received. At the beginning, for example, we could open a database connection, which is typically a relatively slow process.

The task runs until the input queue is not closed. If we use TThreadedQueue for messaging, we can close it by calling its DoShutDown method and check whether it is closed by testing the ShutDown property.

If the input queue is correctly initialized, the PopItem call will wait forever. It will only return if there's new data in the input queue or if the input queue was shut down. If the return value is wrSignaled, all is well and we can continue. Any other result indicates an unexpected error and the only thing the stage can do is shut down.

This code also assumes that ProcessInput cannot throw any exceptions. If that is a possibility, data processing should be wrapped in a try..except handler and errors should be appropriately handled.

This sample code generates one processing unit on the output for each received processing unit. This is not a requirement, and in practical applications, this will most often not be a case you need to worry about. As you will see later in this chapter, one input processing unit can result in multiple or no processing units being sent to the output queue.

Web spider

To show a more complex example that you can take and adapt to your own needs, the Pipeline demo from the Pipeline folder implements a simple web spider. This code accepts a URL and retrieves all of the pages on that website.

This project is not meant to be a fully functional web spider application, but a relatively simple demo. It may not work correctly on all sites. It may also cause you to be temporarily locked out of accessing the site that you are trying to crawl as it can generate a big amount of http requests, which may trigger security measures on the website.

This example is significantly more complicated than the pipeline concept I have discussed so far. It extracts data (URLs) from the retrieved pages and feeds them back into the pipeline so that new URLs can be processed. As we'll see later, this makes it hard for the pipeline to determine when the work has finished. Still, a self-feeding pipeline is a useful architecture and you should know how to write one.

The web spider pipeline is fully implemented in the `WebSpider` unit, which provides a very simple interface, as shown here:

```
type
  TWebSpider = class
  public
    procedure Start(const baseUrl: string);
    procedure Stop;
    property OnPageProcessed: TProc<string>
      read FOnPageProcessed write FOnPageProcessed;
    property OnFinished: TProc read FOnFinished write FOnFinished;
  end;
```

We can only start and stop the pipeline, nothing more. The pipeline triggers the `OnPageProcessed` event each time one web page has been processed. It also calls the `OnFinished` event when the work is done. (We can, of course, always stop the process by calling the `Stop` method, even if the website hasn't been fully crawled yet.)

The main form uses this class in a fairly straightforward manner, as we can see in the following code:

```
procedure TfrmPipeline.btnStartClick(Sender: TObject);
begin
  if not assigned(FWebSpider) then begin
    FWebSpider := TWebSpider.Create;
    FWebSpider.OnPageProcessed :=
      procedure (url: string)
      begin
        lbLog.Items.Add(url);
      end;
    FWebSpider.OnFinished := StopSpider;
    FWebSpider.Start(inpUrl.Text);
    inpUrl.Enabled := false;
    btnStart.Caption := 'Stop';
  end
  else
    StopSpider;
end;

procedure TfrmPipeline.StopSpider;
```

```
begin
  FWebSpider.Stop;
  FreeAndNil(FWebSpider);
  inpUrl.Enabled := true;
  btnStart.Caption := 'Start';
end;
```

To start the process, the code creates a `TWebSpider` object, sets up event handlers, and calls the `Start` method, passing in the initial URL. If the user later clicks the same button, the web spider will be stopped and destroyed – as it will be if the `OnFinished` handler is called.

The process works in three stages:

1. The first stage receives a URL. It checks whether this URL has already been processed. If not, it passes the URL to the second stage. The first stage functions as a filter.
2. The second stage receives a URL and retrieves its contents. If the operation is successful, both the URL and returned HTML are passed to the third stage. The second stage is a downloader.
3. The third stage parses the HTML, extracts all URLs that are referenced by that page, and sends them back to the first stage. (The first stage then makes sure that the process doesn't cycle indefinitely.) The third stage functions as a parser.

The whole process is set up in the `Start` method, as follows:

```
procedure TWebSpider.Start(const baseUrl: string);
var
  i: integer;
begin
  FPipelineInput := TThreadedQueue<string>.Create(100);
  FHttpGetInput := TThreadedQueue<string>.Create;
  FHtmlParseInput := TThreadedQueue<THttpPage>.Create;

  FPageCount := 1;
  FPipelineInput.PushItem('');

  FThreadPool := TThreadPool.Create;
  FThreadPool.SetMaxWorkerThreads(TThread.ProcessorCount + 3);
  FThreadPool.SetMinWorkerThreads(TThread.ProcessorCount + 2);
  FTasks := TList<ITask>.Create;
  FTasks.Add(TTask.Run(
    procedure
    begin
      Asy_UniqueFilter(baseUrl, FPipelineInput, FHttpGetInput);
    end,
```

```
          FThreadPool));

    for i := 1 to TThread.ProcessorCount do
      FTasks.Add(TTask.Run(
        procedure
        begin
          Asy_HttpGet(FHttpGetInput, FHtmlParseInput);
        end,
        FThreadPool));

    FTasks.Add(TTask.Run(
      procedure
      begin
        Asy_HtmlParse(FHtmlParseInput, FPipelineInput);
      end,
      FThreadPool));
  end;
```

First, the code creates three message queues. `FPipelineInput` functions as an input to the filter stage; the downloader reads data from `FHttpGetInput` and the parser reads from `FHtmlParseInput`.

Then, the code sets the number of unprocessed work items in the pipeline to one and pushes the initial item (an empty string indicating the starting `baseUrl`) to the input of the first stage. We'll see how `FPageCount` is used to stop the pipeline when all the work is done later.

The code then creates its own thread pool and makes sure that we'll have enough threads at our disposal.

Finally, the code sets up all the tasks and passes the appropriate message queues to the workers. Since we don't care about the order in which the pages are crawled, the code creates multiple copies of the slowest stage, downloader. The web download doesn't use much CPU when it performs this process, so we can start lots of downloader threads. They will be mainly waiting for data anyway.

To shut down the pipeline, the `Stop` method merely shuts down the first message queue and waits for all tasks to finish their work, as follows:

```
procedure TWebSpider.Stop;
begin
  FPipelineInput.DoShutDown;
  TTask.WaitForAll(FTasks.ToArray);
  FreeAndNil(FTasks);
  FreeAndNil(FThreadPool);
end;
```

Filter stage

The filter stage creates a `TStringList` object, which holds the names of all the URLs that have already been processed. For each URL received on the input, it checks whether the URL is already in the list. If so, the URL is thrown away. The code also checks if the URL belongs to the site we are crawling. If not, it is also thrown away. (We certainly don't want to crawl the entire internet!) If all of the tests pass, the URL is added to the list of already processed links and is sent to the output queue.

The `Asy_UniqueFilter` method implements the filter stage, as follows:

```
procedure TWebSpider.Asy_UniqueFilter(baseUrl: string;
  inQueue, outQueue: TThreadedQueue<string>);
var
  baseUrl2: string;
  url: string;
  visitedPages: TStringList;
begin
  TThread.NameThreadForDebugging('Unique filter');

  visitedPages := TStringList.Create;
  try
    visitedPages.Sorted := true;
    if not (baseUrl.StartsWith('https://')
            or baseUrl.StartsWith('http://'))
    then
      baseUrl := 'http://' + baseUrl;
    if baseUrl.StartsWith('http://') then
      baseUrl2 := baseUrl.Replace('http://', 'https://')
    else
      baseUrl2 := baseUrl.Replace('https://', 'http://');

    while inQueue.PopItem(url) = wrSignaled do
    begin
      if inQueue.ShutDown then
        break; //while

      if url.IndexOf(':') < 0 then
        url := baseUrl + url;
      if (url.StartsWith(baseUrl) or url.StartsWith(baseUrl2))
        and (visitedPages.IndexOf(url) < 0) then
      begin
        visitedPages.Add(url);
        outQueue.PushItem(url);
      end
      else if TInterlocked.Decrement(FPageCount) = 0 then
        NotifyFinished;
```

```
    end;
    outQueue.DoShutDown;
  finally
    FreeAndNil(visitedPages);
  end;
end;
```

In addition to the standard `while inQueue.PopItem` loop that we described previously, the code also sets the name for this thread (`TThread.NameThreadForDebugging`). This enables us to quickly locate this thread in the debugger's Thread Status window.

Additional complication in the code comes from the fact that many websites nowadays quietly redirect you from a `http://` address to a `https://` address. I want such URLs to be treated as part of the website that is crawled. The code sets up two strings, `baseUrl` and `baseUrl2`, that are later used for testing whether an URL belongs to the website we are crawling.

The most important part of this stage are the following lines:

```
if (url.StartsWith(baseUrl) or url.StartsWith(baseUrl2))
   and (visitedPages.IndexOf(url) < 0) then
begin
  visitedPages.Add(url);
  outQueue.PushItem(url);
end
else if TInterlocked.Decrement(FPageCount) = 0 then
  NotifyFinished;
```

If the URL belongs to the website (`StartsWith`) and was not processed before (`IndexOf`), it is passed to the output stage. Otherwise, we are done processing this URL and it can be thrown away. As we do so, however, we must decrement the shared `FPageCount` counter, which holds the number of processing units in the pipeline. If it falls to zero, the pipeline is now empty and can be stopped. The code calls `NotifyFinished` to signal this, as shown here:

```
procedure TWebSpider.NotifyFinished;
begin
  TThread.Queue(nil,
    procedure
    begin
      if assigned(OnFinished) then
        OnFinished();
    end);
end;
```

This code uses the messaging approach we explored previously in this chapter to execute the `OnFinished` handler in the main thread.

This approach of queuing the event handlers to the main thread is also the reason why we must use a custom thread pool in the web spider code.

I have mentioned before that the RTL makes sure that all queued anonymous methods are executed in the `TThread.WaitFor` call. In the web spider implementation, however, we are using tasks and not threads. If we were using the common thread pool, the worker thread would not be destroyed after a task has completed its job. Although the `TWebSpider` would be then destroyed, the worker `TThread` would be not and the queued message would still be delivered, which could cause all kinds of problems.

As we are using a custom thread pool, however, all of the threads are destroyed when the thread pool is destroyed (in the `Stop` method), which makes sure that all the queued anonymous methods are processed before the `TWebSpider` is destroyed.

Downloader stage

The downloader stage uses a `THTTPClient` object to download the web page. This task is implemented in the `Asy_HttpGet` method, as follows:

```
procedure TWebSpider.Asy_HttpGet(
  inQueue: TThreadedQueue<string>;
  outQueue: TThreadedQueue<THttpPage>);
var
  httpClient: THTTPClient;
  response: IHTTPResponse;
  url: string;
begin
  TThread.NameThreadForDebugging('Http get');

  httpClient := THTTPClient.Create;
  try
    while inQueue.PopItem(url) = wrSignaled do
    begin
      if inQueue.ShutDown then
        break; //while

      try
        response := httpClient.Get(url);
      except
        if TInterlocked.Decrement(FPageCount) = 0 then
          NotifyFinished;
      end;
```

```
    if (response.StatusCode div 100) = 2 then
      outQueue.PushItem(THttpPage.Create(url, response))
    else if TInterlocked.Decrement(FPageCount) = 0 then
      NotifyFinished;
    end;
    outQueue.DoShutDown;
  finally
    FreeAndNil(httpClient);
  end;
end;
```

As the `Start` method creates multiple tasks, there are multiple `Asy_HttpGet` methods being executed in parallel. This is OK, as each uses its own local variables and there is no conflict between them.

If the web download fails (raises an exception or the response code is not 2xx), the code throws the input URL away. As before, the code then decrements the shared `FPageCount` counter in a thread-safe manner and notifies the owner about job completion if the counter drops to zero.

If everything is OK, the code pushes a `THttpPage` record to the output queue. This record is defined as follows:

```
THttpPage = TPair<string, IHTTPResponse>;
```

Parser stage

The parser stage parses the returned HTML and extracts all hyperlinks (`<a>` tags). Delphi does not contain a HTML parser in a standard distribution and as I wanted to remove any dependencies on third-party HTML parsers, I cheated a bit and used regular expressions to detect `<a href="..."` in the page.

The parser doesn't check whether the returned content is actually in HTML format or not. It merely scans the result for a simple regular expression.

In production code, you should never parse HTML with a regular expression. This doesn't work. Regular expressions are too limited to parse HTML.

The parser stage sets up the regular expression parser and then loops through all the data in the input queue. Each input is parsed and all detected URLs are sent back to the first stage for filtering. This task is implemented in the `Asy_HtmlParse` method, as follows:

```
procedure TWebSpider.Asy_HtmlParse(
   inQueue: TThreadedQueue<THttpPage>;
   outQueue: TThreadedQueue<string>);
var
   hrefMatch: TRegEx;
   match: TMatch;
   page: THttpPage;
begin
   TThread.NameThreadForDebugging('Html parse');

   hrefMatch := TRegEx.Create('<a href="(.*?)"\s.*?>', [roIgnoreCase,
roMultiLine]);
   while inQueue.PopItem(page) = wrSignaled do
   begin
     if inQueue.ShutDown then
       break; //while

     try
       match := hrefMatch.Match(page.Value.ContentAsString);
       while match.Success do
       begin
         if outQueue.ShutDown then
           break; //while;
         TInterlocked.Increment(FPageCount);
         outQueue.PushItem(match.Groups[1].Value);
         match := match.NextMatch;
       end;
     except
     end;

     NotifyPageProcessed(page.Key);
     if TInterlocked.Decrement(FPageCount) = 0 then
       NotifyFinished;
   end;
end;
```

Each detected a href hyperlink represents a new work unit. For each hyperlink, the code increments the number of work units in the pipeline (FPageCount) and then pushes the hyperlink into the output queue.

After the input is parsed, the processing of this URL is done. The code therefore decrements the number of processing units and calls the OnFinished event handler if necessary.

The need to always maintain the correct state in the shared FPageCount counter is what makes writing self-feeding pipelines a complicated process. You must absolutely make sure that you increment the counter for each addition to the pipeline and decrement the counter when the processing unit is not needed anymore.

Always increment the shared counter before pushing data to the output queue.

Always add data to the output queue before dropping the current processing unit.

This code also triggers the OnPageProcessed event, which notifies the main thread that a page was processed, as shown here:

```
procedure TWebSpider.NotifyPageProcessed(const url: string);
begin
  if assigned(OnPageProcessed) then
    TThread.Queue(TThread.Current,
      procedure
      begin
        if assigned(OnPageProcessed)
          OnPageProcessed(url);
      end);
end;
```

The test, queue, and test again pattern is used here for optimization. The second if assigned(OnPageProcessed) (inside the anonymous method) test is required, while the initial if assigned(OnPageProcessed) test is only used as an optimization step. After all, there is no need to spend time in the Queue call if the event handler is not set.

The following screenshot shows the web spider in action:

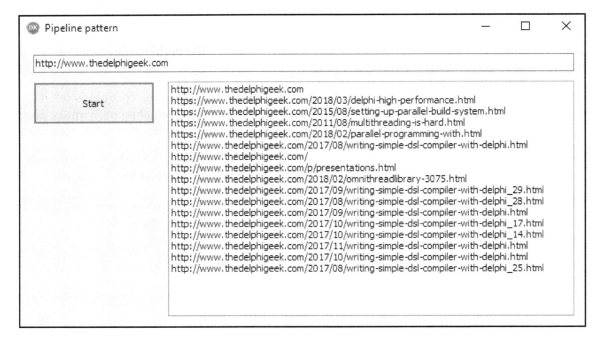

Web spider browsing my blog

Admittedly, the current web spider doesn't do any useful work (except providing a complete example of a complicated pipeline). To convert it into a more useful application, however, you only need to add one stage, which will either save received HTML pages to a disk or store them in a database. This part is left as an exercise for the reader.

Summary

In this chapter, we have explored four more concurrency patterns, in which two of them have been designed as simple drop-in replacements for the original code and two are required for rearchitecting parts of the code.

The thread pool pattern is a variation of an object pool pattern, and is designed to store threads. Instead of creating a new thread each time we need to execute some code in the background, we can take the already created thread from a thread pool and ask it to run our code. This speeds up the performance of the program and allows for some other interesting tricks.

After that, we were introduced to the concept of messaging. Although it belongs to architectural patterns, a proper use of this concept requires detailed knowledge of the tools that are offered by the operating system and the programming environment. This chapter explored three implementations of a messaging subsystem – the first used the Windows messaging infrastructure, the second was based on messaging support that's built into Delphi, and the third was based on being fully built with custom code.

The next section introduced the future pattern. We saw how this pattern allows us to easily push function calculations into the background and do something else while the result is being calculated. Although the future pattern is intentionally very simple, we can make it more powerful by combining it with the messaging pattern.

The last pattern in this chapter, pipeline, is more architectural than a design pattern because it requires a program redesign from standard code to a solution based on messaging. Still, it allows us to parallelize code that cannot be put into multiple threads with other approaches and because of that it's a powerful tool for any programmer's toolbox.

This brings our journey of standard design patterns to an end. In the next chapter, we will focus on the specifics of programming with Delphi.

6
Section 6: Miscellaneous Patterns

This part will discuss a number of interesting borderline topics that do not fall under the design category, but that are still useful for all programmers.

This section will comprise the following chapters:

Chapter 10, *Designing Delphi Programs*

Chapter 11, *Other kinds of Patterns*

Designing Delphi Programs **10**

Design patterns are important programming tools, but they are not the beginning and end of everything you should know about. There are other pattern groups beside design patterns and in the next chapter we will look into some of them but there are also important programming concepts that cannot be directly marked as patterns.

Besides design patterns, this book covers lots of Delphi idioms concepts that are related to one programming language and are not language independent like patterns. In this chapter, however, I would like to cover some important Delphi programming concepts that are more than idioms, but are still closely related to Delphi and cannot be treated as patterns.

Still, there is a close relation between the topics of this chapter and patterns in general. We'll see that some of the concepts that are described here are direct implementations of design patterns, while others spring from well—known programming paradigms and object—oriented programming.

In this chapter, you will learn about the following topics:

- Creating multicast events
- Using actions, the Delphi implementation of the command pattern
- Programming without writing code by using LiveBindings, an implementation of the *observer* pattern
- Using object—oriented programming in form design
- Modularizing form design by using frames
- Creating visual storage for components by using data modules
- Using data modules to implement a table module pattern

Event-driven programming

Creating applications by writing event handlers is a basic tenet of rapid application development with Delphi. From responding to button clicks to reacting to an application being resized, from overriding paint mechanisms to writing code that executes when the application is idle everything is done by writing event handlers.

Event-driven programming is not a Delphi invention. It was introduced a long time ago with the appearance of the first **Graphical User Interface** (**GUI**) libraries. Before this programming paradigm was introduced, programs were written as big ugly loops that checked the position of the mouse against each GUI element, checked whether a button had been pressed, called some code if it was, checked the keyboard, and so on and so on. All in all, creating user interfaces in that manner was extremely slow and boring.

With event-driven programming, all of that is replaced with a similar loop that runs at the heart of your GUI framework library. In Windows/VCL, for example, this is the main message loop. This code does all the boring and time—consuming tasks while allowing your code to modify the program's behavior by writing event handlers. For example, if you want the code to do something when a button is clicked, you create a `OnClick` event handler for that button.

In Delphi, the event driven paradigm is used in all parts of the runtime library, not just for managing the user interface. We create periodically executing code by writing an `OnTimer` event handler, react to changes in a dataset by providing an `AfterPost` event handler, follow the location of the device by writing an `OnLocationChanged` event handler, and so on. Events can be found in every part of the runtime library.

The true power of event—driven programming comes from a well-designed library. It must provide event hooks (places where event handlers are called) at all important places but no more than that. A library that doesn't call an event handler when a button is clicked is not good to anyone, as is a library that calls event handlers at places in code that are of no interest to anyone.

Technical details behind event—driven programming in Delphi are actually not very complicated. An event is just a procedure of object, which is a native Delphi data type that describes the method of an object. The real magic comes from the tooling. The integration between the compiler, the IDE's Object Inspector, and the editor brings event-driven programming to life.

I will not talk about that part of event-driven programming here. Rather, I'll look into how we can enhance our code by providing event hook extensibility in any class, even if it is not a component or a control. I'll also look into the concept of multicast events, something that Delphi doesn't provide out of the box.

The `Events` application in the `Event-driven programming` folder demonstrates a few different aspects of event-driven programming in Delphi. To show how user interfaces are written in Delphi, the code implements `OnClick`, `OnMouseEnter`, and `OnMouseLeave` events for two buttons, `Button1` and `Button2`. The event handlers are shared between the buttons. Both `OnClick` events point to the same method, `Button1Click`, both `OnMouseEnter` events point to `Button1MouseEnter`, and both `OnMouseExit` events point to `Button1MouseExit`.

All three methods are shown in the following code:

```
procedure TfrmEvents.Button1Click(Sender: TObject);
begin
  ShowMessage('You clicked button ' + (Sender as TButton).Tag.ToString);
end;

procedure TfrmEvents.Button1MouseEnter(Sender: TObject);
begin
  (Sender as TButton).Caption := 'Mouse is over the button!';
end;

procedure TfrmEvents.Button1MouseLeave(Sender: TObject);
begin
  (Sender as TButton).Caption := 'Button' + (Sender as
TButton).Tag.ToString;
end;
```

When we share event handlers between components, as in this case, we have to know which control triggered which event. To support that, event handlers in Delphi are written so that they pass this control as a first parameter (`Sender`) to the event handler. This is just a convention, not a requirement, but it is best if it is always followed.

Also by convention, the `Sender` parameter is always of type `TObject`. To use it in the code, we have to *cast* it into the appropriate type. The `Sender as TButton` construct in the event handlers does just that.

Sometimes, we want to associate some additional information with a control and then later use this information in the event handler to facilitate that Delphi's components all implement a `Tag` property. This component, of type `NativeInt`, is not used anywhere in the VCL or FireMonkey libraries and is there just for your convenience. The code in the example program stores 1 in `Button1.Tag` and 2 in `Button2.Tag` so that it can simply display the name of the button by using the expression `'Button' + (Sender as TButton).Tag.ToString`.

To demonstrate how we can add events to any class or record, the example program implements a class called `TDeltaTime` in the `DeltaTime` unit. This class has a settable property called `Delta_h: integer` and a function called `Now: TDateTime` that returns the current date/time, offset by `Delta_h` hours. It also contains three different implementations of an event that's triggered whenever the `Delta_h` property is modified. The declaration of this class is shown in the following code:

```
type
  TDeltaTime = class
  strict private
    FOnDeltaChangedProc: TProc;
    FOnDeltaChanged: TNotifyEvent;
    FDelta_h: integer;
    FOnDeltaChangedMulti: TMultiNotifyEvent;
  strict protected
    procedure SetDelta_h(const value: integer);
  public
    constructor Create;
    destructor Destroy; override;
    function Now: TDateTime;
    property Delta_h: integer read FDelta_h write SetDelta_h;
    property OnDeltaChanged: TNotifyEvent read FOnDeltaChanged
      write FOnDeltaChanged;
    property OnDeltaChangedProc: TProc read FOnDeltaChangedProc
      write FOnDeltaChangedProc;
    property OnDeltaChangedMulti: TMultiNotifyEvent read
FOnDeltaChangedMulti;
  end;
```

Before I show you the implementation of this class, let's see how it's used in the main form. It contains a field called `FDeltaTime: TDeltaTime`, which is created in the `OnCreate` event handler and destroyed in the `OnDestroy` handler, as follows:

```
procedure TfrmEvents.FormCreate(Sender: TObject);
begin
  FDeltaTime := TDeltaTime.Create;
  FDeltaTime.OnDeltaChanged := ReportDeltaChanged;
```

```
FDeltaTime.OnDeltaChangedProc :=
  procedure
  begin
    ReportDeltaChangedProc(FDeltaTime);
  end;
FDeltaTime.OnDeltaChangedMulti.Add(ShowTimeInPanel);
FDeltaTime.OnDeltaChangedMulti.Add(ShowTimeInListBox);
end;

procedure TfrmEvents.FormDestroy(Sender: TObject);
begin
  FreeAndNil(FDeltaTime);
end;
```

The `TDeltaTime` class contains an `OnDeltaChanged` method, which is implemented in the standard Delphi way as a procedure of object. The class defines `OnDeltaChanged` as a property of type `TNotifyEvent`, which is defined in `System.Classes` as follows:

```
type
  TNotifyEvent = procedure(Sender: TObject) of object;
```

The `ReportDeltaChanged` method of the `TfrmEvents` form accepts the `Sender: TObject` parameter. Because of that, it is assignment compatible with a property of type `TNotifyEvent` and we can simply assign `ReportDeltaChanged` to `OnDeltaChanged`.

When a `Delta_h` property is changed (and we'll see soon how that is handled), the `OnDeltaChanged` event is triggered and the `ReportDeltaChanged` method is called. The following method shows the current state of the `Delta_h` property:

```
procedure TfrmEvents.ReportDeltaChanged(Sender: TObject);
begin
  Log('New delta (via object method): ' +
    (Sender as TDeltaTime).Delta_h.ToString);
end;
```

In standard Delphi fashion, we have to cast `Sender` to `TDeltaTime` to access its `Delta_h` property. We can make the code cleaner if we change the type of the event property from procedure of object to an anonymous method.

The `TDeltaTime.OnDeltaChangedProc` property is of type `TProc`, which is defined as `reference to procedure` in the `System.SysUtils` unit. That makes `OnDeltaChangedProc` an anonymous method that takes no parameter. The initialization code then captures the `FDeltaTime` parameter and uses it inside the anonymous method, as follows:

```
FDeltaTime.OnDeltaChangedProc :=
  procedure
  begin
    ReportDeltaChangedProc(FDeltaTime);
  end;
```

The real event handler, `ReportDeltaChangeProc`, now accepts a parameter of type `TDeltaTime`, so we don't need to bother with casting. It is implemented as follows:

```
procedure TfrmEvents.ReportDeltaChangedProc(const deltaTime: TDeltaTime);
begin
  Log('New delta (via anonymous procedure): ' +
    deltaTime.Delta_h.ToString);
end;
```

Both of these examples implement a singlecast event, that is, an event that can only have one event handler. Sometimes, it is useful if we can attach multiple event handlers to one event. We call that concept a multicast event.

Multicast events are implementations of the observer pattern. Chapter 7, *Iterator, Visitor, Observer, and Memento*, discussed the observer pattern in detail. In this chapter, you can also find an implementation of a multicast event with the Spring4D programming library. In this chapter, we'll show a simple implementation that requires no external libraries.

The `TDeltaTime` class implements a multicast event called `OnDeltaChangeMulti`. The initialization code in the main unit attaches two event handlers to it by executing the following code:

```
FDeltaTime.OnDeltaChangedMulti.Add(ShowTimeInPanel);
FDeltaTime.OnDeltaChangedMulti.Add(ShowTimeInListBox);
```

Both event handlers accept a `Sender: TObject` parameter so that they can access the properties of the `TDeltaTime` class, just as the singlecast event handler did. They are implemented as follows:

```
procedure TfrmEvents.ShowTimeInListBox(Sender: TObject);
begin
  Log('Time is ' + FormatDateTime('dd hh:nn:ss',
    (Sender as TDeltaTime).Now));
end;
```

```
procedure TfrmEvents.ShowTimeInPanel(Sender: TObject);
begin
  pnlTimeNow.Caption := FormatDateTime('yyyy-mm-dd hh:nn:ss',
    (Sender as TDeltaTime).Now);
end;
```

The last part of the program represents a `TSpinEdit` control called `inpTimeOffset`. Each time it is modified, its `OnChange` event calls the `inpTimeOffsetChange` method, which sets the `Delta_h` property, as follows:

```
procedure TfrmEvents.inpTimeOffsetChange(Sender: TObject);
begin
  FDeltaTime.Delta_h := inpTimeOffset.Value;
end;
```

If you run the program and change the spin edit a few times, you'll see that each change results in three lines being logged to the list box (via `ReportDeltaChanged`, `ReportDeltaChangedProc`, and `ShowTimeinListBox`). The text on the panel is also updated from the `ShowTimeInPanel` event handler. The following screenshot shows the program in action:

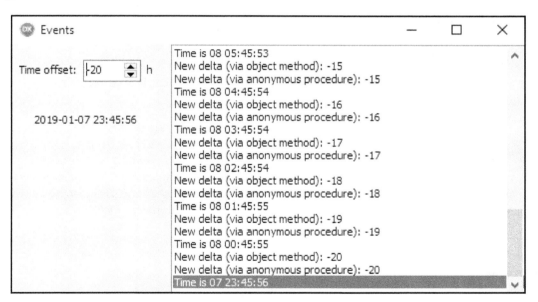

Singlecast and multicast events in the demonstration program

Now, let's move our focus to the implementation of event hooks in the `DeltaTime` unit. Each time the `Delta_h` property is changed, the `SetDelta_h` writer modifies the internal field `FDelta_h` and then calls event handlers. It is implemented as follows:

```
procedure TDeltaTime.SetDelta_h(const value: integer);
begin
  if value = FDelta_h then
    Exit;

  FDelta_h := Value;

  if assigned(OnDeltaChanged) then
    OnDeltaChanged(Self);
  if assigned(OnDeltaChangedProc) then
    OnDeltaChangedProc();
  OnDeltaChangedMulti.Notify(Self);
end;
```

The code quickly exits if the new value of `Delta_h` is equal to the old value. If that happens, the property did not actually change and there's no need to call the event handler. After that, the internal field `FDelta_h` is changed so that event handlers will be able to read the new value when they access the `Delta_h` property.

The code then calls the `OnDeltaChanged` property, but only if it is set. If the code had have not assigned an event handler to the `OnDeltaChanged` property, its value would be `nil`, and in that case any attempt to call `OnDeltaChanged` would result in an access violation exception.

Event handlers should always be *optional*. The code that calls the handler should always check whether the handler is assigned at all. If you find out that in your program design the event handler is *required* for proper functioning of the code, your should redesign the code. A better pattern to use in such a case is dependency injection. For more information about the dependency injection pattern, see `Chapter 2`, *Singleton, Dependency Injection, Lazy Initialization, and Object Pool*.

The second event handler, `OnDeltaChangedProc`, is called in the same way, except it doesn't take any parameters.

The last part, `OnDeltaChangedMulti.Notify(Self)`, calls all registered multicast event handlers. The `OnDeltaChangedMulti` property is internally represented as an instance of a `TMultiNotifyEvent` class, which provides a simple wrapper around a list of `TNotifyEvent` methods. This class is implemented in the same unit and is defined as follows:

```
type
  TMultiNotifyEvent = class
  strict private
    FList: TList<TNotifyEvent>;
  public
    constructor Create;
    destructor Destroy; override;
    procedure Add(event: TNotifyEvent);
    procedure Remove(event: TNotifyEvent);
    procedure Notify(sender: TObject);
  end;
```

As `OnDeltaChangedMulti` is of type `TMultiNotifyEvent`, this allows the code in the main unit to directly call the `Add` method of that interface to register event handlers. This method simply adds an event handler to an internal list, as follows:

```
procedure TMultiNotifyEvent.Add(event: TNotifyEvent);
begin
  FList.Add(event);
end;
```

The `Notify` method walks this internal list and calls all event handlers, as shown in the following code:

```
procedure TMultiNotifyEvent.Notify(sender: TObject);
var
  event: TNotifyEvent;
begin
  for event in FList do
    event(sender);
end;
```

You can check out the rest of the `TMultiNotifyEvent` implementation in the source code of this book.

Actions

In the previous section, we saw how to write event handlers for user interface components. This works great in small applications, but for larger projects, such hardwired connections between the UI and code leads to a pretty big mess. A solution is to separate the user interface from the actual code and connect them with a command pattern.

 Chapter 6, *Nullable Object, Template Method, Command, and State*, discusses the command pattern in more detail.

As you are programming with Delphi, you're in luck. There's no need to write the complicated infrastructure that's required for the implementation of a command pattern as Delphi already implements this pattern in the form of *actions*.

In Chapter 6, *Nullable Object, Template Method, Command, and State*, I wrote about four important parts of any command pattern:

"A command is an action, wrapped inside an object. It is created by the client object, for example, as a response to the user input. When a command is executed, it operates on a target object called a receiver. The last part, the invoker, is responsible for executing commands."

In the Delphi implementation, a command is represented as a TAction object (or some other descendant of the TBasicAction class). The client is the user interface framework itself either VCL or FireMonkey which creates all TAction objects when a form is created.

A receiver is not so well—defined. It may either be specified explicitly in code or it may be automatically determined by the user interface framework. We'll see how both variations are used later.

The last part, the invoker, is also implemented in the user interface framework. Actions are usually executed from a TControlActionLink object that resides inside each TControl and connects this control with an associated action. They can, however, also be executed by other means. For example, you can manually execute an action from the code.

To start using actions, you first have to drop a `TActionList` component on a form. This component functions as a container for `TAction` objects. Double—click the component and Delphi will open an editor where you can create new actions, arrange them into categories, edit their properties, and so on. The following screenshot shows the action list editor and the `TAction` properties being displayed in the Object Inspector:

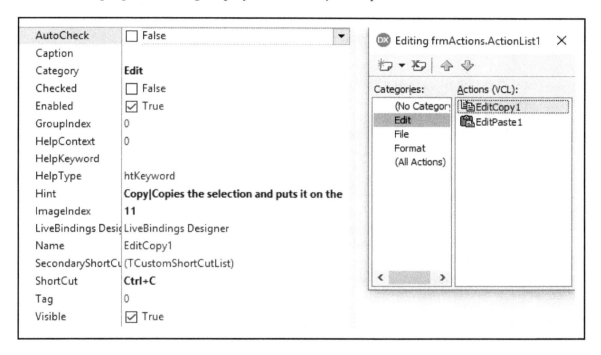

Action list editor (right) and TAction properties (left)

To link an action to a control, use the control's `Action` property to select an existing action, or use the `New Action` or `New Standard Action` options on the action selector. In addition to binding them together, this will also copy some properties of the action object to the properties of the bound control. For example, when you link an action and a button, the action's `Caption` property is copied to the button's `Caption` property (effectively changing the text on the button), the action's `Enabled` property to the button's `Enabled` property, and so on.

This process also changes the control's `ImageIndex`, `Checked`, `Shortcut`, `Hint`, and `Visible` (if the control has them) properties. From this point on, you should not try to modify these `bound` properties on the control but directly on the action object. All changes will also affect the bound control.

An action can be linked to multiple controls, for example, to a speed button and a menu item. In this way, you can only create the action (the code to be executed) once and then link it to all the appropriate places in the user interface.

Each action can implement three events – `OnExecute`, `OnUpdate`, and `OnHint`. The `OnExecute` event handler provides the code that is executed when an action is activated. The exact moment of an activation depends on the control to which the action is linked, but usually that happens when a control is clicked that is, when the `OnClick` event handler would be called. An action is also executed if it defines a shortcut and that shortcut is pressed. You can also execute the action manually from the program by calling its `Execute` method.

The `OnUpdate` handler allows the programmer to enable or disable the action according to the current state of the program. When an action is enabled or disabled, all linked controls are also enabled or disabled. The `OnUpdate` handlers are called periodically when an application is not doing anything and at some other occasions, for example, immediately before an action is executed. You should keep in mind that `OnUpdate` handlers are called very frequently. The code that's executed in these handlers should therefore be as fast as possible.

The last event, `OnHint`, allows us to provide a hint string that is displayed in the user interface when a mouse hovers over a control.

Besides the custom actions that execute our code in the `OnExecute` handler, Delphi also implements a large collection of standard actions. These actions are built into the user interface framework and don't expose an `OnExecute` handler. Rather, they execute code that is part of the framework.

A list of standard actions would be really extensive. There are actions to manipulate the clipboard (cut, copy, paste), manipulate rich edit controls (bold, italic, underline, align), open and close files and images, navigate datasets, and much, much more. To see the full list, open the action list editor by double-clicking on the `TActionList` component and selecting **New Standard Action** from the drop-down menu of the first icon in the toolbar.

The beauty of standard actions is that they adapt to the situation in a program automatically. For example, a TRichEditBold action is disabled unless a TRichEdit control has focus. When it is executed, it toggles the bold status in a focused TRichEdit. In that way, a standard action can automatically determine the receiver.

The Actions project in the Actions folder demonstrates how actions are used in Delphi programs. The main form contains a TActionList component that stores actions, a TImageList containing some images, and a TMainMenu with a few menu items. The form also contains two buttons, some speed buttons, and two TRichEdit controls. This form is shown in the following screenshot:

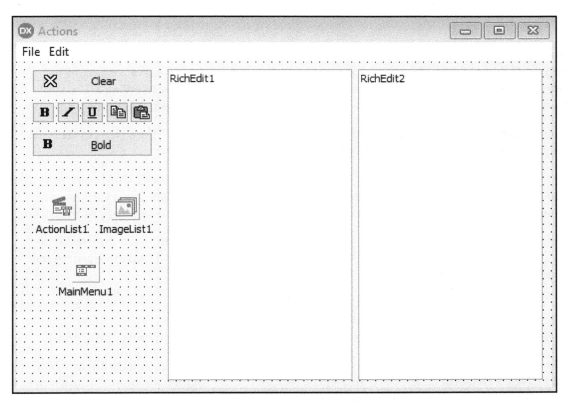

Main form of the Actions project

The form implements only one custom action, **Clear**. It defines both the `OnExecute` and `OnUpdate` event handlers, as follows:

```
procedure TfrmActions.actClearExecute(Sender: TObject);
begin
  RichEdit1.Clear;
  RichEdit2.Clear;
end;

procedure TfrmActions.actClearUpdate(Sender: TObject);
begin
  (Sender as TAction).Enabled :=
    (RichEdit1.Text <> '') or (RichEdit2.Text <> '');
end;
```

The `actClearUpdate` method makes sure that at least one of the rich edit controls is not empty. If that is `true`, the action's `Enabled` property is set to `true`. As we saw in the previous section, Delphi's event handler receive the invoker of the event as a `TObject` parameter and we have to cast it to `TAction` before we can access the action's properties.

This action is linked to a **Clear** button and to a **Edit, Clear** menu. These two controls are enabled and disabled in sync with the action's `Enabled` property.

The `actClearExecute` method is called when the action is executed. This happens when the **Clear** button is clicked or when the **Edit, Clear** menu is selected. The event handler clears the content of both rich edit controls, which makes them the receivers of the action.

Besides the custom action `actClear`, the form implements five standard actions. Three modify the rich edit control's font style (bold, italic, underline) and two manipulate the clipboard (copy, paste).

Let's take a look at one of these actions, `FormatRichEditBold1: TRichEditBold`. When created, its properties are automatically configured `Caption` to "&Bold", `Shortcut` to *Ctrl+B*, and so on. It is linked to the second button and to the menu entry, **Edit, Bold**.

We don't have to write any code to use this standard action. It is automatically enabled whenever a rich edit control is active and it automatically toggles the bold status for active rich edit control whenever the action is executed.

If you run the program, you'll see that you can use the action through the **Edit, Bold** menu or by using the *Ctrl+B* shortcut. You cannot, however, use it by clicking the **Bold** button. The reason for this is that clicking the button activates it, which takes the focus away from the rich edit control and that disables the action before it can be executed.

You can, however, use a speed button to execute the action. The form contains five speed buttons that are linked to five standard actions, and you can use them to format the text in rich edit controls and use the clipboard.

To exit the program, the form implements a standard action called `FileExit1`: `TFileExit`, which is linked to the **File, Exit** menu. When you select this menu, the action is executed and the program is closed.

LiveBindings

Besides the concept of actions, which are implementations of the command pattern, Delphi also contains a well—integrated implementation of an observer pattern in the form of the LiveBindings mechanism.

The observer pattern is discussed in `Chapter 7`, *Iterator, Visitor, Observer, and Memento.*

LiveBindings, which is partially implemented in the IDE and partially in the runtime library, helps create applications without any line of code. Of course, that is only the best—case scenario and in almost any useful application you will have to write some code.

The LiveBindings mechanism is very powerful and quite complicated, so I cannot do it any real honor on these few pages. I will therefore present just a short recipe, which will show you how to use LiveBindings to display data from a table. It will hopefully give you a taste of LiveBindings and the possibilities behind it. If you would like to learn more, I'd recommend reading an extensive white paper that was published by Embarcadero, which can be downloaded at `https://www.embarcadero.com/images/dm/technical-papers/` `understanding_rad_studio_livebindings.pdf`.

The `LiveBindings` folder contains two projects. `LiveBindingsStart` contains just one form with one `TClientDataSet` component preloaded with data. In the rest of this section, you'll get instructions on how to extend this project by using the LiveBindings mechanism so that you'll be able to view and edit the data in this `TClientDataSet`. The folder also contains the `LiveBindingsFinished` project, which contains the resulting functional application.

The LiveBindings mechanism is useful in VCL applications, but it is even more important for FireMonkey users. As FireMonkey contains no database-aware controls (such as VCL's `TDBGrid`), LiveBindings presents the only way of presenting data in a grid without doing a lot of coding. For this reason, the example application uses the FireMonkey framework.

To start, open the `LiveBindingsStart` project, right—click on the `CDSChapters` component, and select **Bind Visually** from the menu. A LiveBindings designer will open below the form editor. Initially, it will contain the `CDSChapters` component, as we can see in the following screenshot:

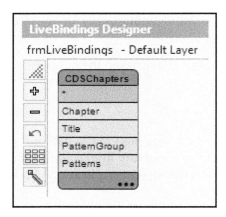

LiveBindings designer

The LiveBindings designer shows which parts of the component can be bound to other controls. All four columns of the table are available **Chapter**, **Title**, **PatternGroup**, and **Patterns** as is the wildcard field, *****, which represents the entire table.

To create a grid representation of the table, right—click the * field and select **Link to new control...** from the pop—up menu. A new dialog will appear, from which you can select the control that will display the data. As the * field represents the entire table, this dialog will only show controls that can display multiple records. With a standard Delphi installation, it will contain only two controls – TGrid and TStringGrid.

Select TStringGrid and click **OK**. This will create two components, BindingsList1: TBindingsList and BindSourceDB1: TBindSourceDB, and a string grid control called StringGridBindSourceDB1. The string grid will also appear in the LiveBindings designer, where you'll also notice a line connecting **CDSChapters:*** and **StringGridBindSourceDB1:***. The data from the CDSChapters table is immediately displayed in the string grid control, as shown in the following screenshot:

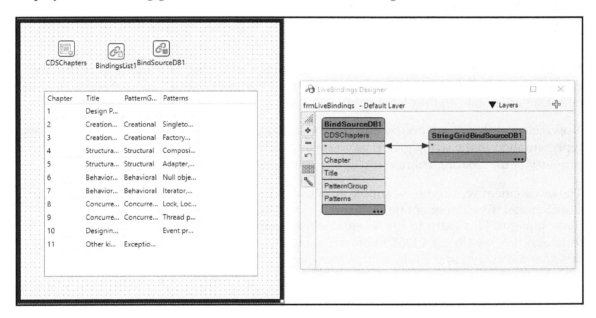

A client dataset bound to a string grid

This line has arrows on both ends, indicating that changes on any side will also modify the other side of the connection. If the table is changed, the string grid will be automatically updated. If the string grid is modified, the data in the table will be updated.

The `TBindingsList` component on the form stores all of the live bindings for that form. You will generally only need one such component on each form. If you double-click the component, an editor will pop up where you can modify existing connections and create new ones.

The `TBindSourceDB` component sits between the `CDSChapters` component and the string grid, and enables LiveBinding functionality.

 You can always change names of automatically created components and controls to something that will carry more meaning in your application.

Next, let's make the string grid look better. Right-click the string grid and select **Columns Editor...**. A columns editor will appear. Click the third toolbar icon (Add All Fields) and the editor will populate all four table fields.

Now, select each column one by one and for each, set the `Header` and `Width` until the data representation in the string grid is as you would like it. Also, change the `ColumnStyle` property of the Chapter column to `IntegerColumn`.

The last element we need for a simple application is a navigator. To add it, right-click the **BindSourceDB1** component on the form designer and choose Add Navigator from the pop-up menu. This will add the **NavigatorBindSourceDB1: TBindNavigator** control to the form and link it with the **CDSChapters** component. The resulting form and LiveBindings designer are shown in the following screenshot:

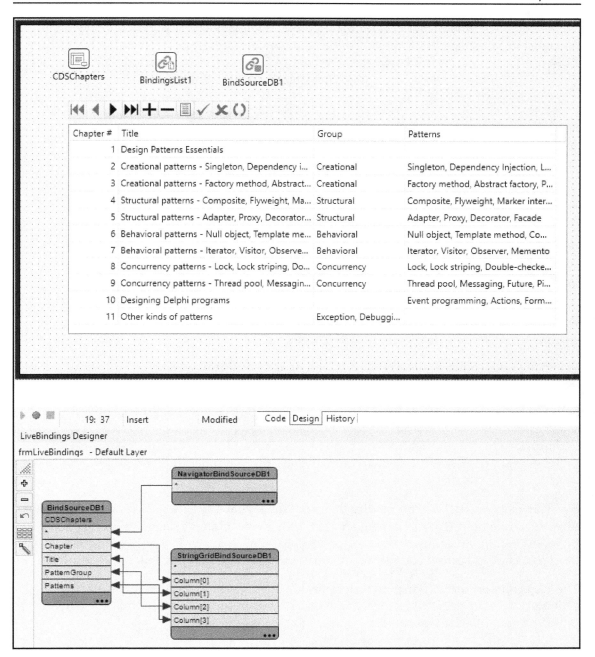

A simple table-editing form

This application already allows you to edit table rows, as well as insert and delete them. To make it useful, however, we need to add some hand—written code. When the application is closed, it should save the **CDSChapters** table to a file. When it is restarted, it should load this file back into the table. The following two form event handlers, `OnCreate` and `OnDestroy`, take care of that:

```
procedure TfrmLiveBindings.FormCreate(Sender: TObject);
begin
  if FileExists('Chapters.xml') then
    CDSChapters.LoadFromFile('Chapters.xml');
  CDSChapters.Active := true;
end;

procedure TfrmLiveBindings.FormDestroy(Sender: TObject);
begin
  CDSChapters.SaveToFile('Chapters.xml', dfXMLUTF8);
end;
```

The `FormCreate` event handler loads the file, but only if it is present. When the application is started for the first time, there will be no `Chapters.xml` file, and the original data that was compiled into the `CDSChapters` component will be displayed. On the next run, the current state from the disk will be loaded and used.

While the application is already useful, we can use LiveBindings *expressions* to make it even better.

Select the `CDSChapters:Title` field in the LiveBindings editor, and then right-click and select Link *to* new TEdit from the menu. This will add a new `TEdit` control to the form and link it to the `Title` field. If you run the program and move around the table, you'll see that the new `TEdit` control always contains the Title column of the currently selected table row.

By using expressions, we can modify the program so that `TEdit` will show the contents of more than one field. To start, create another `TEdit` control that's linked to the `Title` field by following the procedure from the previous paragraph again. In the LiveBindings designer, click the arrow connecting `CDSChapters:Title` and the new `TEdit` control.

The Object Inspector will display properties for the LiveBindings connection called `LinkControlToFieldTitle2: TLinkControlToField`. Enter the following text into the `CustomFormat` property:

```
Self.Owner.CDSChaptersChapter.AsString + ' - ' +
Self.Owner.CDSChaptersTitle.AsString
```

As a result of evaluating this expression, the text in the new `TEdit` will change to 1 - Design Pattern Essentials. If you run the program and click on the different rows in the string grid, you'll see that the `TEdit` contents will always display the chapter number, followed by a dash and the chapter's title.

For the last example, we can modify the code so that the comma-delimited *Patterns* field is displayed in a more readable manner. To start, open the Columns Editor of the string grid and remove the Patterns column. Drop a `TListBox` control on the form and name it `LBPatterns`.

Next, double-click the `BindingsList1` component. A bindings list editor will appear. Click the first toolbar icon. From the resulting dialog, select `TBindExpression` and click **OK**.

This will add a new expression called `BindExpression1` to the bindings list. Set the following properties of that expression in the Object Inspector:

- `SourceComponent` = `CDSChaptersPatterns`
- `SourceExpression` = `AsString`
- `ControlComponent` = `LBPatterns`
- `ControlExpression` = `Items.DelimitedText`

This expression is equivalent to the following line of code:

```
LBPatterns.Items.DelimitedText   := CDSChaptersPatterns.AsString;
```

If we configure the `LBPatterns` control correctly, this will split the Patterns field into multiple listbox items. Add the following two lines to the `FormCreate` method:

```
LBPatterns.Items.Delimiter := ',';
LBPatterns.Items.StrictDelimiter := true;
```

In all of the previous examples, the bound component was automatically updated when the selected row in the string grid changed. The LiveBindings mechanism made sure that everything was in sync. This expression, however, needs to be manually updated whenever the active row in the table is changed or the data in the table is updated.

To do that, select the `BindSourceDB1` component and select the Events tab in the Object Inspector. Click the **+** sign next to the `DataSource` property and double-click the `OnDataChange` event. Write the following code in the newly created event handler:

```
procedure TfrmLiveBindings.BindSourceDB1SubDataSourceDataChange(Sender:
TObject; Field: TField);
begin
  BindingsList1.Notify(CDSChaptersPatterns, '');
end;
```

This will notify the LiveBindings mechanism that the `Patterns` field changes when data source is modified. The LiveBindings mechanism will take care of the rest.

For a final touch, we have to do some preprocessing on the `Patterns` field value. It contains the data in the format of "`pattern 1, pattern 2`", which gets split into "`pattern 1`" and "` pattern 2`". The second field starts with a space, and we would like to get rid of that.

Double-click the `BindingsList1` component again and select `BindExpression1` in the editor. Go to Object Inspector and create an event handler for the `OnAssigningValue` event. Write the following code:

```
procedure TfrmLiveBindings.BindExpression1AssigningValue(Sender: TObject;
AssignValueRec:
  TBindingAssignValueRec; var Value: TValue; var Handled: Boolean);
begin
  Value := StringReplace(Value.AsString, ', ', ',', [rfReplaceAll]);
end;
```

This will change all occurrences of "`, `" to "`,`" in the value taken from the Patterns field before that value is assigned to `LBPatterns.Items.DelimitedText`. When data is split into multiple items, they will contain no leading spaces.

Run the program. The result should look similar to what's shown in the following screenshot:

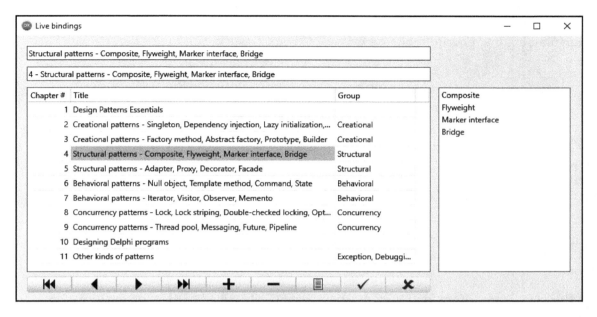

LiveBindings-based table editor in action

The LiveBindings mechanism is extremely powerful. It can, however, perform quite slowly in some situations. You should always test it well before deciding to use it in your application.

Form inheritance

Delphi is an object-oriented language and it is no wonder that objects and inheritance are used throughout the runtime libraries. That includes both user interface frameworks, VCL and FireMonkey, where every user interface element from a label to a form is represented as an object.

It is no big surprise that we can use the object-oriented approach to create new user interface elements by deriving from existing ones. As each form is represented with its own class (usually inheriting from TForm), we can even use inheritance to create new forms. Even more, the IDE implements tooling support for creating inherited forms and maintaining the repository of base forms.

 Chapter 5, *Adapter, Proxy, Decorator, and Facade*, discusses how inheritance can be used to create a *proxy* object for a button in the *Delphi idioms – replacing components in runtime* section.

Form inheritance is useful in two common situations. First, it functions great when you need the same functionality in multiple projects but you cannot share the same form directly. You can then create a base form that implements the common functionality and then inherit from it and do some final design changes to each project.

Second, form inheritance allows you to set up common design guidelines for an application. You can, for example, design a common dialog form that contains **OK** and **Cancel** buttons at the correct positions, to ensures that it is set up to scale correctly, and so on.

When we create a form by inheriting, we automatically get all of the functionality of the parent form. All design elements (controls) that are placed on the parent form are automatically visible in the inherited form, as are all event handlers and other methods from the parent form. Of course, all the normal Delphi inheritance rules are still followed, so we cannot access fields and methods from the strict private, private, and strict protected sections, but everything else is available to us.

We can add to the new (inherited) form as if it were a "normal" form. We can also modify the properties of inherited controls and components to change position, size, event handlers, and so on. The only limitation is that we cannot delete inherited components and controls. If the parent form implements too rich a functionality (design elements that we don't want to use on the inherited form), we can hide the extraneous controls by settings Visible to False, but we cannot remove them fully.

Interestingly, we *can* delete event handlers. Deleting an event handler just sets the appropriate property to `nil`.

The Delphi IDE supports two ways for the quick creation of an inherited form. If your base form is part of the same project, you can select **File| New | Other** and then find the Inheritable Items branch under the Delphi Projects node. Then, you can select the appropriate parent form and click **OK**. Delphi will create a new form, derived from the selected parent form, and open it for editing:

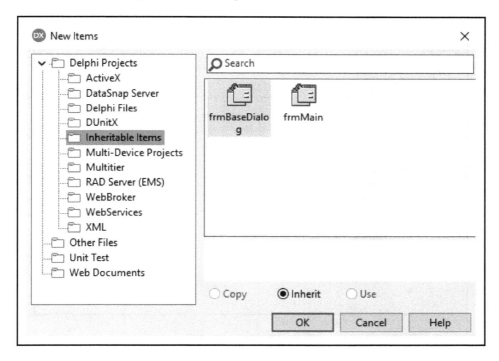

Creating a new form by inheriting from any form in the project

The bad side of this approach is that in a large project, the **Inheritable Items** branch gets very crowded. Because of this, is also not useful if the parent form isn't part of your project.

The second approach requires you to manually add a parent form to the object repository. To do that, open the form in the editor, right-click somewhere on the form designer, and select the menu entry **Add to Repository...** near the end of the menu. A dialog will pop up where you can select the location in the repository tree, set the form title, and add a description and author. By pressing **OK**, the form will be saved in the object repository:

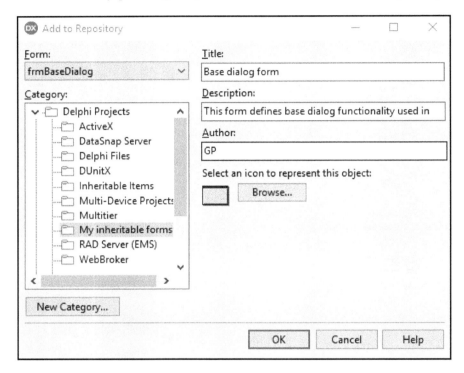

Adding a form to the object repository

To use such a form as a parent, proceed as before by selecting **File** | **New** | **Other** Instead of looking in Inheritable Items, select the category that you put the parent form in (My inheritable forms, in this example) and select the parent form from there. You will be given some additional options so that you can simply add the form to the project (Use) and make a copy in the current project (Copy):

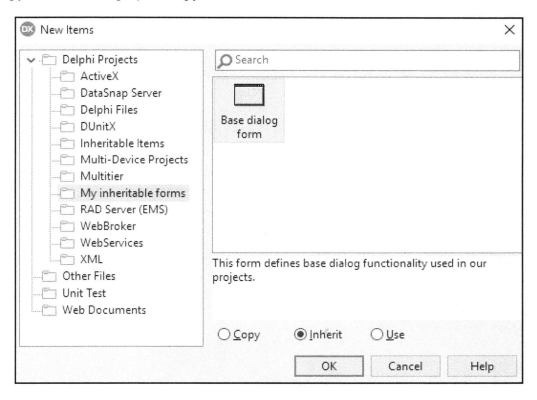

Creating a new form by inheriting from the object repository

As an example, the `FormInheritance` project from the `Form inheritance` folder implements a base form called `TfrmBaseDialog`, which is implemented in the `BaseDialogForm` unit. This form contains three buttons, **Help**, **OK**, and **Cancel**, which are placed on a bottom-aligned panel. Both **OK** and **Cancel** are also anchored to the right-hand side and not to the left so that they stay in the right-hand corner when the form is resized. This form is shown in the following screenshot:

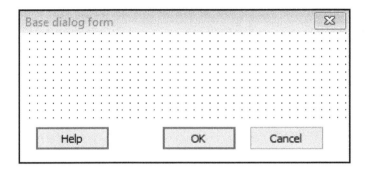

Base dialog form, opened in the form designer

The form also implements an `OnCloseQuery` event, which asks the user if they really want to close the dialog, as follows:

```
procedure TfrmBaseDialog.FormCloseQuery(Sender: TObject; var CanClose:
Boolean);
begin
  CanClose := MessageDlg('Do you really want to close this dialog?',
                    mtWarning, mbYesNo, 0) = mrYes;
end;
```

The example program contains two forms that are derived from the `TfrmBaseDialog` form. `TfrmDialog1` from the `DialogForm1` unit contains only one modification, which is an `OnClick` event handler for the **Help** button. This form is as follows:

```
type
  TfrmDialog1 = class(TfrmBaseDialog)
    procedure btnHelpClick(Sender: TObject);
  private
  public
  end;

procedure TfrmDialog1.btnHelpClick(Sender: TObject);
begin
  ShowMessage('No help available for this dialog');
end;
```

We can see that this form class is not derived from the standard `TForm` parent class, but from the class of the parent form, `TfrmBaseDialog`. This enables form inheritance to function when the program is executed.

The form designer uses the `dfm` file to find out whether a form is of a normal or inherited type. A `dfm` file for a normal form starts with an `object` keyword, as shown here:

```
object frmBaseDialog: TfrmBaseDialog
  Left = 0
  Top = 0
  BorderStyle = bsDialog
```

This code fragment shows the beginning of the parent form, `TfrmBaseDialog`. The inherited form, `TfrmDialog1`, however, starts with the `inherited` keyword, as follows:

```
inherited frmDialog1: TfrmDialog1
  Caption = 'Dialog 1'
  inherited pnlButtons: TPanel
    inherited btnHelp: TButton
      OnClick = btnHelpClick
    end
  end
end
```

This short description fully defines the `TfrmDialog1` form. It only lists the properties that were modified – the `Caption` text and the `btnHelp.OnClick` handler.

The second inherited form, `TfrmDialog2`, from the `DialogForm2` unit, contains more modifications:

- Th form's caption was changed to Dialog 2
- The form was resized
- The OK button was resized and repositioned and its `Default` property was set to `False`
- The `OnCloseQuery` event handler was removed

As you can see from this extensive list, the form inheritance mechanism allows us to centralize the design and behavior, but does not in any way enforce that either the design or behavior will be respected. The programmer can inherit from a form and then completely change the imported behavior.

If you make a mess when changing a control in an inherited form, you can right-click the modified control and select **Revert to Inherited** from the drop-down menu. This will reset the selected control to the inherited state.

To test the new forms, run the program. It contains two buttons, both of which open modal dialogs with the following code:

```
procedure TfrmMain.btnDialog1Click(Sender: TObject);
begin
  frmDialog1.ShowModal;
end;

procedure TfrmMain.btnDialog2Click(Sender: TObject);
begin
  frmDialog2.ShowModal;
end;
```

Frames

Another concept that allows us to make parts of a user interface reusable are frames. A frame is similar to a form. It is implemented in a separate unit, can be visually edited in the IDE, and you can place controls and components on it. A frame, on the other hand, cannot be directly displayed on a screen. To use it, you must place it on a form, or on another frame, which is then placed on a form.

Frames function more like composite controls than full forms. You can even put a frame on the component palette and use it as a normal component later. Similarly to forms, frames can be added to the object repository and can be inherited from.

To create a new frame, select **File** | **New** | **Other...** Then, select the **Delphi Files** branch and find the **VCL Frame** icon. (The name of the icon will be FireMonkey Frame if you are designing a FireMonkey application.) Click **OK** and a new unit will be created. It will look and function similarly to a form. You can place components and controls on a designer, write event handlers, add methods to the frame class, and so on – exactly like would modify a form.

When you want to *use* a frame on a form, select the Tool Palette window, open the Standard category, and double-click Frames. (Alternatively, you can type `<Ctrl>+.` `frame<Enter>`.) A dialog with the available frames from this project will appear. Select the appropriate frame and click on **OK**. This will place a frame on a form:

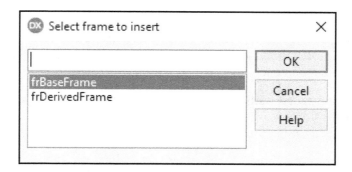

Placing a frame on a form

The placed frame behaves much the same as inherited forms. You can edit components on the frame, but you cannot delete them. Unlike the inherited forms, you also cannot add to the placed frame. Any control that you drop on it will be added to the form instead. You can, however, modify the original frame and all modifications will be immediately visible on the form.

Frames can be added to a component palette. To do that, open the frame unit, right-click on the designer, and select **Add to Palette**. A dialog will pop up where you can define the frame's name, palette page (category)m and icon, as follows:

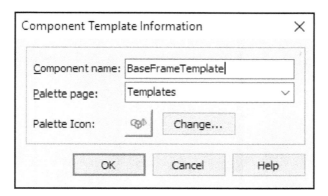

Adding a frame to a palette

After that, you can place the frame on a form in the same way as any other component or control.

To create an inheritable frame, use the same approach that you used for the form inheritance. Frames can be created from the Inheritable Items items or from frames that have been explicitly added to the object repository.

While we can use frames for normal user interface design, they are also useful for creating adaptable interfaces. To show this, the sample application `Frames` from the `Frames` folder implements a very simple tabbed web browser. The user can create any number of tabs and open a different web page in each one.

This example is implemented with the FireMonkey framework just to show that frames work in both of the UI frameworks that are included with Delphi. The application is intentionally very basic; for example, there is no styling and the form looks quite ugly.

 To learn more about FireMonkey and styling, see the great *The Delphi Cookbook* book, which was written by *Daniele Teti* and *Daniele Spinetti*, published by Packt Publishing.

The basic frame functionality is implemented in the `TfrBaseFrame` frame, which is defined in the `BaseFrame` unit. It contains two components – a top-aligned `TEdit` and a client-aligned `TWebBrowser`, as shown in the following screenshot:

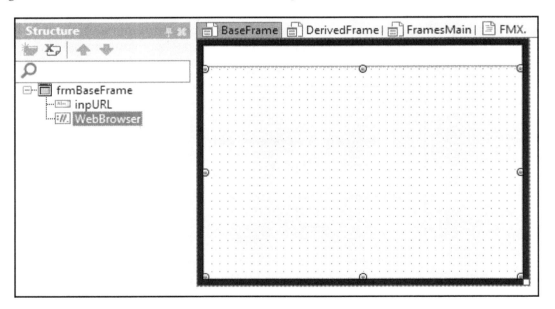

The basic frame opened in the frame designer

The implementation of the frame class `TfrBaseFrame` is shown in full in the following code:

```
type
  TfrBaseFrame = class(TFrame)
    WebBrowser: TWebBrowser;
    inpURL: TEdit;
  private
  public
  end;
```

We can see that is is very similar to a standard form class, except that it derives from `TFrame` and not `TForm`.

The functionality of this frame is enhanced in the derived frame `TfrDerivedFrame`, from the `DerivedFrame` unit. This frame leaves the inherited user interface elements unchanged, but adds some runtime functionality. The `TfrDerivedFrame` class is as follows:

```
type
  TfrDerivedFrame = class(TfrBaseFrame)
    procedure inpURLKeyDown(Sender: TObject; var Key: Word;
      var KeyChar: Char; Shift: TShiftState);
  private
    FOnStartLoading: TNotifyEvent;
    function GetURL: string;
    procedure SetURL(const value: string);
  public
    procedure SetFocusToURL;
    property URL: string read GetURL write SetURL;
    property OnStartLoading: TNotifyEvent read FOnStartLoading
      write FOnStartLoading;
  end;
```

The frame implements the `URL` property, which allows the main program to read and write the contents of the `inpURL: TEdit` control. In this way, the main program is decoupled from the actual implementation of the frame. Instead of working directly with the user interface element `inpURL.Text`, the frame implements a facade property `URL`, as follows:

```
function TfrDerivedFrame.GetURL: string;
begin
  Result := inpURL.Text;
end;

procedure TfrDerivedFrame.SetURL(const value: string);
begin
  inpURL.Text := value;
end;
```

For a longer discussion of the *facade* design pattern, see `Chapter 5,` *Adapter, Proxy, Decorator, and Facade.*

Another small helper, `SetFocusToURL`, sets the focus to the edit field, as follows:

```
procedure TfrDerivedFrame.SetFocusToURL;
begin
   inpURL.SetFocus;
end;
```

This function will be used later in the main program when a new tab is created.

The last part of the code implements the `inpURL.OnKeyDown` event handler. When a user presses then *Enter* key, the browser is directed to the URL that's written in the `inpURL` control. The code also triggers the `OnStartLoading` custom *event* if it is set, as follows:

```
procedure TfrDerivedFrame.inpURLKeyDown(Sender: TObject; var Key: Word;
   var KeyChar: Char; Shift: TShiftState);
begin
   if Key = vkReturn then begin
     WebBrowser.URL := inpURL.Text;
     if assigned(FOnStartLoading) then
       FOnStartLoading(Self);
   end;
end;
```

This frame implements a very basic web browser. To browse to any web page, the user has to enter its URL in the edit field and press *Enter*. To present this frame to a user, however, we first have to place it on a form.

In this example, the user can open any number of web pages. Because of that, we cannot create them in the form designer in advance. Instead, we have to create them in code.

The main form, `TfrmFrames`, which is implemented in the `FramesMain` unit, contains only two user interface elements a `TTabControl` that uses the whole client area and a small button with the text +, which is placed in the upper right corner. When a user clicks this button, a new tab is created and an instance of the `TfrDerivedFrame` is placed on it with the following code:

```
procedure TfrmFrames.btnNewTabClick(Sender: TObject);
var
  tabItem: TTabItem;
  webBrowser: TfrmDerivedFrame;
begin
```

```
tabItem := TabControl.Add;
tabItem.Text := '<blank page>';

webBrowser := TfrDerivedFrame.Create(tabItem);
webBrowser.Parent := tabItem;
webBrowser.Align := TAlignLayout.Client;
webBrowser.OnStartLoading := FrameStartLoading;

webBrowser.SetFocusToURL;
TabControl.ActiveTab := tabItem;
end;
```

First, the code creates a new tab and sets its caption to "blank page".

A frame is created after. For the user interface logic to function correctly, both the owner and the parent of the frame must be set correctly. The code passes tabItem to the constructor, which sets the owner, and sets the Parent property immediately after that. The frame is then expanded over the full tab area and OnStartLoading is assigned.

At the end, the edit control on the frame is focused and the new tab is activated.

The user is then presented with a new tab with the text "blank page", an empty edit control, and an empty web browser. The user can then type any URL in the edit control and press *Enter*. TfrDerivedFrame.inpURLKeyDown will then open that URL in the web browser and call the OnStartLoading event, which was set to call the FrameStartLoading method, as follows:

```
procedure TfrmFrames.FrameStartLoading(Sender: TObject);
var
  webBrowser: TfrDerivedFrame;
begin
  webBrowser := Sender as TfrDerivedFrame;
  (webBrowser.Parent.Parent as TTabItem).Text := webBrowser.URL;
end;
```

This method sets the text on the tab that owns the frame to the entered URL. The TfrDerivedFrame instance is passed as the Sender parameter. The code then converts it into the correct type so that it can access the TfrDerivedFrame.URL property.

To find the tab item that is associated with the frame, the code walks up the parent chain. Even though we have set the Parent property of the frame to be the tab item, the code inside the FireMonkey library changes that so that the parent of a frame is an intermediate TTabItemContent control. We have to climb another step in the relationship, to TTabItemControl.Parent, which represents the actual TTabItem that we want to modify.

A different approach to the same solution would be to store associations between tab items and frames into a `FDictionary`: `TDictionary<TfrDerivedFrame, TTabItem>`. When creating a new tab, the code would add the relationship into that dictionary by calling `FDictionary.Add(webBrowser, tabItem)`. The code in `FrameStartLoading` would then access `FDictionary[webBrowser]` to get the associated tab item.

The following screenshot shows the example application with three open pages:

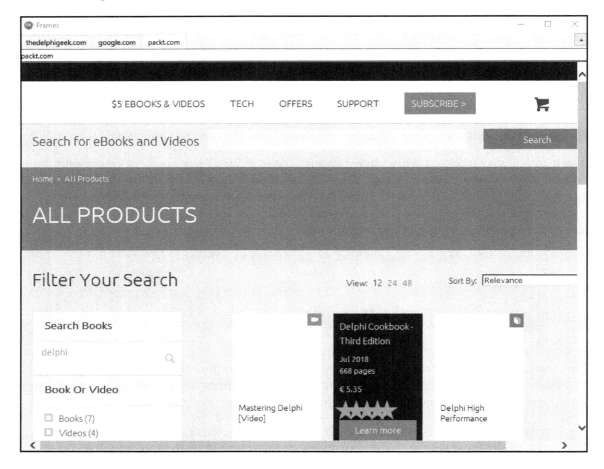

The tabbed browser application with three open web pages

The frames are a powerful concept, especially in FireMonkey applications where we can enhance their functionality with an open source component such as `TFrameStand`, which was written by Andrea Magni. You can find it at `https://github.com/andrea-magni/TFrameStand`. (Andrea also wrote a great FireMonkey book called *Delphi GUI Programming with FireMonkey*, published by Packt Publishing.)

Data modules

Data modules are another form-like container that we can find in Delphi. Like forms and frames, they are available both in VCL and FireMonkey frameworks. Unlike them, however, they don't accept controls, but only components. As such, they cannot be used to create graphical user interfaces. Nevertheless, they are excellent storage for datasets, SQL connections, and other non-visual components.

To create a new data module, select **File** | **New** | **Other** and then pick the Data Module icon in the Delphi Files branch. After pressing *OK*, Delphi will create a new unit and open the form designer. You will not be able to place controls on the design form, and the component palette will reflect this. While the data module is being edited, the component palette will not contain any controls, just non-visual components.

A data module can appear in three different types – VCL, FireMonkey, and framework-neutral. As you would assume, the VCL type is intended to be used with VCL applications, the FireMonkey type with FireMonkey applications, and the framework-neutral type with other applications such as console applications and services.

To set a data module type, change the `ClassGroup` property. It can take the following values: `Vcl.Controls.TControl`, `FMX.Controls.TControl`, and `System.Classes.TPersistent`. Changing the type also changes the list of available components, so you cannot place a framework-specific component on a framework-neutral data module by mistake.

The following screenshot shows how the list of components in the *System* category changes when the data module type is modified:

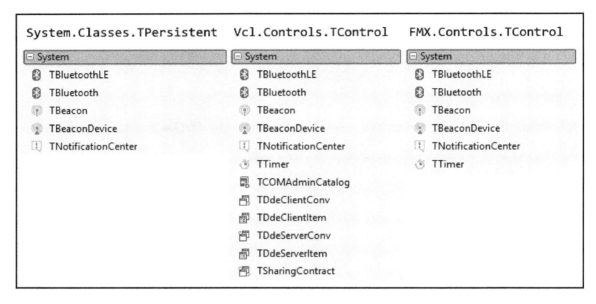

The list of *System* components that are available for each of the three data module types

Just like forms, data modules are inheritable. You can create an inherited data module in the same way as you would create an inherited form. All data modules in the project can be found in the **Inheritable Items** branch of the object repository. A data module can also be added to the object repository manually by right-clicking on the designer and selecting **Add to Repository....**

As an example, the sample application `DataModules` from the `Data modules` folder uses a data module to implement a table module pattern. This enterprise pattern, which is part of a domain logic group, specifies how one class should take care of one table and expose business logic as methods.

 This is just one of the possibilities of how database access can be managed. You could also use the domain model pattern or other possibilities. In some cases, however, wrapping just a single table is a correct choice.

To simplify the code and to remove any external dependencies, this example does not connect to a SQL server. Rather, all the data is stored in a `TClientDataSet` component, which is placed on a `TdmChapters` data module, and implemented in the `DataModulePatterns` unit.

`TClientDataSet` contains a simple table with four columns that describe the content of this book. The `Chapter` field stores an integer chapter number, the Title field contains a chapter title, the `PatternGroup` field holds the name of a pattern group that is described in this chapter, and the Patterns field lists the names of patterns that are described in this chapter. The following screenshot shows the data that's stored in the client dataset:

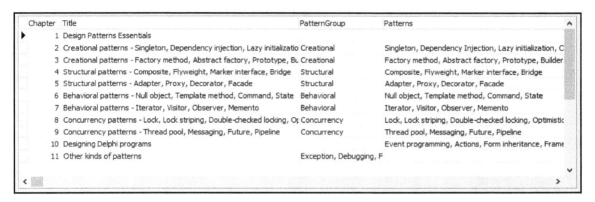

Contents of the TClientDataSet component on the TdmChapters data module

A beginner Delphi programmer would just drop a `TClientDataSet` on a form and then access the table fields directly in the code. That way surely works and is great if you are just putting together a simple program but in a complex application, such an approach typically ends in a mess.

If the program is accessing the table in multiple places, any modification of the table's structure ends in lots and lots of code fixing. It's better if we put the knowledge about the table structure in only one place and just expose the operations on the table – the business logic in a simple API.

`TdmChapters` does that by implementing an `IChapters` interface that defines the business logic, as shown here:

```
type
  IChapters = interface ['{0C8601E7-C15E-45FB-BA24-705838D3F036}']
    function GetChapters: TArray<integer>;
    //
    procedure Close;
```

```
      function GetCategory(chapter: integer): string;
      function GetPatterns(chapter: integer): TArray<string>;
      function GetTitle(chapter: integer): string;
      function Open: string;
      function IsOpen: boolean;
      property Chapters: TArray<integer> read GetChapters;
    end;
```

This API, which will be explained in a moment, is implemented by the `TdmChapters` data module, which is shown here:

```
  type
    TdmChapters = class(TDataModule, IChapters)
      CDSChapters: TClientDataSet;
      CDSChaptersChapter: TIntegerField;
      CDSChaptersTitle: TStringField;
      CDSChaptersPatternGroup: TStringField;
      CDSChaptersPatterns: TStringField;
    strict protected
      function GetChapters: TArray<integer>;
    public
      destructor Destroy; override;
      procedure Close;
      function GetCategory(chapter: integer): string;
      function GetPatterns(chapter: integer): TArray<string>;
      function GetTitle(chapter: integer): string;
      function Open: string;
      function IsOpen: boolean;
      property Chapters: TArray<integer> read GetChapters;
    end;
```

Besides the `TClientDataSet` table, the data module contains four `Field` fields that map directly to the table columns. They are used in the code to simplify access to table data.

The `Open` method prepares the data module for operation. It loads the contents from the `Chapters.xml` file, which must be present in the same folder as the `.exe` file. The code archive for this chapter already contains this file in the `Win32\Debug` subfolder, so everything should work if you just open the project and press *F9*. The code, which is as follows, returns any error as a function result:

```
  function TdmChapters.Open: string;
  begin
    Result := '';
    try
      CDSChapters.LoadFromFile('Chapters.xml');
    except
      on E: Exception do
```

```
      Result := E.Message;
    end;
  end;
```

The `IsOpen` method checks whether the dataset is open. The `Close` method closes the dataset. They are implemented as follows:

```
function TdmChapters.IsOpen: boolean;
begin
  Result := CDSChapters.Active;
end;

procedure TdmChapters.Close;
begin
  CDSChapters.Close;
end;
```

The `Chapters` property contains an array of all of the chapter numbers that are found in the table. The data is generated in the `GetChapters` method, as follows:

```
function TdmChapters.GetChapters: TArray<integer>;
var
  chap: TList<integer>;
begin
  chap := TList<integer>.Create;
  try
    CDSChapters.First;
    while not CDSChapters.Eof do begin
      chap.Add(CDSChaptersChapter.AsInteger);
      CDSChapters.Next;
    end;
    Result := chap.ToArray;
  finally
    FreeAndNil(chap);
  end;
end;
```

This code represents a standard way of iterating over a dataset. The result is returned as a `TArray<integer>`, which is a managed type and therefore doesn't require life cycle management on the client side.

The `GetCategory` and `GetTitle` functions return the values of the `PatternGroup` and `Title` fields for a given chapter, respectively. They are implemented as follows:

```
function TdmChapters.GetCategory(chapter: integer): string;
begin
  Result := '';
```

```
      if CDSChapters.FindKey([chapter]) then
        Result := CDSChaptersPatternGroup.AsString;
    end;

    function TdmChapters.GetTitle(chapter: integer): string;
    begin
      Result := '';
      if CDSChapters.FindKey([chapter]) then
        Result := CDSChaptersTitle.AsString;
    end;
```

The last API function, `GetPatterns`, returns the value of the `Patterns` field for a given chapter. The code knows that the patterns are stored in a comma-delimited list internally, and splits this list into a `TArray<string>`. This way, the API client (the rest of the application) doesn't have to deal with this implementation-specific detail. The `GetPatterns` function is implemented as follows:

```
    function TdmChapters.GetPatterns(chapter: integer): TArray<string>;
    begin
      if CDSChapters.FindKey([chapter]) then
        Result := CDSChaptersPatterns.AsString.Split([',', ', ']);
    end;
```

The main form contains four buttons that call the `IChapters` functions and two buttons that deal with data module life cycle management. In complex applications, data modules are frequently created when needed, and this example demonstrates how to do that.

The **Load data module** button's `OnClick` handler creates the data module, as follows:

```
    procedure TfrmDataModulesMain.btnLoadDMClick(Sender: TObject);
    begin
    FChaptersDM := TdmChapters.Create(nil);
    FChapters := FChaptersDM as IChapters;
    end;
```

The code creates a `TdmChapters` object and stores it in the `FChapterDM` field. The owner of the data module is set to `nil` and not to the form itself (`Self`) because we don't want the form to own the data module. After that, the `IChapters` interface is accessed and stored in the `FChapters` field so that we don't have to type `FChaptersDM as IChapters` over and over again.

To close and destroy the data module, the `UnloadDataModule` method calls the `Close` API, clears the `FChapters` reference, and destroys the `FChaptersDM` object, as follows:

```
procedure TfrmDataModulesMain.UnloadDataModule;
begin
  if assigned(FChapters) then begin
    FChapters.Close;
    FChapters := nil;
    FreeAndNil(FChaptersDM);
  end;
end;
```

The rest of the code just calls the `IChapters` functions. For example, the following code lists all of the chapters in this book:

```
procedure TfrmDataModulesMain.actGetChaptersExecute(Sender: TObject);
var
  chapter: integer;
begin
  for chapter in FChapters.Chapters do
    lbLog.Items.Add(Format('%d. %s', [chapter,
FChapters.GetTitle(chapter)]));
end;
```

To list the patterns that are described in each chapter, the code similarly loops over the `Chapters` property, calls the `GetCategory` and `GetPatterns` helper functions, and then merges the `TArray<string>` array that's returned from the `GetPatterns` function into a simple string by calling the `Join` helper. This method is defined as follows:

```
procedure TfrmDataModulesMain.actGetPatternsExecute(Sender: TObject);
var
  category: string;
  chapter: integer;
  patterns: TArray<string>;
begin
  for chapter in FChapters.Chapters do
  begin
    category := FChapters.GetCategory(chapter);
    patterns := FChapters.GetPatterns(chapter);
    if (category <> '') or (Length(patterns) > 0) then
      lbLog.Items.Add(Format('%d: [%s] %s',
        [chapter, category, string.Join('/', patterns)]));
  end;
end;
```

The following screenshot shows the result of these two methods:

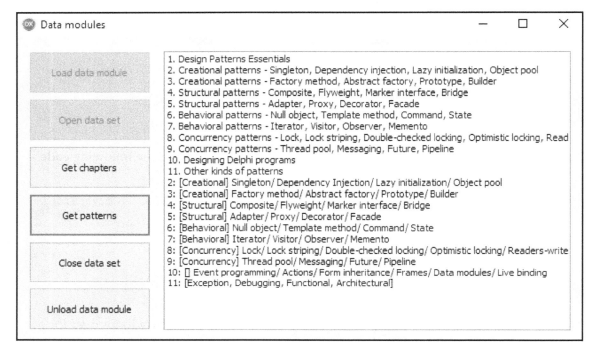

List of all the chapters in this book, followed by a list of all the patterns

Summary

This chapter looked into some important Delphi programming concepts that cannot be directly classified as *design patterns* because they are language-specific, while they are too rich to be called *idioms*.

Event-driven programming is a basic tool for rapid application development in Delphi. It has its roots in the first GUI libraries and is also important for writing objects that are created and used in code, not just for components and controls.

Delphi *actions* are implementations of the *command* pattern, which was covered in Chapter 6, *Nullable Object, Template Method, Command, State*. Actions can be used to separate the user interface from the code and to reduce the complexity of a complicated Delphi program.

Next, we looked into LiveBindings, which is a Delphi mechanism that can be used to write programs without writing code. LiveBindings is an implementation of an *observer* pattern, which was discussed in `Chapter 7`, *Iterator, Visitor, Observer, and Memento*. It is especially useful for database application development with the FireMonkey framework.

After that, we covered three different form and form like topics. All Delphi programmers know how to design forms, but form inheritance is a less well-known and used concept, and is based on object—oriented programming. It can be used to simplify form design and introduce common elements and code through inheritance.

Another concept that helps with form design is frames. They represent a way to put a collection of controls and associated code in a separate unit. A frame can be placed on one or more forms in the project and can be easily created during program execution.

At the end of this chapter, the data module concept was presented. Data modules are similar to forms, but cannot host visual components. They can be used in visual and non-visual applications (console, service) and are especially useful when we are working with database components.

In the next chapter, we will round up this book by looking into other categories of patterns, such as architectural, enterprise, and more.

11
Other Kinds of Patterns

In this book, we have discussed design patterns, anti-patterns, idioms, programming techniques, and more, but that barely scratches the surface. There are many other kinds of patterns that we could talk about, and there are many more roads to discover.

I have intentionally stayed away from architectural and enterprise patterns. On the one hand, they are not that interesting to the intended audience of this book programmers while, on the other hand, they really cannot be summarized in a few pages. A very thick book would need to be written to cover these two topics and summarizing them on a few pages would only give them injustice.

Instead of that, I have decided to focus on three concepts that don't fit into our previously covered categories but are still very important to an everyday Delphi programmer. I will discuss exceptions, debugging, and functional programming.

In this chapter, we will cover the following:

- Learning about exceptions
- Finding out how exceptions can be used and abused
- Learning a proper way to handle exceptions
- Looking at debugging processes from a new perspective
- Seeing how functional programming can be used in Delphi

Exceptions

Exceptions are mechanisms that bypass normal program execution flow. Although the specific details are language-specific, many modern programming languages follow the same principles.

A piece of code may signal invalid condition by raising an exception. (This is also called **throwing** an exception.) This exception may be a hardware exception that's generated in the hardware (on the CPU) or a software exception that's generated in the code.

Typical examples of hardware exceptions are access violations (where a program tries to access an invalid memory location) and division by zero. Software exceptions are more diverse, as they are frequently raised in different places of the Delphi runtime library. Probably the most well-known of all is the range check error exception, which is raised when the code, tries to access elements of a list that don't exist.

When an exception is raised, the code immediately exits from the current method, its caller, the caller's caller, and so on until it encounters an exception handler. This handler may optionally execute some code and then either raise the exception again or catch the exception and continue with the normal program execution. We say that an exception is handled if it is caught by an exception handler.

If the exception is not handled in our code, a special application level handler catches and displays an exception. In a Delphi GUI application, a message box pops up displaying the exception details while in a console application the exception is logged to the console output. A console application will then exit, while a GUI application would continue execution.

A small demo will demonstrate the difference between unhandled and handled exceptions in a GUI Delphi application. The Exceptions project from the Exceptions folder contains all of the examples for this section. A click on the Unhandled exception button executes the btnUnhandledClick method, which is shown here:

```
procedure TfrmExceptions.btnUnhandledClick(Sender: TObject);
begin
  Method1;
end;

procedure TfrmExceptions.Method1;
begin
  Log('Method1 start');
  Method2;
  Log('Method1 end');
end;

procedure TfrmExceptions.Method2;
var
  a: real;
begin
  Log('Method2 start');
  a := 0;
  a := 1 / a;
  Log('Method2 end');
end;
```

The `btnUnhandledClick` logs the `Method1 start` text to a listbox (the logger method, `Log`, is not shown here, but you can look it up in the source code). This method then calls the `Method2` method.

The `Method2` method logs the `Method2 start` text and then does some floating-point computation. The line `a := 1 / a;` tries to divide by zero, which results in a hardware exception, `EZeroDivide`.

Exceptions in Delphi are actually objects, derived from the base class `Exception`. The most frequently encountered Delphi exceptions are defined in units, such as `System.SysUtils` and `System.Classes`. `EZeroDivide`, for example, is derived from `Exception`, as shown here:

```
type
  Exception = class(TObject) ... end;
  EExternal = class(Exception) ... end;
  EMathError = class(EExternal);
  EZeroDivide = class(EMathError);
```

If you are running the program in a debugger, a message box will pop up at that moment, notifying you about the exception. Click **OK** to continue with its execution.

The code will now jump out of `Method2` and will not log the `Method2 end` text. The line that logs `Method1 end` in `Method1` will also not be executed. The exception will only be caught by the application-level exception handler, which will display a message box describing the exception, as shown in the following screenshot:

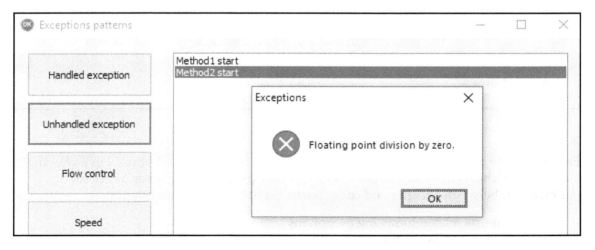

Unhandled exception caught by the application-level handler

You can now click **OK** and continue working with the application.

For comparison, the handled exception button shows how to catch and handle such an exception. It calls the `btnHandledClick` method, which is defined as follows:

```
procedure TfrmExceptions.btnHandledClick(Sender: TObject);
begin
  try
    Method1;
  except
    on E: Exception do
      Log('Exception caught: [' + E.ClassName + '] ' + E.Message);
  end;
end;
```

The code wraps the call to `Method1` in a `try..except..end` statement. This statement catches any exception that may be raised while `Method1` is being executed. If there's no exception, the `except..end` part of the statement is skipped; otherwise, it is executed. The `on E: Exception do` filter tells the compiler that we are interested in handling all exceptions and the `Log` statement logs some information about the exception.

The following screenshot shows the program after clicking on the **Handled exception** button:

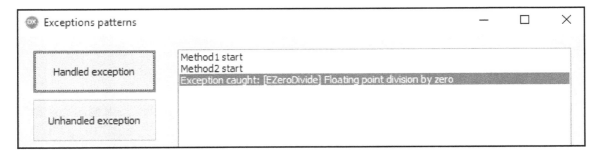

Handling exceptions in code

Exceptions are a powerful mechanism, but they can easily be abused or used in a way that leads to code that is hard to maintain. As with other programming tasks, a nice set of patterns will help you design good code. We can split them into two categories:

- Patterns related to raising exceptions
- Patterns related to handling exceptions

In the remaining part of this section, we'll look into the most important patterns from both categories.

Reserving exceptions for abnormal conditions

Like all powerful tools, exceptions can be used to solve all kinds of problems. The first pattern of exception usage therefore tries to limit the damage that would come out of such overuse. When working with exceptions, you should hold back and use them only to signal and handle abnormal conditions. You should not use them to report conditions that can be reasonably expected to happen.

As it is sometimes hard to draw a line between the two, a few real—world examples will help you decide what to do in a specific case.

Hardware exceptions are a good example of exceptions that signal abnormal conditions. In well—written code, a hardware exception such as division by zero or access violation simply should not happen. Any such exception indicates a broken program that should be fixed as soon as possible.

Another great example of a well-placed exception is a range check error, that is, ERangeError. It is raised by the runtime library when you try to access an invalid element of a list (TList, TObjectList, TStringList, TList<T>, and so on). For example, the following code would raise a range check error exception:

```
function TestRCE(list: TStringList): string;
begin
  Result := list[list.Count];
end;
```

Every Delphi list container starts by numbering its elements with 0. The last element in the list therefore has an index of list.Count - 1. The element with an index of list.Count does not exist and if we try to access it, an ERangeError is raised.

This exception is also raised if you try to access a string or array element that does not exist, but only if the code is compiled with Range checking turned on. Otherwise, the behavior will be unpredictable. The code may raise an access violation or may just proceed by returning an invalid result or, even worse, by overwriting some part of memory that is used by other data structures in the program.

My recommendation is to always turn on Range checking in **Project | Options | Compiling**. If required, you can always turn off Range checking just for a part of code by using the {$R} compiler directive. My book, *Delphi High Performance* (https://www.amazon.com/dp/1788625455), published by Packt Publishing, covers this in more detail in Chapter 3, *Fine-Tuning the Code*.

Another good example of using exceptions is the Design by contract methodology. If we follow this approach to software design, we treat a method as a piece of code that conforms to a contract that specifies certain conditions that are to be guaranteed on entry to the method (preconditions), guaranteed at exit (postconditions), and maintained during the execution (invariants). The easiest way to implement preconditions and postconditions in Delphi is to add some condition—checking code that raises an exception if the condition fails, as shown here:

```
function Shorten(s: string): string;
begin
  // precondition: String is not empty
  if s = '' then
    raise Exception.Create('String is not empty');

  Result := s;
  Delete(Result, Length(Result), 1);

  // postcondition: Result is 1 char shorter than input
  if (Length(Result) + 1) <> Length(s) then
    raise Exception.Create('Invalid result length');
end;
```

This code also demonstrates the name of the problem, not the thrower pattern, which will be discussed later.

An exception should not be raised when the calling code can be expected to handle the problem. For example, code that opens a file should not just raise an exception if the file name is invalid. A missing (or misnamed) file is a common problem and should be handled in code as a part of regular program flow, not as an exception. The *Exceptions should not cross API boundaries* section later in this chapter discusses this in more detail.

Exceptions also shouldn't be used for flow control. Delphi contains a rich set of statements for breaking the normal flow of execution – break, continue, and exit – that should be enough for all purposes. (There's even a goto statement that can be used for extreme situations.)

Just for a demonstration, the **Flow control** button in the `Exceptions` project triggers the following code, which uses an exception to break out of a loop:

```
procedure TfrmExceptions.btnFlowControlClick(Sender: TObject);
var
  i: integer;
begin
  try
    for i := 1 to 10 do
      if not Test(i) then
        raise Exception.CreateFmt('Failed at %d', [i]);
    Log('All OK');
  except
    on E: Exception do
      Log('Test failed');
  end;
end;
```

The code loops from 1 to 10, calls the `Test` function for each element, and writes out `All OK` if `Test` always returned `True` or `Test failed` otherwise.

Such code gets hard to read, especially if the program logic is split into multiple methods. Such programs are hard to debug and maintain. Even worse, each such exception stops the program's execution if you are running the program in a debugger! Testing such code in a debugger is a big problem and this alone should be a reason for staying away from such constructs.

We can fix this code in many different ways. One possible solution is shown in the following code:

```
procedure TfrmExceptions.btnFlowControlClick(Sender: TObject);
var
  i: integer;
begin
  for i := 1 to 10 do
    if not Test(i) then
    begin
      Log('Test failed');
      Exit;
    end;

  Log('All OK');
end;
```

If I still didn't convince you, look at this code with the eye of a programmer that wants to create fast programs. The **Speed** button in the `Exceptions` project calls the `btnSpeedClick` method (not shown in this book), which measures the execution time of the following four methods:

```
procedure TfrmExceptions.NoExceptions;
var
  i: integer;
begin
  for i := 1 to 100000 do;
end;

procedure TfrmExceptions.NoExceptionsTryExcept;
var
  i: integer;
begin
  for i := 1 to 100000 do
    try
    except
    end;
end;

procedure TfrmExceptions.NoExceptionsTryFinally;
var
  i: integer;
begin
  for i := 1 to 100000 do
    try
    finally
    end;
end;

procedure TfrmExceptions.WithExceptions;
var
  i: integer;
begin
  for i := 1 to 100000 do
  try
    raise Exception.Create('Test');
  except
  end;
end;
```

From top to bottom, the methods run 100,000 repetitions of an empty loop, the same number of repetitions of a loop with an empty `try..except` statement and with a `try..finally` statement, and 100,000 repetitions of a loop that raises and eats (throws away) an exception.

The following screenshot shows timing information for these four methods. The test was repeated three times:

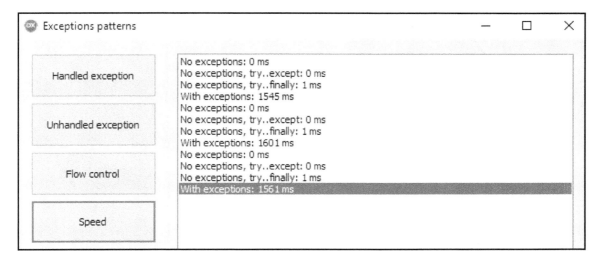

Comparing execution time for exception-free and exception-raising code

We can see that the code is fast if there are no exceptions. The `try..except` and `try..finally` statements by themselves don't slow down the code much. Raising and handling an exception, on the other hand, is a different matter. If your code depends on exceptions to handle flow control, exception handling can easily become the biggest factor for regulating the speed of the program.

Name the problem, not the thrower

An exception should tell you what went wrong, not where the problem occurred. All of the previously mentioned hardware and software exceptions behave in that way. Division by zero, access violation, range check error – they all tell you what went wrong and not where in the code this happened.

A standard counter-argument to that says, yes, but when my code crashes I want to know where that occurred, otherwise I cannot fix it! That is, of course, correct, but let's look at it from another perspective. You don't want to know where in the code the problem occurred, but who called that code. In other words, knowing that `ERangeError` occurred inside `TList<T>.Delete` is completely irrelevant. You need to know which part of your code called the `Delete` function.

If you are running this code in a debugger, the execution stops when an exception is raised and you can browse through the call stack to see exactly which function called which and how the current situation occurred. If the program is not run in the IDE, however, this information is not available and you only get the exception text, which is not very useful at that point. This can be solved by using exception loggers, a topic that will be discussed later in this chapter in the *Using an exception logger* section.

Saying all that, I still like to report both the location and reason when raising exceptions on precondition and postcondition checks. I would, for example, write the previously shown `Shorten` function as follows:

```
function Shorten(s: string): string;
begin
  // precondition: String is not empty
  if s = '' then
    raise Exception.Create('Shorten: String is not empty');

  Result := s;
  Delete(Result, Length(Result), 1);

  // postcondition: Result is 1 char shorter than input
  if (Length(Result) + 1) <> Length(s) then
    raise Exception.Create('Shorten: Invalid result length');
end;
```

I do that because in such a case, the name of the class and method where the check failed actually adds some relevant information. Unlike in the `ERangeCheck` example, in this code, the source of the problem could also be the `Shorten` function itself and not the caller.

Don't raise exceptions in destructors

Technically, you are allowed to raise an exception from inside a destructor (`TSomeClass.Destroy`). This raises a perfectly normal exception that can be caught with a `try..except` statement, just like in all of our previous examples. The problem, however, is that raising an exception in the destructor bypasses the final parts of object destruction in the RTL code and such an exception will prevent the memory that was used for the object from being released.

Let me repeat this again. Each time you raise an exception inside a destructor, the code causes memory to be leaked. Do this in a loop and the program will crash sooner rather than later with the `EOutOfMemory` exception.

Raising an exception from a destructor should only be reserved for critical conditions, after which the program will not continue execution. In all other cases, the destructor should report the exception via some mechanism (a global logging object or injected error handler) and then ignore the exception. Such a destructor would look as follows:

```
destructor TSomeObject.Destroy;
begin
  try
    // do the cleanup
    // an exception can be raised here
  except
    on E: Exception do
      LogExeptionDetails(E);
  end;
  inherited;
end;
```

While raising exceptions in a destructor is inherently bad, raising an exception in a constructor is supported by the Delphi compiler and runtime library. If you raise an exception in a constructor, the exception is caught in the code and a destructor is called automatically to clean the partially constructed object. After that, the exception is raised again.

If there's a possibility of an exception being raised inside the constructor, the destructor for that class must know how to handle the partially constructed object. In most cases, this does not represent the problem, as the code initializes the complete object to zeroes before calling the constructor. Since the `TObject.Free` works correctly if we invoke it on a `nil` object, the constructor can call `Free` or `FreeAndNil` without taking special care. This situation is different if the destructor wants to do some additional processing on object fields before destroying them.

To demonstrate the correct behavior, the **Exception in the constructor** button creates and destroys a `TExceptClass` object with the following code:

```
procedure TfrmExceptions.btnConstructorClick(Sender: TObject);
var
  obj: TExceptClass;
begin
  obj := TExceptClass.Create;
  try
    // do something with obj
  finally
    FreeAndNil(obj); // this will also never execute
  end;
end;
```

The `TExceptClass` constructor is shown in the following code:

```
constructor TExceptClass.Create;
begin
  inherited Create;
  FStream1 := TMemoryStream.Create;
  FStream2.Position := 0;
  FStream2 := TMemoryStream.Create;
end;
```

The preceding code contains an intentional mistake and uses `FStream2` before it is initialized. This results in an access violation exception on the `FStream2.Position := 0` statement. When that happens, a `TExceptClass.Destroy` destructor is automatically called. After that, the exception is re-raised. Since the code doesn't handle the exception anywhere (the `btnConstructorClick` method is still inside the `TExceptClass.Create` call at that moment), the exception is caught by the application-level event handler and displayed in a message box.

The `TExceptClass.Destroy` destructor shows one example of how such an exception can lead to problems. Let's say that the destructor doesn't expect that the exception can be raised inside the constructor and is implemented as follows:

```
destructor TExceptClass.Destroy;
begin
  FreeAndNil(FStream1);
  FStream2.Size := 0;
  FreeAndNil(FStream2);
  inherited Destroy;
end;
```

In this implementation, the `FStream2.Size := 0` statement tries to set the size of a `nil` object. This results in an access violation exception inside the destructor and that, as we have seen, is a bad thing. A proper way to implement such a destructor is shown here:

```
destructor TExceptClass.Destroy;
begin
  FreeAndNil(FStream1);
  // constructor failed, so FStream2 is not initialized at that point!
  if assigned(FStream2) then begin
    FStream2.Size := 0;
    FreeAndNil(FStream2);
  end;
  inherited Destroy;
end;
```

Exceptions should not cross API boundaries

One of the major reasons for the introduction of the concept of exceptions was that handling an exceptional situation in classical code results in messy code. For example, let's assume we have a function called `CheckFile` that accepts a file name and returns a `boolean` that indicates whether the data inside the file is valid or not. A declaration of such a function would be as follows:

```
function CheckFile(const fileName: string): boolean;
```

What should such a function return when a file is not found? It cannot return `false` as that value already has a contractual, meaning that the data inside the file is not valid; that is, a file not found is a different state and requires a different result.

We cannot fix this problem by changing all of the places in the code where the `CheckFile` is called to:

```
if FileExists(fileName) then
    Report(CheckFile(fileName));
```

After all, a file can be deleted after the `FileExists` is called and before `CheckFile` is called.

Taking that into account, we end with the following messy implementation:

```
type
  TCheckResult = (DataIsValid, DataIsInvalid, FileNotFound);

function CheckFile(const fileName: string): TCheckResult;
```

This approach mixes two different concepts into one result type and that is a bad idea from a software architecture viewpoint. One possible solution is to split the result into two values one carrying the result of the validity check and the other carrying the error status. Another is to introduce the concept of exceptions and raise an exception if the file was not found. The caller code must then handle that exception somewhere.

While I agree that exceptions are great for signalling exceptional conditions such as programming errors and failing preconditions or post conditions, I don't approve of using them in such situations. To me, it clearly breaks the reserve exceptions for abnormal conditions pattern, specifically the part saying that an exception should not be raised when the calling code can be expected to handle the problem. A file not being found is not such an uncommon situation that it should be treated as an abnormal condition. It is, however, something that needs to be handled.

Let me illustrate this with a short demonstration. Delphi comes with a `TFileStream` class, which is a `TStream` descendant wrapping a file. A fresh Delphi programmer who knows a bit about creating and destroying objects would use it in the following way:

```
var
  fs: TFileStream;
begin
  fs := TFileStream.Create(fileName, fmOpenRead);
  try
    // process the file
  finally
    FreeAndNil(fs);
  end;
end;
```

This looks fine and works great until the code tries to use a file that doesn't exist. When that happens, the code as the inexperienced programmer will be surprised to discover raises an exception inside `TFileStream.Create`. If we want to handle this situation in our program, we end with quite ugly code, as you can see here:

```
var
  fs: TFileStream;
begin
  try
    fs := TFileStream.Create(fileName, fmOpenRead);
    try
      // process the file
    finally
      FreeAndNil(fs);
    end;
  except
    on E: Exception do
      Log('Failed! [' + E.ClassName + ']: ' + E.Message);
  end;
end;
```

While simple to solve once you are aware of its existence, this problem neatly demonstrates the problem of raising exceptions from code that is hidden besides a well-known interface. In modern programming, we like to stick to programming to the interface and when we do that, we don't look inside the class to see how the code is implemented. The whole point of programming to the interface is to ignore the implementation details and work strictly with the interface (or, in broader terms, an API – an application programming interface).

When we program to the interface, we simply don't know that a method of that interface (of that API) can raise an exception. We say that exceptions are not discoverable in this context. The only way of knowing that such a situation can occur is to read the documentation (if it exists) or, more commonly, to encounter it in practice.

To prevent this problem, I posit a pattern that says that exceptions should never cross the API boundary. Using exceptions such as EFOpenError (meaning that the file cannot be open for reading) inside a tightly coupled code, for example, in methods of a class, is completely fine and can greatly simplify the code. Allowing such exceptions to leak out of the interface that external code will use to work with that class, however, is a bad idea that will sooner or later get you into trouble.

To be clear, I am not advocating catching and handling all exceptions. Exceptions that clearly indicate programming errors, such as division by zero and range check error, should still be raised. To catch some exceptions and let others be raised, the code must correctly implement the exception catching filter. This will be discussed in the *Catching exceptions selectively* section later in this chapter.

If we don't want to raise an exception, we can return the error result as an exceptional value. For example, the Windows CreateFile API returns a file handle (an integer) if the operation is successful or a special constant called INVALID_HANDLE_VALUE if the operation fails. The code can then call GetLastError to get detailed information about the problem. Similarly, code that creates and returns an object can return nil of operation fails.

The Exceptions project demonstrates the original approach in the btnFileStreamClick method, which is activated by clicking on the TFileStream button. The code is shown here:

```
function TfrmExceptions.OpenFile(const fileName: string;
  mode: word): TFileStream;
begin
  Result := TFileStream.Create(fileName, mode);
end;

procedure TfrmExceptions.btnFileStreamClick(Sender: TObject);
var
  fs: TFileStream;
begin
  try
    fs := OpenFile('com1', fmOpenRead);
    try
      // process the file
    finally
```

```
      FreeAndNil(fs);
    end;
  except
    on E: Exception do
      Log('Failed! [' + E.ClassName + ']: ' + E.Message);
  end;
end;
```

An alternative implementation in that it returns `nil` when `TFileStream` creation fails is triggered by clicking on the `OpenFile` / `nil` button. This code is implemented as follows:

```
function TfrmExceptions.OpenFileNil(const fileName: string;
  mode: word): TFileStream;
begin
  Result := nil;
  try
    Result := TFileStream.Create(fileName, mode);
  except
  end;
end;

procedure TfrmExceptions.btnOpenFileNilClick(Sender: TObject);
var
  fs: TFileStream;
begin
  fs := OpenFileNil('com1', fmOpenRead);
  if not assigned(fs) then
    Log('Failed to open file!')
  else
    try
      // process the file
    finally
      FreeAndNil(fs);
    end;
end;
```

This solution is much cleaner than the original approach, but still requires the user of the `OpenFileNil` function to understand that the code can return a `nil` object. In other words, the discoverability is still quite bad.

 This implementation of `OpenFileNil` has a big problem of eating all exceptions. You'll learn how to fix that in the *Catching exceptions selectively* section.

Returning an exceptional value has the same problem as the `TCheckResult` that we mentioned previously. It mixes two different concepts a result of the operation and an error status in one entity. Another solution is to return the result as one value and the error status as another. The `OpenFile` / `status` button in the demonstration program calls the following code, which demonstrates this approach:

```
function TfrmExceptions.OpenFileStatus(const fileName: string; mode: word;
  var fs: TFileStream): boolean;
begin
  fs := nil;
  try
    fs := TFileStream.Create(fileName, mode);
    Result := true;
  except
    Result := false;
  end;
end;

procedure TfrmExceptions.btnOpenFileStatusClick(Sender: TObject);
var
  fs: TFileStream;
begin
  if not OpenFileStatus('com1', fmOpenRead, fs) then
    Log('Failed to open file')
  else
    try
      // process the file
    finally
      FreeAndNil(fs);
    end;
end;
```

`OpenFileStatus` returns the newly created `TFileStream` object in the `fs` variable. It also returns a `boolean` result. As both are part of the function definition (the API), the programmer can see at a first glance that the function returns a `boolean`. The fact that the function returns both a value and a status thus becomes discoverable.

In the *Catching exceptions selectively* section, we'll see how this code can be improved even further.

Exceptions should not cross thread boundaries

At the very beginning, I said that exceptions in Delphi are normal objects, derived from the common parent `Exception`. That is why standard exception-raising code starts with `raise Exception.Create`. The code must first create an exception object (`Exception.Create`) and only then can it be raised.

Similarly, in the following code, `E` contains the exception object, which can be passed to logging code, `LogException`:

```
try
  // do something
except
  on E: Exception do
    LogException(E);
end;
```

This exception object, however, is destroyed at the end of the exception handler. The following code, for example, wouldn't work:

```
var
  tmp: Exception;
begin
  try
    // do something
  except
    on E: Exception do
      tmp := E;
  end;

  LogException(tmp);
end;
```

At the time the `LogException` is called, the `tmp` variable would contain the address of an already destroyed object.

To allow code in which event handling is decoupled from event catching, Delphi introduces two methods, `AcquireExceptionObject` and `ReleaseExceptionObject`. Their use is demonstrated in the following code, and are triggered by clicking on the `AcquireExceptionObject` button:

```
procedure TfrmExceptions.btnAcquireEOClick(Sender: TObject);
var
  excObj: TObject;
begin
  excObj := nil;
```

```
try
  Method1;
except
  on E: Exception do
    excObj := AcquireExceptionObject;
end;

if excObj <> nil then
  LogException(excObj as Exception);
end;
```

The code in `btnAcquireEOClick` calls `Method1`, which calls `Method2`, which raises an exception. This exception is caught in the exception handler.

The `AcquireExceptionObject` method creates a permanent copy of the exception object and returns it as a result of type `TObject`.

Once the execution exits the exception handler, the code checks whether an exception occurred and, if so, calls the `LogException` method to log the information about the exception on the screen. As this method excepts a parameter of type `Exception` while `AcquireExceptionObject` returns a `TObject`, the code casts the `excObj` variable into the appropriate type. The `LogException` method, which is shown in the following code, logs the information about the exception object:

```
procedure TfrmExceptions.LogException(excObj: Exception);
begin
  Log('Exception was caught: [' + excObj.ClassName + ']: '
    + excObj.Message);

  ReleaseExceptionObject;
end;
```

The preceding code extracts the relevant information (`ClassName` and `Message`) from the exception object and then calls `ReleaseExceptionObject` to destroy the exception object. After that statement, `excObj` points to an object that has been destroyed and should be no longer used.

This approach works fine in single-threaded code, but fails spectacularly in multi-threaded code. Let's assume that the previous code has been changed so that one thread calls `AcquireExceptionObject` and then uses some mechanism (either shared data or messaging) to send an acquired exception to another thread. The second thread then calls the `LogException` method, just like in the previous code.

While this looks fine at first glance, we must never forget that in multi-threaded code, many things execute at the same time. What if, after the `AcquireExceptionObject` was called but before `ReleaseExceptionObject` destroys the exception, another thread is called, `AcquireExceptionObject`. Which exception will be destroyed by the `ReleaseExceptionObject`? We cannot know. It's quite possible that the one we are expecting to be destroyed isn't.

In real code, an exception object should never travel from one thread to another. Doing so will get you into trouble. Instead of that, the exception should be processed while still inside the exception handler and converted into a form that can safely travel between threads. The **Serial exception button** shows one possible way of doing that:

```
procedure TfrmExceptions.btnSerializeExceptionClick(Sender: TObject);
var
  s: string;
begin
  try
    Method1;
  except
    on E: Exception do
      s := '[' + E.ClassName + ']: ' + E.Message;
  end;

  if s <> '' then
    Log('Exception was caught: ' + s);
end;
```

In this solution, the important data from the exception object is stored (serialized) inside a string. This string can be then safely sent to another thread for processing.

Catching exceptions selectively

I have hinted several times that catching exceptions with an `on E: Exception` filter is not a very good idea. Let's revisit the code demonstrating `TFileStream.Create` to show why this is the case.

The code that created a `TFileStream` object and converted exceptions into a `boolean` status was implemented as follows:

```
function TfrmExceptions.OpenFileStatus(const fileName: string;
  mode: word; var fs: TFileStream): boolean;
begin
  fs := nil;
  try
```

```
      fs := TFileStream.Create(fileName, mode);
      Result := true;
    except
      Result := false;
    end;
  end;
```

This code catches all possible exceptions (an `except` statement without a filter works the same as `except on E: Exception`), but that is usually not what we're aiming for. This will not only catch the exceptions carrying the operation status (such as file not found), but also exceptions signalling other abnormal conditions (for example, out of memory). In most cases, the code should not be written in a catch-all manner, but should only catch exceptions that carry the operation status.

In this case, doing things properly requires catching two different types of exceptions. `TFileStream.Create` raises `EFOpenError` when it cannot open the existing file and `EFCreateError` when it cannot create a new file. Both exceptions are defined as follows:

```
type
  EFCreateError = class(EFileStreamError);
  EFOpenError = class(EFileStreamError);
```

A better way to implement `OpenFileStatus` is to catch only `EFileStreamError` exceptions and ignore all others, as shown in the following code fragment:

```
function TfrmExceptions.OpenFileStatus(const fileName: string;
  mode: word; var fs: TFileStream): boolean;
begin
  fs := nil;
  try
    fs := TFileStream.Create(fileName, mode);
    Result := true;
  except
    on E: EFileStreamError do
      Result := false;
  end;
end;
```

This converts `EFCreateError` and `EFOpenError` into a `false` status, while ignoring other exceptions that will be re-raised at the end of the exception handler. If you want to know which of the two exceptions has occurred, then you have to handle them separately, as in the following method:

```
type
  TOpenFileError = (ofeOK, ofeCannotCreate, ofeCannotOpen);
```

```
function TfrmExceptions.OpenFileStatus2(const fileName: string;
  mode: word; var fs: TFileStream): TOpenFileError;
begin
  fs := nil;
  try
    fs := TFileStream.Create(fileName, mode);
    Result := ofeOK;
  except
    on E: EFOpenError do
      Result := ofeCannotOpen;
    on E: EFCreateError do
      Result := ofeCannotCreate;
  end;
end;
```

This method converts a successful operation into the ofeOK status, a file open error into the ofeCannotOpen status, and a file create error into the ofeCannotCreate status. All other exceptions are left unhandled and would be displayed by the standard application-level exception handler.

A click on the **OpenFile / status 2** button activates the following event handler, which calls OpenFileStatus2 and processes the result:

```
procedure TfrmExceptions.btnOpenFileStatus2Click(Sender: TObject);
var
  fs: TFileStream;
begin
  case OpenFileStatus2('com1', fmOpenRead, fs) of
    ofeOK:
      try
        // process the file
      finally
        FreeAndNil(fs);
      end;
    ofeCannotCreate: Log('Failed to create file!');
    ofeCannotOpen: Log('Failed to open file!');
  end;
end;
```

As the code is now, OpenFileStatus2 results in a ofeCannotOpen status and the code logs **Failed to open file!**. If, however, fmOpenRead is changed to fmCreate, the code results in ofeCannotCreate and logs **Failed to create file!**.

Don't ignore exceptions

Another bad example of exception catching is code that catches and ignores exceptions. This approach is equivalent to the infamous **On Error Resume Next** from Visual Basic. For example, the following code just silently ignores that a file was not opened and no processing was done:

```
procedure IgnoreExceptions;
var
  fs: TFileStream;
begin
  try
    fs := TFileStream.Create('com1', fmOpenRead);
    try
      ProcessFile(fs);
    finally
      FreeAndNil(fs);
    end;
  except
  end;
end;
```

The problem here lies in the empty `except end` block. An exception handler should always do something to convert an exception into a different kind of error (as in the examples from the previous section), log the exception, or re-raise it.

Using an exception logger

We saw at the beginning of this chapter that finding which part of code called the method that raised the exception is not a problem when running in a debugger. Real problems occur only when the program is running outside of debugger such as in a testing environment or, if you're unlucky, in production.

The solution to this problem is an exception logger. Such a tool will link some additional code into your program and generate a full stack trace (a list showing how the methods were called) when an exception occurs. An exception logger will at least allow you to save such a stack trace in a file, while some of them also integrate a dialog that allows the end user to directly send a stack trace to the support.

Examining the capabilities of different exceptions loggers is outside the scope of this book, so I will only list three good Delphi solutions – two that are commercial and one that's open source:

- EurekaLog, `http://www.heaventools.com/eurekalog-exception-logger.htm`
- MadExcept, `http://www.madshi.net/madExceptDescription.htm`
- JvExcept, `https://github.com/project-jedi/jvcl`

It isn't important regarding which exception logger you use as long as you use one!

Simplifying try..finally

The last pattern in this section does not deal with raising or catching exceptions, but with the resource finalization and `try..finally` statement.

As Delphi is not a garbage collected language, the code must make sure that objects are correctly destroyed, files are closed, and so on when an exception occurs. To do that, programmers must implement a standard way of creating and destroying objects, as shown in the following code fragment:

```
procedure Test;
var
  sl: TStringList;
begin
  sl := TStringList.Create;
  try
    PrepareList(sl);
    ProcessList(sl);
    WriteOut(sl);
  finally
    FreeAndNil(sl);
  end;
end;
```

The preceding code creates a string list object and then runs three methods on it. At the end, the object is destroyed.

The difference between the `try..except` and `try..finally` statements is that `try..finally` always executes the `finally..end` part, whether the exception was raised or not. If, for example, `ProcessList` raises an exception, `WriteOut` is not executed but `FreeAndNil` is. If there is not exception, `FreeAndNil` is still executed.

Another difference is that `try..finally` automatically re-raises the exception so that it can be caught by the next `try..finally` or `try..except` handler.

The problem with this approach is that it can lead to the arrow anti-pattern. For example, if you need to create three string lists and then destroy them all, you have to nest `try..finally` statements, as follows:

```
procedure TfrmExceptions.btnArrowClick(Sender: TObject);
var
  sl1: TStringList;
  sl2: TStringList;
  sl3: TStringList;
begin
  sl1 := TStringList.Create;
  try
    sl2 := TStringList.Create;
    try
      sl3 := TStringList.Create;
      try
        //DoSomethingWith(sl1, sl2, sl3);
      finally FreeAndNil(sl3); end;
    finally FreeAndNil(sl2); end;
  finally FreeAndNil(sl1); end;
end;
```

 The arrow or pyramid anti-pattern got its name from the shape of the whitespace at the beginning of lines.

In not so well-written programs, you can find arrows of such depth that the actual code drops off the right-hand side of the screen. Such code can be split into multiple methods, or it can be flattened out by using the following approach:

```
procedure TfrmExceptions.btnFlatTryFinallyClick(Sender: TObject);
var
  sl1: TStringList;
  sl2: TStringList;
  sl3: TStringList;
begin
  sl1 := nil;
  sl2 := nil;
  sl3 := nil;
  try
    sl1 := TStringList.Create;
    sl2 := TStringList.Create;
    sl3 := TStringList.Create;
```

```
      //DoSomethingWith(sl1, sl2, sl3);
    finally
      FreeAndNil(sl1);
      FreeAndNil(sl2);
      FreeAndNil(sl3);
    end;
  end;
```

Unlike the previous code, which called the constructor before entering the `try..finally` statement, this approach initializes all objects to `nil` and then creates them after the `try` statement.

If, for example, sl3 cannot be created, the `finally..end` block destroys sl1 and sl2. The sl3 variable will still contain the initial `nil` value and as `FreeAndNil(nil)` is a legitimate do nothing operation in Delphi, `FreeAndNil(sl3)` will not cause any problems. (`sl3.Free` can also be used as `Free` does nothing when executed on a `nil` object.)

The only problem with such code occurs if a destructor raises an exception. If, for example, `FreeAndNil(sl2)` would somehow raise an error (which should not occur with a `TStringList`), sl3 would not be destroyed at all. As raising exceptions from destructors is not a good idea and should be avoided, this does not represent a serious problem.

Another solution for such a problem is to use shared objects from the Spring4D library and replace the code with the following solution:

```
    procedure TfrmExceptions.btnFlatTryFinallyClick(Sender: TObject);
    var
      sl1: IShared<TStringList>;
      sl2: IShared<TStringList>;
      sl3: IShared<TStringList>;
    begin
      sl1 := Shared.New(TStringList.Create);
      sl2 := Shared.New(TStringList.Create);
      sl3 := Shared.New(TStringList.Create);
      //DoSomethingWith(sl1, sl2, sl3);
    end;
```

The Delphi compiler automatically initializes such objects to `nil`. It also inserts a `try..finally` statement that cleans up the variables at the end of the method. This drastically simplifies the code and allows you to focus on parts of the code that really matter, not on object management.

To learn more about Spring4D and shared objects, see the discussion of the proxy pattern in `Chapter 5`, *Adapter, Proxy, Decorator, Facade*.

Debugging

Fixing bugs in a complex program can be a complicated task. Sometimes, bugs are straighforward, while others are hard to reproduce or fall into the "there's no way that the current code produces this result" area.

A good programmer doesn't use random changes to the code to fix problems but approaches debugging methodically. Different people use different debugging approaches, but they can be typically summarized in the following steps:

1. Gather the data.
2. Develop a hypothesis.
3. Test the hypothesis.
4. Repeat until the test succeeds.
5. Add a test to the unit tests.

The last step (regression testing) is especially important as it prevents the bug to be accidentally reentered into the code by merging the incorrect version of the source.

To really fix a bug, you have to *reproduce* it first. Fixing a bug that you can't repeat is just performing guesswork. Your fix may work, or it may not, and even if it works, you won't know whether your changes really fixed the bug or whether it is not reappearing for some other reason. Sometimes, a bug appears on your first try and sometimes you need to work hard to get it reproduced. The following debugging patterns will help you with hard cases.

The recurring bug pattern is the simplest one. If the bug can be simply repeated, write a unit test for it. Then, fix the problem and add the unit test to the standard test suite.

The reproduce environment pattern helps with the bugs that cannot be repeated with the default program configuration. In such cases, you should reproduce the client's working environment. In most cases, you'll be able to repeat the bug after using the same program configuration, as used by the person who reported the bug. Other times, the environment problems go deeper. The bug may depend on the specific version of the operating system, installed drivers, numbers of monitors, or who knows what. A good understanding of the program will usually allow you to guess the important factors.

The time-specific bug pattern will help you if a bug is not easily repeated. In such cases, you should write a test that runs the problematic code continuously until the code fails. This is usually the only way to repeat problems in multi-threaded programs. Once the problem can be repeated, proceed with the fixing part.

Sometimes, you can repeat the problem but are unable to find the real cause for it because there's too much going on in the program. This happens a lot with multi-threaded applications. In such situations, you should eliminate noise by turning off parts of code. This is usually done in the develop hypothesis/test hypothesis part of the process.

In the first step, you develop a hypothesis that some part of the code (or a module or a thread) doesn't play a part in reproducing a bug. You can do that by examining the code or even by using pure guesswork. In the second step, you test this hypothesis by disabling that part of the code and rerunning the test. If the bug can still be repeated, you are now debugging a simpler version of the program, and that will help with finding the reason for the bug. You can even reapply the eliminate noise pattern and try disabling some other part of the program.

On the other hand, if the bug is now gone, you may have removed the part of the program that's responsible for the bug. Especially in multi-threading applications, however, this is not always the case. Stopping one thread can change the situation in the program just enough for a bug to disappear, even though the bug has nothing to do with that thread. In any case, your hypothesis has failed, so you should re-enable the disabled code and make a new hypothesis.

When you find a bug, you should always reduce to the smallest case. When you have minimal code that reproduces the problem, you can be sure that you really understand it. A smallest reproducible case will also help you create good a unit test that can be used for regression testing.

Sometimes, it will be hard to think of a good hypothesis. Maybe you can repeat the problem but you can't understand how the current code could possibly result in that bug, or you get stuck eliminating the noise and the program is still not working. Maybe you just cannot repeat the problem. Each time you're stuck, remember that you are not alone in this world. We programmers tend to get fixated on a problem and don't want to let it go, even if we are stuck. A good way to find new ideas is to discuss the problem with someone.

As it turns out, it doesn't matter much whether the person you are explaining the problem to understands how your program is working or not. The very act of explaining the problem activates parts of the brain that are not active during debugging and that frequently gives us a new perspective and new ideas. This process works even if you are not explaining the problem to a person. Many programmers that work from home use a rubber duck debugging technique in which you explain the problem to a rubber duck. You can also use a teddy bear, or a unicorn – whatever you want.

When you really get stuck, debugging by bisection can help. Go back into the revision history and find a version of the code that worked correctly. You can, for example, try with a version from the previous month or year and check if it works fine. If not, go back further.

When you find a good version, pick a revision that lies in the middle between the good revision (without the bug) and the bad revision (containing the bug). Test that revision. It will either work or not. In any case, you now have a half smaller interval where one revision works and one doesn't. You can now repeat this process until you find the exact revision that introduced the bug. Check the code that was committed in this revision and you'll have a much better idea about the possible sources of the problem.

If you are using a Git repository, you can use the `git-bisect` tool to automate this process (`https://git-scm.com/docs/git-bisect`).

Functional programming

Functional programming is a way of programming that is not well-known in the Delphi community. It is nevertheless an interesting concept which, although it cannot be directly transplanted into Delphi code, offers insightful ideas that we can use in our programs. Before I start talking about patterns in functional programming, though, we have to answer a seemingly simple question – *what is functional programming, anyway?*

Functional programming is one of the programming paradigms, a way of coding that treats computing as an evaluation of mathematical functions. It is part of a bigger family called **declarative programming**. Declarative languages focus less on defining the flow of the program and more on describing the program logic. Think about how SQL works (indeed, SQL is a declarative language). When writing a SQL program, you tell the database what needs to be done but not how it should do it.

 Some functional programming languages include F#, Scheme, Erlang, and Haskell.

As opposed to declarative programming, the imperative programming style uses program statements to control the program flow and change the program state. The Delphi language is a member of the object-oriented programming group of languages, which is a subset of imperative languages.

The main paradigm of functional programming is that it allows no mutable data. Once a variable is assigned a value, we cannot modify it anymore. This leads to a programming style that differs a lot from the standard Delphi code, but also brings some big improvements into our programs.

Once we accept that the data can't be mutated, all of the methods become idempotent. If we call one function multiple times with the same input, it always produces the same output. As data cannot be modified, this function cannot store any state that would affect computation. Because of that, the computation depends only on the input and produces the same output for the same input.

This is very much not the case in Delphi. Consider, for example, `TStream.Read`. It reads some data from a stream and its output depends very much on the current position inside the stream. `TStream.Read` changes this position (modifies the state) and by that causes the code to return different data each time it is called.

Idempotence is useful because it makes programs easier to understand and analyze. It also simplifies multi-threaded programming. The calculation in different threads only depends on the input and not on the shared state, and that makes all of the threads in the program fully independent.

To be fair, functional programming cannot solve all problems. For example, a pure functional program (one that never modifies state) is incapable of reading and writing data. Reading from a file, writing into a list-box – all of this modifies the external world and that requires handling mutable state (a state that can be changed).

Functional programming languages solve this problem by allowing some kind of interaction with the outside world. The core of the program can stay completely functional and just use a small set of functions to communicate with the real world. Another solution is to use an imperative language to write a user interface and a functional language to program business logic. In .NET, a common approach is to use a combination of C# and F#.

Another important concept in functional programming is the use of high-order functions. A high-order function takes a function as an argument or returns a function as a result, or does both. This style of programming was possible in Delphi for a very long time and is, for example, used for event-driven programming, but it became much more useful and powerful with the introduction of anonymous methods.

It is hard to write functional code in Delphi, simply because the language was not designed to do so. The compiler does not prevent modification of shared data and it is very easy to make a mistake and introduce a mutable state into the code. We can, however, use concepts of functional programming to simplify the code and make it more maintainable.

The concept of immutable data was used in the *pipeline* pattern from Chapter 9, *Thread Pool, Messaging, Future, and Pipeline*. In a pipeline, each processing stage reads data from a communication channel, uses some code to process the data, and writes the result to a second communication channel.

If the processing code doesn't use any state, we have a purely functional solution. Even is there is a state, the code is simple to understand. as the state affects only the processing code inside the processing stage and not the whole program.

Using functional programming ideas in Delphi implies the use of managed data types dynamic arrays and interfaces. I have prepared two simple examples. One uses out-of-the-box Delphi and dynamic arrays, while the other uses the Spring4D library and its extensive set of interface-based collections.

The Functional project from the Functional programming folder demonstrates the concept of immutability and high-order functions in a Delphi program.

Clicking the Filter & Map button executes the following code, which processes a list of numbers and generates a short output:

```
procedure TfrmFunctional.btnFilterMapClick(Sender: TObject);
var
  data1: TArray<integer>;
  data2: TArray<integer>;
  data3: TArray<integer>;
  isEven: TFunc<integer,boolean>;
begin
  data1 := GenerateData(500);
  isEven :=
    function(value: integer): boolean
    begin
      Result := not Odd(value);
    end;
  data2 := Functional.Filter<integer>(data1, isEven);
  data3 := Functional.Filter<integer>(data2, DivisibleBy17);
  WriteOut(Functional.Map<integer,string>(data3, IntToStr));
end;
```

In the first step, the code generates a list of all integer numbers from 1 to 500 and stores it in the `data1` variable. The `GenerateData` function is a short Delphi method, which is shown here:

```
function TfrmFunctional.GenerateData(count: integer): TArray<integer>;
var
  i: integer;
begin
  SetLength(Result, count);
  for i := 1 to count do
    Result[i-1] := i;
end;
```

The `btnFilterMapClick` method then defines a function that accepts one integer parameter and returns a `boolean` input which is `True` if the parameter is even. This anonymous function is stored in a local variable called `isEven`.

The code then calls the `Functional.Filter` function, which takes a dynamic array and a filter function as parameters. It calls the filter function for each input and returns a dynamic array containing elements for which the filter function returns `True`. This function is implemented in the `FunctionalDelphi` unit, as follows:

```
class function Functional.Filter<T>(const input: TArray<T>;
  const filter: TFunc<T, boolean>): TArray<T>;
var
  iIn: integer;
  iOut: integer;
begin
  SetLength(Result, Length(input));
  iOut := 0;
  for iIn := 0 to High(input) do
  begin
    if filter(input[iIn]) then
    begin
      Result[iOut] := input[iIn];
      Inc(iOut);
    end;
  end;
  SetLength(Result, iOut);
end;
```

The `Filter` function shows how we can use a function parameter in code.

You may have noticed that the result of the first `Filter` call is stored in the `data2` variable and the result of the second call is stored in the `data3` variable. As we are trying to write functional code, we must not modify the same variable twice.

The result of two `Filter` calls is a list of integers from 1 to 500 that are divisible by 2 (filtered in the first call) and by 17 (filtered in the second call).

In the last step, the code converts an array of `integer` data into an array of `string` and then passes the result to the `WriteOut` function, which logs the data to the listbox. The `Functional.Map` function, which converts data from one type to another, is implemented in the `FunctionalDelphi` unit, as follows:

```
class function Functional.Map<T1, T2>(const input: TArray<T1>;
  const mapper: TFunc<T1, T2>): TArray<T2>;
var
  i: integer;
begin
  SetLength(Result, Length(input));
  for i := 0 to High(input) do
    Result[i] := mapper(input[i]);
end;
```

If you run the program, you'll see a list of all integer numbers from 1 to 500 that are divisible by 34:

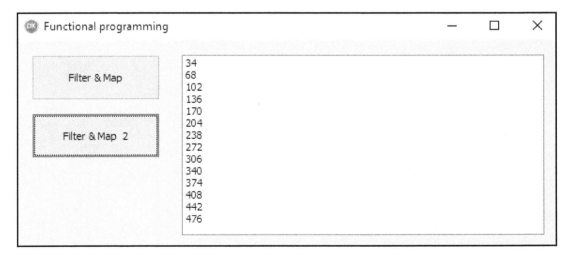

Result of running the demonstration functional program

To prove that all operations in the demonstration program are indeed idempotent, the program includes another method, btnFilterMap2Click, where every operation is repeated twice. The code is executed by clicking the **Filter & Map 2** button. You can check the code and the output it generates in the Functional project.

The second example uses interface-based collections from the Spring4D library (https://bitbucket.org/sglienke/spring4d). To run the program, you'll have to install this library and then add its folders, that is, Source, Source\Base, and Source\Base\Collections, to Delphi's Library path or to the project's Search path. If you unpack the library into the Chapter 11\Spring4D folder, the project's Search path will already be correctly configured and you can simply press *F9* to run the program.

 If you have git installed, you can execute the following command in the Chapter 11 folder to install Spring4D: git clone https://bitbucket.org/sglienke/spring4d.

The FunctionalSpring project from the Functional programming folder implements similar code to the Functional project but uses the IList<T> and IEnumerable<T> interfaces instead of the dynamic array TArray<T> to store data.

The btnIEnumClick method is activated by clicking on the **IEnumerable** button. It is implemented as follows:

```
procedure TfrmFunctionalSpring.btnIEnumClick(Sender: TObject);
var
  data1: IList<integer>;
  data2: IEnumerable<integer>;
  data3: IEnumerable<integer>;
  data4: IEnumerable<integer>;
  data5: IEnumerable<string>;
begin
  data1 := TCollections.CreateList<integer>(GenerateData(1000));
  data2 := data1.Where(
    function (const value: integer): boolean
    begin
      Result := (not Odd(value)) and ((value mod 17) = 0);
    end);
  data3 := data2.Take(10);
  data4 := data3.Reversed;
  data5 := TEnumerable.Select<integer, string>(data4, IntToStr);
  WriteOut(data5);
end;
```

The preceding code generates an array of integers from 1 to 500 by calling the GenerateData function and wraps that array in an IList by calling TCollections.CreateList<integer>.

Next, the code filters the list to remove all of the numbers that are not divisible by 2 and 17. This is done in the Where function, which is part of the IEnumerable<T> interface that's implemented in the Spring.Collections unit. The Where function returns data of type IEnumerable<T>, which cannot be modified in the same way as a list can be as it doesn't support Add and Delete methods. By that, IEnumerable<T> enforces immutability of its contents.

> You will find many other interesting kinds of filters in the IEnumerable<T> interface and in the TEnumerable<T> class. Both are defined in the Spring.Collections unit.

The code then uses another Spring function, Take, to take only the first 10 elements from data. All other elements are thrown away. After that, Reversed is called to reverse the order of elements.

At the end, the class function Select of the TEnumerable class converts data from integer to string. The result is written to a listbox, just like in the previous example.

This code is more or less the same as the array-based code from the previous example. The beauty of Spring, however, is that we can use fluent programming and chain processing steps one by one. The **IEnumerable fluent button** calls the btnIEnumFluentClick event handler, which is shown in the following code:

```
procedure TfrmFunctionalSpring.btnIEnumFluentClick(Sender: TObject);
var
  data: IEnumerable<integer>;
begin
  data := TCollections.CreateList<integer>(GenerateData(1000))
    .Where(
      function (const value: integer): boolean
      begin
        Result := (not Odd(value)) and ((value mod 17) = 0);
      end)
    .Take(10)
    .Reversed;
  WriteOut(TEnumerable.Select<integer, string>(data, IntToStr));
end;
```

This method executes the same steps as `btnIEnumClick`, except that it uses only one variable. All intermediate steps are stored in hidden variables that are maintained by the compiler and destroyed at the end of the method.

Summary

In this chapter, we have looked into three concepts that are important to an everyday Delphi programmer but didn't find their place anywhere else in this book.

The first part of this chapter discussed the idea of programming with exceptions. We saw why exceptions were introduced to modern languages, how they should be used, and how they can be abused. We also saw how exceptions should be correctly handled in the code and what alternatives are available if we don't want to use them.

The second part discussed the debugging process. As this is a highly abstract topic, this book could only give some advice and hints that could improve that part of your programming.

The final part of this chapter focused on functional programming. This programming paradigm cannot be directly transplanted to the Delphi language, but we can still use some concepts from functional programming, such as data immutability and high-order functions, to create programs that are simple to write and to maintain.

Other Books You May Enjoy

If you enjoyed this book, you may be interested in these other books by Packt:

Delphi Cookbook - Third Edition
Daniele Spinetti

ISBN: 9781788621304

- Develop visually stunning applications using FireMonkey
- Deploy LiveBinding effectively with the right object-oriented programming (OOP) approach
- Create RESTful web services that run on Linux or Windows
- Build mobile apps that read data from a remote server efficiently
- Call platform native API on Android and iOS for an unpublished API
- Manage software customization by making better use of an extended RTTI
- Integrate your application with IOT

If you enjoyed this book, you may be interested in these other books by Packt:

Delphi High Performance
Primož Gabrijelčič

ISBN: 9781788625456

- Find performance bottlenecks and easily mitigate them
- Discover different approaches to fix algorithms
- Understand parallel programming and work with various tools included with Delphi
- Master the RTL for code optimization
- Explore memory managers and their implementation
- Leverage external libraries to write better performing programs

Leave a review - let other readers know what you think

Please share your thoughts on this book with others by leaving a review on the site that you bought it from. If you purchased the book from Amazon, please leave us an honest review on this book's Amazon page. This is vital so that other potential readers can see and use your unbiased opinion to make purchasing decisions, we can understand what our customers think about our products, and our authors can see your feedback on the title that they have worked with Packt to create. It will only take a few minutes of your time, but is valuable to other potential customers, our authors, and Packt. Thank you!

Index

example 133, 136
hashers 137
string interning 131
form inheritance
about 397
using 398, 400, 402, 404
frame
about 404
creating 404, 406, 408, 411
functional programming 449, 450, 453, 455
future pattern 354, 356

G

Gang of Four
about 20
don't inherit—compose philosophy 20, 23, 25
git-bisect tool
reference 449
GpSQLBuilder project
reference 117
graphical user interface (GUI) 148

H

hasher 138
Highlander problem 182

I

idioms 12
injection 93
interfaces 93
Inversion Of Control (IOC) 55
invoker 384
iterator pattern
about 234, 236
custom enumerators, implementing 240
iterating, with for..in 237
iterator interface, using 241, 246, 250, 252

J

JvExcept
reference 444

K

KISS principle 35

L

lazy initialization pattern
about 64, 67
Spring, using 68, 70
LiveBindings mechanism
using 389, 392, 394, 396
lock striping pattern
about 304, 306, 308
bitwise operators, using 313, 314
single bit locks 309, 311, 313
locking pattern
about 287, 289, 294, 297
implementing 297, 299, 301, 303
Lock (custom) button 297
locking pattern 292

M

MadExcept
reference 444
marker interface pattern
about 140, 142
attributes, declaring 142
re-implementing, with attributes 144, 146
memento pattern 272, 274, 275, 277
messaging pattern
polling process 351, 353
queue option 349
Queue option 346
Synchronize option 346, 349
using 342, 344
Windows messages 344, 346
method injection 63
mock object 165
MSFT (Microsoft) 72
multiple readers, exclusive writer (MREW) 323
multiple readers, single writer (MRSW) 323
multithreaded programming
in Delphi 282, 284, 285, 286

www.ingramcontent.com/pod-product-compliance
Lightning Source LLC
Chambersburg PA
CBHW060643060326
40690CB00020B/4502